Vicissitudes of the Goddess

VICISSITUDES OF THE GODDESS

Reconstructions of the Gramadevata in India's Religious Traditions

SREE PADMA

OXFORD
UNIVERSITY PRESS

OXFORD

UNIVERSITY PRESS

Oxford University Press is a department of the University of Oxford.
It furthers the University's objective of excellence in research, scholarship,
and education by publishing worldwide.

Oxford   New York
Auckland   Cape Town   Dar es Salaam   Hong Kong   Karachi
Kuala Lumpur   Madrid   Melbourne   Mexico City   Nairobi
New Delhi   Shanghai   Taipei   Toronto

With offices in
Argentina   Austria   Brazil   Chile   Czech Republic   France   Greece
Guatemala   Hungary   Italy   Japan   Poland   Portugal   Singapore
South Korea   Switzerland   Thailand   Turkey   Ukraine   Vietnam

Oxford is a registered trademark of Oxford University Press
in the UK and certain other countries.

Published in the United States of America by
Oxford University Press
198 Madison Avenue, New York, NY 10016

Library of Congress Cataloging-in-Publication Data
Sree Padma, 1956–
Vicissitudes of the Goddess : reconstructions of the Gramadevata in India's religious
traditions / Sree Padma.
pages cm
Includes bibliographical references.
ISBN 978-0-19-932503-0 (pbk : alk. paper)—ISBN 978-0-19-932502-3 (cloth: alk.
paper) 1. Hindu goddesses—India—Andhra Pradesh. 2. Folk religion—India—Andhra
Pradesh—History. I. Title.
BL1216.4.A54S74 2013
294.5'2114095484—dc23
2013004847

9 8 7 6 5 4 3 2 1
Printed in the United States of America
on acid-free paper

For my dear mother, Vuyyuru Annapurnamma,
and in loving memory of my father, Vuyyuru Venkatrao.

Contents

Acknowledgments

IT WAS ALMOST twenty years ago that this project was first conceived. A year of field work in 1993 with a couple of scholarly presentations was what I brought with me as I came to participate in the Study of Women and Religion Program at Harvard Divinity School during 1994-1995. During that time, I resided at the Center for the Study of World Religions as a Senior Fellow. Thanks to lively conversations that year, I decided to study the discrepancy between how the divine (goddess) and mundane (women) worlds were articulated in India and specifically in Andhra Pradesh. While this issue continued to be relevant to my research and teaching, my preoccupation with other research projects over the years made me greatly expand my research focus to incorporate the examination of the influences of goddess religion on many other forms of Indic religious culture. This necessitated the investigation of a range of sources, including contemporary ritual practices, oral traditions, literature, art, inscriptions, and other archaeological materials.

Some of the preliminary research for this project began while I was at Andhra University as a research associate and was teaching graduate students in the department of history and archaeology. I owe my original inspiration for research to my professors, including the late K. Sundaram, C. Somasundararao, A. Kamalavasini, K. Krishnakumari, and B. Mastanaiah, and to the dedicated staff of the main library at Andhra University.

My fieldwork for this book took place in two phases. While the first phase of my intensive field trips to temples, ritual sites, archives, libraries, and archaeology museums had taken place in 1993 and 1994, the second phase spread over a number of years into 2012, when I made irregular visits to India from the United States. During these field trips I was assisted by a number of people, to whom I am grateful. Some of these are priests of the Brahmin and non-Brahmin castes who served in *gramadevata* and popular goddess temples and who enthusiastically narrated to me the details of rituals and mythologies germane to their goddesses. Most inspirational of all was the late Dr. Kundurti

Satyanarayanamurty, who served at Kanaka Durga temple in Vijayawada. I interviewed Dr. Kundurti in 1993 and went back in 1994 when he gave me a copy of his PhD thesis. While the thesis proved to be a very useful reference, my discussions with him were a milestone in confirming my belief that the goddess Kanaka Durga received animal sacrifices and that she was treated as a *gramadevata* not very long ago.

I owe a debt to the friendly staff at the Andhra Pradesh State Archaeology office, library, and museums. Dr. E. Sivanagireddy and Dr. B. Subrahmanyam were always ready to share their knowledge, either at excavation sites or at their offices. Mr. Narasimharao in the photography section went out of his way in digging through the photo archives to locate needed photos or to take pictures of objects, even when the museum was closed for repairs. I am especially grateful to the late Dr. V. V. Krishnasastry, long-time director of the Andhra Pradesh State Archaeology office, library, and museums, who enthusiastically engaged in extensive discussions with me. I regret that he did not live to see the finished product of my efforts. I am also grateful to the staff at the State Archives in Hyderabad and in Visakhapatnam for helping me to find many sources.

I am greatly appreciative of the help and support that I received from my family and friends. Conversations with my mother, Vuyyuru Annapurnamma, inspired me review my childhood memories of watching various rituals and hearing songs in praise of the village goddess. My conversations with her about her own childhood also helped me to cross-check and to substantiate my other sources about the ways in which middle-class girls lived their lives in the first half of the twentieth century. My brother-in-law, Parupalli Murali Mohan Rao, is not only an avid reader of all literature, especially Telugu, but commands an enormous amount of knowledge about Telugu traditions and Telugu culture in general. Listening to his passionate narration of literary accounts was useful to identify the right Telugu literary sources for my project. My sister, Parupalli Leela, who is not much older than me but acts like my mother, made sure that I was well-cared-for, even when I was distracted with my work. My brother, Vuyyuru Murali Krishna Rao, accompanied me on some of the field trips and in my absence acted as mediator and supervisor to my field assistant, providing my assistant the necessary equipment, means, and advice. Thanks to my field assistant, Sunkara Siva Krishna, who taped many interviews of devotees and priests on my behalf by going to some remote areas of Andhra Pradesh. Thanks also to my close friend, Gogineni Mani, and to my cousin, Kala, who accompanied me on field trips in and around Hyderabad. I also benefitted from enthusiastic friends such as Garnepudi Rattaiah, who accompanied me on some field trips, and Vedullapalli Vivek, who documented some of the rituals that took place in my absence and who shared that documentation generously with me.

I received help in several libraries in India and elsewhere, including Harvard and the University of Calgary. But because I have been at Bowdoin College since 1995, it was Bowdoin's Hawthorne/Longfellow Library that I used the most. Most of my secondary sources came either from Bowdoin's library or were borrowed through it. Thanks to all the staff, especially Ms. Katie Sasser, whose help I sought over these many years and who became one of my good friends.

This book has been shaped by many of my presentations in scholarly conferences in India, the United States, and Bhutan, and in my public lectures given at institutions like Harvard University, Bowdoin College, the University of Calgary, and Loyola University, Chicago, as well as in classroom lectures. Thanks to my students at Harvard and Bowdoin who read portions of my manuscript as part of their class readings and who gave their feedback in the form of their own essays.

While I managed collecting material over many years from different sources and preparing papers for presentations, what turned out to be tricky was finding a healthy stretch of time to write the book. My responsibilities as executive director for the Inter-Collegiate Sri Lanka Education (ISLE) Program and my course offerings at Bowdoin did not leave very much time to make a good progress. But whenever I was away from Bowdoin during my husband's (John Holt's) sabbaticals, I substituted my teaching time with working on drafting my manuscript. My first such attempt was at the University of Calgary in the fall of 2006 where, as a research associate in the Dept. of Religious Studies, I wrote my first chapter. This momentum continued into 2007 when I was a resident at the idyllic Rockefeller Foundation Bellagio Study Center (Italy). During the next few years I continued my writing at Bowdoin whenever I could. A big breakthrough came in 2011, when I was a research associate at the Center for Southeast Asia at Kyoto University, Kyoto. It was in Kyoto that my book began to take on its final shape. I am very grateful to Professor Yoko Hayami for inviting me to be a research associate.

I have used photographs and line drawings to illustrate the meanings of various motifs and their evolutions over many centuries. I was helped in this regard by Mr. Tilak Jayatilake, librarian for the Inter-Collegiate Sri Lanka Education (ISLE) Program in Kandy, Sri Lanka, who made the line drawings. I am grateful for all the after hours and weekends he spent in studying the photographs before trying his hand at these representations.

At Bowdoin, I acknowledge my thanks to two of my colleagues, Professors Thomas Conlan and David Collings, who were both kind enough to read portions of the book when it was in its initial stages. My thanks are also due to the staff of Bowdoin's informational technology force for providing assistance when needed. My special thanks goes to Jennifer Snow for helping me produce maps for the book.

I am deeply grateful to my husband and children. This project literally matured to its present stage along with my two children, Sasi Kanth and Sireesha, as we together made our journeys from India to the United States. My children graciously indulged me for whatever demands the project required, either by bearing my absences from home or by helping me out in various ways to free up my time. Throughout these many years, they supported me enthusiastically, inquired curiously, listened patiently, and grew anxious to see the project come to its fruition. My husband, John Holt, is also my intellectual companion. He gave himself untiringly as a sounding board to my ideas as they evolved. I needed his valuable critiques and his editorial suggestions for my many drafts. He proved to be an enormous help. This project could not have been completed without his emotional, practical, moral, and intellectual support.

Maps

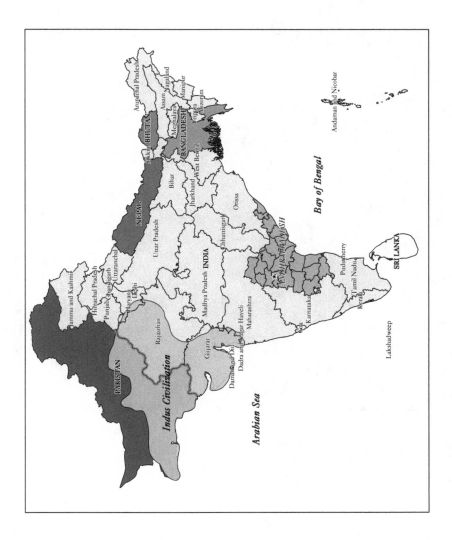

MAP 1 Location of Andhra Pradesh.

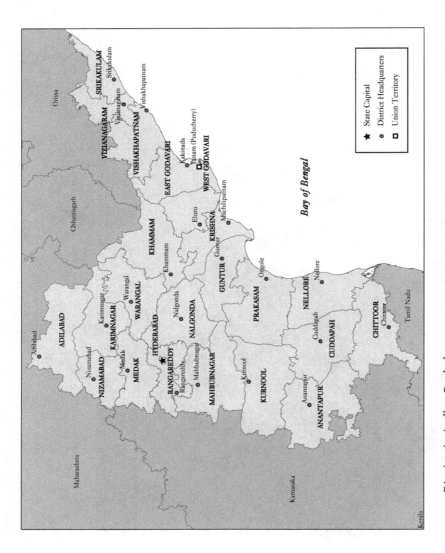

MAP 2 Districts in Andhra Pradesh.

Introduction

ANDHRA PRADESH, LIKE most of the states in India, has always been primarily rural in character. In spite of the major urbanization process that has been underway since the middle of the twentieth century, this rural character continues to dominate Andhra into the first and second decades of the twenty-first century. One of the key aspects of this rural character, despite these days of globalization, is the ubiquitous worship of tutelary and other female deities of local importance, deities that I refer to in this book as *gramadevatas* or "village goddesses." The worship of *gramadevatas* is now just as prevalent in the big urban sprawls of Andhra, where villages have become part of major cities in Hyderabad, Vijayawada, and Visakhapatnam, as it is in rural areas. This prevalence is the result of the migration of vast rural populations to urban centers. The pattern of worship of these *gramadevatas* assumes regional variations depending on geographical location, political vicissitudes, and other circumstantial factors, with the result that some age-old traditions have been generally sustained, while in other instances transformations have occurred so that contemporary worship has been accommodated into various urban religious, social, and political milieux.

Gramadevatas are understood as part of Hindu tradition, though at times they seem to exist in juxtaposition with the religion of the *brahman* priests, who have been responsible for the invention and proliferation of most of the well-known religious myths, rituals, and ascetic practices in India and with whom most of western scholarship has been preoccupied. The *gramadevatas* with whom this book is concerned are not of one type or category. In their various types, they correspond to different dimensions and spiritual strategies of popular Hindu religious sentiment and magic. In my research, I have become primarily interested in two of these types of goddesses. The first are those goddesses who are associated with powers of fertility and the outbreak of disease. The second are those goddesses who are clearly deified women whose lives came to an abrupt or unseemly end. As my study reveals, these two are not as exclusive as they appear to be on the surface. I am interested in tracing the historical vicissitudes of the first category of goddesses to see how they influenced various religious traditions and how gender became a factor in qualifying the religious meaning of these various religious traditions. This study also shows the resilience and survival of *gramadevata* cults in the face of their transformation into *brahmanic* deities. By studying the second category of deified women, my aim is to examine how feminine power has been imagined, symbolized, and thus conceptualized in Hindu religious tradition.

There are some *gramadevata*s that continue to be popular at the local level even after they become widely recognized as *brahmanic* deities. Examples of this include the famous Hindu deities Durga and Kali, whose profiles have grown to encompass many *gramadevata* cults. In the study that follows, I refer to these types of goddesses as "popular goddesses." I argue in this book that these goddesses, as well as the *gramadevata*s that they have absorbed, either share a common origin or have been conflated with the worship of pre-historic goddesses, those I labeled as "fertility goddess." Hence in this book, the terms, "*gramadevata*," "popular goddess," and "fertility goddess" are intrinsically related to each other, but I have deployed them in different contexts, depending upon historical circumstances.

In addition to popular goddesses that I mentioned above, I have also traced the origins of goddesses of Buddhist, Jaina, Saiva, and Vaishnava traditions to the fertility goddess. The goddesses of Saiva and Vaishnava affiliation who acquired Sanskrit mythology and a performance liturgy in permanent temples on a daily basis by *brahman* priests are identified in this book as "*brahmanic*" goddesses. Although there are some previous studies dedicated to these different groups of goddesses, there is no study probing into the important interconnections between these various types of goddesses. As such, I have explained in my book how these disparate groups of goddesses (*gramadevata*s, *brahmanic*, Buddhist, and Jaina) are connected historically.

This project has absorbed nearly twenty years of research. I have examined a variety of sources: material remains of archaeological excavations, archaeology reports, published inscriptions, archives, etc. I have also conducted years of fieldwork. The project started in 1993 and 1994 when I engaged in extensive field trips visiting temples, observing goddess rituals, and interviewing devotees and priests. I continued with fieldwork through 2011 and 2012, all the while updating a record of the changes since my first visits in 1993 and 1994. As the source material suggests, this study is interdisciplinary in nature. As a trained archaeologist and historian, my approach to this study has been overwhelmingly historical. As a native Telugu speaker who has lived for many years in both rural and urban areas, I present something of an "insider's perspective" in analyzing the *gramadevata*s of Andhra as a whole, but my views are not normative. The "insider's perspective" obviously provided me with many advantages, but I was also forced to transcend that perspective, especially when I confronted a lot of important questions that demanded historical explanation beyond the answers provided by traditional sources.

I also changed my perspective regarding some of the central problems germane to understanding Indian history. For example, when I started this study, I was skeptical that any contemporary traditions of *gramadevatas* could be traced back to the culture of the Indus period, for I am fully aware of the dangers of anachronistic readings and the limitations we face owing to the paucity of historical and linguistic evidence. And, in fact, I did not see any connections until I had a chance to study in depth the various symbols used in contemporary rituals to represent the goddess by comparing them closely with the sculptural motifs from the historic and proto-historic periods. I need to be very clear here. As I try to explain in this book with the help of illustrations, some important religious scenes and symbols point toward a *possible* continuation of some *gramadevata* traditions that *may* stem from the Indus period. This does not mean that I aver that all of the contemporary traditions of *gramadevata* have roots in the Indus period. Far from it. But I have tried to elucidate, abetted by examples of material evidence, that the prehistoric fertility goddess, of Indus orgins or not, not only managed to remain an important dimension of the social and cultural experience of agricultural communities throughout history into the contemporary period in the form of *gramadevatas*, but also that these cults changed in significant ways to become part of major religious traditions such as Buddhism, Jainism, Saivism, and Vaishnavism.

In the same way, in the initial stages of the project, I was not quite sure whether to take up the topic of deified women as part of my study. Analyses of *sati* and *perantalu* are fraught with many types of difficulties. But as I worked on various case studies, it became clear to me that there has developed an unmistakable connection between some *gramadevatas* and the cults of deified human women. In short, what I often found is this: if a woman dies as a victim of patriarchal proclivities in village society, it is sometimes the case that the collective guilt emanating from her family and others or their attempt to tame her malevolent spirit results in her deification. This deified woman, in some instances, is then transmogrified within the village as a *gramadevata* who, in turn, gains the potential of becoming a *brahmanic* deity as well.

To contextualize an understanding of the subject matter in this book, I have also undertaken an inquiry aimed at discerning reasons for the historical discrepancy between the veritable and sustained popularity of village goddesses on the one hand and the reluctance to acknowledge the status of goddesses as independent deities by religious leaders, missionaries, and academic cultural and religious historians on the other. I bring the following new trajectories of inquiry to this study: 1) a historical narrative about how the *gramadevata*s in their more recent popular forms (as Kali and Durga, for instance) have been understood first by Christian missionaries, and then by colonial and post-colonial scholarship, and finally how my methodology and understanding agrees or differs from this body of scholarship; 2) a historical analysis of the roots of Andhra *gramadevata*s (whom I have referred to in prehistoric and historic contexts as fertility goddesses) through a consideration of symbolism, iconography, inscriptions, textual sources, and mythology; and 3) an analysis of the stories and worship of deified women in Andhra (who in some instances are regarded as *gramadevata*s) to understand issues of gender, caste, and religious belief.

In the last few decades, scholarship dedicated to understanding *gramadevata*s has finally gained some scholarly momentum after centuries of relative neglect. The first scholarly study, conducted by a Protestant Christian missionary in the eighteenth century, was not actually published until more than a century later.[1] It took yet another century following this missionary's lead for his pioneering interpretation to find print. Later accounts in the late nineteenth and early twentieth century were a mix of informal missionary and colonial writings that recorded aspects of mythology, folk stories, and ritual practices. Coastal sections of the present state of Andhra Pradesh comprised some of the venues of attention.[2] After another lull of half a century, some resumed scholarly interest on the subject was developed by late twentieth- and early twenty-first-century scholars. In the case of Andhra, these studies were either focused on the rituals of a specific *gramadevata*, or the subject of *gramadevata*s formed part of an anthropological study of village or folk literature.[3] An exception to these limited patterns of inquiry was the monumental study undertaken by Madeleine Biardeau in which the rituals of *gramadevata*s were traced to *puranic* and *vedic* sources.[4] While early twentieth-century studies are helpful in ascertaining the changes that have taken place in the worship and ritual of the *gramadevata*s since, Biardeau's study illuminated an understanding of the historic nature of village rituals and their deeper meanings.

In this book, I have studied the symbols, mythology, and meaning of current rituals and have traced them back beyond the *puranas* and *vedic* literature to the proto-historic period in an attempt to build an unbroken history of the traditions of goddesses from agricultural and hunting origins to the twenty-first century. Not only have I traced out continuity but also have determined the transformations that have occurred throughout history. Particularly I have studied the influences of divergent streams that give rise to different versions of mythology and to a variety of rituals that have often culminated in the cults of *gramadevata*s.

In more particularity, the specific issues broached in the book are as follow: 1) how to distinguish *gramadevata*s from the goddesses of textual traditions; 2) what terminology to employ to recognize devotion to the *gramadevata*s; 3) the manner in which groups of people participating in the rituals to the *gramadevata*s have been identified; 4) what historical links the *gramadevata*s share; 5) how the worship of the *gramadevata*s reflects on gender and caste relations; 6) what ideologies they represent; and 7) what relationship these cults share with *brahman*ical forms of Hinduism. With this scheme in mind, I have organized the book in the following manner.

The first chapter is useful for the readers who are new to scholarship on Indian goddesses. Others may wish to begin with the second chapter. The first chapter discusses colonial, post-colonial, and modern scholarship on goddesses that are still popular as *gramadevata*s at the village level. As mentioned earlier, and to clarify further, I use the term "popular" broadly to mean the goddesses who are widely worshiped in rural and agricultural contexts and, at the same time, are considered as *brahman*ic deities supported by textual traditions and Sanskrit liturgy. The prime examples, as I have said, are Durga and Kali.

The first chapter is divided into three major sections. The first section investigates the circumstances that led to the composition of an early eighteenth-century work entitled "Genealogy of the South-Indian Gods," by the first notable Protestant Christian missionary, Bartholomaeus Ziegenbalg; the rejection of its publication by ecclesiastical authorities in Germany; and how, a century and a half later, his work was considered so valuable by Halle clergy that a project was undertaken to translate and publish it in both German and English. After looking into the background and context in which Ziegenbalg had undertaken such a controversial work and the reasons why his superiors in Halle came to reject it at first, this section also documents the changes that took place in the next century and a half within Indological studies and discusses how these changes, in turn, influenced European missionaries in such a way as to eventually recognize Ziegenbalg's work as extremely valuable. The second section looks at the ways that racial theory developed and in what ways popular religiosity was used in legitimating it. It also assesses the ways that these racially motivated interpretations changed western perspectives about Indian people, culture, religion, and society and how this perspective further shaped future scholarship on popular religion, especially the worship of popular goddesses. The discussion in the third section shows how post-colonial scholarship, for the most part, critiqued colonial scholarly categories and proposed newer ones with the intention of interpreting Indian society and religion in more realistic terms. Even so, as this discussion reflects,

there have been some pitfalls and disagreements about which proposed categories or frameworks are utilized and how Indian society, religion, and its
past should be understood. While presenting a number of salient theoretical
discussions engaged in by various scholars in relation to the religion of *gramadevata*s, I explain how my own methodology agrees or disagrees or takes a
different route.

Chapters 2, 3, and 4 are devoted to ferreting out the historical vicissitudes
of Andhra village goddesses.

The second chapter serves as an informational resource, laying the foundation for the following two chapters. As such, this chapter introduces the
first known symbols and proto-anthropomorphic images of the goddess from
proto-historic Andhra. As a way of explaining the nature and forms of *gramadevata*, the chapter also discusses rituals observed in the worship of *gramadevata*. Within this discussion, I demonstrate the ancient nature of shared
similarities with the religious culture of Indus River Valley times on the one
hand, and on the other the continuation of their cults throughout history in
influencing current goddess mythology and ritual practices. The chronological sequence introduced in this chapter informs the discussion of the third
chapter.

The third chapter builds upon the ground laid in the previous chapter to
trace the history of goddess symbolism. I do this by examining specific symbols in their evolution over time, their adaptation into the Buddhist, Jaina,
Vaishnava, and Saiva traditions and their current relevance to contemporary
goddess mythology and rituals. I have employed three lines of inquiry in analyzing these symbols: 1) how some symbols have changed their meanings as
they entered into other religious traditions; 2) how some symbols evolved into
the anthropomorphic form of the goddess; and 3) how contemporary mythologies and rituals of the goddess consider these various symbols as actual material forms of the goddess.

The fourth chapter looks at anthropomorphic representations of the
goddess as well as some specific profiles of *gramadevata*s such as Ellamma,
Erukamma, Durga, Kali, and Sammakka, known through mythology, literature, inscriptions, and ritual practices. In this chapter, I highlight three different but indirectly related aspects: 1) the ancient nature of goddess symbolism
and its continued relevance to the present day; 2) the constant creation and
evolution of goddess cults to fit into an ongoing historical reification process;
and 3) the cultic diversification, multiplication, and evolution of the goddess
over time.

The rest of the chapters analyze the stories and worship patterns of deified
women and their relationship to *gramadevata*s. The stories I discuss in these

chapters are varied and diverse, and so are the reasons given for the deification of these women, though they all share the theme of an unspent power of *sakti* now being tapped. Another common theme among these deified women is that, in almost all cases, they experienced tragic and premature deaths despite the fact that the circumstances and ages of these women are different. The central question in this part of the book is the relation between the concept of women's deification and traditional notions of gender and caste.

Chapter 5 discusses the category of deified virgin goddesses, women who met sudden deaths either by natural causes or self-immolations. Through a discussion of how young girls are raised and regarded in Andhra society, I provide a framework to analyze the stories leading to sudden deaths of young girls. I then look into how and why these young girls came to be worshiped posthumously and the meaning that is attached to their deifications. I compare these cases with *gramadevata*s and ascertain a close relation in terms of function.

In the sixth chapter, I consider the stories of married women who took their lives either to join their dead husbands or for other specified reasons. Sacrifices of women, on the other hand, fit into the larger practice of sacrificial religion arising from divergent beliefs of pre-Vedic, Vedic and post-Vedic tribal origins. I examine the historical context of this practice and its continuation into the present day. For this, I probe into the history of *sati* to understand its probable origins and to determine the kinds of influences that Andhra received. I also look into the aspect of whether the *sati* cult in Andhra influenced other regions of India. To contextualize the meaning of self-immolation, I discuss the demands placed on adult women in traditional Andhra society and the consequences for women who fail to meet them. As with the discussion of deified virgins, deified married women also share the theme of the unspent power of *sakti* being tapped.

In the seventh chapter, I treat two different but somewhat related cases of deaths: human sacrifices and murders of women. In the case of human sacrifices, I consider religious reasons and justifications of sacrifice and their consequent influence on the practice of deifying a sacrificed female. As a prelude to the discussion of the cases of murders and their causes, I discuss the moral and social restrictions placed on women in order to explain what constituted infractions and why relatives reacted so violently. The profiles of deified women are then compared with *gramadevata*s to analyze shared as well as unique features.

In short, this book begins by examining how goddesses have been perceived by westerners (missionaries, colonialists, and post-colonial scholars) and what motivations these westerners have brought to their understanding of goddesses. The second but major line of inquiry, in contrast, refracts the ways that goddesses have been not only an important element of the ancient religious past, but one whose features have been appropriated and transformed by emergent Indian religious traditions (e.g., Buddhism, Jainism, Saivism, and Vaishnavism) on the one hand and yet have continued to appeal independently to contemporary Indian devotees on the other. Within this trajectory, I have attempted to determine the various processes that have contributed to the diversification of goddess cults throughout Andhra Pradesh.

I

Goddess Explained—Perspectives from the West

FOR MANY CENTURIES India remained a very exotic land in western imaginations. Accounts such as Nearchus's and Megasthenese's that were written during the time of Alexander's invasion were quoted and recycled by late medieval and early modern European historians, regarded for centuries as authentic sources of knowledge about India.[1] Indeed, there was a paucity of direct observations of India by Europeans until the twelfth and thirteenth century CE, when a few curious travelers drifted into different regions of the country. Their observations were a jumbled mix about whatever caught their fancies. European Christian missionaries to India in the sixteenth through eighteenth centuries made the first serious and systematic attempts to describe the indigenous religions of the subcontinent. They did so in order to dismiss Indian's religious traditions and to promote their own. Next came colonial administrators who, for a variety of reasons, became the first proponents of an emerging western academic Indology. I discuss how these westerners portrayed the popular goddess (whose origins lie in village religion) and with what intentions and motivations they recorded their observations. Some of their views continue to be propounded today, mainly to buttress Eurocentric and evangelical Christian perspectives. Post-colonial scholarship, as I intend to show in the latter portions of this chapter as a way of strategizing my own study, critiqued pre-colonial western understandings and proposed novel approaches to study Indian culture and society including its goddess religion. The chapter ends with a debate on the source of goddess traditions to set the context for the following chapters. Although my main focus is on the scholarship of the goddess in south India, which includes the present state of Andhra Pradesh, the geographical area of my study, I also consider writings about the goddess in other regions of the Indian subcontinent, so far as those are useful to my emerging argument.

Early Encounters with the West: Ziegenbalg's Rendering of South Indian Popular Goddesses

Among missionary studies of Indian religions, the first clear attempt to study village goddess religion in south India is an early eighteenth-century work entitled "Genealogy of the South-Indian Gods," composed by Bartholomaeus Ziegenbalg, who lived in south India in his capacity as a Lutheran mission-ary.[2] The importance of Zieganbalg's ethnographic work to my discussion lies specifically in the material that he presented about *gramadevatas* (village goddesses):

> Besides the gods and goddesses that have been described in the second part of this Geneology, these heathens worship also another set of dei-ties, called ... Gramadevatas, i.e. tutelary deities, which are supposed to protect the fields, villages, and towns from evil spirits, and to ward off all sorts of plagues, famine, pestilence, war, conflagration, and inunda-tion, and are, in short, regarded as beings who, though they cannot bestow positive blessings, are able to prevent evil.[3]

While the issue of whether the *gramadevatas* can or cannot bestow positive blessings is highly debatable, Zieganbalg's work was unique in many ways. As a foreigner and a Christian missionary, he presented information on the worship and nature of various gods and goddesses of south India that was col-lected from indigenous sources, oral and textual.[4] Although he was preceded by a host of Jesuit missionaries who published their own studies about Indian culture and religion, it was Zieganbalg who first recognized the importance of *gramadevatas* within the pantheon of south Indian deities. He ascertained that *gramadevatas* were worshiped by almost all people within villages, especially those of its lowest castes,[5] and regardless of sectarian affiliation. Ziegenbalg knew fairly well that the information he compiled was relevant not just in and around Tranquebar, where he was stationed, but throughout the whole of peninsular India, as well as on the island of Sri Lanka.[6] That was why he was convinced that future Christian missionaries ought to possess knowledge of this widespread popular religious orientation in order to learn how to pitch the Christian gospel more successfully.

The Beginnings of a Pioneer's Work. In July 1706, Ziegenbalg, accompa-nied by his missionary colleague Henry Pluetschau, arrived as an evangelical Lutheran minister at the Danish Colony at Tranquebar to start his first mis-sion. Trained as a pietistic minister at the Halle University in Germany with professors August Hermann Francke (1663–1727), Joachim Lange (1670–1744), and Johann Anastasius Freylinghausen (1670–1739), Ziegenbalg brought with him a confessional zeal that fueled his determination.

Initially, like other pietists of this time, August Hermann Francke was afraid that the purity of the Bible and its teachings would be perverted if Christianity were to spread outside of Europe. The fear of these pietists was directly related to the perceived compromises that earlier Jesuit missionaries had made in relation to Christian ideals in Asia in order to convert heathens to Christianity. Ziegenbalg had been greatly influenced by the ideas of pietists, especially Francke's understanding of the Bible as direct and inspired revelation. He was determined that he would not fall into the rut that Jesuits had created by making various compromises.

By the time of Ziegenbalg's arrival, Jesuit missionaries had worked among south Indians for nearly a century and a half since the time that the Portuguese had begun to occupy Goa. During this long period of time, their regard for south Indian religious culture took many different twists and turns: from loathing it to embracing it. To speed up the rate of conversions, on the recommendation of one of the first Jesuit missionaries, the famed Francis Xavier (1502–1552), the Portuguese imposed an inquisition that lasted for more than a century and a half from 1560 CE to 1712 CE.[7] The inquisition was so severe that it created something of a controversy in Europe, the general sentiment of which was expressed by French philosopher Voltaire (1694–1778) in the following words:

> Goa is sadly famous for its inquisition, which is contrary to humanity as much as to commerce. The Portuguese monks deluded us into believing that the Indian populace was worshipping The Devil, while it is they who served him.[8]

Branding Indian gods and goddesses as devilish in nature gave the Portuguese and the Jesuits a moral authority to be intolerant toward many expressions of Indian religiosity.[9]

Given Xavier's low opinion of the natives and their cultures, it was hardly a secret that he did not have any interest or curiosity in learning anything about Indians except for their language, the essential component he needed to communicate his version of the gospel.[10] Unlike Xavier, Alessandro Valignano (1539–1606), an educated aristocrat turned missionary, in an attempt to assist missionary work, wrote an elaborate but prejudiced account of the sub-cultures that he observed while traveling along the peninsula of India's west coast from Diu to Cape Comorin.[11] Valignano's racist view of Indians may have stemmed from failed attempts to evangelize high-caste Indians. Following his predecessor Xavier, he later decided to move on to Japan and China.

Even though Valignano and Xavier gave up in frustration in their attempts to convert Indians, there were other Jesuit enthusiasts who came to India with different strategies. Supported by a liberal pope, a number of other Jesuit missionaries, such as the Englishman Thomas Stephens (1549–1619) and the Italian Roberto de Nobili (1577–1656), educated themselves in south Indian cultures by studying south Indian languages and Sanskrit texts. Both wrote Christian propaganda tracts in local languages. Obviously, religious culture and language cannot be completely decoupled. Although Stephens developed a love for the local languages, he was clear in noting the difference between the Hindu religion and Christianity: "...as great as that which exists between light and darkness, truth and falsehood, heaven and hell, God and the devil."[12] De Nobili took a step further by becoming enamored with the *brahman* way of life, especially many aspects of Hindu ascetic lifestyle, a lifestyle that he, himself, came to adopt. In the same way that Stephens had separated language from religion, de Nobili separated *brahman* lifestyle from the idolatrous religion that *brahmans* subscribed to, a religion he labeled "gentilism" or "gentile religion." His explanation and defense for adopting the lifestyle of *brahman* ascetics was to attract *brahmans*, the gentiles, to the Christian faith.[13] To put this in perspective, even Ziegenbalg in the next century would not have chosen de Nobili's path, although he might have agreed with Nobili about the direct correlation between studying Indian religious texts and achieving effective Christian missionary work. In fact, by adopting revolutionary lifestyles and by introducing indigenous forms of worship and rituals into the Christian church service, de Nobili and his followers created a controversy among their fellow Jesuit missionaries and an outrage among future Protestant groups such as the Halle Pietists.

Although de Nobili's aim was the same as other Jesuits, his approach was a significant departure from theirs. While his observations on south Indian religion were not apologetic, it was not in any way sympathetic either.[14] In fact, de Nobili used his understanding of Hindu religious aspects effectively in his several publications to argue for the superiority of Christianity.[15] With his sophisticated theological arguments, he won over some influential *brahmans* locally. Because of his effective missionary work, de Nobili managed to convince the pope of his strategy. Thus, with Rome's support, a certain number of "Malabarian rites" were allowed into Madurai churches. This conciliation with south Indian forms of religious culture was ridiculed by Protestants in Europe. They scorned how Catholic missionaries in the name of conversion corrupted the Christian faith and compromised the Christian value system.[16] It seems that in the beginning of his mission, Ziegenbalg was in agreement with Halle pietists on this matter. What factors influenced a change in his view and consequently how he revised his missionary strategies are now addressed.

Onsite Lessons Learned. In spite of the reluctance of Danish authorities to welcome him and his colleague, Ziegenbalg started his missionary work with great enthusiasm and with an ambition of converting as many people to Christianity as quickly as possible.[7] Like his Jesuit predecessors, Ziegenbalg arrived in south India without any knowledge of the local language but with a particular trait of temperament that led his biographer to call him a "hot head."[8] His own report to his Halle authorities shows both his inability to understand local religious sentiments as well as his tactlessness in how to express his feelings:

> Yesterday taking a Walk in the Country, we came to an Idol-Temple, wherein Ispara's [Isvara's] Lady (he being one of their first-rate Gods) is worshipped. Her Ladyship was surrounded with abundance of other Gods made of Porcellain. We, being deeply affected with the Sight of so foppish a Set of Gods, threw some down to the Ground, and striking off the Heads of others, endeavour'd to convince this deluded People that their images were nothing but impotent and still Idols, utterly unable to protect themselves, and much less their Worshippers.[19] [brackets mine]

It is not a surprise that Zieganbalg's eagerness to convert too many locals in too little time to Christianity without understanding local sentiment resulted in a rebellion by a certain section of Hindus. Because of this, within a year of his arrival, Ziegenbalg found himself jailed by the Danish authorities for disturbing the social equilibrium.[20] At this juncture, Ziegenbalg seemed to begin in earnest a serious and sustained reflection upon his frustrated methods of conversion. For, upon release, his next step toward understanding south Indian society, its religion, ethics, and culture, was to start studying Tamil and Tamil manuscripts. This study turned out to be an eye-opener. Zieganbalg was impressed by Tamil Saiva *bhakti* (devotional) works that question the religious authority of *brahmans*. Other Tamil texts on ethics seemed to astonish him, as he saw how closely they compared to his own pietistic principles.[21]

Zeigenbalg's studies of Tamil literature were followed by his discussions with Tamil scholars who would teach him about local practices, especially religious rituals and worship. Ironically, it was the nature of his German pietistic devotional background that helped him to see potential among Tamils, including their lower castes, a potential that he understood was dormant because of their unacceptable ways of heathenish ritual observance. Tensions with Halle pietists began when Ziegenbalg, influenced by the Enlightenment belief in natural religion imbued in all people, put his ideas into experimental practice in Tranquebar.[22]

Experience Rejected. Ziegenbalg achieved a measure of success in converting south Indians among the lower castes by educating their children of both
sexes and by translating the New Testament into colloquial Tamil. Attributing
his accomplishment to his acquaintance of native people and their culture,
he wanted future generations of missionaries to understand the nature of
south Indian religions so that "they will learn to grow in grace and truth and
defeat the devil forcefully in his kingdom of darkness through him [i.e., Jesus
Christ]."[23] With this inspiration he collected information from locals about
their gods and goddesses.

> In Europe, as he [Ziegenbalg] puts it, they had such "strange ideas
> about the Malabarees". They considered them to be not "reasonable,
> sensible, and clever people, but wild, untamed and coarse folks, whom
> one could never bring under a human order, let alone to Christianity".
> In spite of the "darkness of Satan" which he saw and all the "horrible
> errors, the beloved reader in Europe could readily see" how far they
> had come by the light of their reason in the knowledge of God and
> of the natural order, and how by their natural powers, they often put
> to shame many Christians by their upright life, also showing a much
> greater striving for the future life".[24] [brackets mine]

Ziegenbalg himself had shared those "strange" notions when he first came to
south India and had thought that Europeans Christians could change the heathen. But now he wanted to share the transformation of his outlook with min-
isterial colleagues and the European public so that they could understand how
the south Indian field was a fertile ground for receiving the gospel. In his own
mind, he believed that the ethical principles of the south Indians were good,
but that what he understood separately to be their religious beliefs needed to
be changed. Here it is interesting to note the proverbial bifurcation between
ethics and religion reflective of the preponderant Protestant reliance upon faith
or belief, in contrast to an understanding of good works being basically con-
stitutive of the Christian religious path. And, for this reason, although it was
unpleasant, Ziegenbalg had thus claimed that, because of what he had learned,
the onus was upon him to compile an account of south Indian religious beliefs
to be published for European consumption so that the European Christian
community would be motivated to take mercy on south Indians in order to
bring them out of their stupidity, their absence of faith in the one true god.[25]

However strong and compelling his petition might be, when his manuscript arrived at Halle, pietists such as his mentor Francke denigrated it, saying
that the missionaries were sent out to extirpate heathenism, and not to spread

such heathenish nonsense in Europe.[26] Francke's view also corresponded to
the position of *sola scriptura* and absolute faith in the god who had inspired
it[27] Eventually, following Ziegenbalg's repeated positions, the Halle authorities
would publish a highly truncated and modified version of Ziegenbalg's manuscript under a different title, in which the author's name was mentioned only
casually toward the end as a provider of the content.[28] With Sanskrit studies
on the rise, European scholars were interested almost exclusively in learning
about the more philosophical aspects of India's religious traditions and considered Ziegenbalg's Halle reports, which contained popular religious aspects, as
naive and worthless to be considered.[29] Another century elapsed before Halle
revised its opinion of Ziegenbalg's work, after it began to recognize its ethnographic significance. What had changed during this century is what I will
consider next.

The Lead of "Oriental Jones." By the late eighteenth century, the English East
India Company, profiteers in trade, found itself unwittingly in control of vast
Indian provinces. To administrate them effectively and to continue to amass
great profits without getting into trouble, the company's lead officials eventually
realized a dire need to understand Indian people and their culture. With the
company's blessings, Sir William Jones (1746–1794), a philologist, who came
to India as a British jurist with a background in classical languages, learned
Sanskrit rapidly and proceeded to found the Asiatic Society of Bengal in 1783.

On the third anniversary of the Asiatic Society, after a considerable comparison of the languages he had learned, Jones proclaimed that Sanskrit
shared a common heritage with Greek, Latin, and probably with Gothic and
Celtic languages.[30] While this statement made him famous in the philological
world, this very statement also bore the seeds for later racial theories. He also
believed that as English derived from Greek and Latin, Sanskrit, by extension,
was also part of the variegated inheritance of the British. For Jones, aspects
of Hinduism based on Sanskrit texts were part of his own past heritage, as
much as it was India's, and thereby needed to be preserved and defended. His
paternalistic European view extended as well to the Sanskritic Hindu goddesses Padma, Lakshmi, Parvati, Kali, Durga, Bhavani, Ganga, and Saraswati,
all of whom he equated with various European deities.[31] He treated popular goddesses Durga and Kali as one and the same. Since he believed that
the higher philosophical aspects of Hinduism could contribute to the great
European heritage, he attributed the negative qualities of Kali or Durga not
so much to the nature of the goddess per se, but rather to deceitful clerics:

> With all my admiration of the truly learned Brahmens, I abhor the sor-
> did priestcraft of Durga's ministers, but such fraud no more affects the

sound religion of the Hindus, than the lady of Loretto and the Romish impositions that affect our own rational faith.[32]

In this way, Jones protected "his" ancient religion from where, according to him, goddesses like Durga and Kali take their origin, as well as the Protestant form of Christianity to which he belonged, while criticizing effectively both the Roman Catholic clerics and the priests of popular goddess cults for encouraging base forms of ritual. Jones's idea of Vedic Aryans sharing their culture with other European ancestors did not catch on among many orientalist scholars until well into the nineteenth century.

Repudiating Missionaries. Toward the end of the eighteenth century, encouraged by the success of Ziegenbalg's first Danish mission in Tranquebar, a second mission was established in Serampore with William Carey, Joshua Marshman, and William Ward as its first missionaries. Ward used negative descriptions of the rituals and worship of the goddess Durga to prove how the British had placed themselves in a unique position to uplift the popular Hindu morality from its shockingly deplorable state.

> The songs and dances which the author has witnessed in the Hindoo temples at the time of the Doorga festival, at midnight, would disgrace a house of ill-fame.... This is the religion of the Hindoo!
>
> The author himself one year saw, from his own window at Serampore, in a procession on the river Ganges of the images of Doorga, sights so shockingly detestable.... Can we wonder, after this, that the Hindoos should be notoriously the most corrupt nation at present existing on the earth?[33]

Around the same time (1792–1823), a French missionary, Abbe J. A., Dubois, who was living in south India, studied Tamil and Sanskrit and composed a book on Hindu manners, customs, and ceremonies through his interviews with locals. He was paternalistic, as well as disparaging, in saying how the notion of God conceived originally by the Hindus was promising but how in the absence of "revelation," it had devolved into "darkness."[34] He highlighted the popular idolatrous religious practices in *brahmanic* temples as well as the worship of *gramadevatas*, such as Tipamma and her six sisters. These he regarded as examples of this degeneration.

> The goddess, placed in a beautifully ornamented palanquin, is carried in procession through the streets. In front of her there is another

divinity, a male. These two idols, which are entirely nude, are placed in immodest postures, and by help of a mechanism a disgusting movement is imparted to them as long as the procession continues. This disgusting spectacle, which is worthy of the depraved persons who look upon it, excites transports of mirth, manifested by shouts and bursts of laughter...

The goddess Tipamma of Mogur is not the only member of her family. She has six sisters, who are not in any way inferior to her in point of decency and politeness....

There are temples in certain isolated places, too, where the most disgusting debauchery is the only service agreeable to the presiding deity.[35]

Dubois's intention in reporting the spectacle as he observed it was obviously to lead his readers to the "consoling...religion of Jesus Christ."[36]

Company Officials Follow Along. Some British administrators took cues from the missionaries, as well as from misconceived observations, to declare the follies of the uncivilized nature of natives and the disastrous effects of worship of female divinities. They postured themselves as saviors whose mission was to bring civilization to the brown man's doorstep. Administrators such as William Sleeman in the middle of the nineteenth century wanted to elevate his own position in the colonial government by parading himself as a hero who had suppressed a seditious group guided by an uncouth female goddess.[37] Supporting the rhetoric of evangelicals, he blamed the culture of devotion to the goddess Kali/Durga/Bhavani as a threat to the basis of humanity.[38]

A Change of Strategy Required. Meanwhile, following William Jones, in the final years of the eighteenth century and then well into the nineteenth, much progress was made in western Indological studies by scholars like Henry Colebrooke, Nathaniel Halhead, Charles Wilkins, and others who were translating Sanskrit works and then offering their interpretations of Indian religions.[39] The learned attempts by these colonial scholars to interpret India's past, as well as their stated rationales for doing so, created a telling effect on the latest generation of Christian missionaries who were officially allowed into British colonial domains.[40] If they were to change India, missionaries like Rev. Alexander Duff understood the importance of gaining a deeper knowledge about Indian tradition.[41] In this process, some missionaries turned into philologists and scholars of India's past.

Prominent among these was Rev. Robert Caldwell, who had studied south Indian languages and published his study on Dravidian grammar in 1856. This work obviously was aimed at helping the missionaries to study south

Indian culture, while at the same time endorsing Jones's line of thought that *Rg Vedic* culture indicates a superior but now lost understanding of religion.[42] While Caldwell identified the legacy of *brahmans* as responsible for the preservation of civilized and more rational aspects of Hindu religion, he vilified the religious devotion of *ammans* (mothers or *gramadevatas*) as sharing many common traits with devils.[43] However, whether Caldwell intended it or not, his study of Dravidian language helped, to some extent, to recognize the independence and ancient character of Dravidian literature while thereby attracting other missionaries and administrators, albeit for the cause of Christianity, to study popular south Indian traditions. It was precisely within this context that the value of Ziegenbalg's work was finally recognized.

Zieganbalg's Work Exhumed. So, now, a century and a half later, the time was ripe to take up Ziegenbalg's work by German missionaries like Dr. Wilhelm Germann, and Rev. G. J. Metzger, who undertook to edit and publish the full extent of Ziegenbalg's work and to translate it into English.[44] Although progress in Indological studies had changed the atmosphere such that a need to publish Ziegenbalg's work was palpable, obviously this historical era also provided its own sets of biases and conditions that prohibited Zieganbalg's work from being published without some revisions. Germann, who added some additional material to the original work, presumably to give it more clarity, and Metzger, who took many liberties in editing and translating the manuscript into English, in the process removed some information that he claimed was repetitious, rewrote the introduction, and added appendices. Caldwell, who then reviewed Ziegenbalg's work in this newly edited form, did not find it as objectionable to change the original content, although he did praise Ziegenbalg's study as invaluable because it recorded the statements and ideas of the local people who at that time were free of any contemporary European influences.[45] The irony here is that although both Germann and Metzger agreed that the elapsed century and a half had not resulted in any change in the relevant aspects of local practice in Hindu religion since Ziegenbalg first recorded his observations, the pretext to change his original composition was to make it more presentable for the nineteenth-century readers who were of a different mindset than Europeans of the previous century. Indeed, what certainly had not changed during the elapsed time period, as it turned out, was the zeal of the missionaries to propagate Christianity or their view of Indians as depraved heathens who needed to be rescued earnestly.[46]

What had changed in a century and a half? As I have noted above, scholarly understanding of Indians and their culture by the west had changed significantly. Indeed, the second half of the nineteenth century saw an increasing number of scholars of mostly European, though some of Indian, origin, contributing to Indological studies either by translating texts like the *Vedas*, epics and *Puranas*, or by interpreting the past with the help of ancient Indian texts. These texts were acknowledged implicitly or explicitly as having derived from an Aryan or Indo-European heritage and hence were viewed as superior to the popular religious culture of south India, regarded as a lower form of religion originating from a non-Aryan source.[47] Whereas Ziegenbalg had acknowledged that the worship and ritual of *gramadevatas* was different from that of the gods and goddesses in urban major temples in important ways, he did not in any way indicate that the two forms had derived from different ethnic or racial origins. Here is an example of the type of comparison that Ziegenbalg offered:

> They [the Gramadevatas and the local goddesses] are not respected in the same way as the Mummurttis [Brahma, Vishnu, and Siva] and also worshipped with entirely different offerings. As a sign that they rule over and deal with devils the South Indians offer them animals which they consider impure, such as swine, goats and other animals. None from the Brahmin-caste serves as priest in the temples of these gods, because people from this caste do not even kill anything that has life and thus allow themselves to be [ritually] polluted.[48]

But a century and a half later, Metzger, like his contemporaries who were influenced by the Aryan theory of Vedic superiority over other forms of Indian religion, added a footnote in his English translation of Ziegenbalg's work to make it apparent that the two forms of religion were idiosyncratic:

> The worship of the tutelar deities and the demons that are associated with them forms, in fact, a distinct religion, which differs very much from that of Siva and Vishnu...The Brahmans and others of higher castes are, in general, ashamed of worshipping the Gramadevatas and their associates."[49]

This separation of popular religion from the *brahmanic* form was a clear shift from an age of innocence when there was no notion of Aryans as the authors of the *Vedas* or their connections to Europeans. This change of view of Indian society as constituting two divergent forms was what determined, to a large degree, the course of the study and the estimation of popular goddess cults for the next century.

Perceptions of the Goddess: Colonial
Interpretations of the Other

In this section, I will explore the appearance of a dominant theoretical pattern of Indological studies that surfaced between the second half of the nineteenth and the first half of the twentieth centuries in order to determine motivations for and assumptions of colonial interpretations regarding Hinduism, particularly in relation to popular goddesses. In my two-pronged approach, I will argue: 1) how the seeds sowed by the late eighteenth-century Indological studies starting from William Jones developed into a fully fledged theory by Max Muller that set the tone for his successors; and 2) how these theories portrayed popular Hindu goddesses in relation to Vedic religion; further, how these opinions matched their theoretical propositions and aims. These two inquiries are then applied to the rest of my discussion of the writings of British scholars, administrators, missionaries, and archaeologists of the twentieth century to assess whether or not, or in what ways, racial biases influenced their interpretations of popular Hinduism and goddess traditions, especially south Indian goddess traditions. The ramifications of this are discussed in the last section to indicate their relevance to my study in the following chapters.

Max Muller's Trademark. Max Muller's public persona was such that he appears as an Aryan supremacist promoting Sanskrit culture. Muller, who never set foot in India, showed in his personal letters his real intention in translating the *Rg Veda* into English:

> It [the *Rg Veda*] is the root of their religion and to show them what the root is, I am sure, the only way of uprooting all that has sprung from it during the last three thousand years.[50] [brackets mine]

While this was his private confession, Vedic literature and the ancient Indian past did receive some credibility in his public lectures. But when it came to the subject of Hindu goddesses, he believed that the goddesses were decidedly of "a non-Vedic spirit," and a "non-Aryan pollution of the true Hindu tradition," a racial slur not only to goddess worship itself but also to the entirety of what was called non-Vedic culture.[51] But then, Muller was not the first linguist who had dismissed the significance of Hindu goddesses. His predecessor, Colebrooke, had expressed the same view. David Kopf has stated that both Muller and Colbrooke held the Vedic world in high esteem but regarded contemporary Hindu practices as pantheistic and especially viewed the worship of fertility goddesses and the popular goddess Kali as a personification of evil.[52] What was essentially a racially biased attitude toward popular goddesses, such as Kali and others, slowly but surely spread to make its mark by the end of twentieth century, as well as throughout much of twentieth-century western scholarship.

As I mentioned above, Muller's theory did not seem to make much impact upon his hardworking contemporary, Sir Monier Monier-Williams, who as the Boden Professor of Sanskrit at Oxford University in 1831 was dedicated to promoting Christianity through his translations and interpretations of Sanskrit works. As Boden Professor, Monier-Williams had been expected to follow the trajectory established by H. H. Wilson.

H. H. Wilson, true to his vocational aim of demonstrating the superiority of Christianity, opined that "the Vedas are human and very ordinary writings, that the Puranas are modern and unauthentic, and even that the Tantras are not entitled to respect."[53] In that order of deterioration, Wilson went on to assert that most of the aspects of the practical religion of Hindus are "of an exceedingly mischievous and disgraceful nature." He referred to Kali as an "impure goddess." One can see his work as resonating with the sentiments of contemporary Christian missionaries.[54] In showing cracks in Hinduism, Wilson's mission was to help the Christian cause and not to emphasize or elevate the contribution of Aryans.

Succeeding Wilson, Monier-Williams's rationale for scholarship was really not very different from Wilson's.[55] What was different, however, is that Monier-Williams did not seem to overly concern himself with showing the dominance of Aryans over non-Aryans. Agreeing somewhat with Jones, but with no passionate tone or suggestion of ancestral links, Monier-Williams suggested the probability that popular Hindu goddesses, who he called "Mothers" and whose variety and extension of worship he enumerated with greater detail, originated from Aryan culture itself.[56] By suggesting this probability, Monier-Williams, in a way, had rebuffed the racially based theory articulated by Muller that there is a major divide in Hinduism along Aryan and non-Aryan racial lines and that the Hindu goddess is non-Aryan. Also, Monier-Williams did not see any inherent contradictions between the Saivite Hindu theistic conception of interrelated male and female energy on the one hand, and the commonplace practical worship by Hindu laity of village mothers in the form of a stone. In this sense Monier-Williams had achieved a remarkably sophisticated understanding of the integration of Hindu religious thought and popular cultic practice.[57]

In spite of his specific agenda to study Hindu culture for the purpose of eventually proving the superiority of Christianity, Monier-Williams's descriptive and analytical portrayal was, by some measure, the most objective and complete understanding rendered when compared to his Indological predecessors and as well as many of his successors.

Muller Deployed. Unlike Monier-Williams, Rev. Robert Caldwell seemed to authenticate the view that the Dravidians, despite being the first inhabitants of India, were indebted to their Aryan counterparts for the sophisticated aspects of Indian civilization. Assisting the British administration as well as the Christian missionaries in the late nineteenth century, John Murdoch, an educator who prepared school textbooks for south Indian students attending Christian missionary schools, took Caldwell's proposition of Dravidian cultural subordination to a further level. The general theme that Murdoch wanted to popularize among south Indian youth was that the civilized presence in the south has been the *brahman* "race" who came from outside, just like the British, with the high probability that these *brahman*s share in the same racial Aryan component as the British. [58] Setting this tone, in one of his textbooks, Murdoch stressed the evils of a degraded popular Hinduism:

> A tutelary god among the Hindus is one that delivers from the calamities believed to be due to demons. The village deities (grama-devata) probably represent the local fetiches (A fetich or fetish is any object, living or inanimate, looked upon as the representative or dwelling place of a god) once held in veneration by uncivilized aboriginal tribes . . . [59]

For Murdoch, the veneration of Dravidian deities was commensurate with the loss of religious credibility. As he put it: "Truly Hinduism is a mixture of sin and folly."[60] Murdoch's proposal, therefore, was whether *brahman*s or Dravidians, that there is only one way for Hindus to redeem themselves from their depraved conditions: to renounce Hinduism and Hindu culture and to embrace Christianity.

Although Max Muller eventually rescinded his racial theory, his successors continued to use it as a basis to study Indian culture. Isaac Taylor was one of those who employed new discoveries in race science to question Max Muller's statement about equating languages with races but not his opinion about the racial superiority of Aryans over their Dravidian counterparts or their "foul Dravidian worship of Siva and Kali, and the adoration of the lingam and the snake."[61]

Gustav Oppert, a professor of philology at the University of Madras and a Telugu language translator for the British Indian government at Madras, was one of the few scholars who did an elaborate study on south Indian culture, using linguistic evidence as well as ethnological observations.[62] He identified south Indians as "Gauda-Dravidians" and made links to European origins.[63] But, at the same time, like Caldwell, he thoroughly bought into the idea of the racial supremacy of Aryans, which led to him to say that the "Gauda-Dravidian" race possesses ugly features, is rude and has inherited a superstitious religious culture, clearly indicating Oppert's derogative stance toward them and their worship of popular deities. [64] In spite of centuries of intermingling between two races, he opined that some Dravidian religious features were still prominent in villages in the form of the worship of *gramadevatas* as chief local goddesses, with Aiyanar as a supreme deity.[65]

Whether they hated the British or considered British rule as a blessing, many English-educated Hindus, in response to the colonial criticism of many aspects of Hindu religion, wanted to rationalize their religion so that it could withstand criticism and meet western standards of rationality. Representing this latter group was an anthropologist, T. Ramakrishna, who documented village life in Andhra at the end of the nineteenth century with the encouragement of a British official, Sir M. E. Grant Duff, the Chancellor of Madras University. Like his colonial masters, Ramakrishna believed that the real Hindu religion was based on Sanskrit Hindu scriptures, while all folk forms were mere aberrations generated by the wicked and followed by the ignorant. His documentation of an Andhra village reveals his view of how well a hierarchical yet interdependent small village society could function if it only could follow hereditary caste professions as prescribed by sacred Hindu scriptures instead of succumbing to deviations such as worshiping the village goddess:

> Worship in the temple of the village goddess is of a very low kind. Animals are sacrificed, intoxicating drugs are taken and crude songs are sung. Hideous dances also form part of the worship.[66]

Ramakrishna hoped that with the help of British education, ignorance could be driven out of the country.[67] However, unlike his western counterparts, the difference with Ramakrishna was that he did not perceive Hindu religion along racial lines. As a native who was put in a defensive situation, it is not surprising that Ramakrishna would be eager to reform those aspects of his society that did not meet the British standards.

Drumming for the British. At the same time, not every colonialist needed the tool of Aryan racial theory to prove the greatness of the British. At the turn of the twentieth century, Edgar Thurston, a British official, compiled an exhaustive ethnographic account of south Indians through culling the British administrative records and consulting ethnological documentaries such as that of Ramakrishna's.[68] In his account, Thurston's aim was to show the changes the British government had wrought in reforming the common people of their superstitions and their practice of "hair raising" rituals to fulfill vows made to village goddesses. Thurston cites the reports of the Government

of Madras, which were collected in 1854, to rationalize the government's interference by banning religious acts such as swinging from iron hooks inserted
through the skin of one's back. [69] Thurston's job in documenting this information was, on the one hand, to show to educated Indians like Ramakrishna what
a noble cause this was and, on the other, to encourage British magistrates to
use their skills in persuading the public that the British government was working for a just cause.

In treating Aryan heritage as related to their own, European Indologists
regarded popular goddess religion as boorish at best. Scholars like Arthur
Berriedale Keith, who published *Religion and Philosophy of the Vedas and
Upanisads*, argued how Vedic religion became so tolerant in absorbing various lower forms that it lost its character when the religion of goddesses
was merged.[70] With this approach, Keith relegated the local goddesses of
sickness under the category of "evil beings" who were nothing but "disease
demons."[71]

While the above authors treated the subject of popular goddesses as a sub-
heading of their broader study areas, it was Henry Whitehead, an Anglican
bishop of Madras in the early twentieth century, who attempted, for the
first time, an extended study focused exclusively on popular village religion.
He published his work with the title *The Village Gods of South India*.[72] As a
missionary, Whitehead studied village religion with the same conviction as
Ziegenbalg.

> To the Christian the study has a still greater interest, because, amid all
> their repulsive features, these rites contain instinctive ideas and yearn-
> ings which find their satisfaction in the highest truths of Christianity.[73]

Village Hinduism prepared, Christianity completed. Make no mistake,
Whitehead agreed with Muller and his followers in identifying Hinduism as
containing "a strange medley of the most diverse forms of religion, ranging
from the most subtle and abstruse systems of philosophy to primitive forms
of animism," the former being the contribution of Aryans who had felt the
burden of civilizing the "simple Dravidian folk" so that "the primitive forms
of Dravidian religion have been modified to certain extant [so] that now both
forms of religion [are] followed by all south Indians except the isolated hill
tribes."[74] [brackets mine]

Overlapping with Whitehead's work, W. T. Elmore, an American who came
to south India to study village religion for the first time with purely scholarly interest, published his own study. Elmore was not a missionary but he,
nonetheless, was convinced that the south Indian village religion was purely

Dravidian, as exemplified by the title he gave to his book, *Dravidian Gods in Modern Hinduism: A Study of Local and Village Deities in South India.*[75] As far as the historical relationship between Aryans and Dravidians was concerned, he shared the same views as his missionary contemporary Whitehead, and other British colonial predecessors like Oppert and Baden-Powell:

> Although the Dravidians were worshippers of "mad gods," they were most tenacious of their religious rites. The Aryans did not attempt to compel them to give up their gods, but adopted the policy of bringing the people with their religion in to the fold of Hinduism.[76]

Elmore did not stop at branding Dravidian deities as "mad." Whether it was his complete ignorance of the Dravidian literary past or whether he was audacious enough to disregard the works of Caldwell and others, he stated:

> The Dravidians are not a literary people, and their religion has no literature. There are no Vedas or other writings telling of their gods.[77]

Somewhat contemporary to Whitehead and Elmore was W. Crooke, who reiterated the normative view regarding the civilizing influence of Aryans on non-Aryan races. Crooke, comparing the scholarship on the subject of goddesses from the time of Ziegenbalg to Bishop Whitehead, mapped out various local goddess traditions in the Indian subcontinent to argue that the worship of cruder and brutal forms of goddesses was the norm in those areas where there is less Aryan influence:

> These cults, in their more ecstatic or hysterical form, prevail chiefly among the Dravidians of the south, where they are connected with practices like devil-dancing, spirit possession and the like, which is less common among the more sober and less excitable races of northern India. In that part of the country it is only in places outside Aryavarta, the original Holy Land in the south-western Panjab, that the more brutal forms of animal sacrifice and ecstatic rites are found, as at the shrine of Kali in Calcutta, Kamakhya in Assam, Devi Patan in northern Oudh, and in Nepal.[78]

Crooke's view was fully consistent with many colonial scholars and missionaries who portrayed non-Aryan forms of religiosity, such as the rituals connected with the worship of goddesses, as vulgar and rough, with the rituals' central location being south India.

No Dichotomies Employed. H. Krishna Sastri, an archaeologist who belonged to the same time period as Whitehead and Elmore but a quarter-century later than Ramakrishna, was one of the very few scholars who studied the images of gods and goddesses both in the large urban Hindu temples and in those worshiped by villagers in humble rural settings. Unlike Ramakrishna, his book aimed not to glorify any particular group, but only to record strictly the iconography, rituals, and mythologies of the images of gods and goddesses as he observed them. He differentiated the worship in the big temples as "orthodox" from the worship at small humble shrines as "village," where he explained how different caste groups of priests, "Brahman" in the former, and "non-Brahman" or "Sudra" in the latter, served:

> In the temples dedicated to the village deities the ceremonial is not much different. Brahmans however rarely officiate and animal sacrifices are generally offered, especially when the village is threatened with an epidemic or with serious scarcity or famine. Vedic incantations are not uttered in these temples.[79]

To show how these two forms of worship are not exclusive, Krishna Sastri also documented the overlap between these two traditions.

> The worship in the shrines of village goddesses is generally performed by non-Brahmans....Sometimes, but very rarely, Brahmans also worship these fearful goddesses installed even within the sacred precincts of orthodox temples....On such occasions it is stated that the Sudra priest takes the place of the usual Brahmana and an entrance opening directly into the outer courtyard of the temple—kept closed on the other days of the year—is now thrown open for the goddess to receive animal sacrifices and worship from her Sudra or other devotees.[80]

Scholars like Krishna Sastri represented a section of Indian scholarship that relied in their interpretations mostly on iconographic manuals as well as contemporary practices, and yet did not seem to be convinced about the racial categories with which the late nineteenth- and early twentieth-century Indologists had been obsessed.[81]

Possible Goddess Origins and Indus Culture. The chance discovery in the 1920s of the ruins of the cities of Harappa and Mohenjodaro along the Indus River and its tributaries provided a different twist to the existing understanding of races and their role in India's past, as well as the historicity of its goddess worship. Aspects of this crucial discovery of a civilization unearthed in

Harappa and Mohenjodaro were first published in 1924 by John Marshall and later substantiated by Henry Sayce and others.[82] These studies pushed the age of the Indus civilization back to 3000 BCE, along with its worship of fertility cults. It also forced the consideration of the possible antiquity of Dravidian speaking groups in India and their capability of developing a high civilization before the migration of Aryan peoples into the region.[83]

Although Marshall believed in the simplistic conception of Aryans as handsome and Dravidians as ugly, as per colonial Vedic translations, he admitted that there was no sufficient archaeological proof to figure out the physical characteristics of those who formed the population of the Indus civilization. Leaving this issue aside, the religion Marshall observed in the ruins of the first great civilization was at odds with that of the Vedas.

> In the Vedic pantheon the female element is almost wholly subordinate to the male, and neither the Mother Goddess nor Siva [with whom, however, the Vedic Rudra was afterwards to be identified] has any place among its members. Among the Indus cults those of the Mother Goddess and Siva are prominent, and the female elements appear to be co-equal with, if not to predominate over, the male.[84] [brackets mine]

Marshall's observations pushed back into the hoary past to find the antiquity of fertility cults in the form of the worship of a "mother goddess" as a central part of the Indus civilization. The unearthed female terracotta figurines, either pregnant or carrying a child, were seen as physical evidence pointing in this direction.[85] In any case, while the antiquity of goddess origins was an impressive find, its association with Dravidians, who continued to be seen as subordinate to Aryans, did not make it a sophisticated religion either. The discovery of Indus civilization eventually led to a healthy debate about the source of goddess traditions that is useful to understand my study, and which I will take up in the next section.

Thus, the use of terms "Aryan," "non-Aryan," and "Dravidian" had become standard by the second half of the twentieth century, although the racial connotations of these words changed significantly since their first application in the eighteenth century. It should also be clear by now, with some exceptions, why it is that goddesses have been viewed in general as marginally religious (or "heathen"), and therefore why it is that only recently the study of goddesses has emerged as an important line of inquiry, both in western and Indian academic contexts. Most Indians, particularly from the south, and most western academics who are well acquainted with Indian religious culture, know that goddesses are the most ubiquitous form of deity veneration in so-called Hindu tradition. Why their study has been neglected historically in western academic circles is blatantly clear from the assumptions intrinsic to the European perspectives that I have outlined so far. Below I discuss how most of the germane post-colonial scholarship has generated different frameworks to study Indian culture and how this framework helped to interpret goddess traditions in a more realistic light. This discussion also indicates the interpretive strategies I have adopted in writing this book.

Goddesses Framed: (Within Theories about Hinduism)

The middle of the twentieth century was a period of experimentation in terms of finding a proper framework to analyze Indian society and Hindu religion. While some scholars in the post-colonial era continued to use "Aryan and Dravidian" either loosely to distinguish north from south or with an agenda to defend a weaker group, others found these terms inadequate or distorting. To interpret their field data effectively, these scholars proposed newer and, in some cases, more accurate and appropriate categories. I quote Louis Dumont in this regard who, while working to understand south Indian village gods and goddesses, found that earlier scholarship on the subject was distorting the present reality. Pointing out how a popular south Indian deity, Aiyanar, was portrayed first by Ziegenbalg and later by Oppert and Whitehead with very different, contrasting opinions and confusing assertions, Dumont reacted in the following manner:

> But the result first of all from hasty interpretations rooted in the idea, which has done so much harm, [is] that Indian culture is merely a juxtaposition of Aryan and so-called Dravidian or other elements.[brackets mine][86]

That India's religious culture cannot be simply reduced to the interplay of "Aryan and Dravidian" became one of the underlying issues for much of post-colonial scholarship in efforts to explore new ways of interpreting the religion and society encountered in Indian villages.

There has been a veritable explosion of goddess studies, especially in the last three decades, that have articulated some promising theories and analyses. What I attempt in this section is a broad-strokes description of the frameworks used by post-colonial and post-modern scholarship to interpret the significance of goddess traditions focused on village and popular goddesses such as Kali or Durga. My aim is to assess how various goddesses have been portrayed and understood by more recent scholarship in order to begin to strategize the vocabulary that I will employ in the following chapters.

My discussion of various models of interpretation that have been proposed by various scholars in the following pages does not fit into any neat chronological order, as often there are many overlaps with one group of scholars following one model for a few decades with others arguing this same model and applying alternatives in their own studies. As such, the material is treated not so much in chronological sequence but under the categories that the scholars proposed.

Sanskritization. "Sanskritization" has been understood by many scholars as a social process that has influenced various levels of hierarchical Indian society, a yardstick to measure how various components of literary and ritual *brahman*ical Hinduism have been deployed within local contexts to bolster status. M. N. Srinivas, a native anthropologist, was first to coin the term to explain how some castes manage to climb up the social ladder by Sanskritizing their life style. Srinivas further identified "Sanskritization" as a process that influenced "[t]he rites and beliefs of the castes occupying the lower rungs of the caste-ladder as well as the rites and beliefs of outlying communities hidden away in the forest-clothed mountains of India" and gave rise to various forms of Hinduism.[87] At the same time Srinivas also recognized the fusion that occurs between Sanskritic and non-Sanskritic systems of rituals and beliefs with *brahman*s and untouchables represented on either end of the hierarchical system, resulting in various new articulations of Hindu tradition.

Geographical Division. Srinivas attempted to classify various forms of Hinduism by geographical division, and suggested the categories of " 'All-India Hinduism,' 'Peninsular Hinduism,' 'Regional Hinduism,' and finally purely 'Local Hinduism.' " [88] In this analysis, the *brahman* caste is seen as the bastion and promoter of the "Sanskritization" process. For Srinivas, many cultural expressions, including local "blood-thirsty goddesses" as the lowest of the categories at the receiving end, can be subjected to this process.[89] Srinivas traced this extensive influence of "Sanskritization" to the propaganda of reformist movements and improvement in the modern communication system. From my own field observations, I think that Srinivas is right about the cause and extent of the recent Sanskritization process.

"Low and High" Culture. Some twenty years after he proposed the "geographical division" in Coorg, Srinivas studied a multi-caste village in the same state of Karnataka. In this study, he ranked the local cultures as "higher/lower" or "superior/inferior," in which "the articulated criteria of ranking were usually ritual, religious or moral resulting in concealing the importance of secular criteria."[90] In this sense, those caste groups that have numerical and economic strength, borrow the customs, ritual, and lifestyle of the higher and more Sanskritized castes to move up the ladder of the caste hierarchy.

In this context, Srinivas wondered whether improved health services, which effectively tackled epidemics, had an impact on the worship of *gramadevatas* and helped to increase the popularity of Sanskritic deities. My study in the following chapters reveals that although Sanskritization is a process influencing many dimensions of the society, including the worship of *gramadevatas*, the improved health services for human beings and domestic animals did not alleviate the need of worshiping *gramadevatas*.

Great and Little Traditions. The categories of "little and great" traditions to distinguish different Hinduisms were originally proposed by Robert Redfield and Milton Singer and were later followed by a host of scholars.[91]

Paul Wiebe, in his study of religious changes in a small town called Peddur in Andhra Pradesh, using Sanskritization as a measure, employed these categories to show how the worship of goddesses and spirits gain more importance among lower castes.[92]

By following great and little traditions on the basis of Sanskritization, Wiebe identified the worship of goddesses and spirits in village Andhra as a "little tradition" containing very little or no Sanskritization that was, therefore, mostly followed by the lowest spectrum of the society in Peddur. It is not clear whether Wiebe was including goddesses like Lakshmi, who is worshiped during certain calendrical festivals by higher castes, in this equation. Wiebe noted that Sanskritization is gaining ground with male deities receiving increasing importance at the cost of the goddesses. In general, goddesses and low castes on the one hand were fit into the little tradition category and male deities and high castes on the other were fit into the great tradition. An interesting question that could be posed at this juncture is this: since it is actually the worship of the *gramadevatas* that is so ubiquitous throughout south India when compared to the cultic presence of the so-called "higher," or Sanskrit deities, which are male deities who are buttressed by extensive literary traditions, doesn't the goddess tradition itself form something of a "great tradition" in its own right, especially since it is far more prevalent throughout the various strata of religious culture?

Parochialization vs. Universalization. Studying Kishan Garhi village, Marriott noticed certain processes that he called "parochialization" and "universalization," which helped to keep both "little" and "great" traditions in coexistence and equilibrium. "Parochialization" occurs as a "downward movement and transformation of contents between great and little traditions," whereas "universalization" happens when a deified spirit of a family becomes public and at times spreads beyond the village.[93] Nav Durga of great tradition, worshiped as "the local female godling Naurtha," serves as example of parochialization, while a deified ascetic of the next district becomes the deity of Kishan Garhi as part of universalization.

While the terminology applied to differentiate the deities of local relevance and the goddesses of pan-India is not as relevant to this study, the processes that Marriott noted hold true in many villages and towns of Andhra, as is illustrated through some examples I discuss in the next two chapters.

Aryan and non-Aryan/Dravidian. Following somewhat in the footsteps of Srinivas was S. C. Dube, who studied a village in Andhra, but who also believed that there was great Aryan fusion with non-Aryan groups, leading to the consolidation of Indian society and its Hindu religion.[94] Even so, he did not seem to perceive how any aspects of village life, including its religion, are divided along Aryan/non-Aryan lines. Instead, like Srinivas, what he identified was various shades of Hinduism fitting into a geographical division, with some deities worshiped at the village level, others in large urban areas, and still others at the pan-Indian level.[95]

Similar to Dube, there were anthropologists like Alan Beals, whose main focus was the functional aspects of religious rituals and who continued to employ terms such as "Dravidian" to imply "non-Brahmanical and non-Sanskritic" origins of the goddesses who accept non-vegetarian offerings. While the diet of the divinities played an important role for Beals in deciding whether their origins were either Aryan or Dravidian, the geographical division as proposed by Srinivas came in handy to substantiate the same.

Each jatra honors a different deity: Mariamma is the goddess of cholera and presumably of Dravidian or at least non-Brahminical origin; Ca Hussayn is a Muslim deity; Mallayya and Bhimayya both seem to be of Sanskritic or Brahminical origin although Mallayya's antecedents are not so easily traced. Mallayya and Bhimayya both receive vegetarian offerings, while Mariamma and Ca Hussayn receive offerings of meat.

The myth and ritual of these jatras involve a weaving together of local, regional, and pan-Indian tradition.[96]

It is clear that the tribal background of deities like Mallayya and Bhimayya was not taken into account by Beals when categorizing them as Sanskritic or *brahmanic* deities. In chapter 4, with the help of some specific cases, I have illustrated the historical process of how tribal cults have been assimilated into mainstream Hinduism.

While introducing the classic text *Devi Mahatmya*, the first exhaustive account of the great goddess written in Sanskrit, Thomas Coburn says that the work "takes as its point of departure the affirmation that the heartbeat of India culture has been the on-going and continuous interplay of the indigenous culture with that of the invading Aryans...."[97] He asserts that he is following "the opinion of scholarship, both Indian and Western" which "is virtually unanimous."[98] In addition, Coburn also noted that there is much Indian and western scholarship that traces the origins of the goddess to non-Aryan sources, and at times, specifically to Dravidian, but without going into any racial descriptions and their implications.[99]

Scholars like Norman Brown also employed the categories of pre-Aryan/non-Aryan as a matter of fact to identify certain components of Hinduism, such as the worship of mother goddesses as "pre-Aryan, or at least non-Aryan."[100]

Not only Sanskritization. Raising the issue of the unity of Hinduism, Milton Singer argued how "Srinivas's ideas on 'Sanskritization' and 'All-India spread' offer one approach to the problem," but do not address the all-India spread of other beliefs and practices, including the forms of "popular Hinduism" that could be either a diluted form of Sanskritic Hinduism or a form that is ancient/indigenous but has incorporated Sanskrit elements.[101] Singer had a critical eye not only in identifying other divergent streams flowing into Hinduism, but also the probability of the existence of another widespread form which he named "popular Hinduism."[102] However, his categorizing this form as a "little" tradition posed further problems.

For example, scholars like David Mandelbaum questioned the usage of categories such as "little" and "great" traditions by arguing how their deployment could lead to a misrepresentation of people's religious practices, since these two traditions are practiced universally in rural India.[103] This is a legitimate concern: rarely does a Hindu worship only local deities without incorporating the deities of all-India significance.

Transcendental and Pragmatic. Mandelbaum's argument was based on the fact that these distinctive aspects of religion are followed by the same people cutting across the hierarchical caste system, irrespective of their position in the order. To explain this phenomenon, he proposed "pragmatic" and "transcendental" complexes. Using a functionalist argument, Mandelbaum asserted that the pragmatic complex is defined as worship for personal gains and local needs, while the transcendental complex is meant for the welfare of community at large and for ultimate human goals, including "salvation." He further discussed the idiosyncratic nature of these two types and their applicability to one and the same divinity, thus changing the divinity's attributes in some minor ways.[104]

Mandelbaum explains how the two modes of worship fit into the realm of a goddess religiosity either at the village level or at the pan-Indian level. If these two complexes are complementary to each other and are applicable to all of the deities, then the question is whether it is necessary to have these markers at all.

Pauline Mahar Kolenda, who published her study earlier than Wiebe, noted a disparity in the observation of two different religious practices among a caste group. Discussing the applicability of the theory of fate among a north Indian sweeper caste, Kolenda noticed an infraction, which she described as "parochialization of philosophical concepts."[105] In this "parochialization," Kolenda stated that the sweepers resolve their paradoxical understanding of sudden deaths before their fated time and their concomitant worship of "supernaturals" ("the mother goddesses, godlings, and *bhuut-preets*") as a function of differences between "fate and God".[106] Kolenda argued that the gap between the "Philosophical Hinduism" and the religion practiced by sweepers was due more to the difference between ideals and their real applicability in day-to-day lives. For example, she reports that although educated men of the sweeper caste under the influence of the Arya Samaj insist that their caste people should believe in only one god, they acquiesced to their worried wives who continued approaching goddesses, godlings, and others to help in critical matters of life and death. This phenomenon of contradictions between theory and practice is present at many levels in popular Hinduism. In my study, I attribute many of these paradoxes to the historical occurrence of the merging of various religious traditions.

Sanskritic and Non-Sanskritic/Textual and Local. In 1959, Edward Harper, in his study of the Totagadde village in the Western Ghats of Mysore State, categorized the supernaturals of the village into what he called "a tentative typology, purposely oversimplified to bring some order to otherwise chaotic data." *Devaru* (vegetarian gods) were considered as ritually pure, *devate* (meat-eating deities), and *devva* (blood-demanding spirits) corresponded to the division of Sanskritic gods, local or secondary deities, and malevolent spirits, in that order.[107] Even though Harper identified *devaru* as "Sanskritic" gods in order to "refer to the way the supernatural realm is organized by contemporary inhabitants of a village," he was not convinced that the categorization of gods into Sanskritic and non-Sanskritic was methodologically sound.[108]

Lawrence Babb identified the religion practiced in his field area of the Chhattisgarh region of eastern Madhya Pradesh on two levels, the gods based on Sanskrit texts attended by Brahman priests as "Sanskrit" and those "primarily" found in villages attended by a "non-Brahman priesthood" with regional lore and usage as "non-Sanskritic."[109] Alternately, Babb also used the terms "textual," represented by a *brahman* priest and "local," with the role of a Baiga (non-*brahman*) as two opposing complexes. Babb made it clear that "local" does not mean unique to any particular locality but rather that it is an "essential parochialism of its [the Baiga complex's] manifestations and functions."[110] Although there is a distinction between these two religious complexes, Babb noted how the sophisticated as well as illiterate villagers recognize that all the deities of different characteristics in the end are one and the same. Babb's report is similar to what I encountered in coastal villages of Andhra, where all the *gramadevata*s are increasingly seen as forms of the goddess Durga. This recognition does not prevent villagers from approaching each of their goddesses differently and attributing to them specific characteristics and functions.

Benevolence and Malevolence. The theme of malevolence vs. benevolence was not new, as it had already been explored by several scholars, including Lawrence Babb. Comparing and contrasting the qualities of male and female divinities in both "textual" and "local" complexes, Babb identified females as "destructive" and males as using their power to restrain the destructive female attitude.[111]

Harper, on the other hand, had identified the upper castes and their gods as ritually pure as compared to the blood-demanding spirits who were likened by him to untouchable castes in terms of their ritually defiled state. In the same way, goddesses such as Mariamma were described as ambivalent deities, "who help and protect people, but who also may cause harm."[112] In Harper's analysis of social hierarchy, which corresponded to the divine hierarchy, what is significant is that Mariamma is described not just as "malevolent," but as "ambivalent," having the potential for both. The water begins to get muddy.

Susan Wadley employed the categories of benevolence and malevolence in a way to analyze the nature of supernatural beings in her study of religion in the north Indian village of Karimpur. Criticizing Babb's inadequate definition of the concept of "supernatural" and Harper's lack of defining the same, Wadley asserted that "the basic characteristic of any god, demon, or ghost is the powers which he/she controls and represents—the fact that he/she is in essence, power."[113] On this basis, Wadley organized the multiple number of powerful beings of Karimpur village under three groups in descending hierarchical order to show how they perform their actions in relation to "salvation," "shelter," and "rescue," containing negative and/or positive involvement with various good and bad results.[114] However, as far as goddesses are concerned, Wadley basically agrees about their impulsive nature and their subordination to male deities: "Their potential for malevolent action makes them more suspect than male deities."[115]

There are anthropologists like Susan A. Bean who took a different route in discussing the character of female deities. In her research on female energy (*sakti*) in the context of a Kannada village, Bean explained how female energy is expressed through mothers, women, *and* goddesses. In her assessment, she has transported the status of women to the realm of goddesses. In this scenario, goddesses fall into two categories, either benevolent or malevolent, depending on their relations to male deities.[116]

Like Bean, many scholars pursued the theme of how independent and unmarried goddesses are viewed as powerful and potentially destructive, while married goddesses are seen as subdued. By taking into consideration not only particular contexts but also their historical background, in my study of some specific goddesses I came to understand that the reasons for this potential destructiveness of goddesses are complex and quite varied according to situations.

Pure and Impure. Edward Harper, in his study of social and religious culture in the Malnad region of Karnataka, explored the malevolence of female deities by deploying the concepts of purity and pollution.[117] In this study, he argued how impurity angers the blood-demanding goddesses (*devates*) such as Mariamma, the "village guarding" smallpox goddess, more than her vegetarian counterparts and how she causes harm as a result.[118] He analyzed goddess anger as issuing from the imagination of ambivalent *sudras* who view any misfortune as a punishment given for their ritual impurity.[119]

On the other hand, he states that *brahmans* were not worried that their gods would take any retribution if they were inadvertently defiled, because it was "not generally part of the religious complex associated with these more pure gods."[120] This is ironic but consistent with my study of the goddesses like Mariamma and other deified goddesses, who help to reiterate the notions of caste hierarchy and patriarchy. The anger of Mariamma in Karnataka, as reported by Harper, reinforces the caste hierarchy, just as in Andhra villages, the appeasement of an angry goddess ennobles caste as well as gender hierarchy.

The notion of purity and impurity in Hindu religion has been explored in many different ritual contexts. Harper has employed this category to separate deities, including goddesses of different kinds, on the basis of the offerings that they receive. Louis Dumont explored the categories of "purity and impurity" further in his various works devoted to the study of south Indian societies. Mentioning the pantheon of deities worshiped by a caste group in the state of Tamilnadu, Dumont categorized them as "the pure (*suttam*) gods who do not eat meat, and the meat-eating gods who are impure (*asuttam*)" and that their relation is the same as the relation between meat-eating and non-meat-eating castes.[121] Stating that "the structure of the divine needs to be considered in relation to the social order," Dumont identified purity and impurity as both caste and divine markers.[122]

Dumont's argument of socially "impure" preferring "impure" deities has come under criticism by some scholars. Gabriella Eichinger Ferro-Luzzi argued "that a god's purity or impurity is a consequence primarily of his food habits and only secondarily of his character," in a study on food offerings in the four south Indian states of Tamilnadu, Kerala, Karnataka, and Andhra Pradesh, and she noted an anomaly of a Harijan caste group that traditionally falls lowest in the caste hierarchy, and hence was considered "impure," turning its "impure" goddess into "pure" by changing her diet.[123] However, treating this as an anomaly, she lays out the stereotypical division in the following words:

> In Hindu religion, several pairs of opposites are discernible....The pure deities include all the gods and goddesses of the great Sanskritic tradition of Hinduism, whereas village deities normally fall into the impure category. As a rule, pure and impure deities also differ in character: pure deities tend to be benevolent..., while impure deities are ferocious, causing disease and drought if not propitiated. There are borderline cases; Siva, for example, is not altogether benevolent, nor is Narasimha, the man-lion *avatar* of Vishnu.[124]

This categorization not only puts the *gramadevata* into a boxed category, but also treats her as a lower kind of deity. However, what is interesting in this division is the recognition of the ambivalent nature among some vegetarian male Sanskritic deities, such as Siva and Narasimha. This is an important observation to show how the ambivalent attitude in the divine arena is not gender-specific.

While fundamentally agreeing with Dumont's theory of divine hierarchy based upon the concepts of purity and impurity, Michael Moffat, in his study of a Harijan village in south India, also expressed some reservations. Moffat agreed to a large extent with Harper and Wadley as well, in that not only do the powers of divine beings diminish as they go down in the divine order, but also their beneficent attitude decreases. But a problem arises, he points out in his explanation, in that there is a possibility that different social hierarchical groups worship the same gods.[125] This "possibility," according to Moffat, does not always lead to a neat pairing of the "pure" caste groups worshiping "pure" deities or their lower caste counterparts worshiping only the "impure" deities.[126] Moffat's hesitation seems well-grounded not just in my own Andhra study area but elsewhere; Mandelbaum, earlier on, pointed out that those who worship *gramadevatas* also worship pan-Indian deities and vice versa.

Questioning Binaries. Bryan Pfaffenberger, a student of Mandelbaum's, questioned the dual categories used by Mandelbaum, Eichinger Ferro-Luzzi, and Babb, saying that these categories do not pay much attention to various Hindu social contexts. Pfaffenberger demonstrated, in his case study of south Indian Hinduism practiced among the Tamil folk in Sri Lanka's Jaffna peninsula, how these binaries would not make sense without taking into consideration the local social framework.[127]

I cannot agree more with Pfaffenberger on this point. This is much like the strategy of Diane Mines, when she categorizes various deities of the village Yanaimangalam in Tamilnadu:

> Scholars have sometimes described the distinction between universally recognized gods and strictly local ones as a distinction between a "great tradition" and a "little tradition" of Hinduism. But residents of Yanaimangalam have their own set of distinctions. They distinguish among three kinds of gods, what I will gloss here as Brahmanical gods (pirmanka tevarkal), village goddesses (ur ammankal), and fierce gods (matan or pey, lit. "ghost").[128]

Also focusing on local frameworks was the study conducted by Bruce Elliot Tapper in a Telugu village, Aripaka. In this study, Tapper argued that "certain cultural ideas about female personality" are used to "conceptualize deities which control human health."[129] The rationalization of females needing male control surfaces because of perceived female "excessive compulsiveness and passion," traits reinforced by ritual symbolism during festivals to the *grama-devatas*.[130] Because Tapper's study incorporates the geographical area, as well as some of the themes I pursue in my study, his findings are quite applicable to my own work.

Peasant Studies. Somewhat relevant to some of the themes I pursue are those "peasant studies" that have explored the diversity of people who inhabit villages and small towns of south India. Brenda Beck, who undertook the study of peasant society in Konku in the state of Tamilnadu in the 1970s, explained the centrally important theme that constituted this new approach:

> Fundamental to this newer historiography is the notion that a group of prior residents, who were tribally organized, pastoral people, were gradually displaced from India's forests and uplands by caste organized, village based communities. The colonization and settlement of new lands by peasant cultivators thus emerges as one of the important themes in the historical development of the south.[131]

In this newer framework, with a focus on a particular region in south India, the terms Aryan and Dravidian and their associated gods were not seen as determinative as terms such as *brahman* and other caste names in order to differentiate each group and their hierarchical order. The social order of castes depends on which caste group is politically or economically dominant at that particular locale and time. Whenever there is a shift in the power of caste groups, it is reflected in the way they worship their local clan goddesses.[132]

While clan deities are rarely seen in Andhra, rituals to the *gramadevatas* do serve as venues to establish and reinforce the social hierarchy. However, power shifts in a typical Andhra village where people pursue traditional occupations is not a frequent phenomenon.

Great vs. Independent and Left vs. Right. Identifying *brahman*ic temples as "great" and "official" and local goddesses such as Mariamman as "independent females" in "lesser" temples, Beck explained how the degree of participation in these temples is divided along local caste divisions such as "left" and "right."[133] Exploring the differences in the ritual roles of *brahman* and various non-*brahman* caste groups, Beck discussed how the division of social order extended to the deities of their caste and clan in Konku.[134] Beck's study suggests that while the goddess remained the focus of worship for all castes, villagers view their goddesses primarily in a way that is dependent on the division of castes to which they belong. In other words, this religiosity emphasizes the local rootedness of peasant castes.

It is interesting to note that most of the peasants under study who purportedly formed alliances with *brahman*s to promote their gods and goddesses migrated from coastal parts of Andhra. I will mention how these migrations play a role in spreading the tradition of *sati* in chapter 8.

Sanskritization/Aryanization? In attempting to define south Indian Hindu religion, Stein reopened the discussion of the relevance of using these traditional categories.[135] He started by questioning the historical origins of *brahmans* of south India in the "pure land" of the Aryans in the north, so called "*Aryavarta,*" and stated that *Aryavarta* is a myth perpetuated by European and *brahman* scholars over the years. While agreeing that the ancestors of most of the populations, including *brahman*s in peninsular India, came from outside, Stein pointed out that there is no evidence to prove that *brahman*s belonged to a separate ethnic group. The usage of terms like "Aryanization," and "Sanskritization" are misleading for Stein; for it is *the mutual interaction* of Sanskrit and Dravidian cultures that helped to create a south Indian Sanskritic tradition. For Stein, the "Dravidian culture," as practiced in pre-modern south India in the absence of any major cities, is neither merely folk, nor simply village, nor only rural. The south Indian Hindu religion, according to Stein, started in the medieval period under the patronage of Pallava and Chola rulers, as the product of a peasant/*brahman* alliance and then came to incorporate many divergent elements such as Vedic lore, heretical sects, and folk elements.[136] While I agree with the assertions that Stein made about pre-modern south India and the development of temple culture as a result of peasant/Brahman alliance, I argue in this book that although there are some high and low periods of cultural amalgamation, the process can be traced as early as to the first civilization that existed in the northwestern parts of Indian sub-continent.

In general, my studies in the following chapters are more radical historically, in that I endeavor to show that the origins of fertility goddess cults go back to pre-Buddhist and pre-*brahmanic* times. I will illustrate how the goddesses of Saivite and Vaishnavite traditions are borrowings from the cults of fertility goddesses.

Pure and High vs. Power Divinities. While Stein argued that there were no separate traditions such as Dravidian and Sanskrit because of their thorough mixture by the thirteenth century, Susan Bayly refuted this by saying that the two traditions remained separate until as late as the fourteenth century. According to Bayly, "the focus on divinities of blood and terror is clearly an ancient feature of south Indian religion" and these power divinities "were never wholly beneficent like some of the region's so-called 'pure' or 'high' gods."[137] Attributing the sudden rise in status of the south Indian goddess and her widespread worship from the fourteenth to the eighteenth century due to the growing power of the newly immigrant martial groups, Bayly argued that this involved neither the "Sanskritization" nor "cultural interaction" processes suggested by Stein.

> "This was not the 'Sanskritization', a term which has been used to describe a shift towards uniformly 'orthodox' and Brahmanical forms of Hindu worship. Here the dominant model came from the world of the warrior and the segmentary clan-based forest and plains dweller."[138]

When the two traditions came to interact with each other, Bayly argued, "it was neither the suppression of one tradition in favor of another, nor was there an attempt to 'purify' or *brahmanize* the worship of *ammans* and other power deities," although "the relationships were often ambivalent and contentious."[139]

To a certain degree, my argument will agree with Bayly's. In the following two chapters I trace the origins of many symbols employed by major religious orientations such as Buddhist, Jaina, Saiva, and Vaishnava to the fertility cult that is worshiped by the agricultural folk. In this sense, the fertility cult serves as a "dominant model" to these different religious traditions. Many surviving goddess mythologies in Andhra that I discuss in the following chapters do display "ambivalent and contentious" relationships between the goddess tradition and other traditions that I mentioned above.

Exclusive goddess studies. Some of the scholarship that focuses exclusively on the traditions of goddesses, either through literature or through ritual obser-vations, has been involved in the debate about whether the goddesses are traced to Vedic or to Indus origins. David Kinsley belonged to the group who traced the majority of goddess traditions to the Vedic or later Vedic contexts.[140]Although Kinsley did not subscribe to the theory of Indian goddesses originating in the Indus civilization very enthusiastically, if at all, he did differentiate village god-dess from that of the "Sanskritic" by referring to this latter category as "great" deities worshiped in large temples.[141] Kinsley also identified popular god-desses like Kali as non-Vedic by labeling them as "non-Aryan/non-Brahmanic" because of their dark complexion and their association with caves and moun-tains.[142] While the term "non-Aryan" and its association with dark complexion is problematic for the reasons discussed earlier, the category "non-*brahmanic*" is what I employed to differentiate goddesses whose origins lie in hunting or agricultural groups who spoke languages unrelated to Sanskrit.

There are other scholars who agreed with Kinsley in stating that there is no clear evidence to show that the Indus was the source for existing Hindu god-dess traditions. Gavin Flood, who understood that Indus culture was primarily Dravidian and that Vedic culture was Aryan, was not quite sure that the Hindu goddess tradition was necessarily the product of Indus civilization.[143] On the other hand, Flood agreed that "there is strong supporting evidence to show that the language of the Indus valley civilization was Dravidian" and "Aryan culture itself, including the Sanskrit language, has absorbed Dravidian ele-ments."[144] Kinsley and Flood may be right in not finding similarities between Indus goddess figures and the later *brahmanic* Hindu goddess figures associ-ated with male deities, but the similarities in concepts and symbolisms in relation to *gramadevatas* can hardly be ignored.

Vedic vs. Indus. Taking the argument of Kinsley and Flood further, schol-ars like Madeleine Biardeau traced the mythology, worship, and ritual of folk goddesses not so much to Dravidian religiosity but to the core of Aryan identity, the *Vedas*. Although this scholarship acknowledged the presence of divergent strains in Hindu religion, it argued that the basic structure of the religion, even in its folk form, was based on Vedic and classical patterns of ritual and mythology.

Biardeau, in her revolutionary study *Stories about Posts*, argued that the rit-uals, mythology, and the present and past practices connected to the goddess point to their origins in Vedic sacrifice.[145] Although Biardeau was not certain about the Aryan identity of *brahmans*, she did find the source of much of the present Hindu religious culture, both its folk and established forms with all its contradictions, in the *Vedas*.[146]

This contradiction is what Biardeau argued was present in contemporary folk rituals to the goddess Mariamma as well as in the worship of the *brahmanic* god Aiyanar.[147] The deities that are separated as non-Vedic, however, are the meat-eating demons. Finding striking similarities between the *asvamedha* sacrifice mentioned in the *Puranas* and contemporary goddess festivals, Biardeau argued that one must look at the worship and ritual of *gramadevatas* to understand the essence of opposing notions in Hinduism that are found in Vedic sacrifices. The reasons for these opposing similarities embedded in the Vedic sacrifices find a different explanation in Asko Parpola's argument, which I will relate shortly.

David Knipe followed the same route as Biardeau in his comparative study of the animal sacrifices to the *gramadevatas* and the ancient sacrifices to Vedic gods as they were performed in contemporary coastal Andhra Pradesh by arguing how the folk rituals to goddesses owe their origins to *Vedas*.[148]

Alf Hiltebeitel's studies fit into this category as well. Hiltebeitel's study of the Draupadi cult is focused on south Indian local mythologies and cultic veneration in the context of establishing their connections to the stories mentioned in the *Mahabharata*. His underlying argument throughout is that the local mythologies might incorporate divergent local elements depending on past history and culture, but ultimately the source for these mythologies lies in the epics whose cultic rituals follow the pattern of Vedic sacrifices.[149]

At a seemingly opposite spectrum of this scholarly argument are philologists such as Asko Parpola, whose focus has been to unpack the mystery of Indus civilization and culture through the decipherment of its script. There are several other scholars prior to Parpola who have traced goddess traditions to the Indus Valley, citing Indus seals and sealings as pictographic evidence.[150] What is new, however, was that with the decipherment of seals and sealings, Parpola illustrated clearly how various concepts and ideas, including the concept of auspicious goddesses, were actually practiced in the Indus Valley by Dravidian-speaking people and then how these got into Vedic and later Vedic culture. According to Parpola, there is, at least, a little less than a millennium separation between the end of the Indus period and the composition of the *Rg Veda* and that this long period of interaction between these two linguistic groups, Aryan and Dravidian, is what is reflected in *Rg Vedic* composition itself.[151]

Parpola's argument, with the theory of the introduction of Megalithic culture by horse-riding and warring nomads who spoke an Aryan language that belonged to the Iranian branch and who adopted the local language (Dravidian) and Black and Red Ware (BRW) culture, is relevant as far as the south Indian context is concerned.[152] This particular point of Parpola's is very significant because it points out once again how languages and racial groups, *contra* Muller, could be very different. This point, in fact, substantiates the earlier theory put forward by Andree Sjoberg and Clarence Maloney about how Dravidian languages came to be spoken by an amalgam of peoples.[153]

As far as the goddess tradition in Indus Valley is concerned, Parpola compared Indus seals and symbols with contemporary civilizations as well as the Vedic and later Vedic Sanskrit resources to prove the prevalence of goddess worship. What he shows is that some of these goddesses were not just of the *gramadevata* type, but that the prototypes of those later labeled as Sanskritic goddesses, such as Savitri, Arundhati, Durga, Sashthi, Prabhasa, Bhutamata, Parvati, Lakshmi, and Rohini, can be identified together with their ancient associations with trees, stars, and animals.[154] Parpola's arguments were supported and used by other Indus scholars such as Jane Mcintosh.[155]

My own study agrees with Parpola's findings only insofar as it is based largely on evidence drawn from material culture, and some of that material evidence is drawn from the remnants of the Indus civilization. Whether the linguistic research of Parpola and others is deemed completely scientific or not, it cannot be disputed that nomadic or semi-nomadic tribes like the Vedic Sanskrit speaking groups came into contact with other nomadic or isolated tribes. History tells us time and again how these groups, either through war or by trade, intermingled and influenced each other's ideas and concepts. Given this scenario, it is not unreasonable to assume that the high culture that appeared in the Indus River Valley must have left some impression on these texts. But given the fuzziness, I apply restraint in claiming that elaborate Hindu rituals known from later times were followed in the Indus, as has been argued by Parpola at times. In this sense, I follow Kinsley's approach of exercising caution in interpreting the Indus data.[156] At the same time, I do not think categorizing goddesses as "Aryan" and "non-Aryan" deities is justifiable, given the complexity of how goddess religious culture evolved. For this reason, my discussions in the next three chapters constitute a comparative study of the pre- and proto-historic goddess symbols and images of Andhra, in which I draw on many similarities with evidence from the Indus. This is to argue how some religious symbols and elements of goddess imagery may derive their origins from the Indus and retain some basic original features, in spite of their constant flux as they interacted with various emerging Indic religions on the one hand and other goddess cults of migrant and isolated groups on the other.

Feminist Theories. The words "Dravidian" and "Aryan" have yet to grow out of usage. Feminist scholars have advanced theories redefining the words Aryan and Dravidian. In one of these theories, women have been regarded as the introducers of goddess religion, who officiated over goddess rituals and continued to play a dominant role until *brahmanic* forces entered the scene. Lynn E. Gatwood described Aryans as bringing "patrifocal values" and a "war-like pantheon of gods" into village contexts that were originally based on peaceful Indus agricultural traditions.[157] In this equation, the Indus civilization stood for egalitarian values over and against the Aryan patriarchal culture that succeeded it. The interaction between these two cultures, Gatwood argued, resulted in a gradual acceptance of the goddess, first in a subordinated spousal position and much later emerging as the independent goddess, Mahadevi.

In a second interpretation, the meaning of the word "Aryan" extended not just to male gender, but to any oppressor. Representing this scholarship is Sarah Caldwell, who assessed the process of subduing goddess religion in two ways: 1) on the one hand, the patriarchal texts in Jaina, Buddhist, and Hindu traditions relegated goddess religion in a negative light; 2) on the other, there has been an attempt, especially by Sanskrit tradition, to incorporate and tame the goddess, as well as the tribal and low-caste women who officiate and participate in goddess rituals, under the umbrella of Sakta Tantrism.[158] In order to explain how and when the process of taming occurred, Caldwell, following in the footsteps of earlier scholarship, employs the word Aryan.

> ... Brahman influence began to be keenly felt due to extensive immigration of upper-caste Aryan groups into the south following the fall of the Gupta empire to the north.[159]

Aryan, in this context, stands for all those who have been oppressors of women in the past two millennia, the authors of patriarchal religions, (Jaina, Buddhist, and Hindu), as well as the patriarchal Mughals, the British colonialists, the founders of various reformist Hindu movements, and, presently, the high-caste groups. On the other hand, the women who were seen as oppressed are equated with those who are recognized as marginal, or at the lower stratum of the society, that is, the aboriginal, Dalit, untouchable, and other low-caste groups.

There are studies also focusing on specific goddess traditions, such as those conducted by Kathleen Erndl and William Sax, or exploring the religious traditions of *sati* in specific contexts, by scholars such as Lindsey Harlan. In a relatively recent book, *At The Feet of The Goddess*, Lynn Foulston conducted an innovative study by comparing local goddesses in two contrasting settlements of Orissa and Tamilnadu to show not just their shared features but also the complexities that make them impossible to compartmentalize.[160]

While there is so much more of relevance written on goddesses by feminists and others, here I will turn to Eveline Meyer, who studied the goddess

Ankalamma in Tamilnadu. In the long quote below, she has captured perfectly the dilemmas I have encountered in my own study:

A major problem in dealing with "folk" Hinduism is the choice of terms. Since Hinduism operates on many levels or combines elements from various levels or strata in the so-called process of "sanskritization", one is somewhat at a loss as to which terms should be applied to these levels. V. Das [Veena Das, *Structure and Cognition*, (1982)] has shown how terms of opposites such as "Sanskritic", "non-sanskritic", "sacred", "profane", "good-sacred", "bad-sacred" may be confusing, if not confined to a particular context. The same may be said for "little" and "big" traditions or for "village" gods....According to V. Das, who uses the terms left (death, inauspiciousness) and right (life, auspiciousness) over pure, bounded (articulated) and impure, liminal (disarticulated), Ankalamman is a goddess who fits only the left category, but both aspects of it (the impure, liminal as well as the pure, bounded) [Ibid., p.102-3, 143, 147]....Although these categories give room for a more precise description of particular aspects of goddesses, they do not suffice to describe a goddess as a whole, especially since a goddess may move from one category to another or even, in her various aspects, take part in all categories at the same time. To place Ankalamman into the left side is telling only half her story, at least with regard to her image in the myths. The myths make clear the problematics of any classification. They show that the goddess can be anything from a sophisticated cosmogonic concept to a very localized and socially clearly defined female deity, that she can be both benevolent and malevolent, pure and impure.[61]

These dilemmas have increased as the theories and categories put forward in the last two and a half decades have made the analytical picture far more complex, which I have discovered while I have proceeded with my own study. After much thought and reflection, and while I have indicated in this summary where some theoretical stances resonate with my findings, I have decided to let my material speak for itself as much as possible.

What follows in the ensuing chapters is my humble attempt to be analytically precise, but not overly preoccupied with theoretical matters. In my reprise of theoretical approaches that constitutes the first part of my book, various elements from recent theories that I have reviewed in this chapter will come to bear in specific instances I have analyzed, but they will not supplant the indigenous categories in play on the village ground. If I have relied in any way on one of the more general trajectories of approach reflected in previous studies, my own approach, as will be seen, is decidedly more historical.

At the same time that I have traced out the trajectories of post-modern and post-colonial scholarship and its relevance to my study, I hope that I have also successfully exposed the very serious problems intrinsic to the scholarship conducted by missionaries and colonials for their mercenary reasons. A closer review of post-modern and post-colonial scholarship might indeed identify traces of residues from earlier European and American scholarship. But suffice it to say that we are now on an improved track, and my hope in the chapters that follow is to make a contribution in that more favorable direction.

2

Contextualizing the Fertility Goddess

AND THE CULT OF *GRAMADEVATAS*

IN THE PREVIOUS chapter, I have discussed how western missionaries, philologists, and colonial administrators viewed popular goddesses such as Kali and Durga with great ambivalence. Thanks to the legacy of colonial western scholarship, some educated natives of Andhra regard the *gramadevatas* in small villages and towns with the same negative or ambivalent attitude as well. In my field study, I often encountered educated people, including archaeologists I have worked with before, steering me away from my research on *gramadevatas*. Intending to direct me to the "right path," they advised me to shift my focus to the goddesses of large urban temples. Unlike the colonialists mentioned above, ambivalence was limited to *gramadevatas*, but not necessarily extended to the goddesses considered as *brahmanic*, in which category Durga and Kali are often grouped. These people believe that the *brahmanic* goddesses have an authentic history to be discovered by scholars while the *gramadevatas* really have none. While this notion is widely prevalent, devotees of those *gramadevatas* who have acquired *brahmanic* identities insist that these goddesses are not lesser deities (*kshudra devatas*), but rather the incarnation of Parvati or Lakshmi or other recognized deities. Of course, there is the other side of the spectrum, where some devotees constantly try to retain the local intimacy of goddesses by either insisting on their special provenance at the village level or by localizing incarnations of *brahmanic* goddesses as special instances that reflect divine preference for their locales. My intention in this and the following chapters is to show how *gramadevatas* and the *brahmanic* pantheon of goddesses not only share the same ancient source, but also influence each other in their constant evolutions and reifications.

What follows here is an attempt to show how the prehistoric goddess, in spite of her changed identities, continues to retain some basic qualities and remains relevant as a goddess independent of *brahmanic*, Buddhist, and Jaina identities throughout history. Taking into account the primary nature of this prehistoric goddess, I refer to her as "fertility goddess." I discuss how this fertility goddess retains her identity in spite of her transformations as the Buddhist, Jaina, Saivite and other Hindu goddesses in the successive centuries in history. At least from the eleventh century, this "fertility goddess" has been referred to in inscriptions as *gramadevata*, a term that continues to be in vogue to the present day. Because there are certain *gramadevatas* transformed as *brahmanic* deities (i.e., Durga and Kali), who continue to be worshipped at the local level as *gramadevatas*, I distinguish these particular goddesses by employing the term "popular goddess." The relationship of the three terms can be described in the following manner: a popular goddess is a transformed fertility goddess who extends her jurisdiction throughout and beyond the South Asian cultural region, functioning both as a goddess in *brahmanic* temples and simultaneously serving at the village or local level as a *gramadevata*. As will be shown in the following chapters, the goddess Durga can bear all three of these identities.

Although there is some surviving evidence of iconic goddess images made of terracotta (very common) and other materials (very rare) coming from very early historic periods, it is a fact derived from common observation, as well as from scholarly studies, that a variety of goddesses at the village or local level or in household rituals have been worshiped for ages in non-iconic forms. Even when the goddess was worshiped in the image form in ritual proceedings, images were made of perishable materials, such as dung, clay, turmeric, rice flour, etc., leaving very little enduring material evidence as a result. With the exception of the Indus civilization that flourished for around two millennia well before the Common Era (CE), all other communities in the Indian subcontinent, especially those in Andhra, seemed to have lived on a subsistence basis until at least the fourth century BCE. In the absence of any major urbanization of the time, it makes sense that there is very little material evidence of the execution of images or symbols[1] in a long-lasting medium.

In any given society, an increase in production is what will give rise to an elite group of people who manage, own, and control excess resources. This elite group will have a capacity to undertake long-lasting projects, including the expression of religious ideas. The evidence of the first occurrence of this in the Indian subcontinent is obviously traced to the Indus valley civilization. This civilization in its heyday produced the first substantial material religious expressions in the form of seals and sealings in terracotta and stone. After the demise of this civilization, modified versions of these art forms started appearing in different parts of the Indian subcontinent, as and when the second urbanization process occurred.

While different areas of the subcontinent showed signs of a second urbanization as evidence through the remains of their art forms at different time periods, in the case of Andhra, the first art forms relating to fertility goddesses started appearing between the eighth and fourth century BCE, when populations living in Andhra engaged in megalithic culture (whose chief marker was the building of large stone burials in commemoration of the dead). As I will show below, almost all of the evidence related to the fertility goddess per se appeared during this proto-historic period in Andhra and seems linked to the Indus civilization. This cultural basis provided Andhra, like its counterparts in other regions of the Deccan peninsula, with a solid ground for the goddess cult, so that it was not easily eradicated, nor was it completely absorbed by Buddhist, Jaina, Saivite, and other Hindu traditions.

One of the main aims of this and the next two chapters is to reconstruct the history of the Andhra fertility goddess and her connection with the *gramadevata*. To achieve this, I will first look at symbols, images, rituals, and mythologies of the *gramadevata*s and trace them to the ancient known past. Reconstructing the history of the fertility goddess that remained distinct in some ways from the goddesses of the literary traditions, who are often endowed with large temples, is challenging, to say the least. For one thing, separating the fertility goddesses from the goddesses that acquired literary traditions means there is scant literary evidence in relation to the former. Moreover, representations of the fertility goddess in art have also been rare. But her transformed identities in the Buddhist, Saivite, Jaina, and Vaishnava traditions are prolific. I study how and in what forms these goddesses initially made their appearance in art and literature in order to trace their origins back to the source of the fertility goddess. I include discussions of these goddesses to depict the process of their transition and to demonstrate its effects on the fertility goddess cult. Most fertility goddesses make their first appearance in Buddhist art, although scholars often misunderstood them as initially *brahman*ic.[2] I will cite the pre-Buddhist and pre-*brahman*ic art to prove, on the one hand, how goddess religion predates both *brahman*ic and Buddhist forms in Andhra, and on the other, how these various religions were heavily dependent upon goddess symbols and imagery. I will also discuss the ways in which the goddess retains independence to continue her popularity at the village and suburb levels while experiencing simultaneous reification and reinvention.

The sources for this study are archaeological, iconographical, inscriptional, and literary, as well as from ethnography generated from my own field data. The main point of this and the next two chapters is to ascertain how the fertility goddess cult, though transformed as it was assimilated by various religious traditions over the centuries, also retained its independent character either in the form of a popular goddess or as a *gramadevata*.

Here, I will proceed to introduce a general understanding of the present *gramadevata* cult and the first known symbols and images of the prehistoric fertility goddess in order to establish elements of their shared identities.

Who is *gramadevata*? A *gramadevata* often is "at home" in the outdoors and usually symbolized aniconically in the form of a shapeless rock, a snake hole, or a tree. While she may also be seen in the form of images within more humbly constructed and appointed shrines at the edge of a village, *gramadevatas* are usually worshiped directly by devotees without any *brahman* priestly mediation and therefore without elaborate liturgical Sanskrit recitations. That is, she is usually addressed in the local vernacular with an accent on familial terminology. Most frequently she is known in familial terms in Telugu as *amma* or *talli* ("mother") or *akka devatalu* ("elder sister goddesses"). At times, she is addressed with the respectful and formal term *ammavaru* ("madam"). In the instance of her transition into a *brahmanic* deity, a *gramadevata*, she might acquire the Sanskrit suffix, "*amba*" or "*ambika*" ("mother") or "*devi*" (goddess). The priests and priestesses of these *gramadevata* are mostly from non-*brahmanic* castes and play a major cultic role only at the time of special festivals. While these characteristics are typical, in fast-changing contemporary Andhra, exceptions are quite common.

A typical traditional village generally propitiates its *gramadevata* as a guardian of the boundaries of the village (and hence is sometimes known as Polimeramma, meaning "mother of the borders"); as a presiding deity of a particular caste or group or craft, or of a household, or of crops, milk and milk products, rains and other water sources (such as rivers, rivulets, tanks); as a guardian of cattle or children; or as the bringer and curer of viral diseases as well as the mistress of the cremation ground. Sometimes the functions of *gramadevatas* may not be so specified, with the result being that goddesses are simply known *as grama devatalu* (village goddesses). In fact, villagers are not always so particular about the name of the goddess as they are about her functions. A village deity may also be simply called Uramma (village mother) or be named after the village itself as in Nandyalamma (mother of Nandyala village). Here it needs to be pointed out that the origin of the worship of a village goddess is usually regarded as the primordial social event of a village. Before any house is built in a village, an oblong stone is planted vertically in the center of what is to become the village. This is called *boddurai* (navel stone) and it is directly worshiped as the *gramadevata* (Figure 2.1). After the formation of the village, the elders of the village decide the extent of its boundaries and will plant another stone at the southern boundary. Whenever they go away from or

FIGURE 2.1 Boddurai

into the village, they will stop at the boundary stone and worship it by adorning it with turmeric and vermillion. What this means for the villagers is that the *gramadevata* is not primarily a symbol for some metaphysical or transcendental otherness, but rather is commensurate with the sacred space of the village itself. This principle of deifying the village is the same operation at work when Indians apply it more generally in deifying "mother India" Herself.[3]

There are common features germane to *gramadevata*s of Andhra, such as their intimate connection with natural rocks, waters, snake holes, serpents, trees, flowers, etc., which reflect their connections with the ancient fertility goddess. In addition to these characteristics, a typical *gramadevata* has an intrinsic connection to the village she represents. In this instance she represents that piece of earth that constitutes a village. In a way, this theme is as ancient as the fertility goddess herself, wherein she represented the earth.

The innumerable ways that villagers perceive a *gramadevata* is illustrated in her myths and annual rituals. Myths of *gramadevata*s are usually preserved in a song form sung by professionals. These professionals, just the same way as the priests of *gramadevata*s, are derived from various non-*brahmanic* castes. For example, the myth of goddess Renuka Ellamma in its many variations is sung by *mala*s or *madiga*s (formerly untouchable castes), the stories of the goddess Gangamma are sung by *golla*s (the traditional cattle/sheep/goat keepers), and the myths of the goddesses Pinnamma and Posamma are sung by the *chakalis* (washermen caste).⁴ That these specific caste singers specialize in the mythology of a particular goddess also indicates that these goddesses were originally worshiped by these caste groups before they became *gramadevatas*. The following myth, which relates the birth of the goddess Mahuramma, otherwise known as Ellamma, is prevalent in the villages of western Andhra.⁵ It is actually of great importance for understanding how goddess culture has evolved in Andhra.

Once, there existed a mountain king (Giri raju) who had several sons but no daughter. Seeking a daughter, Giri raju and his wife Parvati took many vows, by offering a numerous variety of green leaves (patri) and many vessels of water to the divinity. Watching their devotion, Adi Maha Sakti (the primordial great goddess) came in the form of a bird to their capital city Bhogavati.⁶ Impressed by the splendor of the city, she took the form of little worms and spread herself all over the city. The guards of the grove complained to the king that little worms had invaded the soil. When the king went to examine this situation, she appeared to him as lightning in the sky and then as an eagle swinging in the bed of the leaves on a white mimosa suma (jammi) tree. When the king's soldiers tried to catch the bird, Adi Maha Sakti quickly transformed herself into a thousand-hooded golden cobra and disappeared into a twelve-holed snake abode. When the king wondered about the meaning of all of this, his counselors explained to him that these signs meant that he would beget a daughter in the form of baby Mahuramma who would be Adi Maha Sakti herself. Hearing this, the king prayed to the goddess by lighting oil lamps, burning incense, and offering food, after which the snake abode grew to a height of many yards. The king then ordered his subordinates to dig into the snake hole, so Mahuramma decided to make it easier for him by appearing in the form of a baby.

Mahuramma, as Ellamma, is a popular *gramadevata* in Andhra's towns and villages. In the above myth, goddess Mahuramma is addressed as Adi Maha Sakti, indicating the villagers' view of her as responsible for the beginning of the universe. The myth also tells us that the goddess can take any form that she pleases. While a snake hole and a tree are her familiar abodes, her forms as bird, snake, and lightning indicates that the goddess has control over the earth as well as the atmosphere surrounding it. In annual rituals held for the *gramadevata*, devotees worship her in many different forms that include the tree, snake hole, and many more. To give an idea of how varied these forms are, I have mentioned variations of the ritual drawn mainly from ritual performances observed in China Waltair, Visakhapatnam.⁷ In coastal Andhra, the ritual for a *gramadevata* is held annually in the autumn just before the beginning of agricultural activities.[8] The colloquial Telugu words employed in this description, the details, the components and the number of days of the ritual, vary from region to region. The usual participants in the ritual come from a range of various non-*brahmin* castes comprising the whole social spectrum, except the *brahmans*.

A typical festival starts with an announcement by the beat of a drum by a *mala* or *madiga*. The following evening, the elders of the village, along with the village priest and drum beaters, go with a basket of food and water to the nearest snake hole, treated as the native place of the goddess. Here, they spray water and offer milk and eggs. They tie a thread to two sticks that are planted on either side of the hole. This is the symbolic way of inviting the goddess to the village festival in her honor and asking her to accept their offerings made during the festival.

Celebrations will commence on the next morning when the priest and village elders from agricultural castes, accompanied by drum-beaters, go again to the snake hole. Two of the village elders will carry on their heads a decorated *ghata/garaga* (clay or brass pot with different shapes and decorations) containing water and topped by an oil lamp. The pot that represents the goddess is smeared with turmeric and vermillion dots and flower garlands (Figure 2.2). The priest also carries on his head another representation of the goddess, a food basket containing cooked rice and lentils. The food is offered at the snake hole after smearing some water over the hole. Then one of the village elders,

FIGURE 2.2 Ghata/Garaga

with a gold finger ring, draws up some of the moistened soil from the snake hole and puts it in the basket. This moist, fertile soil is called *putta bangaram* (gold from the snake hole) and is symbolic of the goddess' presence. Then, they proceed to the *chadanampattu*, the center of the village, often marked with a spacious stage around the trunk of a pipal (ficus religiosus; the Sanskrit name is *asvattha*; Buddhists refer to it as the *bodhi* tree), margosa, or banyan (Indian fig or ficus bengalensis) tree that also represents the presence of goddess. (If they do not have this kind of permanent setup, the villagers will erect a small canopy as their temporary goddess shrine.) There, they keep the pot and "golden soil" with an oil lamp. These symbols "receive" worship from the devotees for the following week until the end of the festival. Whenever the pot of water is taken in procession through the village streets for worship and offerings, the golden soil remains behind to be worshiped by other devotees. In processions through the village for the next eight nights, the carrier of the pot, possessed by the goddess, dances rhythmically to an accompanying traditional orchestra and torchbearers. There are two or so other pot carriers who collect cooked food offerings given by the householders. These pots are also smeared with turmeric and vermilion dots, which indicate the presence of the goddess. After the symbols of the goddess and her offerings are brought back to the *chadanampattu*, many forms of entertainment, such as dances, dramas, and songs are performed in honor of the goddess. Later, the participants and other devotees who participate in the daily celebrations partake of the food that has been blessed by the goddess. During some nights, a ram or a male pig, washed and smeared with turmeric and vermilion, may be sacrificed. On the seventh night of the eight days of the festival, a special program called *pathana* (offerings to the goddess) is conducted. Farmers bring all of the varieties of agricultural produce reaped from their lands and offer these to the goddess along with turmeric and vermilion. The new produce itself is treated as a form of the goddess and is accompanied by turmeric and vermilion, the auspicious signs of the goddess.

On the eighth day, a ceremony called *toliyerlu* (the first tilling of the soil) is held around the *chadanampattu*. Farmers, including the village headman, first worship their plows and oxen by decorating them with turmeric, vermilion, and garlands and then bring them to the goddess.[9] The village headman takes the lead in plowing around *chadanampattu*. Making the first furrow with the blessings from the goddess is important. Sometimes, two men replace the oxen to hold the plow as a way of getting blessings from the goddess. There is a belief that after this act of plowing, there will be some rain showers as a sign of approval from the goddess for starting agricultural work. At this time, decorated bullock carts also go round in a procession.

The next morning, i.e., the last day of the celebrations, is called *anupu* or *ampakam* (send-off). It is the time to send the goddess back to her abode. On this day, the sacrificial animals are brought to the *chadanampattu*. The priest (in some village rituals, a male priest wears a female dress to please the goddess) brings *chaldi* (food cooked the night before and mixed with curds or buttermilk, which is considered good for the empty stomach) and offers this to the goddess (and is later eaten by the participants). On this day, a special anthropomorphic image of the goddess is carved out of margosa wood by a carpenter. In some areas, a potter makes the image out of clay. These images are nude and crudely made. Then the priest, along with village elders, goes in a procession to bring the image from the house of a carpenter or a potter. The carpenter/potter is offered beetle leaves, areca nuts, and some money.[10] Later in the evening the decorated pot with water, the golden soil, and the image are carried by the priest, accompanied by drummers and *poturaju* (a person who plays the role of "the brother or servant of the goddess," in some cases accepts offerings of chicken on behalf of the goddess, drinks the chicken blood, and beats himself with a rope).[11] Devotees vie with each other to receive a thrashing from the rope held by *poturaju*, as they believe that this brings luck (Figure 2.3). A female *ganachari* ("possessed by the goddess," one who speaks out on behalf of the goddess) joins the procession (Figure 2.4). The *ganachari* (who usually leaves her hair down and smears her face with turmeric and a big vermilion mark on her forehead) eats margosa leaves while dancing to the

FIGURE 2.3 Poturaju

FIGURE 2.4 Ganachari

beat of the drum. Village elders pursue her to speak out on the behalf of the goddess to know whether she is satisfied with their offerings and whether the following year will bring good rains and good crops. At each house, female devotees wash the feet of the priest and offer coconuts and fruits. After going through the main streets of the village, the procession finally reaches the shrine of the goddess. In big cities like Hyderabad, devotees offer *bonums* (decorated pots of food) to the goddess after drawing a pattern with rice powder on a cleared piece of earth. This pattern representing the goddess is called *patam* (picture). These *bonums* then are treated as the form of goddess and are carried by women on their heads in a procession. All these *bonum* pots are smeared with turmeric and vermilion. Some contain either special marks of the goddess, such as *svastika* (Figure 2.5), *trisula* (Figure 2.6), or an anthropomorphic image of the goddess (Figure 2.7).

At this point in the ritual, formerly it was a common practice to sacrifice a buffalo.[12] Since the Indian government's ban on animal sacrifices in 1960, a sheep or goat has replaced the buffalo, except in some remote villages. The sacrificial animal, always bathed, smeared in turmeric with a vermilion dot on its forehead and a flower garland on its neck, will be led in the procession before it is sacrificed (Figure 2.8).[13] The sacrifice is understood as a means of fulfilling the vows of the entire village. The animal is taken for sacrifice only if it shivers during the bathing. This shivering (an indication that the animal is possessed by the goddess) is interpreted as the approval given by the goddess.

FIGURE 2.5 *Svastika* Marks on the *Bonum* (Pot)

After cutting off the head of the animal, the foreleg is then cut from the body and put into the mouth of the animal's head and then offered to the deity. The sacrificial animal is regarded as a demon-lover that the goddess has subjugated. In other words, by killing the demon, it is said that the goddess accepts

FIGURE 2.6 *Trisula* Mark on the *Bonum* (Pot)

FIGURE 2.7 Goddess Lakshmi Images on the *Bonum* (Pot)

him to unite with her, as it is mentioned in the fifth century CE Sanskrit text, *Devi Mahatmya*.[14] In temples maintained by the government, the animal is symbolically sacrificed by touching its ear with a knife in front of the goddess. During the procession, both the sacrificial animal and the pot carrier, who is

FIGURE 2.8 Sacrificial Animals

also understood to be possessed by the deity, receive worship by householders. In the case of some of the *gramadevatas* like Nukalamma in Anakapalle
(Visakhapatnam District), clay pots full of toddy are offered at this time. Later,
in the midnight hour, some of the rice offered to the goddess is taken in a
toddy pot, after mixing it with the blood from the sacrificial animal, to spread
around the village with shouts of "food," in an attempt to drive evil spirits away
from the village. This procession is led with so much commotion that few, at
that time, are willing to be in the streets due to the fear of evil spirits. In some
village rituals, there is a practice of placing various grains in a pot of water
or blood collected from the sacrificed animal and putting this in front of the
goddess for three days to see what grains have sprouted well. Blood signifies
fertility.[15] The best-sprouted kinds are believed to have been selected by the
goddess to sow in their fields for that coming year. At the end of the ceremony
the temporary wooden or clay image of the goddess is taken in procession in a
small cart through the village (Figure 2.9). In some villages, these images are
taken apart and left out on the outskirts of the village or taken in procession to
be submerged in the nearby river, tank, or well.

FIGURE 2.9 Goddess Image in Procession

During the last day of the ritual to the goddess, married daughters in the vicinity are invited to their natal homes. During this festival, or whenever there is another major religious ritual of any kind, hearths are worshiped as the form of the goddess. After applying the paste of cow dung mixed with soil and water on the hearth, various auspicious and intricate patterns are drawn in front of the hearth. The first cooked meal on this hearth is a matter of boiling milk until it spills over the hearth and into the fire. This is considered an offering to the goddess. The goddess is also invoked every morning at the entrance of the house. Before sunrise, the courtyard and the entrance to each house in the village is swept, water mixed with cow dung is sprinkled to settle the dust on which auspicious patterns of rice flour are drawn. Many households keep a *tulsi* (Indian basil) plant in the back of their houses as the form of goddess. As part of worship the area around the plant is cleaned and auspicious patterns representing the goddess are drawn (Figure 2.10). The everyday ritual of drawing patterns in the front yard gets elaborated annually in a harvest festival called Sankranti, which is celebrated for three days in the middle of January, when the farmers reap their crops. In these instances, these auspicious patterns are worshiped (Figure 2.11). In the center of each pattern a cup made of cow dung is placed in which turmeric, vermilion, curds, flowers, fruits, grains, and vegetables are placed. Young girls worship this as Gobbemma, a form of Sri Lakshmi, the goddess of

FIGURE 2.10 *Tulsi* in Worship

FIGURE 2.11 Intricate Pattern

grains and abundance. While there are many festivals at which Sri Lakshmi is worshiped throughout the crop growing season, the month of Sravana (August) is especially dedicated to this goddess. During this time, the patterns at thresholds take many vegetative forms, with the lotus (Figure 2.12) especially prominent. In addition, on Tuesdays and Fridays in Sravana, Sri Lakshmi is worshiped as Gauri (the golden one) in home shrines in the form of a turmeric mound (Figure 2.13). The turmeric mound in Figure 2.13 is on the right, on a stool placed on new saris decorated by flowers and bangles, which are the auspicious signs of the goddess. The lotus pattern is also prominent in the rituals to *gramadevatas*. Matangi, a professional *ganachari* (a woman possessed by the goddess) devoted to the *gramadevata* starts her career in a ceremony by sitting on a lotus pattern drawn on the earth that had been smeared with cow dung.[16] In this context the lotus pattern symbolizes the power of the goddess that the Matangi is about to possess. The comparison of these patterns and symbols from the ancient past (as illustrated in the line drawings in Figures 2.14 through 2.22) helps us to identify the continuation of the usage of auspicious signs as the representation of goddess. Specific instances of worshiped patterns drawn on a wall symbolizing

FIGURE 2.12 Vegetative Pattern

FIGURE 2.13 Sri Lakshmi in Many Forms—Image, *Kalasa*, Turmeric Mound, Flowers, Leaves, and Bangles

a *gramadevata* in the form of sun, moon and other marks what came to be known as "Saivite" were reported by Whitehead:

> Sometimes, animals are sacrificed to Gangamma by the people in Ellore in the courtyards of their own houses. They then clean the wall of the house outside with cow-dung and make three horizontal lines with kumkuma (a red paste of turmeric and lime) [vermilion], with a dot above and below, and a semicircle on the right side with a dot in the middle, thus :-
> [2.14 Sacred Symbols on a Wall]
> The symbol on the right represents the sun and moon (the sun has to be drawn): that on the left is the Saivite sectarian mark (not drawn). They sacrifice to these symbols sheep, goats, and fowls. [brackets mine][17]

Like the goddess Ganga, Sri Lakshmi, in some areas outside of Andhra, is reported to have received animal sacrifices.[18] This is another feature of her ancient nature derived from the fertility goddess. The sacrificial animal is considered as the form of goddess herself. Some myths, such as the myth of Renuka that will be explained in the next chapter, illustrate how her violent death leads to her deification as a *gramadevata*. Analogous to this are the stories of several deified females who have become *gramadevatas*. I will analyze the significance of these in successive chapters. In all these cases, before they became *gramadevatas*, these females were victims in the same way as the sacrificial animal. While their stories and myths indicate the connection of their sacrifice with rebirth and rejuvenation, the reenactment of sacrifice in the annual worship of the goddess through an animal victim ensures this revitalization. One of the explanations of the ritual enactment is that the *gramadevata* is a victim at the hands of males (who are sometimes her husband). In turn, she asks for the sacrifice of a male animal representing her husband. In the act of sacrifice, the goddess is understood as uniting with her husband. Whether the sacrificial animal represents the goddess or her husband or a male relative, the goddess becomes the bloody sacrifice causing renewal and rebirth because blood is the potent symbol of the goddess, in which she establishes her seminal nature.

In the above descriptions of ritual, the symbolic presence of the goddess is seen in many different forms and contexts. Forms such as a basket, snake, snake hole, pot, tree, plows, carts, flowers, wooden or clay images, as well as substances like the sample soil from the snake hole, cow dung, turmeric, vermilion, rice flour, water, food, flowers, grain offerings, and sprouted seeds are all treated in the ritual as forms of the goddess. Living beings such as the priest, *poturaju, ganachari,* and the sacrificial animal possessed by the goddess are also seen as forms of the goddess. These contexts indicate that any living being that comes into contact ritually with the goddess also possesses her spirit or power. While possession is an expression derived from worshiping the deity, sacrifice by suffering, such as the *poturaju* beating himself and devotees vying with each other to receive his beatings, are ways of expressing devotion to the goddess in order to receive her grace in return. Discussing various sacrifices made to the goddess Bavaniyamman in Kerala by devotees in fulfillment of vows, some of which involve physical suffering while others "diminish their egocentric delusions," Elaine Craddock asserts that these are ways in which devotees "reaffirm their connection to her [the goddess] and her connection to the place and the devotional community."[19]

It is also clear from discussing the myth and ritual observances of the goddess that she inhabits varied and diverse living and non-living organisms of the earth. At the same time there is a clear recognition by villagers that the goddess, as earth mother, is the personification of fertility who creates, nurtures, and destroys on her own volition. In the context of ritual plowing, the furrow is understood as the symbol of opening up the womb or yoni (female sexual organ) of the earth goddess with the expectation of the delivery of good crops. While each of these animate and inanimate objects and substances carry specific meanings in the ritual contexts, the patterns using auspicious symbols, a few of which will be introduced in the next section, can be traced to the ancient past.

In the next section, I will first describe some traces of the goddess in Andhra to underline her connections to the first known goddess representations in India and their continuations with contemporary goddess traditions. Although these first traces constitute only a few symbols and a couple of images, they provide us with some initial links to the Indus civilization and to successive historical periods in Andhra where these symbols have been continuously appropriated.

Early Forms of the Fertility Goddess. The first signs of the fertility goddess in Andhra are noticed during the late Neolithic (new stone age) and early Megalithic (iron age) periods of the eighth to fourth century BCE, in the form of many auspicious symbols on materials such as pottery, burial slabs, burial goods, rock paintings, terracotta art, coins, etc.[20] These symbols became popular in their later incarnations with Sanskrit names such as *chakra* (a wheel represented in concentric circles: 2.15); *kamala* or *padma* (the lotus: 2.16); the *naga* (serpent [not illustrated]); *nandipada* (resembling the footprint of a bull which later came to be known as *triratna* or the "triple gems" in Buddhist and Jaina religions: 2.17); *srivatsa* (an endless knot evolved over time into different shapes of vegetation and the anthropomorphic shape of the goddess: 2.18); *svastika* (a cross with arms at right angles: 2.19); the *trisula* (trident), and the Ujjain symbol (a square with intersecting lines at the corners terminating in loops representing four quarters of the world: 2.20). All the symbols of this period, including a lone presence of a stamp on a solar disc with radiating circle in the middle, have their origins in the Indus period.[21] The *srivatsa*, represented in early Andhra as an unending knot, closely resembles the *srivatsa* symbol coming from Mohenjodaro.[22] This symbol later evolves to take many vegetative forms and ultimately to represent the goddess in human form. An even more popular symbol made to represent the universe, now known as *yantra* and portrayed in a star shape, also comes from this early period (Figure 2.21). Some symbols, including the *srivatsa*, are still used in their original or modified forms in *gramadevata* rituals, as well as in the form of rice flour patterns drawn in the earth every morning as a welcome sign to the goddess at the entrances of houses in village Andhra (as discussed above and shown in Figures 2.10 and 2.11). The significance of these symbols and their adaptations by other religious orientations, their relevance in contemporary goddess rituals, and their evolution is discussed in detail in the following chapter.

While symbolism has been predominant in goddess myth and ritual, it is not unusual to use anthropomorphic images of the goddess even in the ancient period. In this chapter I will assess a rare couple of examples of anthropomorphic representation of nude images of the goddess from the prehistoric period of Andhra, as a prelude to the discussion in chapter 4.

The first of these two figures is part of a primitive art rock carving at Mudumala village (Mahaboobnagar District), dating from the period between the eighth and fourth centuries BCE.[23] The illustration represents the original carving of the goddess with a bull (Figure 2.22). This nude figure, with upraised hands and legs apart, is flanked by a humped bull and four *trisulas* (tridents [not illustrated]). The nudity of the goddess is not an anomaly, as a second nude goddess figure made of terracotta and dating from the Megalithic levels of fourth century BCE has been found in the same vicinity. These two findings, and evidence of other nude goddess figures from other parts of India starting from 2500 BCE, confirm that nudity was equated with the fertility of goddesses for many centuries.[24] In fact, the combination of a nude goddess with a bull and trident is also not rare, as this combination appeared first in the Indus where a bison bull approaches a prostrate naked goddess to have intercourse.[25] This theme of the naked goddess with a bull continued later, as is seen in 1200 BCE in the present states of Maharashtra and Rajasthan.[26]

The *trisula* is a popular representation of the Neolithic and Megalithic periods seen either in association with the anthropomorphic image of goddesses, or in connection with her symbolic form, such as *nandipada, srivatsa, svastika,* and *naga,* represented in rock paintings and incisions and on pottery, coins, and burial slabs.[27] The goddess who protected villages carried the *trisula* to control the wild and to punish the wicked. Note that in the succeeding periods, the *trisula* served as an emblem for goddesses like Durga before it became popular with the Saivite cult.

As far as the representation of the bulls in Mudumala rock art is concerned, their prominent genitals and horns pointing forward appear to be sexually charged. The economic and religio-cultural significance of a sexually charged bull must by no means be underrated. A pair of healthy bullocks is crucial to a farmer to till his farm and carry the burden. To ensure a good stock of bullocks in Andhra, there has been a tradition of stamping a young sturdy bull as the stud for the village cows. The stamped bull is attached to the village goddess temple and allowed to roam freely in the village to get his fodder as well as to mate with the cows. As such, it is not surprising to see how the bull occupies a significant role in agricultural societies where fertility is the pulse. It is for this reason that the Mudumala bull shares a similarity with the representation of charged bulls in Indus seals.[28] Susan Huntington, who studied Indus art forms meticulously, stated, "perhaps the prowess of the bull [was] also used in the Harappan context to symbolize procreative and progenitive powers."[29] Referring to a multi-faced anthropomorphic god wearing a crown of buffalo horns and a fig branch and squatting on a throne that has hoofed legs, Asko Parpola argues that this god might be the anthropomorphic evolution of the bull.[30] To support this, he cites two amulets: one is from Harappa containing a deity with a human body and bull face and another is from Mohenjodaro showing a horned deity sitting in "yogic" posture on a throne with hoofed legs.[31] A third representation in a seal from Mohenjodaro shows a multi-faced anthropomorphic deity squatting on a throne with hoofed legs.[32] The virility of the bull is similarly esteemed highly in much later periods. Famous religious personalities such as Gautama the Buddha and Adinatha (the first Jain Tirthankara) are each portrayed in art as a bull, indicating their superior physical natures.[33] For this reason, as well as, perhaps, the fertility symbolism, the bull becomes the vehicle of Siva.

The depiction of the goddess in her nude form with her legs apart next to the sexually charged bull can be interpreted as a metaphor both for the cow and the earth, as a sexually charged virulent bull is important for the cows to get more sturdy bullocks, who in turn help the farmer to till the soil and make it fertile. The goddess, as illustrated in the next chapter, is seen both as the form of earth as well as a cow. An Indus seal depicting the goddess giving birth to vegetation can be understood as the mother earth itself.[34] The prehistoric naked goddesses appeared either in association with the bull of twelfth century BCE in the present states of Maharashtra and Rajasthan, or alone as in a gold plaque from the eighth or seventh BCE from Bihar, which came to be identified by scholars as Prthivi, who is known as the earth goddess in the *Rig Veda*.[35] Another goddess, whose motherhood is central in *Rig Veda* and who is seen as a divine cow providing nourishment with her milk, is Aditi.[36] This does not mean to say that the concept of earth as mother or holy cow is only as old as the *Rig Veda*, the composition of which is commonly agreed to be between fifteenth and twelfth BCE. In fact, as noted earlier, the archaeological evidence suggests that the fertility related goddess traditions and her connection to the earth and cows could be traced to several centuries earlier than the composition of *Rig Veda*, a text considered in popular imagination as the root of present-day Hinduism. For example, the notion of mother earth or holy cow needing the virility of a bull is represented in a seal belonging to the Indus civilization. This Indus seal shows a bull in intercourse with a figure that has been later identified as the *Rig Vedic* goddess Aditi, known as the mother of gods.[37] This is because the conflation of Aditi with Prthivi occurs in later Vedic literature, where both goddesses are seen as the form of earth.[38]

Therefore, it is no surprise that Neolithic agricultural communities in Andhra venerated the mother earth in a naked human form accompanied by bull. An incised figure of a plow flanked by a solar disc and an Ujjain symbol in the early historic levels of Andhra show the veneration extended to the plow that was used by a pair of bullocks to till the soil.[39] This veneration, in turn, shows the role of the bullocks and their relation to the earth. There are many references in the epics and *Puranas* about rulers undertaking ritual plowing.[40] In this context, the first plowing with the bullock undertaken in the annual ritual to the *gramadevata* may be recalled. Now, because the bull came to be identified with Siva as his mount, Nandi, it is hard for many to see the connection between the goddess and the bull. However, there are scholars like Carol Bolon, who understand the early association of goddess with the bull. Showing some specific examples of pre-Saivite representations of the goddess and her affinity with bull, Bolon argues that the bull as Siva's vehicle came as a much later development.[41] This, in fact, is the case in Andhra, as the Saivite presence is not evident until the second century CE.

While there is sufficient evidence to prove the continuity of the worship of the naked form of the goddess in the following centuries, as I demonstrate in chapter 4, I will also mention here some inscriptional evidence to show her connection with the present *gramadevata* cult. One instance pointing us in this direction is a short third-century inscription on the base of a large-sized stone image of a naked goddess, the upper part of which is broken. According to this inscription, in order to seek long life for her husband and son, Mahadevi Khanduvata, a queen of the Ikshvaku dynasty, arranged for the image of the goddess to be installed for worship.[42] The second inscription, issued five centuries later than the first one, involves Lokamavva, the queen of the Chalukya ruler, Bhima II. The queen made a donation to the temple of Ellamma, who is a popular *gramadevata* in many villages, towns, and cities of Andhra and whose name is used in many myths. In any case, the first record makes it clear that the Ikshvaku queen approached Ellamma in the same way as contemporary women devotees approach her, seeking either offspring or the health and longevity of their family members. Thus, Ellamma, for more than two thousand years, has been understood as the goddess of fertility and protection. Probably because of her strong associations with fertility, Ellamma is almost always worshiped in her naked form. For example, a seventh century naked image of goddess Ellamma is still in worship at Alampur (Mahaboobnagar District). Ellamma, with Renuka as her other name, remains popular in Andhra and in the neighboring states of Tamilnadu and Karnataka as well.

While Ellamma was a popular name, as known from inscriptions issued from the twelfth to the sixteenth centuries, many *gramadevatas* were named after their villages, villages that often shared the same mythology connecting them with the goddess Ellamma.[43] As in contemporary *gramadevata* worship, sometimes the *gramadevata* was just called Mother, as known from a ninth-century grant made by a ruler of the Chola dynasty. This grant of four villages is found near the temple of *gramadevata* Dasanamma in Pulapatturu (East Godavari District). These inscriptions point out the attention some *gramadevatas* received by the elite and the ruling class. Royal patronage sometimes led to changes in iconography, functions, and characteristics of the *gramadevata* cult. In these instances, *gramadevatas* acquired permanent shrines. Their primary function extended from fertility to providing victory in battles, while their iconography shifted from naked images to fierce feminine forms wielding many weapons. This does not mean to say that royalty did not favor the fertility aspect of goddesses, as there are some clear examples that I will discuss in the next chapter to prove otherwise. It is just that the warrior nature of the goddess received much emphasis as the rulers engaged in constant warfare with their neighbors.

Thus, the inscriptional evidence shows that the fertility goddess, on the one hand, retained her features in the form of *gramadevata* in agricultural and village contexts, and on the other hand, changed her persona under the patronage of royalty. While this is one aspect, there are multiple other factors at work in the evolution and multiplication of various forms of what originally was a fertility goddess. I now turn to a discussion of these factors in the succeeding chapters.

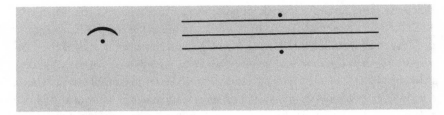

FIGURE 2.14 Patterns on Wall

FIGURE 2.15 Chakra

FIGURE 2.16 Lotus

FIGURE 2.17 Nandipada

FIGURE 2.18 Srivatsa

FIGURE 2.19 Svastika

FIGURE 2.20 Ujjain Symbol

FIGURE 2.21 Star

FIGURE 2.22 Goddess & Bull

3

Fertility Symbols of Goddesses

HISTORICAL RENDERINGS AND CONTEMPORARY PRACTICES

SYMBOLS ARE VITAL to ritual articulations in all religious traditions. They embody what is regarded as sacred. Without understanding ritual context, the religious meaning of a symbol is by no means apparent. For instance, a tree is a tree without any religious meaning unless it is known that the tree is worshiped because it embodies a spiritual force, i.e., the presence of a goddess. Within the logic of the religious context I am tracking, I can elaborate further: since a tree springs out of and draws its nourishment from the earth, and the earth is a mother goddess, the tree is imbued with the spirit of the goddess.

In this chapter, I introduce important symbols associated with the goddess within mythic and ritual contexts. I discuss symbols that are ancient artifacts—art forms and sculptures. In order to connect contemporary goddess worship with the historic past, I will also discuss symbols embedded within mythology and ritual before surveying their historical religious significance. I assess how important goddess symbols have somewhat changed their meanings when appropriated by the Buddhist, Saivite, Vaishnava, and Jaina religious orientations. I also illustrate how these symbols have evolved into the anthropomorphic shape of goddesses now incorporated into those particular traditions. This inquiry is done with the aim of finding how and why goddess symbols have been appropriated by various religious traditions of India and in what ways some of these symbols have evolved to take on an anthropomorphic shape. At the same time, I will indicate how many of these symbols have remained aniconic and still vital in the contemporary ritual worship of *gramadevatas*.

I have organized the data for various symbols categorically. To illustrate the continuity of these symbols that function as veritable expressive forms of the goddess, each category of symbol, or each symbol, is studied in three distinctive periods or contexts in relation to: 1) contemporary *gramadevatas*, 2) ancient independent fertility goddesses, and 3) the fertility goddess transformed within India's various religious traditions. This is something of a circular method, at least when considered historically, for my aim in this scheme is first to contextualize each of these symbols in contemporary mythology and ritual, and then to study these symbols in their early pre-Buddhist, pre-Saivite, pre-Vaishnavite or pre-Jaina fertility goddess guises. With this understanding established, I will proceed to discuss succeeding periods when these symbols were absorbed within Buddhist, Saivite, Vaishnavite, and Jaina art. Since most of the transformations of fertility goddess symbols in Andhra occur initially in Buddhist art and are then followed by Saivite, Vaishnavite and Jaina representations, the discussions will proceed first with Buddhist art.

Vegetation Goddess. Among the symbols present in proto-historic Andhra, the *srivatsa* was considered symbolic of the primary vegetative force of the fertility goddess. In addition to the *srivatsa*, the symbolic representation of the tree and its historical evolution is discussed in this section.

In the previous chapter, I noted mythic and ritual traditions that refer to how the tree is often understood in the contemporary cultic context as an abode of the *gramadevata*. Moreover, ritual proceedings indicate that *the tree is actually regarded as a form of the gramadevata*. That is, there is no discrimination between the natural abode of the goddess and the goddess herself: as a bird living in the tree, or as a cobra living in the snake hole, all of those (the bird, tree, snake and snake hole) are regarded at the village level as possible forms of the goddess. I came across an interesting and imaginative shrine in Gandepalli (Krishna District), for instance, where the *gramadevata* Mutyalamma's head had been carved on a stone and placed in the hole of a Banyan tree trunk (Figure 3.1). In this instance, both the stone image and the tree are regarded as veritable forms of the goddess.

In many instances, anthropomorphic images of *gramadevatas* are worshiped in a formal shrine as well as in the form of a tree within the precincts of her temple. Types of trees that are worshiped as goddesses include the margosa or neem or *melia azadirachta (vepa)*, mimosa suma *(jammi)*, *philanthrus umblica (vuciri)*, *acacia arabica (tumma)*, *ficus racemosa* (glomerous fig tree), banyan or *ficus bengalensis (marri)*, and pipal or *ficus religiosus*. While it is common to worship a tree along with the image form of *gramadevata*, it is rare to decorate the tree as the anthropomorphic form of goddess. An instance of the worship of tree as a *gramadevata* with a sari wrapped around its trunk, with a bend in the trunk as head, can be seen in the shrine dedicated to Mahankali in Hyderabad (Figure 3.2). A small image of the head of the goddess is placed in the bend to make the intention clear. This attempt is not novel, as artists and

FIGURE 3.1 Mutyalamma in *Marrimanu*, Gandepalli

FIGURE 3.2 Tree as Anthropomorphic Shape of Goddess

religious teachers in the ancient past have attempted to give anthropomorphic form to trees. I will refer more to this phenomenon later.

A striking instance of how a tree comes to be worshiped as a goddess is evident in the cult of Maridamma, a popular goddess venerated widely in one of the colonies of Visakhapatnam City. According to oral tradition, four generations ago, a young married couple, formerly of the untouchable caste, were travelling to visit their relatives when they spotted a beautiful little *brahmin* girl.¹ This girl revealed to the couple that if they would worship her, their lot in life would greatly improve. The couple agreed, and the next morning they saw a tiny margosa or neem tree—a tropical tree which has cooling shade and medicinal values—growing in front of their camp exactly where the *brahmin* girl had stood the day before. They believed that the girl herself had been transformed into the sapling, which they then brought home carefully to plant, nourish, and worship. As the sapling eventually grew into a large tree, the number of worshipers increased, and a platform was built around the tree to more formally enshrine the goddess's presence. Today, devotees worship the tree by applying turmeric and vermillion to its trunk and by offering fruits and coconuts at its base. During annual festival days, both male and female descendants of the founding couple's family act as the goddess's priestly intermediaries. Since the goddess is believed to be a *brahman* herself, she does not receive any animal sacrifices. Village, caste, and *brahmanic* elements all contribute to the identity of the goddess and her forms of worship, but in this case it appears that *brahmanic* elements are primarily ornamental and are present essentially for the purpose of social prestige.²

The margosa tree, in general, is very popular as a form of the goddess associated with the outbreak and curing of viral diseases. Indeed, throughout regions of Andhra, the margosa goddess is known by variety of names: Mutyalamma, Ellamma, Posamma, Gangamma, Sitalamma, Pallalamma, Peddamma, Nukalamma, and Maridamma. These goddesses' association with the neem tree is established in many ways, from worshiping the tree directly to decorating the entrances and porticos of their respective temples with neem branches (Figure 3.3).

In contemporary Andhra, although diseases like smallpox have disappeared and cholera is under control, chickenpox and measles are still prominent in the hot season. The myth of the pox goddess, Nalla Pochamma in Secunderabad, well illustrates the nature of this aspect of *gramadevatas*.³ Because Pochamma is dark-skinned, she came to be called Nalla (black) Pochamma. Her story is related as follows. Peddamma, the older sister of Nalla Pochamma, had many children. Nalla Pochamma loved to caress these children. But Peddamma was afraid that her children would get her dark skin color by continuously coming

FIGURE 3.3 Margosa Leaves for Erukamma

into contact with Nalla Pochamma. So she began to hide her children when-ever her sister visited. As Nalla Pochamma left the house, the hidden children would come out, some laughing, some crying, and others playing, but they all contracted different viral diseases. That is, they were possessed by Nalla Pochamma in the form of viral diseases. When Peddamma pleaded with her sister for forgiveness, Nalla Pochamma gave her the remedy: that Peddamma, for eleven consecutive days, should perform a circumambulation around her (Nalla Pochamma) with a pot of cool water, margosa leaves, and turmeric, and on the eleventh day she should offer her a pot of fresh toddy. The pox goddess likes cooling substances such as margosa leaves and toddy.

Since margosa leaves have a calming effect on a patient's body, branches with its leaves are used as fans for comfort. During the recovery from illness, to kill germs, the paste of these leaves is mixed with turmeric and applied while bathing. In this case, the goddess is seen as both cool and hot: cool in the form of margosa and hot in the form of disease; for, she is seen as the disease as well as its remedy. For the same reason, those who are possessed by the goddess in the *gramadevata*'s annual rituals are given margosa branches both to fan themselves and also to chew the leaves. In the case of goddess Ellamma's annual ritual, in Ellamma Rangapuram (Mahaboobnagar District), women devotees wear nothing but the margosa leaves around their bodies.[4]

This practice, performed as a vow, is also prevalent in Tamilnadu in the cult of goddess Mariamman.[5] Craddock mentions this in the context of explaining how sacrifice and suffering are incorporated into vows performed to identify with the sacrifice and suffering of the goddess herself.

Myths about "the goddess of viral disease" illustrate the goddess's vengeance or displeasure on the one hand, and her association with the margosa tree on the other. Like many of the myths of *gramadevatas*, there are many variations of this story. The version I relate here is prevalent in Chittoor District and is told specifically in relation to the goddess Gangamma.[6] An outcaste man, pretending that he was a *brahman*, solicited and received his traditional education from a certain *brahman* teacher and eventually married the teacher's daughter. One day his mother came in search of him. When she had located her son, he immediately informed her of his socially transformed situation. Before being introduced to his in-laws, he instructed her to assume the attire of a *brahman* widow by wearing a saffron sari and asked her to shave her head. She was also instructed to pretend that she was dumb in order that her true caste identity not be discovered. Soon, one day while eating some delicious food, the "widow mother" forgot her pretense and exclaimed a phrase that betrayed her non-*brahman* identity. Ganga, the daughter of the teacher, thus discovered her husband's mischief, and mused despondently on how she had been utterly polluted by intimate contact with these outcaste people. To purify herself, she locked herself inside a room and burned herself to death. Later, her husband found her spirit form among the branches of the margosa tree and asked her to resume her human form. She refused and remained in the tree. Instead, she cursed him and his mother to be reborn as a he-buffalo and sheep respectively, to be sacrificed to her year after year in an annual rite. This story, of course, reveals something of the tensions between *brahmans*, who are at the top on social hierarchy, and the untouchables, the lowest on the social ladder. In defending their purity at all costs, the *brahmans* gain an upper hand by not only being identified as innocent victims of the untouchables' chicanery, but in ultimately claiming the *gramadevata* of the village as a wronged daughter of their families. In this instance, that is, they have justly, on their moral grounds, claimed responsibility for the origins of goddess veneration prevalent among the lower castes. Moreover, an exclamation point to their superiority in purity is added by portraying the untouchables as the scapegoats that deserve to be regarded as nothing but beastly sacrificial animals for the goddess's placation. This myth would also seem to serve as a kind of warning to the lower castes not to go beyond their limits and not to aspire beyond their status. Clearly, the myth articulates a case of appropriation of the fertility goddess cult by *brahman* priests. Nonetheless, the non-*brahman* castes in this area, as elsewhere in Andhra, affirm the veracity of this story and continue to play prominent roles in the rituals of *gramadevata* cults that have been taken over by *brahman* encroachment.

In a contrasting myth to the one just related, another goddess renowned in Saiva tradition is worshiped as a *gramadevata* in villages like Munsabpeta in Srikakulam District. This is none other than Parvati, famously known in pan-Indian tradition as the spouse of the great god Siva. But in Munsabpeta, she is simply worshiped in the form of a palm tree.[7] Her annual festival, called *Gowri Purnima Varalu* celebrated each year in the bright fortnight of Asvayujam (September-October), identifies Parvati as Gowri. Parvati, like a typical *gramadevata*, presides over epidemics and pests that ravage the village. In addition to the offerings of sweetmeats in the annual festival, cooked food and curries, fowls and sheep are also sacrificed. When offering blood sacrifices, branches of the tree *alangium lamarcku* (*udugu*) are dipped in the blood of the sacrificed animals and planted on the bunds of the village's adjoining fields. This act is believed to promote the crop yield. This practice of spilling blood on the twigs before planting them in their fields during the time of ritual is a tradition that is very well-known in this district.[8] It also specifies the fertility aspect associated with blood sacrifices, where the spilled blood is believed to help promote new life. In this cultic context, we see how the principles of the fertility goddess have been sustained in the contemporary context and that the later Saiva identity of the goddess has not been acknowledged. This is one of the rare instances of a goddess whose character as a *gramadevata* has been sustained, despite the fact she has been given a *brahmanic* identity at the pan-Indian level.

Not just one tree, but a whole grove can also be regarded as a form of the goddess, as seen at Pedatadivada in the Visakhapatnam District. In this village, the *gramadevata* Pyditalli is just that. She is invited annually into the village from her grove. A fasting priest goes in procession ceremoniously to the grove to cut a branch off one of its trees. Possessed by the goddess, the priest then sits on the branch while he is carried round the village in a procession.

There are other goddesses in rural Andhra, like Batukamma and Boddemma, who represent the seasons of weather that abet the growth and harvesting of crops. They are worshiped in the form of shrubs like the purple galega (*vempali*), cassia accidentals (*tangedu*) and a variety of other flowers. Boddemma, who in ritual context is associated with the soil from the snake hole that is then topped by flower arrangements, is considered as Batukamma's younger sister. Boddemma represents the rainy season and Batukamma, the winter season. The literal meaning of Batukamma is "come alive, mother." The word "amma" can also be used to address a daughter affectionately. In this sense, the word can be translated as "darling mother." In the same fashion, the name Boddemma can be translated as "younger darling," referring to a little daughter who is younger than her older sister. Batukamma's festival is observed by married women for eleven days starting on the last day of the lunar month of Bhadrapada until the day after the Dasarah festival (in October) in order to procure her blessings for the well-being of their families. Following Batukamma's festival, unmarried girls seeking early marriages worship Boddemma for nine days. However, in Adilabad District, the worship lasts for a month, culminating with the festival of Deepavali (festival of lights), in the lunar month of Ashwayuja (October and November).

While these contemporary examples all illustrate how a *gramadevata* is identified with vegetation in many forms, the discussion in the immediately following pages demonstrates that goddess associations with vegetation are quite ancient. In these discussions, I will also show how these vegetal associations of the goddess were later incorporated by the Buddhist and Hindu religious traditions.

The general sacredness attributed to vegetation and its interrelation with the fertility goddess is represented in an oblong sealing from the Indus civilization where a goddess is shown giving birth to vegetation.[9] The association of naked goddesses with vegetation, especially the fig tree, is shown in various Indus seals.[10]

Standing for vegetative fertility, the *srivatsa* symbol, as noted at the outset of this discussion, has its origins both in the Indus civilization and in proto-historic Andhra. Two major processes have occurred with this symbol. The first process has to do with its meaning. The symbol eventually came to represent the superhuman quality of the Buddha and *tirthankaras* (enlightened Jain teachers). For example, the *srivatsa*, along with the *chakra* and the *svastika*, are marks that frequently designated the presence of the Buddha before he was routinely carved in human form. At Nagarjunakonda (Guntur District), the empty throne with a *svastika* mark on the pillow at the back is conspicuous as a symbol functioning precisely in this way (Figure 3.4). The same is conveyed by the *srivatsa* on the pillar standing behind the throne (Figure 3.4). Here, the *srivatsa* mark resembles a frog or an anthropomorphic female in a birthing position, the details of which will be discussed in the next section. The *srivatsa* and *svatstika*, along with the *chakra* (Figure 3.5), the lotus (Figure 3.6), and the *naga* (Figure 3.7), have become very popular symbols associated either with the Buddha or with the stupa (itself a symbol of the Buddha) in Andhra's Buddhist art. These symbols were also carved on the soles of the Buddha's feet at places like Amaravati (Krishna District) and

Phanigiri (Nalgonda District) (Figure 3.8), constituting *mahapurusha lakshana* (auspicious symbols marking a superhuman being).[11] In general, these symbols convey the meaning that the Buddha possesses superhuman abilities to alleviate suffering (*dukkha*), the fundamental problem of existence. In short, they have been utilized by early Andhra Buddhists at Nagarjunakonda and Amaravati as symbols to interpret the presence of the Buddha.

The appropriation of these symbols is not specific to Andhra; it has spread throughout the entire Buddhist world. For example, a Central Asian painting of the Buddha contains the mark of *srivatsa* on his bare chest, along with other symbols to reflect his character as *mahapurusha*.[12] The *svastika* and the *srivatsa* became part of the *asthamangala* (eight auspicious signs) that Jainas would adopt into their art.[13] Like the image of the Buddha, the icons of Jain *tirthankaras* are dotted with auspicious marks as shown in the tenth- and eleventh-century *tirthankaras* of Nizamabad and Chittoor Districts.[14]

The *srivatsa* has been adapted into Vaishnava religious culture as well, with its original meaning intact, i.e., as the fertility goddess herself. But in doing so, Vaishnavites subordinated the Buddhist renderings by providing an abode for the fertility goddess who came to be known as Sri.[15] By possessing Sri, Vishnu

FIGURE 3.8 Buddha *Padas*.
Source: Photo provided by the Director, Andhra Pradesh State Archaeology Museum

also acquired the splendor of royalty, as shown in an early representation of a seated Narasimha (his lion form) from Kondamotu in which he bears the *srivatsa* on his chest (Figure 3.9).[16] Although the image of this fourth-century depiction of a seated Narasimha is accompanied by five other standing figures on a panel of limestone, his superiority and regal status is understood by his seated posture on a throne and his holding of a club and a *chakra*. While the *srivatsa* takes human form to become Vishnu's spouse, the *chakra* becomes an important weapon for Vishnu.

The initial appearance of the *srivatsa* in the Megalithic period of Andhra (eighth to third century BCE) is in the form of an unending knot (Figure 2.18) or as a triangle or a creeper on pottery and coins.[17] In proto-historic Andhra, it sometimes assumes the shape of two pot motifs, one inverted over the other. This may not be a mere coincidence, as the pot shares with *srivatsa* the common motif of fertility. It was not unusual for the *srivatsa* to incorporate other goddess symbols as it took on different vegetative shapes to show its complementarity with other symbols. For example, Andhra rulers during the fist century BCE to first century CE issued coins with the symbol of the goddess on the obverse side as a blessing sign.[18] Here, the *srivatsa* appears as though two *nagas* are facing a lotus bud (Figure 3.10). Altogether, the symbol gives the appearance of a seated anthropomorphic figure of the goddess. What a firmly seated goddess indicates is the security of royal power.

In the same way, the *srivatsa*, as integral part of living organisms, is reflected in a couple of early Buddhist panels. The first one is on a carved slab at Tirumalagiri (Karimnagar District) belonging to the fourth to third century

FIGURE 3.9 *Srivatsa* on Narasimha
Source: Photo provided by the Director, Andhra Pradesh State Archaeology Museum

FIGURE 3.10 *Srivatsa* on Coin
Source: Photo provided by the Director, Andhra Pradesh State Archaeology Museum

BCE in association with a jumbled mix of life in the wild, with water, vegetation, aquatic and land animals (Figure 3.11).[19] Surrounded by this, the *srivatsa* shows how the goddess stands for life in its many forms. This depiction can be explained as the fecund nature of the goddess in the form of *srivatsa* giving birth to crocodiles, *nagas*, other wild animals and vegetation. This also shows the identical nature of the goddess with wilderness in its many forms.

A second variation of the *srivatsa* in Andhra is seen in a third-century CE Buddhist entry step stone at Kesanapalle (Guntur District), where the symbol is portrayed with lotuses issuing from it, giving an illusion of the abdomen of the goddess with hands and legs attached (Figure 3.12).[20] It shares some similarities with the earlier depiction in which the fish replace crocodiles. Both convey her association with life-giving waters. Like the *srivatsa*, a pair of fish representing the sacred rivers become part of the *ashtamangala* (eight auspicious) signs for the Buddha. Another *srivatsa* symbol of the same period, portraying vegetation in a partial anthropomorphic shape of the goddess, is seen at Amaravati, where her belly area is shown as a lotus medallion (Figure 3.13).[21] Here, the symbol assumes more or less the same headless anthropomorphic form as was seen on the pillar behind the throne of the Buddha at Nagarjunakonda (Figure 3.4). With what could be conceived as arms and splayed legs, these two figures share a resemblance to the naked goddess figure of Mudumala rock carving. These symbols bear a lotus in their bellies. The lotus forming part of the head is an evolving *srivatsa* motif seen in places outside of Andhra, such as at Sanchi in Madhya Pradesh.[22] This motif repeats itself as part of a creeper known as *kalpavalli* (wish-fulfilling creeper). The *kalpavalli* producing material goods is often depicted in Buddhist and Hindu sites, such as at Bharhut in Madhya Pradesh and at Nachna in Rajasthan.[23] The representation of the lotus as the head of an anthropomorphic naked image of goddess is not uncommon, as is discussed in the following pages. An interesting combination of *purnakumbha* and lotuses issuing out of *srivatsa* is also seen in a different panel at Sanchi.[24]

While the above are Buddhist renderings, the further evolution of the *srivatsa* in *brahmanic* art is apparent where the symbol is given due status as a goddess by installing her on a pedestal in the company of other deities. Two examples of this are seen in the fourth-century CE sculptural panels in Peddamudiyam (Cuddapah District).[25] The symbol in one of these two panels appears in combination with the *chakra*. The *chakra* with an added crown gives an illusion of the head of the anthropomorphic shape of the goddess (Figure 3.14). The *srivatsa* in the second panel appears as the outline of a diminutive anthropomorphic goddess under the hood of the *naga* (Figure 3.15). Thus, it would seem as if the *srivatsa* was conjoined with other goddess symbols to abet the evolution of goddess representations in anthropomorphic form.

The *srivatsa* and its evolution into the anthropomorphic shape of goddess is also noticed in other places in the Indian subcontinent, including Sri Lanka, as early as 1000 BCE.[26] An almost full evolution of the *srivatsa* into the anthropomorphic shape of the goddess comes from Thanjavur in the state of Tamilnadu (Figure 3.16). In this depiction, the goddess is flanked by elephants, thus forming a harbinger of her later popular form as Gaja Lakshmi (Sri Lakshmi accompanied by elephants) (Figure 2.13). (An early example of a fully evolved anthropomorphic form of Gaja Lakshmi is discussed in the following chapter.)

With regard to the representation of trees in ancient art, the frequent depictions of the pipal (*ravi*), or *asvatha*, or *bodhi* tree and its leaves in the Indus period and its uncanny continuation in early Buddhist art shows that the tree as a representation of goddess was held sacred for centuries.[27] Trees in enclosures are shown on coins of pre- and early Satavahana rulers.[28] Referring to a scene of an uprooted tree from a relief at Bhaja Vihara in Maharashtra, Susan Huntington observed, "the uprooting of trees may relate to pre-Buddhist cults (such as that of the *Yaksas*) that the Buddhists had to overcome."[29] The relief contained many sacred trees enclosed by railings, indicating the prevalence of tree worship. Huntington is correct in her assumption that the followers of the Buddha had to struggle to replace earlier worship patterns with Buddhist ideals. But it seems that the Buddhists understood the futility of trying to eradicate this widespread cult, and instead, learned the wisdom of manipulating the same cultic symbols of the goddess to their advantage. According to the *Vinayapitaka*, the Buddha meditated under different trees for seven weeks after his enlightenment experience. Some of these episodes are portrayed at Nagarjunakonda.[30]

In later Buddhist art, we see a change of strategy by accepting the fertility aspect of trees in such a way that fits more appropriately with fertility goddess themes. Huntington states that the typical representation of the birth of Siddhartha is shown in various sculpted renditions with "Queen Maya grasping a sal tree, with the *bodhisattva*-child emerging from her right side."[31] Here, the Buddhists clearly utilized the fertility function of the tree held by Queen Maya to depict her birthing of Siddhartha. Moreover, this specific strategy is also seen at Amaravati, Nagarjunakonda, and Chandavaram (Prakasam District), where tree spirits are shown protecting the newly born Siddhartha, an event mentioned in Jataka stories.[32] A second-century BCE sculpture of a tree, now in the Indian Museum at Bharhut, Madhya Pradesh, is represented as having an extended pair of hands offering food and water to passersby.[33]

While analyzing Amaravati art, Fergusson observed that tree worship was more prevalent in the early stages of Buddhism than it was later.[34] This was simply because trees evolved into anthropomorphic forms of the goddess in later art. Among the earlier depictions is the introduction of the tree as the *kalpavriksha* (wish-fulfilling tree) parting a panel depicting the *Mandhata Jataka* at Amaravati.[35] Similar to the meaning attached to the *kalpavalli*, that is, the concept of the gift-giving, the *kalpavriksha* itself derived from the worship of the tree as a fertility force that connoted abundance and wealth. In a transformative stage in the BCE Buddhist art of Amaravati, trees with *yakshis* or *vrikshadevatas* (tree goddesses) emanating out of them are often shown.[36] At Nagarjunakonda, by the first two centuries in the CE, *yakshis* in youthful forms are seen standing under trees either alone or accompanied by a male figure.[37] The fully developed image of the forest goddess, *vanadevata* or *vriksha devata*, evolved from these *yakshis* in the later stages of Buddhist art at Amaravati and Nagarjunakonda.[38] In Theravada Buddhist countries such as Sri Lanka, the bodhi tree, where devotees seeking offspring pour milk on its roots, basically serves the same function as the fertility goddess. In Myanmar, another Theravada Buddhist country, the wish-fulfilling *kalpavriksha* is prominent during the annual Kathina (robe-giving) rites, when the laity present their gifts in the form of a money tree to monks.

The *srivatsa* stands for vegetation in all of its forms. The synonymous nature of the *srivatsa*, lotus, tree, and the anthropomorphic shape of the goddess, is well-illustrated in a second century CE Amaravati sculpture (Figure 3.17). The anthropomorphic form (a female spirit of fertility who in her later Buddhist

representations came to be identified as goddess Sirima or Siri) is seen standing under a *kalpataru/kalpavriksha* (fruits hanging from all over its branches
represent the all-giving nature of the fertility cult) in a *kudu* (niche) in the
shape of *srivatsa* with lotus embedded.[39] The lotus symbol can be seen simultaneously as a *chakra*, with spokes coming out of the center, representing the
fruition of the universe. The Buddhist goddess Sirima or Siri later is identified
in the *brahmanic* context as Sri. From Sri, she eventually becomes *brahmanic*
Sri Lakshmi, a goddess who resides in a lotus flower in the water.[40]

The above discussion makes it clear that the popularity of viewing the fertility
goddess, who informs the contemporary profiles of the *gramadevatas* of Andhra
villages, goes back to the Indus and continues to evolve throughout the development of Indian religious culture in various forms. The evidence of this continuation is known especially through early Buddhist adaptations within the context
of their attempts to make their own message familiar to the people. In the first
stage, Buddhists included trees symbolically in their portrayals of the Buddha's
presence or in their depictions of major events in his life. But soon they were
forced to acknowledge the fertility aspect of these trees by deploying youthful
female figures in their ensembles, figures who eventually became identified as
the Buddhist goddess Sirima or Siri. In the same way, the *srivatsa* symbol that
stands for the vegetative nature of the goddess was adapted to indicate the superhuman power of the Buddha and Jaina Tirthankaras. The Vaishnavites, on the
other hand, incorporated the symbol more intimately, by displaying it on the chest
of Vishnu. They maintained its original associations, but in a subordinated fashion. Simultaneously, both the Buddhists and the Vaishnavites eventually created
a female form for what the *srivatsa* symbolizes in their goddesses, who came to
be known as Siri or Sri or Sri Lakshmi. The Buddhist Siri, who clearly developed
from associations with trees and vegetation, anticipates the Vaishnava goddesses
Sri Lakshmi and Gaja Lakshmi, who also became popular among the Jains, as
shown in the twelfth-century temple in Chippagiri (Anantapur District).[41] Gaja
Lakshmi, in fact, has specific antecedents in the ancient naked goddess tradition,
as will be explained in the next chapter. Suffice it to say at this juncture that Sri
Lakshmi can still function as a fertility goddess in some Andhra villages while at
the same time constituting an august figure of wealth and auspiciousness within
the context of Vaishanava orientations.

Pot-bellied Lotus Goddess. Two prominent symbols of the goddess, the
brimming pot and the lotus, are often seen together in art. Although they are
also depicted separately, they frequently appear together to develop the anthropomorphic shape of the goddess.

A brimming pot is referred to variously as *purnaghata, purnakumbha, pur-
nakalasa, mangalakalasa, kalasa,* or *garaga.* The prefix *purna* in the first three

words indicates "full to its brim." The words, *ghata, kumbha,* or *garaga* are synonymous with the meanings of both "pot" and "womb." In other words, the pot represents the womb of the goddess holding life in its seed form. At times the goddess is called the name of the pot. When a pot is filled with water or other nourishing liquid, along with leaves or flowers or fruits or grains, then it is called *"kalasa"* (Figure 2.13). This *kalasa* indicates the womb of the goddess that gives forth life in the form of leaves, flowers, etc. A prefix *mangala* or "auspicious" may be added to *kalasa* to affirm its propitious nature.

As a part of vegetation, the lotus is understood as a primary form of the goddess. Because the lotus comes out of mud and water, the elements that are understood as fecund forms of the goddess, it receives special significance in representing her, as in the case of Sri Lakshmi. When the lotus is placed in a pot, it stands for the sap of life coming out of the womb of the goddess.

In contemporary household and village rituals in Andhra, lotuses are not as common as other flowers. This might be because they are water-bound and thereby are not prolific. Yet lotuses are still regarded as preeminent symbols of the goddess. The lotus design is frequently drawn in ritual contexts to represent the goddess, as in the daily worship of the *tulsi* plant (Figure 2.10), and on special occasions when Sri Lakshmi is worshiped (Figure 2.13). As far as the ceremonial pot is concerned, its present-day relevance in ritual observations cannot be stressed enough, as there is rarely a household or village ritual to the goddess that is performed without it.

In *gramadevatas'* ritual processions, a ceremonial pot is called *Ammavari Ghatam* ("Madam's pot") (Figure 2.2). Each night after the *ghatam* is brought back from the procession, it is customary to sing the story of Ammavaru, a song usually by *pambala vandlu* (untouchable minstrels) and known as the *Jamba Purana.* While there are many local variations to the mythic version, the song, which I have translated from the Telugu, goes like this:[42]

> *In the midst of the oceans—Ammavaru as Adi Sakti was born—*
> *she laid eggs like a hen—and hatched them like a peahen.*
> *The three eggs became a trio—first Brahma*
> *white like cotton—like milky cream.*
> *The skin of Vishnu was black—like a dark moon night.*
> *Sun and moon also came from the same egg as Vishnu.*
> *Resembling a full moon—Siva came from the third egg.*
> *Adi Sakti then looked at them—they were the only males in the uni-*
>   *verse and thinking that they were not born directly to her—she*
>   *wanted to have sexual union with them.*

When she expressed her wish—rejection came from Brahma
saying that she is his mother—this relation would exist only in the
Kali Yuga.
She was fired with anger—a third eye appeared on her forehead.
Bell, club, trident and lotus were in her hands—and she possessed the yogic
      power of the three mantras.
Brahma was subdued with the power of her yogic incantations—
the same was Vishnu's fate but Siva agreed to fulfill her wish—
if she gave him her third eye, weapons and power—
this she did and went to bathe in the river Ganga.
With this power, Siva brought back Brahma and Vishnu—
and killed Sakti. The ashes of the goddess were divided into four heaps—
      Siva brought life to each. There came Sarasvati, Lakshmi, Parvati,
      and the power om as sakti—
  The trio accepted the first three as their consorts.
The remaining sakti, though one—became the innumerable saktis
      (gramadevatas) of the universe.[43]

Unlike the version I will relate in the following pages, in this version, the goddess is imagined as a peahen, does not sustain her absolute superiority, but is willing to share space with the three male gods of the *brahmanic* pantheon, especially ceding her power to the Saivites. The song not only establishes the superiority of Siva over Vishnu and the *gramadevatas*, but does so in a way that recasts the origins of the pantheon. While the origins of the goddess is not disputed, in this version she must conform to the norms of *brahmanical* tradition according to which she must be brought under the control of Siva. This song also relates the history of goddess religion in a nutshell. The goddess as *sakti* dominated the religious culture prior to the prevalence of the *brahmanic* pantheon of deities. When the three male deities, Brahma, Vishnu, and Siva, arrived to share the religious space, they needed to derive resources from the goddess. The result was that they each acquired a spouse out of the fertility goddess in the form of Saraswati, Lakshmi, and Parvati respectively. Although there are various versions of the song, none mention any conflict with the Buddhists or Jains, either because the conflicts were long forgotten or because the adjustment between them and the goddess religion was complementary. In any case, what is important to note is that all of the versions of the myth agree that there was nothing but the goddess at the beginning and that the world was procreated by her. Since she alone gave birth to the world, as discussed in the following pages, she is understood in ritual and other contexts as sexless or as a hermaphrodite. In either case, my basic point here is that the pot refers to the universal womb of the goddess.

In some villages like Pudivalasa and Mugada (Srikakulam District), *gram-adevata*s are seen in multiple numbers. For this reason, during the annual festival in these villages, three brass or earthen pots are worshiped.⁴⁴ After decorating the pots with vermilion, turmeric, and sandalwood paste, every evening for a month, three women—possessed by the goddess and in a trance state, accompanied by a drumbeat—carry these pots on their heads through the village, collecting special food from each household.

Garagalamma, a name of a *gramadevata* worshiped in several villages in East Godavari District, means the "mother of pots." This is not specific to Andhra, as we know of other examples, such as a rural goddess in the state of Karnataka who is named Kel Mari, which means "earthen pot."⁴⁵ The following story relates how the name Garagalamma was given to the *gramadevata* of this region.⁴⁶

Nearly two centuries ago, a young woman, assuming her bridegroom was handsome, agreed to a marriage arranged by her father. In traditional marriage arrangements, it was common in those days that bride and bridegroom would not see each other until the formal ceremony of marriage. On the day of her marriage, the bride found the groom to be disgustingly ugly and became very upset. As she could not prevent the marriage, she jumped into the fire that had been prepared for cooking the food for the marriage party. Later, her father saw her in his dream wearing ankle bells (indicating that she was in a happy mood) and carrying *garaga* on her head. After the father's dream, the dead young woman was propitiated as Garagalamma in a temple constructed for her. Soon, her cult spread to other villages and she was adopted as a *gramadevata*.

In this story, the dream of the father resonated with his villagers and a number of others because the young woman who was expected to be married and to give birth to many children, although disappearing abruptly, continued to retain her potential fertility on a different plane. This potential is what the dead woman was indicating to her father through the medium of a dream by carrying the *garaga*, a symbol of her fertile energy. It must be noted here that in some *gramadevata* rituals, on the final day of the great celebration, women carry decorated pots of water or milk rice or rice with curds or buttermilk to offer to the goddess to fulfill their vows for being blessed with children or keeping their children out of illness. These pots containing food offerings are also treated as a form of the goddess. Since the *garaga* is the symbol of a *gram-adevata*, it is interpreted that the dead woman is ready to assume the responsibility of a *gramadevata*. This deification also exhibits two opposing processes simultaneously at work, the reification and reinvention of the fertility cult: reification in the sense that the deified woman is understood as becoming the *gramadevata* to perform all the functions expected of a *gramadevata*; but at the same time, she is understood as effective in certain functions such as blessing women with children or caring for their well-being.

As far as the ceremonial pot is concerned, its forms and names vary from place to place. In Velkatte village (Warangal District), the pot, which contains several holes and has a light in it, is carried by a priest for the *gramadevata* Mutyalamma. This form of pot, called *veyikandla bonam* ("offering of a thousand eyes"), shares similarities with the ancient form of ritual pots mentioned below. The *gramadevata* is often envisioned as containing a thousand eyes and this might be the reason that the pot is prepared in this manner. At places such as Bethupalli and other villages in the Khammam District, the pot is attached to a frame of flower arrangements. At times, the flower arrangement may take the anthropomorphic shape of the goddess. In East Godavari and Visakhapatnam, a *garaga* is a brass pot topped by a snake hood containing five or seven heads. This form cleverly combines both the pot and snake forms of the goddess as shown in the picture where the coils of snake forms the base of the brass pot with its seven headed hood spreading over the pot (Figure 3.18). In the city of Hyderabad, the ceremonial pot called *karagam* is decorated to give an iconic form of a beautiful young maid in a gold and silver brocaded pure silk saree, gold jewelry, and flower wreaths. In this scenario, the pot

FIGURE 3.18 *Garaga* with Snake Hood

assumes the shape of the abdomen of the goddess. This is analogous to the evolution of the *purnakumbha* motif that I discuss below.

Sometimes, as in the village Lolla (Srikakulam District), a *gramadevata* is worshiped in the form of a *kalasa*. The *kalasa* of the goddess Lollalamma, named after the village, is kept in a temple for regular worship.⁴⁷ Lollalamma, as a presiding deity of epidemics, is invoked on this *kalasa* for three days during the harvest festival of Sankranti (January 13–15). In addition to the annual ritual, whenever epidemics erupt the village worships the goddess by placing the *kalasa* in the center of the village under a temporary canopy and singing songs in her praise throughout the night, while keeping a vigil.

The *kalasa* is a small copper pot, full of water, with turmeric and vermilion dots on the surface, mango leaves placed inside, topped by a coconut wrapped with a blouse piece. This ensemble is used in household rituals to worship the goddess Gauri or Sri Lakshmi, the very form that evolved from the fertility goddess but is now identified as a *brahmanic* deity, though still worshiped at the household level as a fertility goddess. As mentioned in the last chapter, an example of this is a ritual called Sri Lakshmi or Gauri *vrata* (ritual vow), which is performed by newly married women on a Friday of the Sravana month for long happy married life with many children. Here the fertility goddess has been completely identified with Sri Lakshmi, Parvati, or Saraswati.

The *gramadevata* can also be worshiped in the form of a winnow, or bamboo basket, which is probably an extension of the pot. A common feature the winnow shares with the pot is that they both are used to store grains, vegetables, or fruits. An example of what I'm referring to is the goddess Bandamma in Agali, Anantapur District.⁴⁸ The *gramadevata*, Bandamma, in fact, is a deified maid who was killed two centuries ago by her relations and is now worshiped as a *gramadevata* in the form of bamboo basket in a temple constructed especially for her. Bandamma shares similarities with Garagalamma in that both were maids and both experienced violent deaths. The same logic that worked to worship Garagalamma in the form of a pot seems to be in place with Bandamma: like the pot, the basket holds vegetation in all its forms (Figure 3.19). They both hold the grains or seeds that are essential for the renewal of crops. Hence, they represent the womb of the goddess that sustains villages.

The depiction of *purnaghata/purnakumbha/purnakalasa/mangalakalasa*, *kalasa* or *garaga* permeates the art and architecture of various succeeding religious traditions in Andhra and elsewhere in the subcontinent. The notion of the pot as the representation of the goddess can be traced to proto-historic Andhra. The earliest evidence of this is traced to the Megalithic period, in which a ceremonial pot with three perforations was placed in the northeastern corner of a cist burial in Peddamarur, Karimnagar district.⁴⁹ This perforated

FIGURE 3.19 Basket Goddess

pot shares similarities with the *veyikandla bonam* used in Warangal District in the ritual for that *gramadevata*. Architectural tenets reflect age-old beliefs indicating that the northeastern corner is considered as the abode of the fertility goddess who is now understood as Sri Lakshmi.[50] Another pot with three perforations with a symbol of *nandipada* at Dhulikatta in early historic levels, assigned between the third century BCE and third century CE, is also noticed.[51] This type of pot was probably used in rituals resembling the present *gramadevata* ritual in Velkote described above. This pot is analogous to the carving of the naked goddess and bull at Mudumala, with the pot representing the goddess and the *nandipada* representing the bull. This pairing of goddess with bull continued to be popular in succeeding centuries, as it is represented in a second-century BCE terracotta plaque from Kosam in the state of Uttar Pradesh (Figure 3.20) and in a third to fourth century CE plaque from Vadagaon in Maharashtra (Figure 3.21).[52] The specialty of the Kosam figure is that it shows how the fertility goddess originally was associated with lotuses, elephants, as well as the bull, and how this goddess gives rise to Parvati and Sri Lakshmi. Parvati, as shown in Vadagaon (Figure 3.21), is in her early stages of evolution out of the *purnakumbha* motif, and is seated next to the bull. An analogous example in which the goddess Saraswati replaces Parvati is found in a coin issued by Gupta rulers (fourth to sixth century CE).[53] On its obverse side, two goddesses are placed on either side of the seated Gupta ruler. On its reverse side, the symbols of these goddesses in the form of a lotus representing Lakshmi and a swan representing Saraswati are depicted. The Gupta queen is flanked by these symbols.

Like the *srivatsa*, the *purnaghata* is also associated with other symbols. Some relevant examples, which are at Bharhut in Madhya Pradesh, or at Sarnath in Uttar Pradesh, include the *chakra* or birds like geese as part of the *purnaghata* motif.[54] The most popular *purnaghata* motif, however, is shown with lotuses. Either together or in their separate forms, these two symbols are adopted to denote auspiciousness and good luck into the art and architecture of various religious traditions from the third through the seventeenth century.[55] The otherwise life-generating motif of *purnakumbha*, along with lotuses, is used in Buddhist art to convey the Buddhist message of life as ephemeral by showing lotuses in three different stages: the bud, the fully bloomed, and the wilted. which can be seen at places such as Nagarjunakonda (Figure 3.22).[56] Comparing the iconography of pots with lotuses at a Mathura Buddhist stupa with examples in Java during the Majapahit period, Susan Huntington says, "the vases represented the urns holding the ashes of the deceased (royalty) while the lotuses symbolize the transcendence of the departed individual and the concept of rebirth."[57] If this is so, it shows how the meanings of pots and lotuses are elaborated to fit into the Buddhist world of soteriological ideals. In Jaina and *brahmanic* art, on the other hand, numerous *purnakumbha* motifs are used to convey auspiciousness.[58] The difference is that in Jaina art, this symbol along with the lotus became part of the eight auspicious signs of Jain *tirthankaras*, while in *brahmanic* art, as in the case of the fertility cult, the symbol is life-affirming.

Representing the pot as the womb of the goddess, artists made use of the lotus bud to indicate her generative organ. Since the fertility goddess is often worshiped in the form of the *yoni* (female generative organ), as will be illustrated later, the lotus in this context is understood as a fertile form of goddess. Indeed, the lotus, in both Hindu and Buddhist *tantric* traditions, is much later understood as a symbol of the female sexual organ, showing how the original meaning was in this case sustained. Along with the *chakra*, the lotus appears in Andhra as graffiti marks on proto-historic pottery (Figures 2.15 and 2.16).[59] The lotus and *chakra* in this context might indicate the goddess as representing the cycle of rebirths. How the fecund goddess is synonymous with lotuses and *purnakumbha* is well-illustrated in a second-century CE sculpture from Mathura (Figure 3.23a & b).[60] Here, the goddess on one side of the sculpture stands and holds her left breast with her right hand, while her left hand points to her pudendum. The sculpture has on the reverse side *purnakumbha* giving forth life in its full bloom with couples like peacock, a peahen, and two fish in cohabitation. This sculpture leads the viewer to understand the nature of cohabitation and how this leads to new life. Citing the plaques from Yeleswaram and other places where the lotus, along with *purnakumbha*, is shown as a vulva of the womb of the goddess, Bolon argues that the lotus demonstrates the cyclical nature of life.[61]

> The botanical characters of the lotus plant give rise to further mean-
> ings. Because of the means of reproductions of the lotus plant from a
> seed that matures within the pod, or calyx, of the plant and then bursts
> out as a new plant, the analogy to human reproduction is made. Thus
> the lotus is seen as a plant carrying the potential for future generations
> and is given meanings of cyclic renewal of life, of regeneration of life,
> or reincarnations.[62]

In addition to conveying the ephemeral nature of life, Buddhist art maneu-
vers the original notion of the lotus to indicate Siddhartha's superior birth. In
these instances, Siddhartha is depicted in the form of a lion, bull, or elephant
mounted on a pillar over inverted lotuses.[63] In later periods when the Buddha
is carved in sculpture, he is seen standing or sitting on lotus pedestals, such
as at Gummadidurru (Krishna District) and Nagarjunakonda.[64] In this context the meaning of the lotus is elaborated to mean supreme consciousness
and spiritual power.[65] In the iconography of the late first millennium, in its
association with Avalokitesvara bodhisattva, the lotus stands for compassion
and transcendence through the purity of wisdom.[66] This departure from the
original meaning of lotus as fertility did not seem to be sustained, as in later
Tantric forms of Buddhism, the lotus made its full circle of going back to its
original meaning, that is, once again symbolizing the female sexual organ.[67]

The lotus as a seat of the deity, as shown in Buddhist art, is favored by other
religious traditions as well, with the *brahmanic* deities from the fourth century
onwards and with Jaina Tirthankaras from the sixth century.[68] Just as with
the Buddhists, the conception of the lotus as a generative force is utilized by
the Vaishnavites. Accordingly, Brahma being born out of a lotus issuing from
Vishnu's navel became popular in Vaishnavite art, as represented in the panel
at Raja Rajesvara temple in Vemulavada (Karimnagr District).[69] This is a clear
manipulation and subversion of the lotus as fertility goddess. Here, the lotus
as the fertility force is seen acting only at the will of Vishnu, as she comes out
of his navel, not from her own source of mud and water. This portrayal is consistent with the scheme of adopting the goddess symbols with their original

meanings, but bringing them under the wing of Vishnu or Siva or other *brahmanic* male deities in the pantheon.

Viewing a pot as the anthropomorphic shape of the goddess is a very ancient notion. Some terracotta figurines of the Indus period described as "fat women," are clearly pots with the superimposition of the anthropomorphic shape of female forms.[70] One of these is a more refined pot with attached rope-like hands, bulbous breasts on the belly of the pot, tiny slender legs with one intact under the pot and a bird-like face superimposed on the neck part of the pot (Figure 3.24). In Andhra, the evolution starts taking shape from the third century CE, when the motif of *purnaghata* appears like a female abdomen crowned by a lotus. The early images are small and made of terracotta or stone carved in a rectangular relief appearing in Buddhist sites such as Kondapur (Guntur District), Karlapalem (Guntur District), Peddabankur (Karimnagar District) and Nagarjunakonda.[71] Only relatively better-preserved images have been illustrated here, where the pot serves as the abdomen of the goddess with legs and hips attached. No breasts and hands were indicated at this stage. One of the intact legs in the image at Kondapur (Figure 3.25) appears like a short post as if to insure the stability of the pot. The image at Karlapalem, (Figure 3.26) on the other hand, shows that a pot is superimposed over the belly part of the goddess. The sculpture at Nagarjunakonda (Figure 3.27),

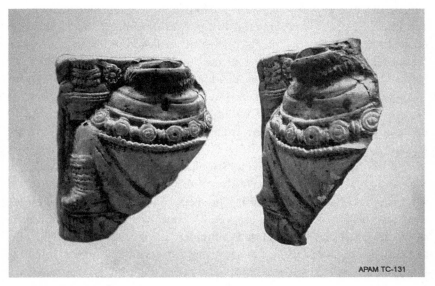

FIGURE 3.25 Kondapur Pot
Source: Photo provided by the Director, Andhra Pradesh State Archaeology Museum

although broken, still looks beautiful, as the shape of the pot is such that it naturally forms part of a beautiful form of female abdomen. The designs half-way around the pot serve as girdle chains for the goddess. In the same way, the decoration on the legs of the pot function as anklets.

A more developed anthropomorphic *purnaghata* goddess image appears in the fourth to fifth century CE plaques as part of the *brahmanic* pantheon illustrated at Darsi (Prakasam District) (Figure 5.28), Keesaragutta (Rangareddy District), Kunidane, Kondamotu, and Uppalapadu (all from Guntur District).[72] Except at Kunidane, where upper arms are seen, the other figures appear armless but with breasts above where, in some panels, a lotus is placed. Here the stage has been set for the lotus to become the head of the goddess. Considering the head as the main part of the body, the lotus indicates the goddess's origins from nature. The main difference in these images, as shown in the illustration at Darsi, is that their sex organs are covered with a piece of cloth (Figure 3.28). Considering that the goddess is the same size as the rest of the *brahmanic* deities in the pantheon within these plaques and her position in the center, Frans Janssen and Bolon argue that the goddess still was independent and was not yet transformed into the wife of either Siva or Vishnu.[73] What is clear, however, is that the goddess had been admitted as part of the pantheon of *brahmanic* deities only after being properly clothed.

In a parallel evolution, there is a group of stone images of the naked goddess carved on the *purnaghata* and functioning as a kind of background. The earliest of these is a third-century CE life-size marble image with its upper part broken. The importance of this image is known from a short inscription on its base, as mentioned earlier, issued by an Ikshvaku queen noting that the installation of this image was for the purpose of seeking long life for her husband and son. This is a clear identification of royalty worshiping the fertility goddess in her original status, but not as part of a *brahmanic* pantheon of deities. This devotion to the fertility goddess by successive rulers can be deduced from the images of the sixth to tenth century CE from Yelesvaram (Nalgonda district), Alampur, Kudavelli, Panchalingala, Miyapuram (all from Mahaboobnagar District), Pratakota, Srisailam, Vemulavada, Bejjinki (all from Karimnagar District), and Yellala (Kurnool District).[74] The outlines of the image at Yelesvaram (Figure 3.29) resemble the shape of a frog. As mentioned earlier, the frog is also associated with rains and fertility. Another significant feature of this image is that the goddess is sitting on a fully blown lotus. The lotus as her bed is an added feature in conveying her essential fecund nature. The image at Alampur is still worshiped by devotees (Figure 3.30). An important feature of the worship of this image is that devotees who approach her to seek offspring make sure to touch her generative organ and apply oil to it. This practice extends to all the naked images of the goddess that are still in worship, highlighting the fertility function of these naked images even to this day. The well-preserved goddess image at Yellala holds lotus buds in her uplifted hands (Figure 3.31). She wears jewelry on her neck, arms, hands, and ankles. Like the third-century CE image, these images were housed in shrines for worship.

The shape of these goddesses with their splayed legs exhibiting their sexual organs has attracted much discussion. Janssen, who has studied the iconography of several sculptures and plaques of India that include many from Andhra, in an attempt to trace the development of *purnakumbha* into the anthropomorphic shape of the naked goddess, has concluded that these are images of goddesses in the birthing position. He writes:

> Conclusive evidence of the interpretation of Lajja Gauri as a birth-giving figure is also furnished by the cloth that covers her thighs and disappears behind the back, sometimes explained as the border of the *langoti* [loin cloth]. In fact, this is the special birth cloth.[75] [brackets mine].

Although the representation of a birthing cloth is not discernible in Andhra images per se, the notion of the pot as the womb of the goddess makes much

FIGURE 3.31 Yellala Pot
Source: Photo provided by the Director, Andhra Pradesh State Archaeology Museum

sense. Taking Janessen's description into consideration, the frog-shaped symbol, the *srivatsa* (Figure 3.4), mentioned earlier, resembles the description of
a goddess in her birthing position. While allusions to female fertility power
are an obvious possible element in play, Bolon, studying the same images
mentioned by Janssen, has argued that the sex of these images, what she calls
instances of Lajja Gauri, is portrayed in such a way that it can be interpreted
either as a lotus bud (female), or as a male sexual organ, or both (the male
organ embedded in the female womb.[76]

> Within the womb of Lajja Gauri, this suggests, is a phallus, or within
> the pot is a lotus bud.... the visual illusion is intended to express union
> and generation.[77]

As seen in the case of evolution of the *srivatsa* with lotus in its womb, the lotus
in these depictions as a vulva is a metaphor for the generative capacity of the
goddess. It is possible that the deliberate visual effect was created by the artist
in such a way that it can be interpreted in either way: the male or female organ
relates to the conception of the fertility cult itself. As the popular myth of the
gramadevata that I have discussed earlier indicates, i.e., how the goddess can
be a hermaphrodite, it might not be unreasonable to think that this conception
of the goddess goes far back in time, one that inspired early artists to illustrate
her nature in this manner.

The images discussed here are shown with their torsos in the belly part of
the pot and contain breasts with attached limbs, legs splayed with the knees
almost touching the neck, and upraised hands holding lotuses at the same
level as the lotus that is placed on the neck part of the pot and that represents
the head of the goddess. In a way, this execution of the goddess's portrayal
reflects the imagination of the popular form of the goddess known through
current myth and ritual. I have mentioned how some of the images such as
the ones at Alampur and Miyapuram are worshiped as the goddess Renuka
Ellamma. As I have noted earlier, the Western Chalukyan inscription of the
eighth century CE mentions the rulers' devotion to the naked goddess known
as Ellamma. An inscription issued in the ninth century CE by Chalukya Bhima
I mentions a goddess named Mukapatala.[78] While Ellamma seems to be popular through the ages, it is possible that there were other names for the naked
goddess, such as Mukapatala.

The presence of life-size naked images of the fertility goddess starting
from the third century CE suggests that the tradition of constructing permanent shrines to the divinities seems to have started during this particular time
and was extended to the fertility goddess as well. While her symbol of the pot

takes her iconic image form to be worshiped in permanent shrines, the goddess continued to be worshiped at the village level in her non-iconic form. In any case, the abundant evidence of the fertility goddess in art as a *purnaghata* and its evolutionary symbolism share striking similarities with the contemporary mythical notions and ritual forms of *gramadevata* worship.

On the other hand, the images of the goddess in the plaques with *brahmanic* deities, although seen with splayed legs and lotus head, hide the sexual organ with a cloth. It is not unreasonable to deduce from this that when the fertility goddess was introduced into *brahmanic* religion, her nakedness was left behind.

Cobra Goddess. One of the common forms of viewing the fertility goddess is as a snake. In Andhra, most snakes often appear during the monsoon season when they are driven from their abodes below by the watery deluge and must seek drier, higher ground. It may be because they are usually seen during the time of life-giving waters necessary for successful agriculture that the fertility of the earth is associated with the appearance of serpents. The association with the snake and fertility of the earth, and therefore the nurturing mother, is but one aspect of the symbolism. The serpent symbolism associated with the goddess also has another dimension that has to do with ensuring purity, propriety, and order. In this connection, the serpent is seen as an enforcer of order, or the means by which punishment by the goddess might be carried out to those who contravene accepted principles of behavior. According to Zimmer, the serpent symbolizes one or more of the following traits: wisdom; a member of a superior ancestral race; the life-giving waters of rivers and seas; regeneration and reincarnation; the fertility of vegetation; and, finally, the guardianship of cows, humans, and valuables, which is also substantiated by Balaji Mundkur.[79] The serpent is also considered as being the controller of the weather, especially of rain, and thus it seems to reveal, in part, an aerial origin.[80] All of these associations are still current among various devotees who worship the *gramadevatas* in the snake form. In Kerala, the devotees of snakes worship them in shrines resembling miniature forests, which are created at home.[81]

Ellamma is not just worshiped in the naked form. In fact, the goddess is more often worshiped in the form of an anthill, as she is especially associated with snake bites in the neighboring state of Tamilnadu.[82] As Elmore reported, the goddess Ellamma, also known as Matangi, is understood as coming out of the anthill holding the heavens in her left hand and the cosmic serpent Adisesha in her right hand.[83] This is a motif not just confined to Ellamma, as there are also other *gramadevatas*, such as Masamma, Jammulamma, Durgalamma, etc., whose myths and symbols identify them with serpents.[84]

The cobra image of *gramadevatas* is either present by itself in her shrines, or seen accompanied by her anthropomorphic image (Figure 3.18). At times, an image of the *naga* may be placed under a tree so that both of them can be worshiped as the *gramadevata* (Figure 3.32). In these instances, the *gramadevata*, in fact, may be represented by a couple of copulating *nagas*. The theme of the goddess being both male and female in her procreation recurs in this symbolism. Many deified women are also worshiped in the form of cobras and trees, the topic of which I will take up in a following chapter. The connection between snakes and trees is often established by priests in Taminadu, who believe that the snakes live in the underground passageway between an anthill and the trees located in the temple precincts.[85]

One of the more illustrative cases of Ellamma worshiped in the form of an anthill is found in the village of Lingampalle (Mahaboobnagar District), where a big anthill, functioning as her shrine, is located under a huge banyan tree.[86] The story behind this location is that a man of low caste carrying *sindhalu* (cymbals that are played in enacting the annual ritual dance for the goddess) of Ellamma in a basket, rested under this banyan tree and fell asleep. When

FIGURE 3.32 Tree and the *Naga*

he woke up, to his dismay, he found that his basket had been replaced by an anthill. And then he heard a mysterious voice announcing that Ellamma had decided to settle there and that he should place five *sindhalu* beside the anthill and assume priestly responsibilities during her annual ritual. While the name "Ella" refers to the type of field where Ellamma prefers her shrine, it is often the case that *gramadevata*s convey their wishes to the villagers of staying outside the village through dreams. During the annual five-day festival in Lingampalle, a woman in the priest's (*madiga*) family covers her naked body with margosa leaves and locks her mouth with a silver wire by piercing it through both cheeks and joins a procession with an accompaniment of music. Some *madiga* men wearing *sindhalu* dance to the beat. Those who fail to keep their vows to Ellamma, it is believed, will have a vision of a cobra on the banyan tree indicating that she will punish them for their failures. If devotees forget their vows of asceticism, the goddess has a sure way of bringing them to their knees.

In several stories of Durgalamma in the suburb Durganagar in Visakhapatanam City, the goddess appears in the very form of a snake. First, villagers noticed a long serpent ranging from four to six yards in length emerge and then suddenly disappear. The serpent was not known to have caused harm to anybody in the village. Then, they witnessed smoke rising from the snake hole, followed by a sweet smell; devotees attributed these phenomena to Durgalamma, who was thought to be assuming the form of a snake to protect the village. Thereby, they started worshiping the snake hole, and eventually a village elder built a temple over it. Following the temple's construction, no one reported any further appearances of the snake. A wooden image of the seated goddess on a lion throne with eight hands was installed in an adjacent chamber, and a *brahmin* priest was appointed to conduct worship (Figure 3.33). Among other weapons and objects, the goddess holds a snake, a remnant of her original form. The worship of this goddess continues to be of a mixed type; devotees not only offer prayers to the image with the help of the priest, but also worship the snake hole directly.

The association of goddesses with snakes, or regarding snakes as the incarnation of the goddess, is clearly seen in one of the many popular Telugu myths describing the nature of *gramadevata*s. I have collected this myth from a temple priest at the temple of Nukalamma, Anakapalle (Visakhapatnam District), and much of it resembles an important myth I related earlier.[87] This myth says that *Para Sakti* (the supreme cosmic transcendental power), the creator of the universe, at the beginning of time gave birth to three eggs. Two of them were spoiled and remained unhatched, but the third one broke open into Brahma, Vishnu, and Mahesvara (Siva), the *trimurti* mentioned earlier. *Para Sakti*

FIGURE 3.33 Durgalamma

suckled and nourished them in their youth as a devoted mother. When they came to age, she gave them each their own cities to dwell in. The name of the city of Siva was Devagiri. In time, they each turned into disobedient sons and completely disregarded her presence. In response, she transformed herself into a twelve-hooded cobra and coiled round the city of Devagiri, where the three had gathered one day. In battle, the cobra defeated all three gods by biting off their heads. Later, in a condition of remorse and compassion, she took pity on them and brought them back to life, whereupon they became obedient sons and good-natured friends.

While this myth illustrates the meaning of serpent symbolism in terms of fertility and the guarding of order on the one hand, it also reflects, as in the case of the similar myth discussed earlier, the tensions between *brahmanic* and goddess cults on the other. Unlike in the last myth, however, here the power balance shifts toward the goddess as the three supreme gods of the *brahmanical* pantheon, namely Brahma, Vishnu. and Siva, learn their true place in the cosmic order as subordinate to the supreme *sakti*, here recognized as the absolute power of the cosmos. On the socio-historical level of interpretation, this myth also expresses that when *brahmanical* religion tried to enter the sphere of the lower stratum of the society, the folk were not ready to accept the superiority of these gods over their goddess. I think that this myth also reflects the reality of socio-political tensions as well: the resistance of the folk who are traditionally seen as the lower strata to the power machinations of upper castes.

In any case, one important point here, as in the last myth, is the theme of the goddess as the creator and mother. And, without a father, she creates and procreates. The notion of the goddess as hermaphrodite is reinforced in myth by recognizing her as a thousand-hooded cobra. In the popular notion of viewing the goddess as cobra, there is no sex differentiation made. This must be the reason why the cobra motif of the goddess is incorporated into various male-oriented religious traditions by subsequently transforming the snake into a male deity. As such, in the *brahmanic* temple religious context, the cobra is a male deity. And this comes to the forefront at the annual festival of Nagula Chaviti, celebrated on the fourth day of the lunar month of Karthika (November). The current mythology of this festival is connected to the Saivite cult of Subrahmanyesvara, the details of which I discuss in tracing the history of *naga* worship in the following lines.

The *naga* in ritual context is seen in an amulet of Indus period in which a horned deity seated on a throne is surrounded by *nagas*, gavials and fish.[88] In its symbolic form, at times, in early art, the *naga* seems to conflate with the symbol of *srivatsa*.[89] It is possible that the belief in the serpent as a protective power and its association with great personalities and divine figures was suggested in Indus times. Its imagery shares striking similarities with later Buddhist representations.[90] Since the pattern of worship is not so much bound to an image, as in the case of the worship of vegetation, there is very little material evidence to trace the antiquity of this worship in Andhra's prehistoric context. The earliest material evidence, however, is a lone sculpture of a standing *naga* in an "S" shape assignable anywhere between the third century BCE to the first century CE.[91] An indication of the veneration of snakes is suggested by some early coins of the first millennium containing the image of a snake.[92] In the excavations at Keesaragutta, a globular terracotta pot encircled by seven snakes and five female figures with demonic features was recovered (Figure 3.34). Assignable to the fourth century CE, this representation shows how the fertility goddesses are understood to appear in the form of cobras.[93] The interesting feature here is a combination of three different symbolisms of the goddess: *purnaghata*, *naga*, and the semi-anthropomorphic form of the goddess. The demonic features of these goddesses indicate their profile as enforcers of law and order.

FIGURE 3.34 Terracotta Pot with Snakes
Source: Photo provided by the Director, Andhra Pradesh State Archaeology Museum

In Buddhist art, the stupa, the relic chamber or the womb, is shown at times with entwined serpents, in the same way as the globular pot is represented in Keesaragutta (Figure 3.35).[94] As in the case of the tree, the Buddhists and other religious traditions incorporated the *naga* into their mythology and art because of its popularity as a fertility cult. While the tree and other symbols discussed earlier evolve into the female anthropomorphic shape of the fertility goddess, the *naga* on the other hand, takes the form of a male deity. In Buddhist understanding, the meaning of *naga* is elaborated to mean "the superior type of progeny" and also "symbolic power and eminence."[95] Comparing the Buddhist art of Amaravati with that of Sanchi, Fergusson observed that the presence of the *naga* is so frequent at Amaravati "that it is sometimes difficult to say to which religion the temple is dedicated."[96] This might be because the *naga*, as the symbol of the fertility cult, was more prevalent in Andhra than in and around Sanchi, so the Buddhists were forced to adopt it into their literature and art. In the *Vinayapitaka*, the *naga* is introduced as a king by the name of Muchalinda who was joined by other *naga*s of different directions to spread their hoods and to protect the Buddha from a cold rainy storm in the weeks following the Buddha's enlightenment. Thus, Muchalinda and other *naga*s, who appear in *Jataka* stories, become frequent subjects in the Buddhist sites of Andhra.[97] How the local form of *naga* worship was incorporated into Buddhist cults is clear in Bhutan, where the *naga* spirits of the land are believed to have been subjugated by the Buddha so that they retain only positive qualities to bless their devotees.[98]

With regard to Siva, he was often perceived as living outside the pale of society, wandering in cremation grounds or courting the wilderness in which snakes are an integral part. Saivites in Andhra are known for converting the Buddhist shrines into Saiva temples. Scholars are unanimous that the famous *Pancharamas* (five important Siva temples) in Andhra were Buddhist temples. A prolific number of *naga* slabs and bodhi trees in these originally Buddhist temples became part of Saivite inheritance. At Alampur temples in Kurnool district and Panagal in Nalgonda District, many images of Siva are seen holding snakes in one of his many hands.[99] In the same way that many *gramadevatas* are understood to be wives of Siva, the *naga* also came to be identified as an essential part of Saivite religion, especially as it has been portrayed in Andhra's many Saivite temples as Subrahmanyesvara, Siva's son who is often depicted as the prominent devotee of Siva.[100] Because the *naga* motif became primary to Saivite religion, it is understood in the Hindu temple context as being more a part of the Saivite cult than a symbol of the goddess that has been incorporated into the *brahmanic* pantheon.

Following, perhaps, the strategy of Saivites, Jains adopted the *naga* as a symbol of the wilderness that the *tirthankaras* courted in their pursuit of *kaivalya*. Serpents are shown in Jaina art either as protective many-headed *nagas* serving as halos to Jain *tirthankaras* or as entwining their bodies around the *tirthankaras* as portrayed in a number of sites in Andhra.[101]

Like the Muchalinda *naga* in Buddhism, in Vaishnavism, the *naga* that was originally a fertility symbol went on to play a protective role for Vishnu. As the name indicates, Adisesha, the cosmic serpent, represents the origins of the universe, reminiscent of the myth of the goddess. The intrinsic connection of Adisesha with the earth is established in Vishnavite traditions that the earth stands on Adisesha's great hoods. By turning his enormous coils as Vishnu's bed and holding his hood to shade Vishnu from all natural elements, Adisesha authenticates Vishnu as the god of the beginning of the universe. While the early representation of Vishnu at the Undavalli cave of the fifth century CE shows him sitting in a lotus posture on a coiled Adisesha, the most popular form is his reclining position on the coiled bed of Adisesha during the interval between world eons.[102] In this sense the serpent becomes the enforcer of time with Vishnu at its helm.

Thus, this prominent symbol of the goddess and the concept behind it has played a major role in various religious orientations of evolving Indian religion. As with other major symbols of the goddess, it is the Saivites who succeeded in claiming the *naga* from very early on and making it an integral part of Saivite imagery at the popular level of *brahmanic* Hinduism, as well as in the textual descriptions. Even so, some scattered records give us a glimpse of the original associations of the *naga* with the goddess. One of these is a twelfth century inscription issued on a slab where the *naga* sculpture is carved, registering a land grant for the goddess known as Pattelamare.[103] Whether the name of the goddess is known to us in the proper form or not, the inscription makes it clear that the goddess was worshiped in the cobra form. Although the context is not clear, a century later another inscription from Srikurmam (Srikakulam District) mentions a temple of *nagas* as *navulagudi*.[104]

Earth Goddess. The concept of the fertility goddess related to forms of the earth occurs probably as early as Indus times. All those features such as the soil, rocks, hills, wilderness, and water that form the materiality of the earth, that is the natural world, have been considered as forms of the fertility goddess. We have seen that even a snake hole or an anthill (where snakes sometimes live) can be considered as a form of the goddess not only because of its association with snakes, but because of its nourishing aspect as well. The soil in which it is burrowed is rich in nutrition and ideal for the growth of vegetation. Hence, a generic name for the village goddess is *puttalamma*, which means "the mother of snake (ant) holes." In the same vein, cow dung and cow urine are seen as the substances representing the goddess because they help enrich the soil.[105] On the most basic level, the goddess is the earth from which all life springs and then depends. All those that live on the earth or those parts of earth such as hills and water are also considered as her forms. The goddess myth I related in the previous chapter illustrates this. This notion is acknowledged in art as well as in contemporary *gramadevata* worship, as I will show below.

The names of *gramadevatas*, such as Kondalamma (mother of hills), Puttamma, Ellamma (mother of borders), Poleramma (mother of fields), Gangamma (water mother), Maisamma (mother of the chase), Boddurai (navel stone of the village), and Gobbemma (cow dung goddess), etc., all indicate the pervasiveness of the goddess in all components and creatures that constitute or spring from the earth. In these cases, the form of worship, or the functions expected of the goddess, indicates the nature of the *gramadevata*.

Stone is one of the forms in which the *gramadevata* is worshiped, as it is common to place the stones within or outside the village or in the fields. There is a temple dedicated to Bata Gangamma near the village of Borrampalem in West Godavari district.[106] The prefix "bata" means a thoroughfare or a road and the reasons for the goddess acquiring this prefix is illustrated in the following yarn. An aged traveler from Borrampalem took rest beside the path under a shady tree when he was close to the village. Soon he fell asleep and saw the goddess Ganga in his dream. She instructed him to worship a stone in her name under that tree. He woke up from his sleep, found a stone and placed it under the tree, and proceeded to worship it. When he got back to his village, he told the villagers what had happened. Soon the villagers followed suit. Whenever they passed that way, each one of them placed a stone there to worship. Now this practice has come to a halt, as there is now a temple at this place, with a brass image of the goddess. Nevertheless, the heap of stones is still worshiped with vermilion, turmeric, and flowers. This temple building indicates that the villagers wanted their goddess to be authenticated for others' sake. Yet, they still believe that the real power of Bata Gangamma lies in the heap of stones, and therefore they continue to pay homage to her accordingly.

There are also natural outcroppings or outgrowths beside springs, fountains, and watery torrents in the hills and rocky areas that are worshiped as forms of the goddess. Two examples of this nature outside Andhra region are Kamakhya from Assam, where a bedrock in the shape of a *yoni* with a spring coming out of it is worshiped as the *yoni* form of the goddess, and Lajja Gauri, a lotus-headed naked goddess at Siddhanakolla, Karnataka, carved from the rock floor of a hill with a spring falling alongside.[107] In these instances, the goddess is conceived as providing the sap of life through her vulva. This is the same understanding of farmers when they till the soil ceremoniously in the annual ritual to the *gramadevata*, that the earth goddess is pleased to open her vulva. If a rain precedes the ceremony, it is assumed that the goddess has given her blessings for a good growing season. Here, the goddess is understood not just as the fertile soil of the earth, but also as the terrestrial and atmospheric water resource as well.

While the above instances illustrate the similarity imagined between the human form of the *yoni* and the naked earth as forms of the fertility cult, there are numerous examples of the goddess symbolized by bedrock in Andhra. The most famous one of them is the goddess Kanaka Durga of Vijayawada (Krishna District), as will be explained in the next chapter. In one of her early forms of worship, the goddess was regarded as the bedrock of the hill called Indrakiladri. Another goddess whose original form is regarded still as bedrock and whose myth as a pox goddess was mentioned earlier is Nalla Pochamma in Secundrabad. Around four centuries ago, Nalla Pochamma is said to have manifested herself in the form of a bedrock of a stream nearby. When the worship started, this bedrock with the shape of a human head was next to a snake hole under the shade of the Margosa and pipal trees that were part of the wilderness where the snakes roamed freely climbing the trees. These conditions were ideal, as the goddess is identified not only with the wilderness and the hills, but also specifically with the trees and snakes. Initially, Nalla Pochamma was worshiped as a goddess of poxes and was offered toddy and chickens by devotees after they recovered from sickness. Over the years the place has been heavily populated to form part of the city of Secundrabad. Now, Nalla Pochamma draws many devotees on a daily basis and a *brahman* priest has been retained to perform daily *puja* (worship). Devotees consist of brides, wives, and young mothers with small children. To accommodate devotees, the goddess is housed in a spacious temple with multiple chambers. The head of the bedrock is decorated with turmeric sumptuously and dressed with a saree, jewelry, and makeup to appear like the goddess Durga on her lion mount. This transition of Nalla Pochamma, from being a pox goddess of occasional worship to the incarnation of the goddess Durga, to receiving regular worship by a *brahman* priest, is a common development for some *gramadevatas* who accumulate many devotees and wealth, especially in an urban context.

At times, a *gramadevata* such as the one in Pukkallapeta (Srikakulam District) may be understood primarily as the earth mother. Here, she is called Bhulokamma ("mother of the world"). The fisher folk worship Bhulokamma to help them in their fishing ventures in the sea. Bhulokamma, in fact, is not only the earth mother who bears oceans in her lap, but also the form of water itself. For this reason, they also call her Gangamma ("water mother"). As is usual with most *gramadeavatas*, villagers treat Bhulokamma/Gangamma as an auspicious married daughter paying a visit to their houses. So, their offerings to the goddess contain a saree, blouse piece, turmeric, and vermilion. For the *gramadevata* Gangamma to receive only vegetarian offerings would be an unusual phenomenon. In prosperous villages like Pullagunta (Guntur District), the character of the *gramadevata* is clearly defined in the image form.[108] Here, the goddess Gangamma is carved with a crocodile as her vehicle, a symbol suggesting that the goddess represents life-generating waters in the same way as the goddess Ganga is often seen in *brahman*ic temples.

As the form of life-giving waters, a *gramadevata* may also preside over tanks, wells, rivers, streams, and rains. This is the reason some *gramadevatas*, such as Poleramma and Mutyalamma, are worshiped on or near irrigation tanks either in image form or simply as a natural rock.[109] Sometimes, a goddess like Nandyalamma in Langanabhavi (Mahaboobnagar District) might live in a well. Her form is a simple pot, believed to appear floating in a village well every year during her annual festival.[110] The well itself is presumed to have been dug out by semi-divine beings called *rasasiddhas*. The villagers get another earthen pot, decorate it with turmeric and vermilion dots, take it to the well in a procession, accompanied by music, and leave it by the side of the pot that has appeared in the well. The two pots will sink together into the well by the next morning, when the villagers celebrate the festival with animal sacrifices and food and cloth offerings.

During drought periods, villagers typically worship their *gramadevatas* by seeking rains. In my native place, Anantharam (Krishna District), the *grama-devata* Mutyalamma is invoked on these occasions in the following manner. At the beginning of the ritual, a person from the washerman caste pours water over himself making his clothes wet, and then applies turmeric and vermilion to the surface of two brass vessels, which he fills with water and around which he ties margosa leaves. He also catches a frog and ties it in a clean thin wet cloth to a bamboo pole of a *kavadi* (two vessels hanging with ropes on either side of a bamboo pole). He places the brass vessels in the *kavadi* and carries them in a procession. The vessels, the frog, and the washerman are treated each as forms of the goddess. Accompanied by a drumbeater and a man carrying a basket on his head to collect grains, the washerman goes from house to house in the village every day for a week singing a song. The translation of the first two stanzas of the song is as follows:

> *The frog mother gave birth.*
> *Pots full of water are brought to wash her*
> *Rains are here.*
> *Floods will follow.*

Each household brings a pot full of water to pour over the washerman, the frog, and the brass vessels. Each household also gives a handful of grains as an offering to another accompanying person who carries a basket. The grains are cooked each day to make an offering to the goddess. Rains are expected during or at the end of this weeklong ritual. After seven days and after witnessing the rain, each household sends their offerings of cooked milk rice, chickens and coconuts in gratitude to the *gramadevata* Mutyalamma, who is then worshiped in the form of a navel stone (*boddurai*) at the center of the village.

The above ritual reflects the function of *gramadevata* as a rain-bearer. Creatures such as frogs, fish, crocodiles, and tortoises, because of their aquatic nature, are identified as assisting the goddess in this task. Simultaneously they are also treated as forms of the goddess. Frogs are especially associated with the rain, probably because after raining, frogs huddle in puddles of water and make their croaking noises. Here, recall the similarity between the shape of frog and that of the evolved shapes of the *srivatsa* (Figure 3.4) and consequently the evolving naked goddess out of *purnakumbha* in Yelesvaram (Figure 3.29).

As mentioned earlier, substances that help boost the fertility of the soil are seen as forms of the fertility goddess. One of the examples of this kind is the goddess Masamma of Vangur (Mahaboobnagar District), who is worshiped in the form of cow dung.[111] During the annual ritual to Masamma, cow dung is made into three cylindrical forms, to which turmeric and vermilion are applied. A *gramadevata* taking this form is not a new phenomenon, as the goddess Gobbemma is also worshiped annually throughout Andhra and elsewhere during the three-day harvest festival (January 13–15) in the form of cow dung (as I have mentioned in the previous chapter). Another name for Gobbemma is Gauramma. David Kinsley records that during the harvest festival in Orissa, and in other parts of the Deccan as well, animal sacrifices are offered to this goddess in just the same way as for a *gramadevata*.[112] The harvest festival in these parts of India is celebrated on Dipavali (the festival of lights) in late October and early November, when the dung hill is worshiped as the form of Sri Lakshmi. During the harvest festival of Sankranti in Andhra, cows are also worshiped as the form of Gauri (Figure 3.36). In fact, the third day of the harvest festival is dedicated to domestic animals, during which time bullock are decorated and worshiped as well. In some Andhra villages, these animals are taken around the *gramadevata*'s shrine to get her blessings.

In Telugu domestic rituals, as mentioned in the previous chapter, Gauri/ Gauramma (the golden one) is also worshiped in the form of a tiny turmeric mound placed on a plate in the home shrine with accompanying songs and

FIGURE 3.36 Worshiping Cows

chants (Figure 2.14). Gauri or Gauramma is the name attributed to both Sri Lakshmi and Parvati, probably indicating their own common origins from this goddess. The household prayer sung in praise of the goddess goes like this:

> *Your divine play, O Gauramma, is strange.*
> *You became Parvati to be a chaste wife.*
> *You also became a spouse to Brahma.*
> *And then you flourished as Sri Lakshmi.*
> *O Gauramma, you are the Kamadhenu*
> *[the divine cow that fulfills all wishes].*

This song is reminiscent of the myth of Adisakti that I related earlier in which her energy is divided to become Parvati, Lakshmi, and Saraswati, and then finally to become many *gramadevatas*. Here, the song recounts that Parvati, Sri Lakshmi and Saraswati are forms of this fertility goddess.[113] It also proceeds to say that Gauramma, in fact, is a divine cow. This theme of cow-as-the-fertility-goddess brings us back to the image of a naked goddess lying next to the charged bull as symbolic of both the earth and the cow at the same time. It is the bull that ties the earth and the cow together. By helping to till the soil and by its dung, the bull boosts the soil and the growth of vegetation. By its semen, the bull also produces offspring with the cow. So, here the cow plays the role of the earth. As such, there are instances, as in Chennamarajupalle (Cuddapah District), where cows are worshiped as *gramadevata*.[114]

Goddess Gangamma is originally the presiding deity of the shepherd (*golla* or *yadava*) caste, whose main occupation was keeping herds of sheep and cows. At the annual festival of Gangamma (*Avula Panduga*, festival of cows), the villagers worship their cows by bathing them, anointing turmeric and vermilion, and offering pulses and cooked rice. An image of a one-horned cow is installed in front of the temple as the image of Gangamma, to which cooked rice, green gram and a pot of liquor is offered. Instead of a buffalo, a ram is sacrificed, placing the ram's leg in its mouth, villagers shouting out *"paluku Gangamma"* (speak Gangamma) upon which the dead ram yawns. A plantain tree is also offered by cutting its trunk. Following this, a vast number of rams are sacrificed as the blood flows before the temple. Later, a drama is enacted in which the story of Gangamma is told. A clay image of Gangamma made for the occasion is taken in procession, after which it is immersed in the nearby stream. The festival concludes with the sacrifice of yet another ram. While the goddess Gangamma in myth is clearly a divine female who encounters Katamaraju, the leader of *Yadava* community, the cow is also seen as the form of Gangamma. In a popular Hindu perspective, the cow is also sacred not just for associations with sustenance, but as a symbol of peace and patience.[115] If a human being is known for being patient and calm in difficult circumstances, then that person is called *Gangi Govu* (a cow who bears the burden quietly). Here, in Chennamrajupalle, the image of the cow is actually offered animal sacrifices. Earlier I have mentioned how a *gramadevata* needs blood to rejuvenate in her fight against demonic forces such as cattle diseases. At the same time the animal that is sacrificed is also worshiped with the understanding that it possesses the form of the *gramadevata*. As is the case with animal sacrifices in *gramadevata* rituals, the ram's yawning is taken as a sign that the animal has been possessed by the goddess. A further proof of identification of the goddess with the sacrificial animal comes from places like Madharam (Mahaboobnagar District), where the image of the *gramadevata* is fashioned in animal form and worshiped in the name of Edamma.[116]

Not just sacrificial animals, but ferocious animals can also be seen as a form of goddess. Although Ellamma is often worshiped as a *gramadevata*, she is claimed especially by the *mala* and *madiga* communities as their goddess. These communities identify Ellamma in the form of a tiger. One way of explaining this is that these communities started worshiping Ellamma from the time that they were hunter-gatherers. Other animal forms of goddesses such as Edamma might have their origins in hunter-gatherer groups too. While those communities merged into the mainstream, pursuing agricultural activities, they must have continued to worship these goddesses, who slowly transformed themselves to meet the needs of an agricultural economy. Agriculture, like hunting, involves its own fierce battles with natural elements, with wild animals as well as other humans of opposing and conflicting interests. So, the goddess would not lose her relevance in the transition from hunting and gathering to farming.

For example, there is a myth about goddess Masamma waging war against the supernatural enemies of these communities. When a particular form of little mushroom erupts in living quarters, *mala* and *madiga* communities assume that this eruption is a form of goddess Masamma or Ellamma and hold a ritual in her honor by narrating her story. Strange as it may seem, the story does not identify the mushroom as the form of goddess. The professional singers of the above mentioned communities, called *pambalavandlu*, sing of the story in which this goddess is identified as Renuka.[117] The name Renuka was used in an earlier myth as synonymous with the popular name Ellamma.

Renuka was the daughter of a mountain king and his wife, Jamilika Parvati. When the mountain king was attacked by *rakshasas* (demons), he hid in a cave. Knowing this, Renuka went to her sage husband, Jamadagni, placing seven pots on her head containing rice and water, with the idea of asking his permission to go to war. To test her deep devotion to her husband, Narada (a divine sage) and Vishnu came to her as beggars and got some of the cooked rice as alms. In a fit of anger that somebody had eaten a portion of his food first, Jamadagni ordered his son, Parasurama, to cut off his mother's head. Parasurama fulfilled his father's order, but afterwards cut his own hand off out of remorse for killing his own mother. The hand of Parasurama became a mushroom, while the head of Renuka took the form of a cobra's hood. Later, Renuka came alive and asked her husband's permission to go to the war with the *rakshasas* (demons) only then to be heckled by him. She then asked her husband to look at her again, by which time she had assumed the form of *sakti* with a thousand hands holding thousands of *sulas* (spears), each piercing an animal. Each of the flayed animals was accompanied by a *sakti* (goddess), holding a *khatvanga* (curved sword) and a *khadga* (sword). When the frightened Jamadagni tried to escape to the underground, Renuka stopped him by holding his garment and retreated back into her human form. And this was how she won his consent to go to the war. During the war, when she killed each of the *rakshasas*, the spilled blood gave rise to the appearance of six thousand more, upon which she ordered her brother, Poturaju, to spread out his tongue on the ground to prevent the blood from falling on the ground. In this way, it is said that Renuka won the war with the *rakshasas*.

The story shares a resemblance to the fifth-century CE text, *Devi Mahatmya*. It also reflects how a *gramadevata* has been understood by villagers as fighting against their enemies. Usually in *gramadevata* shrines, her brother Poturaju is seen as a stake or as an image in the front or back side of the shrine where the animal sacrifices are made. In this story, Poturaju is assigned his familiar job of drinking blood, but in this instance it is the blood of demons.[18] Because of this, sometimes the sacrificial animals are conflated with demon enemies. As discussed earlier, even the sacrificial animal or the demon enemy is understood as a form of goddess. This is the same principle we encountered when I explained that the goddess is at once the disease and its cure.

In this story, Renuka is introduced as the daughter of Siva and Parvati (by a vague reference to him as a mountain king). Despite this introduction, she, as *gramadevata*, is the protagonist of power in the story. Yet, the *gramadevata* as Renuka respects her sage husband, thereby meeting Hindu patriarchal norms, and takes his nominal approval before acting on her own, despite the fact that it is clear that it is not her king father, nor her sage husband, but only she who is capable of crushing the otherwise invincible demons.

The enemies in the form of *rakshasa*s are not just the wild animals that encroach into the fields, or the diseases that attack the fields, domestic animals, and the people who live in the village, but they could also be enemy soldiers. Incessant wars waged by chieftains and rulers demanded men in agricultural communities to serve in the army. For these reasons, a *gramadevata* as a guardian deity not only helped to boost the village's fertility, but also defended them in any peril. This guarding and defending becomes a primary function of a *gramadevata* when adopted as the family deity of a ruler or a ruling dynasty. As the rulers fade and the dynasties disappear, these *gramadevatas* resume to their functions of fertility and protection.

This is also the case of Ankamma, known for her fierce form in villages like Vadavalur (Nellore District). In memory of her victory over seven Odiya (Orissa) kings, a mock battle is enacted during her annual ritual. During the ritual, a cart loaded with a lizard, a pig, a goat, a fowl, and a man (nowadays an image in human form has replaced the actual human being) accompanied by music is taken in procession to Ankamma's temple. The mythology associating Ankamma with wars corresponds with Susan Bayly's argument about how rituals to goddesses like Ankamma are similar to warrior rituals, in that the defeated enemy army represents the animal victims sacrificed to the *gramadevata*.[119] In this scenario, the sacrificial victims of Ankamma—the lizard, pig, goat, fowl and human being—possess the spirit of the goddess. But if these animals represent the enemy army, they must have possessed the spirit of the goddess as well.

The worship of the warrior goddess is extended to the weapons she is assumed to wield in defending her people. Weapons like the axe and sword are worshiped as *gramadevatas* in villages like Nondrukona (Srikakulam District). with the names Jakaramma and Jobemma, respectively.[120] Whenever these goddesses are worshiped, villagers do not work with axes and swords. If they deviate from that norm, they believe that the goddess may come as a tigress and kill them. The deities of the axe and sword are worshiped annually at both village and household levels. The worship of tools or weapons is not confined to this particular village, as there is a warrior tradition of worshiping the weapons of the goddess during the annual festival of Vijaya Dasami to celebrate the victory of the goddess over demons. On this day, many families with a warrior background take out their stored-away weapons of inheritance to polish and worship them.

The early evidence of the earth goddess as the mother of vegetation can be traced to an oblong seal from the Indus civilization, in which a goddess is shown giving birth to vegetation (Figure 3.37).[121] Water is recognized as an important element of the earth goddess, as acknowledged at least from Indus times in the form of *gharial* or *makara*.[122] The *gharial* might have been understood as the form of goddess at this very early period, a theme that seems to have been continued in later art. The *Rig Veda*, which was composed several centuries after the Indus period, with a focus on male deities, does incorporate the prevalent concept of the earth (Prthivi) and water (Saraswati) as goddesses of bounty.[123] The *Bhumisukta* in *Atharvaveda* is a prayer to a goddess described as the earth and its surrounding atmosphere that causes rains.[124] However, the concept of waters representing the fertility aspect takes a diverse route eventually in that it comes to stand for intellect. The concept of earth as mother is also known from early Sangam literature. In addition to the reference to the earth as mother, the Tamil epic of second century, the *Cilappatikaram*, has abundant references to guardian goddesses of cities, groves, waterfronts, crossroads, etc.[125]

Many representations of the fertility goddess in early Andhra wear a *makara* (a composite animal of crocodile and lion amidst the rushing flow of water) type of headdress.[126] As a goddess representing the earth containing water, the fertility goddess, when she acquired her anthropomorphic forms, was probably perceived as riding the lion as well as crocodile, and this perception is what has been articulated in the form of the *makara* headdress.[127]

This ancient notion of earth as the fertility goddess, venerated by agricultural folk in their worship of the earth, the rocks, the hills, the forests, and the water, was apparently so prevalent that the Buddhists were obligated to incorporate this conception of the goddess into their cosmology. The *Digha Nikaya* connects the goddess to the major events of the life of the Buddha, such as Queen Maya's conception of him, and the acknowledgment of his birth and his enlightenment by Bhudevi, the earth goddess.[128] The earth goddess is also introduced into the life of the Buddha during his departure from the city of Sravasti, and during his calling the earth as his witness to meet Mara's challenge before his enlightenment experience. At Amaravati, both of these events are portrayed.[129] In Theravada Buddhist Thailand, Laos, and Cambodia, the earth goddess is portrayed as a young woman, Nang Thorani, who in sculptures found in both public and monastic contexts is wringing her soaked hair to squeeze out waters. These waters generate a flood to confound Mara's army, which was sent to prevent the Buddha from gaining enlightenment.[130]

In the context of Andhra, the depiction of the earth goddess in relation to the Buddha might have been difficult for the masses to understand. For example, the earth goddess is depicted as commanding the animal world or as representing the waters. The goddess at Nagarjunakonda is shown resting one of her legs on a composite animal made of lion and elephant heads. However, the composite animal alone is represented in the illustration (Figure 3.38). This representation is also found in other Andhra Buddhist sites like Amaravati and Phanigiri.[131] A more popular form of the *makara*, showing the association of goddess with water, animals, and aquatic creatures is the combination made up of lion and crocodile heads. This combination is known as *makara sardula* and becomes the mount (*vahana*) of the goddess. This depiction becomes popular in later art as well. In the same way as the *srivatsa,* the lotus, the tree, etc., represent the goddess, the different combination of composite animals shown how the goddess represents the animal kingdom. The female figures in the Buddhist art of Amaravati, Jaggayyapeta (Krishna District), and Nagarjunakonda that are shown holding the branches of a tree, or kicking them with one leg, are often seen as resting one of their feet on a mythical *makara vahana* (Figure 3.39).[32] While the goddess riding a *makara* came to represent rivers in later art, here it is of interest to note that the Buddhist *jataka*s, such as *Losaka Jataka* and *Mahajanaka Jataka*, mention goddesses in command of the oceans.[33] In several Buddhist shrines, the *makara* is also portrayed as part of a *torana* (medallion) with creepers and lotuses issuing out of its mouth, signifying sacred waters that contain fecund auspiciousness as well as the power of transcendence. This representation of the *makara torana* continued to appear in the art of Saiva and Vaishanava shrines starting from the fifth century CE, as shown in the Undavalli caves of Vijayawada and in other places.[34]

The *makara* (crocodile) becomes part of the *srivatsa* to form part of a *torana* at the entrances of Buddhist gateways, and at Jaina, Saiva, and Vaishnava temples. As the *srivatsa* evolves into the anthropomorphic form of the fertility spirit or *yakshi* cult, and the goddess of abundance either as Sri Lakshmi or the goddess representing rivers such as Ganges, the *makara* in some of her many forms, serves as her vehicle, as depicted in the Buddhist art of Bharhut in Madhya Pradesh (third to second century BCE) and at Amaravati in the Krishna District (second century CE) in its mythical form (Figure 3.39).[35] By this time, the goddess riding the *makara* came to be identified as Ganga in Buddhist *jataka* literature.[36] Thus, in later representations, the *makara* became the specific identifiable mount for Ganga, the goddess of life generating waters. Also, the tortoise, as a counterpart of the *makara*, started appearing as a vehicle of one of the river goddesses that adorned either side of Vaishnavite, Saivite, and Sakti shrines as auspicious signs of abundance and prosperity. These and other animal forms of the goddess were incorporated into Vishnu's mythology in such a way that four of his ten *avataras* take the forms of fish, boar, tortoise, and lion, the last of which came to be represented as half-lion and half human. Usually these various incarnations of Vishnu are found in niches of Vishnu temples, and at times even in the Siva temples of Andhra.[37] In some cases, Vishnu temples are dedicated to one of these incarnations, like the Matsyagiri Swamy temple at Kalesvaram in Karimnagar district, where Vishnu is carved on a big granite boulder as a big fish accompanied by Sri Lakshmi.[138] At the same time, the earth as a goddess is identified as a second wife to Vishnu with the name Bhudevi who, as we noted earlier, is known in early Buddhist literature as well.

The frog as a form of goddess is not so favored in temple art. A rare but clearly illustrated example comes in the form of a double-sided terracotta plaque from Mathura dated to the second century CE, which shows the identification of the frog with the goddess.[139] According to Bolon, the carving on one side is the image of the frog, and on the other side is an image of the naked goddess with her feet flexed in the same way that the goddess figures in their birthing position are portrayed in the *purnakumbha* motif. This motif led me to think that the present-day ritual of seeking rain held when the *gramadevata* is worshiped in the form of a live frog might have had its origins at this early period. Within this rite, as noted earlier, there is a Telugu folk song that says that the frog mother gave birth and the mother needs water to bathe. If the villagers offer her water, then the goddess will be pleased and release the waters from the clouds.

A donation is recorded in an early fourteenth century inscription issued by a governor of Macherla who worked under the Kakatiyas to make provisions for the worship and food offerings to Gangamma, who is a goddess of the *yadava* clan and a popular guardian deity of many villages and towns in Andhra Pradesh. As in the case of many *gramadevatas*, Ganga acquires the Saivite epithet—Paramesvari, acknowledging her as the form of Parvati.[140] Her image form was probably similar to that of the *gramadevata* image with the crocodile that is still worshiped in the Guntur District. Her Sanskritized name as Gangamamba is mentioned as the *gramadevata* of Gurizala (Guntur District). She was worshiped as a family deity by the heroes in the Telugu poem, *Palnativiracharitra*.[141]

The tiger form of the goddess, on the other hand, is known from Indus seals, where the tiger with half a human body is seen.[142] Some scholars have argued that this was the prototypical form of the goddess Durga. On one of these seals, tigers flank both sides of a fully anthropomorphic goddess who holds the animals by their throats (Figure 3.40).[143] The goddess Durga, who is known to have tribal and village associations, with her mounts as the tiger and lion, and her worship and ritual resembling the *gramadevata*, is noticed on the Satavahana coins of the Kolhapur series from the second to third century CE.[144]

Durga's next appearance in Andhra is in a plaque of the fourth- to fifth-century CE period in the company of other *brahmanic* deities and with the fertility symbol of the *srivatsa* (Figure 3.14).[145] This is the early form of the fully anthropomorphic figure of the goddess seen as part of the *brahmanic*

pantheon. Here, she appears in the act of slaying the buffalo demon by trampling him with her right foot and thrusting the *trisula* into his back with the
upper left hand. Possessing only four hands, the goddess otherwise stands
on the ground without any mount. It is said that the *madiga* community,
who were once rulers known by the name Matangas because of their claim
as children of goddess Matangi, worshiped this goddess, otherwise known as
Durga.[146] As related in the myth of the pox goddess earlier, the sacrifice of the
buffalo is understood as relating to her husband who belongs to the *madiga*
community. *Mala* and *madiga* communities, in fact, are the performers of the
buffalo sacrifice; they decorate the animal and take him in procession to be
worshiped by the whole village before the sacrifice. Slaying buffalo as a part
of religious sacrifice can also be traced to Indus culture, where the motif of
buffalo being speared by a naked man with one of his feet on its head recurs
in Harappan glyptic art (Figure 3.37).[147]

Durga, who is understood to have mountain origins like the goddess
Ellamma or Edamma, also shares similarities with the typical *gramadevata*
of Andhra, i.e., the bloody rituals held in her honor and her associations with
fertility involving agriculture.[148] The fact that Ellamma as Renuka is worshiped
as Matangi connects her with the goddess Durga. This connection probably
has something to do with their shared tribal origins. As mentioned earlier, the
women dedicated to goddess Ellamma who come from *mala* and *madiga* communities are known as Matangi. Considering how the rulers of the *madiga*
community were known as Matangas, it is possible that they called their tutelary goddess deity Matangi. Here we can see how a goddess with origins in a
hunting-gathering culture was transformed not only into a *gramadevata*, but
into a warrior goddess as well.

Another important form of the earth goddess mentioned at the outset is
the cow. The *Bhumisukta* in the *Atharvaveda* likens the earth to a cow that
contains perennial udders that yield treasures. This notion of earth as a cow
recurs in later literature such as in the *Mahabharata* to show that she is the
kamadhenu who fulfills the wishes of devotees through her divine udders.[149]
The affiliated relation of the fertility goddess to the *kamadhenu*, along with her
other symbols of the lotus and the *srivatsa,* is clearly seen on a first-century CE
coin issued by the Kuninda dynasty in northern India (Figure 3.41).[150] On one
side of this coin, the goddess Sri stands by a *kamadhenu* bearing the symbol of
the *srivatsa* on its head. Here, Sri with her hands on her hip is seen wearing a
skirt-like garment. On the reverse side, a goddess is seen flanked by a *svastika*
and a *kalpavriksha* ("wish-fulfilling tree") but she appears in nude as there is
no sign of clothing on this figure. This coin has a very special significance in

that it shows the fertility goddess in her many forms: anthropomorphic, zoo-morphic, botanic, and symbolic (*svastika* and *srivatsa*).

So far, my study of the symbols of the fertility goddess in ancient and current contexts indicates that some of her ancient symbols, such as the *srivatsa*, *nandipada*, the bull, the bird, etc., have ceased to function as forms of goddess because of the manner in which they have been appropriated by evolving Indian religious traditions. Other symbols, such as the *svastika, chakra, trisula, naga, purnakumbha,* and lotus also ceased to be exclusively related to the goddess, as they assumed specific identifiable meanings within other cultic contexts. These symbols still remain as an integral part of the goddess culture. It is interesting and noteworthy that "live symbols," such as plants, trees, the tiger, lion, elephant, buffalo and ram, also remained prominent fixtures in goddess religious culture. The *gramadevata*s in question did not necessarily remain independent fertility goddesses, as her forms often appear in conjunction with the cults of other *brahman*ic deities. Meanwhile, the fertility goddess cult itself elaborated its meaning by incorporating various tribal goddess cults, on the one hand, and deified women cults on the other. The independent goddesses who remained at the village level have also, in turn, drawn back influences of her own forms that had been subsumed within other religious traditions, a kind of "kickback" effect. I will examine these issues further in studying the iconographic forms of the goddess.

FIGURE 3.4 *Svastika & Srivatsa* N Konda

FIGURE 3.5 *Chakra* N Konda

FIGURE 3.6 Lotus N Konda

FIGURE 3.7 *Naga* Amaravati

FIGURE 3.11 *Srivatsa* with lotuses

FIGURE 3.12 *Srivatsa* Tirumalagiri

FIGURE 3.13 *Srivatsa* Pattern

FIGURE 3.14 Mounted *Srivatsa* & *Chakra*

FIGURE 3.15 Mounted *Srivatsa* with *Naga*

FIGURE 3.16 Goddess with Two Elephants

FIGURE 3.17 *Srivatsa* and Goddess

FIGURE 3.20 Kosam Goddess

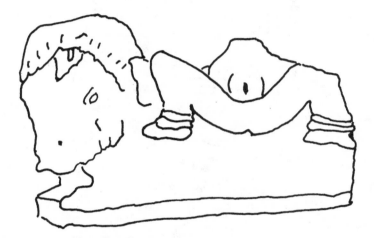

FIGURE 3.21 Goddess & Bull

FIGURE 3.22 *Purnakumbha*

FIGURE 3.23A Naked Goddess

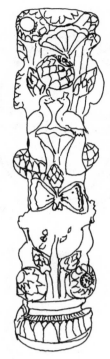

FIGURE 3.23B Birds & Flowers

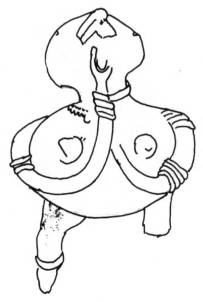

FIGURE 3.24 Indus Pot

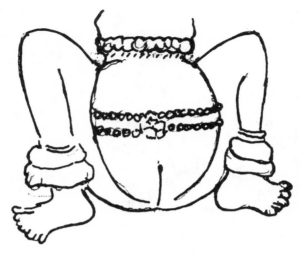

3.26 Karlapalem Pot

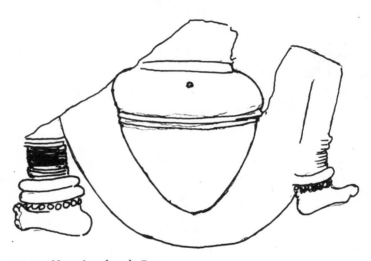

FIGURE 3.27 Nagarjunakonda Pot

FIGURE 3.28 Darsi Panel

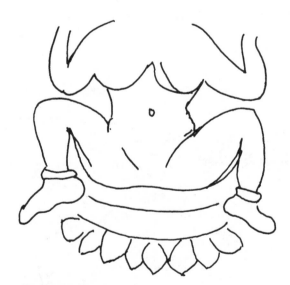

FIGURE 3.29 Yeleshwaram Goddess

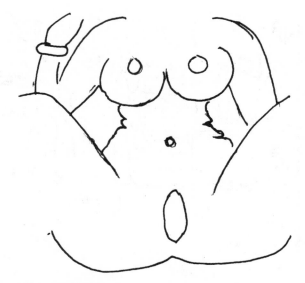

FIGURE 3.30 Alampur Goddess

FIGURE 3.35 Stupa Relic Chamber

FIGURE 3.37 Indus Gharial

FIGURE 3.38 Elephant Lion

FIGURE 3.39 *Makara Vahana*

FIGURE 3.40 Indus Goddess with Tigers

FIGURE 3.41 Goddess & Cow

4

Profiles of Anthropomorphic Goddesses

IN MYTH, RITUAL, AND HISTORY

IMAGE WORSHIP PLAYS a major role in contemporary Hindu religion. But how and when image worship started is not clearly known. Vedic religion was not based on image worship. In goddess worship, however, the image is complementary to other forms of symbols used in the ritual. The complementary role of images can be traced to the prehistoric past when anthropomorphic forms served a temporary ritual function, as a number of terracotta images of the proto-historic and early historic periods indicate. As small and scattered agricultural societies evolved into organized chiefdoms and kingdoms in the late and early centuries of pre- and post-Common-Era of Andhra, and as the building of permanent religious shrines began, a few life-size stone images of the fertility goddess started emerging for regular worship. One of the issues I discuss in this chapter is how and why the anthropomorphic forms of the goddess became popular in the succeeding centuries of the Common Era. This discussion also brings forth the issue of how the fertility goddess emulated her own transformed incarnations while absorbing various tribal and other cults to become the present *gramadevata* or the popular goddess. Examples are Durga and Kali, who qualify as ancient fertility goddesses and who later entered *brahmanic* literature and temples acquiring certain iconographic features that eventually influenced their portrayals as *gramadevatas* at the village level. In order to track this process, I will consider four different profiles of the fertility goddess: 1) the naked goddess, 2) the Buddhist Hariti cult, 3) sister goddesses, and 4) tribal goddesses.

In her study of the evolution of goddess symbols into anthropomorphic forms, Carol Radcliffe Bolon opined that the goddess evolved into anthropomorphic shape by means of the transformation of her symbols, just in the same way as the evolution of Buddha's aniconic representation moved from the symbolic to the human form. In this process, Bolon has identified various phases of gradual evolution of the goddess Lajja Gauri that she argues paralleled the development of Buddha images.

> The four forms of Lajja Gauri I have identified show a broad progression through time and region from the minimal, and nearly aniconic to the fully human. The process of change is fascinating, especially given the comparable early aniconic configuration of the Buddha, before he was given human shape.[1]

While it is true that the Buddha was not depicted in human form in the early stages of the Buddhist art, the same cannot be said about the development of goddess iconography. In fact, the evidence in Andhra and elsewhere shows that the image form of the fertility goddess is, in some instances, perhaps as ancient as her symbolic representations. Only a few images have survived because these were fashioned in terracotta. These few weathered images, however, reflect a major factor in evolving goddess iconography. In the absence of other religious forms of evidence in this early period of Andhra, these images, along with the few symbols I have discussed earlier, lead us to believe that veneration of the goddess, sometimes in anthropomorphic forms, played a significant role in people's lives.

Naked Goddess. The anthropomorphic images of the goddess that were discussed briefly in the previous chapter evolved out of symbols such as the lotus, the tree, *srivatsa, purnakumbha,* etc. Those evolutions, in most cases, were cultivated in Buddhist, *brahmanic,* and Jain traditions. The early images of the goddess in Andhra that I discuss in this subsection are the precursors of those evolutions. Most of these early terracotta images were nude. The nudity of the fertility goddess continued to be popular for many centuries, even when stone was used to represent her anthropomorphic form.

Although the contemporary portrayal of fertility goddesses in naked form is a rare phenomenon, some of the naked stone images of the goddess in past centuries are still in worship. The remnants of these images are seen as *gramadevatas* in certain villages. One of these images comes from Rangapur from Mahaboobnagar District.[2] The goddess known as Gajjela Papamma stands nude, but holds a sword and a shield in her two hands. While her nudity shows her essential function of fertility, the weapons on her person indicate her warrior spirit. Another example of naked imagery is the goddess Gantalamma, carved crudely on a stone and placed in a small shrine for worship in the poor colony of the *mala* community in Gandepalle (Krishna District) (Figure 4.1).[3] The goddess Gantalamma receives an annual ritual in which the whole village

FIGURE 4.1 Gantalamma

participates. Women devotees entreat the goddess to remove barrenness or to care for their sick children. Yet another contemporary example of the naked goddess is an old image of goddess Kanaka Durga of Vijayawada (Krishna District). This naked image of the goddess is carved inside the entrance to a cave wall (Figure 4.2). This cave remains part of the present temple premises. Here, the naked goddess is seen holding demons by their heads in each of her two hands. As discussed in the last chapter, goddesses like Durga accumulated a long history of evolving to meet the needs of early communities such as hunter-gatherers, village farming communities, and ruling classes. What this means is that the worship of a naked female form as the fertility goddess is both ancient and current. This is also known from the examples mentioned in the last chapter, such as the seventh-century CE image of the naked goddess still worshiped in a sub-shrine in the Balabrahmesvara temple at Alampur (Kurnool District) (Figure 3.30).[4] Another naked goddess sharing this long history of worship is in Miyapuram (Mahaboobnagar District).[5] Both these images are currently worshiped as the goddess Renuka or Ellamma, a goddess mentioned in multiple contexts as a popular *gramadevata* with differing accounts of mythology and symbolism in various parts of Andhra. These two images are not fully anthropomorphic, as their heads are represented by lotuses. As discussed in the previous chapter, like many images of the

FIGURE 4.2 Naked Kanaka Durga

naked goddess with lotus heads in Andhra and elsewhere, these images are seen in their birthing position. The continuing tradition of worshiping these naked images is not limited to Andhra, but also in places like Mahakuta and Siddhanakolla in Karnataka and in the Malaprabha valley of Maharashtra.[6] The function of this kind of naked goddess that exhibits the vulva remained more or less unchanged as women devotees wanting children still approach these goddesses, in the same manner as the third-century CE queen mentioned in the last chapter.

As far as the myth of Renuka Ellamma is concerned, the version at Alampur is somewhat different from the one related earlier but shares affinities with the tale mentioned in the *Mahabharata*.[7] The substance of this version is as follows: Renuka was a devoted wife of sage Jamadagni. Through her devotion to Jamadagni, after bathing in a river, she made a pot out of sand, filled it with water and brought it home. On a fateful day, Renuka witnessed a Gandharva couple making love and lost her concentration in making the pot. When she returned distressed and empty-handed, the sage was angry and asked one of his sons to decapitate their mother. Parasurama, his fourth son, agreed and did his bidding. In the process, he also ended up decapitating an untouchable woman first who had given shelter to his mother. When the sage was pleased and granted a boon, Parasurama asked for his mother to be revived.

On his father's direction, Parasurama joined the head and the body. But in his haste, he attached the head of the untouchable woman to his mother's body. Thereafter, the goddess was worshiped both as Renuka and Ellamma. So, Renuka is the goddess of *brahmans* and Ellamma the goddess of *mala* and *madiga* communities.

There are many symbolisms in this story, one of which is that Renuka, whose body is visualized as the form of a pot in her annual rituals, loses her life in failing to create a pot. Since this pot is regarded as the womb of the goddess, this refers to her essential fecund nature for which women approach her. This might be the reason for her naked representation. The myth establishes that she is a split goddess sharing origins from *brahman* and previously untouchable castes, who stand at the opposite ends of the social hierarchy, thus bringing the whole gamut of castes together in her worship.

However, it is interesting to note that Ellamma is worshiped in Undavelli, a nearby village to Alampur, in the form of a head wearing a crown. This perpetuates the myth of the spilt goddess Renuka-Ellamma with her body in the *brahman* colony in a *brahman*ic temple as the goddess Renuka and her head in the untouchable community in the Undavalli shrine containing the head of the goddess Ellamma.

There is another explanation of how Ellamma is the representation of naked goddess. The name Ellamma is said to have originated from the Marathi word *verul*, meaning pot or the vulva of the earth.[8] This not only explains why the naked images in places like Alampur are shown exhibiting the vulva, but also the reason for using pots in goddess rituals as her forms. This notion has its roots going back to the proto-historic Andhra when naked images like that of Mudumala were carved. This naked goddess, as mentioned hitherto, represents the fertile earth that is ready to be tilled and sowed.

In this connection, the role of Matangi women who were mentioned earlier as possessed by the *gramadevata* during annual rituals, can be explained further. The alternative names for Matangi are *basavi* or Ellamma *dasi* (servant), as they are known in the state of Karnataka. Matangis usually serve the goddess Ellamma, who is also known as Matamma.[9] Matangi women who are possessed can be either chosen formally by means of elaborate rituals or informally by the village elders or the elders of the caste group who treat goddesses like Ellamma as their caste deities. Some women appoint themselves as the would-be possessed.[10] In some villages of Andhra, especially in Kurnool District, where the naked goddess as Renuka-Ellamma is still worshiped, a Matangi is selected from one of the virgin girls of the *mala* or *madiga* community after the girl passes through some trying initiation ceremonies. On an appointed day, the virgin goes to the popular temple of Ellamma in

Malinthapadu (Kurnool District) for her final confirmation, since Ellamma is considered as the incarnation of a Matangi. At this temple, as in some regionally popular *gramadevata* temples, a *brahman* priest conducts ceremonies for a group of selected virgins coming from many villages for five consecutive days. On their return to their villages, these Matangis are married to a tree, a symbolic marriage that allows them to take any man of their liking while at the same time retaining their independence.[11] In other words, they do not have to fulfill any wifely duties or take orders from any man. In the past, Matangis have been given some land to live on their own. This custom of the Matangi is, in some ways, analogous to the tradition of stamping a virile young bull as the property of the village. While the Matangi tradition has been desecrated, such that several Matangis have gone into prostitution during recent adverse economic circumstances, the point here is how Matangis have represented the paradoxical situation of being perpetually married yet independent goddesses. In fact, the tale of the Matangi's origins relates her to the goddess.[12]

The outline of this tale is similar to the genesis story of Adi Maha Sakti that I related in a previous chapter. When the mountain king and his wife, Jamilika Devi, were holding court, a beautiful maiden who was the incarnation of Parvati appeared in front of them. As the king tried to catch the maiden with his right hand, she receded and eventually disappeared into an anthill. After many efforts of trying to retrieve her out of the anthill, which grew hard like a stone, the king drove a spear into the anthill out of frustration. As the king pulled the spear out, he found blood from the brain of the maiden beginning to flow. Seeing this, the king and his followers fell into a swoon. The maiden then appeared in front of them in her full glory and in "divine proportions," holding the heavens in her left hand, the great *naga* in her right. She held the sun and moon as plates carrying spilled blood and parts of her scattered brain in each of them.[13] She made a mark with the brains and the blood on the foreheads of the people who were in a swoon, upon which they recovered and witnessed the goddess. The king and the queen took the goddess as their daughter and married her to the sage Jamadagni, with whom she then had five sons.

In addition to identifying Matangi with the Adi Maha Sakti, this tale explains the ritual role of Matangi in the annual festival of the goddess. The Sanskrit word *matangi* (*mata*: mother; *angi*: body) can be understood as "the person whose body is the vehicle to the mother goddess." To represent the goddess in her divine form, the Matangi holds a basket in her right hand representing the heavens, a stick in her left representing the *naga*, and two plates containing vermilion and turmeric, symbolizing the blood and brains on the one hand and the sun and moon on the other. These symbols signify the identity of the goddess with the universe on the one hand and her fertility nature on the other. In the form of a human Matangi, the goddess emphasizes her fundamental identity with blood and brains[14] ritually by applying vermilion and turmeric to the forehead of devotees. In the accompaniment of music and during an invocatory song, the Matangi becomes possessed by the goddess and performs a dance. The translation of a portion of this Telugu song goes like this:

> *Sathya Surabesa (human-lion-bird) Kona (forest)! Gowthama's Kamadhenu*
> *(wish-fulfilling cow)!*
> *The headless trunk in Sathya Surabesa Kona! Your father Giri Rāju*
> *Kamadēva Jamadagni Mamuni beheaded the trunk.*
> *Silently Jamadagni cut off the arms.*
> *Did you, the headless trunk in Kamadhenu vanam (forest), the headless*
> *trunk of Jamadagni, your father's golden sword, did you ask to be born a*
> *virgin in the snake pit?*[15]

This hymn conforms to the tale of the Matangi's origins, that she is the daughter of Giri Raju (as in the earlier version) and that her husband is Jamadagni. Thus it shares similarities with the Renuka/Ellamma's myth related earlier. The difference in this song however, is that her sage husband, Jamadagni, himself cuts off Renuka's head as well as her hands. While the goddess image at Alampur has hands, it is interesting to recall that the third to fourth century CE semi-anthropomorphic images possessed no head or hands. Other names attributed to the goddess in this song are: *surabesa* (human-lion-bird), *kamadhenu* (wish-fulfilling cow), and the golden sword. These are popular forms of the goddess known through mythology, art, and worship, as discussed previously. While the word Surabhi is mentioned in the epic *Mahabharata* as one of the names of the mother goddesses, the goddess as bird is known from the first myth mentioned in chapter 2.[16] That the goddesses are sometimes represented as composite animals, such as the *makara*, has been discussed in the previous chapter. Also discussed was how the cow and the substances the animal produces are regarded as fertile and are considered as forms of the goddess, while the weapons wielded by the goddess are also considered as her forms as well. Claims of various rulers receiving swords from their guardian goddesses, and their worship of them as her forms, are frequently mentioned in Telugu literature and inscriptions. The goddess known as Matangi in this song clearly has an ancient provenance. In fact, Buddhist and other texts identify the goddess Durga as Matangi or Matangirala.[17] Probably because Parvati's origins derived from the fertility goddess, she is also known as Matangi.[18]

According to the Tamil lexicon, *matangi* or *matanki* can also refer to Kali, Parvati, the goddess of the lute, and a female dancer singing in devotion to god Murugan.[19] In this context, it is appropriate to mention that Tamil literature of the Sangam period mentions a human *matangi* tradition similar to what has been described above that existed as early as in the seventh century.[20] The various features of the goddess mentioned in the song, and her name as Matangi, connects goddesses such as Renuka, Ellamma, Durga, and Parvati to show that their cults have something of the same ritual origins. Although their cults seem to hearken back to a common source, these goddesses came to be known later for other specialized functions and hence developed definitive characters reflected in their iconography. In any case, it is clear that the Matangi tradition points out the custom of females acting as priestesses from *mala* and *madiga* communities since ancient times. This custom continues today in remote and small goddess shrines in Andhra. There are many cases, however, when these small shrines have changed hands from female to male priests and then eventually to the appointment of a *brahmin* priest for a regular *puja* (worship).[21]

There are references in early Sangam literature in which some females of tribal culture in the Western Ghats are described as consuming meat and liquor, and dancing, singing, and drumming in a frenzy, while worshiping their forest goddesses.[22] It is possible that the practices of *mala* and *madiga* communities who venerate Matangi by eating meat, drinking liquor, and dancing wildly within the context of *gramadevata* rituals have their origins in tribal culture. In the same way that the fertility goddess has entered *brahmanic* temples, the Matangi tradition under royal patronage was incarnated as the *devadasi* tradition in south Indian temples.[23] In Andhra, the colloquial term used for *devadasi*s was *sani*s, women who were associated with large temples and who formed themselves into guilds as known from inscriptions issued between the eleventh and thirteenth centuries.[24] Deification of a *sani* by the name Manikyamba is evident by an inscription issued at Draksharama temple (East Godavari District) dedicated to Siva.[25] In this historically famous Siva temple, which is one of the five major Saivite pilgrimage sites (Pancharamas) in Andhra, Manikyamba, not Parvati, is considered as the consort of Siva. Manikyamba as *devadasi* or *sani* or *matangi* achieved her potential and became the goddess through devotion.

As discussed in chapter 4, the earliest anthropomorphic images of the fertility goddess in Andhra date back to the Megalithic period between eighth and fourth century BCE. Many terracotta goddess figures of fourth century BCE that have been unearthed in places like Peddabankur (Warangal district), Dhulikatta (Karimnagar district), Nelakondapally (Khammam district), Yeleswaram (Nalgonda district), etc., indicate that at least some goddess

FIGURE 4.3 Naked Terracotta Goddess

images were consistently portrayed as naked.[26] Because most of these figures are not well-preserved, we cannot ascertain many iconographic details except for the fact that they are naked (Figure 4.3). Ultimately, the portrayal of naked anthropomorphic goddesses is traced to the Indus terracotta figurines and carvings on seals.[27]

A relatively well-preserved image, next in chronological order, is a terracotta seal of the first century BCE from Peddabankur in which the naked goddess stands in a lotus pool flanked by two elephants with pails of water held by their trunks (Figure 4.4).[28] This was the first pictographic evidence in Andhra to show the combination of an anthropomorphic representation of the goddess with elephants, lotuses, and water. This sealing becomes a popular motif throughout the art of various religious orientations with one striking difference: the famous goddess who comes to be known as Gaja Lakshmi leaves her nudity behind. Yet the evidence supports the fact that before the goddess came to be popular as Gaja Lakshmi, she was a fertility goddess standing naked not just with elephants but also with her famous companion, the bull, as it is seen from the second-century BCE. terracotta plaque at Kosam in Uttar Pradesh (Figure 3.20). This form of fertility goddess later split into Sri Lakshmi (with the elephants and lotuses), Parvati (with the bull), and the goddess with lotuses known as Kamala, to become part of the group of goddesses known as the Mahavidyas.[29] In Andhra, however, another terracotta figure of the first to second century CE from Yeleswaram holds a child and is accompanied by a humped bull, resembling the combination of Mudumala and other similar representations discussed earlier.[30] This particular figure, wearing a conical

FIGURE 4.4 Peddabankur Gajalakshmi

headdress, shares similarities with the goddess that evolves out of the *srivatsa* symbol of the eighth to ninth century CE to become Gaja Lakshmi in the *brahmanic* art of Tamilnadu.[31] While these similarities and combinations of motifs show how later goddesses such as Sri Lakshmi and Parvati share their origins with the fertility goddess, the interesting detail of this Yeleswaram figure is that the goddess, in the company of the bull, is no longer shown alone as in the past representations, but instead with a child. While the Mudumala figure lying naked next to the charged bull can be explained in an agricultural context as the goddess representing the earth in its virgin form waiting to be plowed and seeded, the representation of the terracotta mother with the child could be a metaphor of the fruit/grain that the earth produces after harvest. The virgin earth has to be furrowed and seeded with the help of bullock and only then does the vegetation spring forth leading to its final stage of harvest. As I have indicated, bullock are a crucial aid from the beginning to the end of this process and, as such, are venerated along with the earth goddess.

The child-bearing images of the above category resemble the terracotta mother figurines of the Indus period about whom Susan Huntington has commented: "this early emphasis on the feminine aspect might be a strong basis for the later importance placed on women in the major Indic religions, and consequently their performance in Indic art."[32] This is, in a way, similar to what happened in Andhra but in a much later period. In the absence of any other symbols intrinsic to the major religious traditions until the third century BCE, except for the presence of fertility symbols and a few nude goddess images, it is not unreasonable to say that the fertility goddess tradition took preeminence in the religious culture of Andhra before the onset of Buddhist, Jaina, and *brahmanic* traditions. As far as the presence of a bull in the company of the goddess is concerned, there is a theory that the bull might be the proto-form of Siva.[33] In the absence of Siva's independent cultic status in Andhra until the second to third century CE, and the representation of the bull only in the context of the fertility goddess imagery, it can be deduced that the goddess played the central role in this imagery at least until then.

The continued representation of naked goddesses with outstretched hands into the second to third century CE is seen in the form of double mold terracotta figures recovered in the excavations at Kondapur (Figure 3.25), Yeleswaram (Figure 3.29), Nagarjunakonda, and other places.[34] The nakedness of the goddess does not mean that these terracotta images are devoid of decoration, as the intricate carving of jewelry on their arms, neck, and waist and their elaborate headdresses signify their special status. Other naked goddesses of the same time period who evolved out of the *purnakumbha* or who have the lotus as their heads have been found at Nagarjunakonda (Figure 3.27), Karlapalem (Figure 3.26), Yeleswaram (Figure 3.29), and Yellala (Figure 3.31), as has been discussed in the last chapter.

Some other goddess images from the same time that are intact only from the waist above are seen holding fruit/s (Figure 4.5), sometimes with a parrot perching on their shoulders or under their arms, and in one instance, a parrot pecking at one of the goddess breasts (Figure 4.6). Bhuvanesvari, one

FIGURE 4.5 Goddess with Fruit

FIGURE 4.6 Goddess with Parrot and Fruits
Source: Photo provided by the Director, Andhra Pradesh State Archaeology Museum

of the Mahavidyas, who is known for nourishing the three worlds, is also represented as holding fruit in one of her hands.[35] These figures, with elaborate double *makara*-shaped headdresses, thus show their connection with water, a fertility-indicating motif since Indus times. The *makara* shape and the head itself seem to be replaced by a lotus in the later naked imagery of the goddess of the third- and fourth-century CE images on *purnakumbha*, or on images of naked lotus-headed goddesses at Alampur, to symbolize the same aspect of fertility but with different connotations. Apart from their nudity, the figures with parrots share an iconography with the current goddess known as Kanyaka Parameswari in Vijayawada. Kanyaka Parameswari is usually portrayed as a youthful figure wearing a saree and blouse with a parrot in one of her hands. The name Kanyaka means "virgin." She is especially worshiped now by the business community as a patron and protectress.

Moreover, a finely carved ivory sealing from this period (third to second century BCE) was found in the excavations of a fortified town, Dhulikatta, with an inscription that reads "AJANI SIRIYA GAME KUMARIYA." V. V. Krishna Sastry opined that the town was named after the goddess Kumari and the two terracotta figures with parrots are representations of this goddess.[36] This is possible because the word "Kumari" is synonymous with "Kanyaka," both referring to a virgin. The epithet, or the suffix "Parameswari," for the present goddess, must have been added to "Kanyaka" during the height of Saivism when most village and suburban goddesses in this region were adapted by the Saivites. The evolving character and representation of goddess Kanyaka is somewhat analogous to the naked Gaja Lakshmi. In both cases, the goddesses left nudity behind to become associated with Vaishnavite and Saivite orientations when fertility ceased to be their primary function. In the non-Sanskritic Sangam age of Tamil tradition, chaste virgin females were worshiped for their sacred power called *ananku*, an earlier Tamil form of concept that later, in Sanskrit, gets called *sakti*.[37]

As should now be apparent, images of the goddess belonging to the period between the eighth century BCE to the third century CE in Andhra, images holding fruits or children in their hands and arms, or images laying next to a bull, serve as forerunners to the images of the fertility goddess that appear later as part of the evolution of symbols such as lotus, tree, *srivatsa, purna-kumbha*, etc., in Buddhist and Brahmanic art.

To further exemplify, I will introduce a third and last category of the double mold terracotta type figures, this one from Dhulikatta (Karimnagar District), from the first to second century CE, an image that is profusely ornamented on her forehead, ears, arms, neck, and waist. She is shown holding her own breasts, smiling with parted lips and narrowed eyes (Figure 4.7).[38] An improvisation of this fertility goddess also has been chiseled in sandstone as part of an architectural detail in a Buddhist railing at Mathura in Uttar Pradesh, where

FIGURE 4.7 Goddess holding her breasts

her left hand is shown holding her right breast and the other hand holding a fruit pointing toward her genital area (Figure 3.23a & b). It is not surprising that this anthropomorphic figure, standing on a *purnaghata* with lotus leaves, buds, and blossoms issuing behind, has been identified as the goddess of fecundity.[39] A pair of peacocks facing each other in the middle of the foliage signals that the goddess's presence stands for peaceful cohabitation and love. By improvising the iconography of fertility goddesses in this depiction, especially by deploying the symbols of the *srivatsa* and *purnakumbha*, Buddhists captured the pulse of the majority population for whom the goddess is not just a motif of fertility and abundance, but also a reverenced symbol of human fecundity.

Images of naked goddesses continued to appear in Andhra in later centuries. The difference, with these later images starting from the third century CE, is that they were carved in relief. As mentioned earlier, these types have been recovered in Buddhist sites such as Karlapalem (Guntur District), Kondapur, Peddabankur (Karimnagar District), Yeleswaram, and Nagarjunakonda.[40] These are naked goddess images with splayed legs, who are described by Bolon as images depicted in their birthing position.[41]

Considering the presence of these fertility cults in Buddhist sites, it is possible that the Buddhists actually facilitated the worship of the fertility goddess to attract the populace to their worship places. Buddhist literature and other evidence suggests that many fertility goddess cults were incorporated into Buddhism to make provisions for the laity to worship these goddesses with vegetarian offerings.[42] In all these cases, it should be mentioned that it was the Buddhists who introduced the fertility cults in their original forms before they attempted any improvisations with symbols and iconic imagery. Janssen has cited an example of a complete evolution of an anthropomorphic figure of the goddess from the *purnakumbha* motif, at Ellora cave XXI, where the lotus is replaced by the head of the goddess. This goddess is identified by Janssen as "proto-Vasudhara," a fertility goddess in the process of becoming Buddhist.[43] This goddess is portrayed with a lotus head, naked, squatting with raised hands. Like the fertility goddess, Vasudhara in her Buddhist incarnation stands for wealth, prosperity, and abundance. The difference, however, is that the fertility goddess symbolized a much broader array of qualities, including the general motifs of life and death per se. These broad symbolisms are sustained in the cults of many *gramadevatas*.

I have discussed earlier how Jains adopted various goddess symbols into *tirthankara* iconography. When compared to other religious orientations, the Jains were very slow in incorporating fertility cults into their literature and art. Perhaps because of this, although they started their missions in Andhra as early as the Buddhists, they were not successful in cultivating many lay supporters until the sixth century CE. At this time, they had made some changes to their art and literature to include some fertility goddesses, when the experiments with the iconography of the fertility goddess had been already made by other religions in such a way that the transformed goddesses met the basic standards of "propriety." As with other Indian religious art, Jaina art embraced the Gaja Lakshmi motif both as part of its Tirthankara iconography and as a good luck sign at entrances to its temples. An interesting representation of how Lakshmi stands for a *kalasa* pot is depicted on porch entrances in a twelfth-century CE pillared cloister in Warangal, where a *kalasa* flanked by two elephants paying homage to it is represented in the same way that Lakshmi is attended by elephants in the Gaja Lakshmi motif.[44] This motif of elephants on either side flanked by a *sankhalata* (creeper coming out of a conch) indicates that the *sankhalata* stands for Sri Lakshmi. Jains favored using the *purnakumbha* on either side of the entrance doorjambs of their shrines in Andhra as a "blessing" to those who entered their shrines.[45] In addition, they introduced their own lotus goddess, Padmavati, who, as her name literally indicates, is the anthropomorphic form of lotus. Padmavati is said to have arranged a lotus seat for the Tirthankara Parsvanatha and this moment is often represented in the Jain sculpture of Andhra.[46]

Saivites, on the other hand, picked up on the third- to fourth-century CE evolutionary phase of the *purnakumbha,* with the lotus as the head and with no hands, as shown in the fourth- and fifth-century CE relief sculptures at Darsi, Kunidane, and Uppalapadu. These sculptures show the goddess squatting next to a *linga* in the company of other *brahmanic* deities such as Brahma, Narasimha (the lion form of Vishnu), and a figure who is probably Kartikeya (Skanda, the son of Siva) (Figure 3.28). Again, the significant difference of the lotus-headed goddess sitting next to a *linga* from that of the fertility goddess that has become a spouse, is that she is not nude any more. While the original nude form of goddess stood for her own great deity status, the evolving goddess next to *linga* was allotted a wifely role to support the cause of Siva. The bull who accompanied the goddess as the proto-form of Siva now becomes the vehicle of the fully evolved and triumphant Siva. Hence the tribal form of proto-Siva merged with that of Vedic Rudra to give rise to a major religious orientation at the expense of other forms, such as the fertility goddess tradition and Buddhism.

Considering the history of Saivite cult, it would not have been necessary for them to clothe their adopted goddess. In fact, with its tribal and fertility origins, Saivite religion was able to incorporate the *yoni* form of the goddess as part and parcel of the *linga* (phallus form of Siva) in the form of a *yoni patta* (a base plate into which the phallus is situated), which later in image form was translated into *Ardhanarisvara* (half Parvati and half Siva).[47] But the *brahmanization* that occurred in Saivism set some restrictions on how they could legitimize their goddesses. As a result, the squatting goddess form of the fertility goddess evolving out of the *purnakumbha* was introduced as the spouse of Siva along with other *brahmanic* deities of the pantheon only after covering her *yoni*. This goddess, in her evolution within Saivite contexts, eventually loses her lotus head and becomes the anthropomorphic figure of Parvati. This clothed Parvati, then, is what later becomes part of the *Ardhanarisvara* iconography. In this imagery there is an attempt to give equal space to the goddess with Siva, although on Saivite terms. Even though Parvati becomes essentially a spouse of Siva, the epithets such as Sailasuta, Giriputri, Girijaputri, and Girisa reveal her original association with mountains and wilderness.[48]

While the evolution of the *purnakumbha* motif was cultivated by the Saivites in order to present the fertility goddess as the spouse of Siva, the Vaishnavites made use of both the symbol of the *srivatsa* and the evolved goddess. The first of the two-pronged approach of the Vaishnavites involved adopting the *srivatsa* as an illustrious mark for Vishnu's chest, as represented in the fourth-century CE plaque at Kondamotu (Figure 3.9).[49] Sri Lakshmi simultaneously is also seen evolving into an anthropomorphic shape out of the *srivatsa* and placed next to Vishnu, as represented at Kondamotu, where Vishnu is seen in his Narasimha form with his lion head (Figure 3.15). In another plaque at Peddamudiyam the variation is that Vishnu stands next to the *srivatsa* that is mounted on a pedestal reaching almost his height (Figure 3.14).[50] In the second instance, the original naked goddess with lotuses and elephants (Figure 4.4), who had also appeared by this time in Buddhist art as Siri or Sirima devata (Figure 3.17), has been adopted as Gaja Lakshmi.[51] The naked goddess that appeared with lotuses in the company of the bull and the elephants was split, for the Saivites adopted the bull as the vehicle of Siva and used the lotus-headed goddess as his spouse, while the Vaishnavites appropriated the goddess in lotuses flanked by the elephants as the spouse of Vishnu. Even so, the Vaishnavites and the Saivites needed to appeal to the fertility goddess to sort out their own disputes, as explained below.

In the waning years of Buddhism in Andhra from the fourth century CE onward, it was the Saivites and Vaishnavites who competed with each other for religious space as they were both incorporating the goddess. The royalty made peace between these two religious orientations by advocating their coexistence. In a sense, it was the independent goddess who tied them together, as if they needed her mediation. In a way, this was ironic, given their attempts to subordinate her. In any case, an eloquent example of this mediation of the

FIGURE 4.8 Goddess Holding Lion and Linga
Source: Photo provided by the Director, Andhra Pradesh State Archaeology Museum

goddess is a stone plaque of the fourth century CE recovered from Keesaragutta (Figure 4.8).[52] On this stone plaque, the goddess sits in the squatting pose with splayed legs and with an inverted lotus as her head, like several other nude goddess figures from the evolution of the *purnakumbha* motif, except that her pudendum is covered with a cloth in the same way as in other Saivite plaques. Here, she holds in each of her palms the *linga* (as Siva) and the lion (as Vishnu). The goddess in this plaque not only supports both Siva and Vishnu in equal manner but also leaves her nudity behind to conform to the moralistic standards set especially by Vaishnavites. Referring to the emblems that the goddess is holding, Bolon interpreted them as Siva and Sakti.[53] While the *linga* as the emblem of Siva is incontrovertible, the lion, as the mount of the goddess in this representation, is highly improbable.[54] Bolon's argument is based on the premise that the lion face is not the same as other depictions of Narasimha in this period. The reason for this difference is that in this depiction, it is the goddess who is central and who is deciding matters for both these religions. In support of my argument, I quote Janssen, who noticed further details in the plaque and compared it to others:

> Next to the lion's head, however, we clearly detect a *sankha* (conch), Vaishnava emblem par excellence. Moreover, in the plaques of

Kunidane and Uppalapadu the lion emerges as Narasimha, while the goddess occupies the centre stage next to the linga. If the lion's head represented Narasimha, the plaque from Keesaragutta could indicate that in the fourth/fifth century this goddess was still independent and not yet "married off" to either Siva or Vishnu. This hypothesis could also shed light on the question of her absence in the texts and her final disappearance.[55]

As discussed earlier, the timeline for Saivite and Vaishnavite adaptations of the goddess fits into Janssen's argument about how the goddess is "married off" to Saivite and Vaishnavite deities. What is problematic, however, is Janssen's last statement about the disappearance of the independent goddess. In fact, right around this time (fourth to fifth century CE), the goddess emerges as Mahadevi and Mahishasuramardini in *brahmanic* literature and art. The first appearance of her in the form of Durga slaying the buffalo demon in Andhra is seen in the plaque of Peddamudiyam, in which she is in the company of *brahmanic* deities and is in the semi-anthropomorphic form of a *srivatsa* (Figure 3.14).[56] In fact, this plaque is a testimony to how the independent goddess in the form of Mahishasuramardini and the subverted goddess in the form of the *srivatsa* symbol are introduced simultaneously into the *brahmanic* fold. Sanskrit texts, like the *Mahabharata,* and the *Puranas*, such as the *Linga, Varaha, Bhagavata,* and *Vishnu Dharmottara and Matsya,* stress the destructive nature of various independent mother goddesses.[57] Following the path laid by the Buddhists, these texts make an attempt to bring these so-called evil goddesses under the control of the post-Vedic pantheon of male deities, such as Skanda, Vishnu, and Siva, with the justification of bringing their negative qualities under control. In spite of these clear attempts to establish the superiority of the male deities over the independent goddess, in the actual religious arena, where the temples of Durga and Kali are concerned, the primary focus of the devotees is Durga and Kali, not Siva or Vishnu, who only function as nominal spouse figures.

While, in Saivite art, the goddess with its lotus head was already clothed and evolved further with an anthropomorphic head and royal clothing as Parvati, the naked goddess image of the fertility cult continued to appear in life-size images installed in shrines attached to Saivite and Vaishnavite temples. This might have been an attempt by the Saivites and Vaishnavites to attract those devotees of the fertility goddess to their temples. Especially if the devotees comprised royalty, it would be difficult to ignore the goddess. The way the torso and the limbs are carved in the life-size lotus-headed images in these temples represents a youthful woman. The earliest image of this type, as noted earlier, was from the third century CE in Nagarjunakonda, where several miniature figures of naked terracotta goddess figures have also been recovered (Figure 3.27).[58] Since this image belongs to a sub-shrine in the small temple area of the *brahmanic* deities adjacent to a large Buddhist complex, it is clear that it denotes the beginning of temple religion, when the images were installed for regular worship and the fertility goddess had her own place in this context. The evidence of this first temple complex explains the reason why the life-size images of the fertility goddess appear only from this period. These nude goddess images continued to be seen in the sub-shrines attached to Saivite and Vaishnavite shrines, as at Alampur (Figure 3.30), Bejjinki (Karimnagar district), Bhavanasi, Kudavelli, Panchalingala, Miyapuram, Pratakota, Srisailam, Vemulavada, and Yellala (Figure 3.31), thereby indicating that royalty constituted her most ardent devotees.[59]

The goddess at Alampur and Miyapuram, as mentioned earlier, is now worshiped as Renuka or Ellamma. There were several other names given to the fertility goddess, some of which are known in the early inscriptions of the seventh and eighth century CE. A late seventh century inscription, for example, makes reference to the son of an early Chalukya ruler, Vijayaditya, as someone who received blessings from the goddess Nanda, otherwise known as "Gauri on the Chalukya Mountain."[60] Going by this description, Bolon identifies Nanda or Gauri with the image of the seventh-century CE Lajja Gauri (lotus-headed naked goddess) carved out of the bedrock on a Chalukya Mountain close to Aihole, the capital of the Western Chalukyas.[61] It is interesting to recall that Gauri is commonly worshiped as the goddess of fertility at the village level. By the eighth century CE, the connection between Gauri and Parvati had been made, as indicated in another Chalukyan inscription recognizing her as the wife of Siva and comparing her beauty to a lotus.[62] But the name Ellamma for the fertility goddess is as old as the name of Gauri, as another eighth-century CE inscription mentions a donation made by one Lokamavva, the queen of the Western Chalukyan ruler, Bhima II, to the temple of Ellamma.[63] That the goddess Ellamma received much attention from the elite during this time period is also known from a small stone temple called Ellamma *gudi*, now in ruins and found on a tank bund at Polas in the Karimnagar district.[64]

The goddess Ellamma continued to be favored by successive rulers of Andhra; the Kakatiyas, who succeeded the Eastern Chalukyas since the early eleventh century CE, considered this goddess, who was simultaneously recognized as Ekavira, Mahuramma, or Polasa, as their favorite deity, as mentioned in the fifteenth-century CE Telugu work, *Kridabhiramamu*.[65] The details of this goddess correspond to the present mythology of Renuka that I related earlier.

What I translate here is one of the poems from *Kridabhiramamu,* sung in praise of the goddess:

> *My reverence to the mother who gave birth to Indiravaru (Kartikeya).*
> *My reverence to the king cobra's hood (phaniraja mandana kunu).*
> *My reverence to the goddess who possesses sun and moon as her two eyes.*
> *My reverence to the mother of the world.*
> *My reverence to the goddess who is served by the sages and gods.*
> *My reverence to the loving wife of Jamadagni.*
> *My reverence to the beautiful goddess.*
> *My reverence to the daughter of the mountain king (Giriraja).*[66]

In the above poem the description of the goddess identifies her with the cobra. The poem also identifies her as the form of universe possessing the sun and moon as her two eyes. This reminds us how the goddess in some villages is reported as worshiped with the symbols of sun and moon drawn on either side of a diagram.[67] In addition, in the poem, Ekavira, or Mahuramma, is identified as the wife of Jamadagni, agreeing with my earlier discussions. However, because the *Kridabhiramamu* was composed at the height of Saivite influence in Andhra, the goddess assumes strong Saivite affiliations. Renuka/Ellamma becomes identified with Saivite Parvati and becomes the mother of Kartiketya (son of Siva). And yet, the second line of the poem identifies Ellamma's essential appearance as a hood of a king cobra or *naga.* In many instances in contemporary Andhra, Ellamma is worshiped in the form of an image of the *naga* attached to a snake hole or anthill. The third line of the poem reminds us of the song of the *matangi,* where the goddess uses the sun and moon as her plates. In the next two stanzas, the goddess with the name Adi Sakti is mentioned as living in some four villages and in the city of Orugallu, the capital of Kakatiyas, indicating that Ellamma, who was a *gramadevata* in those four villages, also served as the guardian deity of the Kakatiya rulers.[68] Her capacity as a guardian deity is explained in the following poem:

> *In a fit of anger*
> *any ruler of valor*
> *is turned into an infant*
> *by the magic of our goddess.*

This warrior mother is what appealed to rulers like the Chalukyas and the Kakatiyas, who needed victory in the incessant wars they waged and in continuation of their royal line.

In one of the inscriptions left by the Kakatiyas, the mythical origins of the Kakatiya ruler, Prataparudra, are described with details that agree with the components of the song collected by Nayani Krishnakumari as *Matapuranamu* (story of the mother goddess).[69] While this mother goddess is said to be Renuka or Ellamma or Mahuramma or yet another name, Akkilidevi ("sister goddess"), the first half of the song tells the story of the mythical origins of the ruler. The story of the goddess is introduced in the song on the pretext of an attempt made by the ministers to straighten up the ruler, who had become an obsessive Saivite and had ignored the goddess. This story also reveals the tensions that existed between the followers of the goddess and the Saivites.

In Warangal district, as mentioned earlier, Renuka/Ellamma is usually identified with the goddess Ekavira, the name often used by Kakatiya rulers for their family goddess. Since the fertility goddess as a *gramadevata* is strongly associated with the protection of boundaries, it is not surprising that royalty found great value in the powers of the goddess; boundaries of empires are simply a conceptual extension of village boundaries. A fifteenth-century Saivite work, *Bhimesvarapuranamu,* mentions that the Saivite temple patronized by the Chalukya rulers appointed the *gramadevatas* to guard the four entrances of the temple located on four corners: Gogulamma at the west, Manda talli at the north, Nukamba on the east, and Ghattambika on the south.[70] The temple named after the Chalukya ruler Bhima is seen as the ruler's cosmos, which is guarded by the *gramadevatas.* This example also shows the role played by rulers in *brahmanizing* the *gramadevatas* by helping to create their iconographic prescriptions, Sanskrit mythologies, and liturgy, with *brahmans* as priests. The most popular myth of *gramadevatas* is the war she wages on the buffalo demon. Since the primary function of the *gramadevata* as a tutelary deity is to guard the empire, she is depicted with fearsome features and with her many hands holding a variety of weapons.

There is another example of a *gramadevata* elevated to tutelary deity status who then acquired *brahmanic* identity. From records and literature, a *gramadevata* named after the village of Mullamguru is known to have received royal donations.[71] This Mullamguramma is mentioned in the early fourteenth-century CE record as the tutelary deity of the *reddy* caste ruler Peddakomati Vema, who built her a temple and set up a donation of three villages for her regular worship.[72] In this record, he praised the goddess as the mother of the whole world. In the succeeding centuries, one of the court poets of Kataya Vema mentioned the existence of a temple to this deity (Mullamguru sakti) in their new capital, Rajamahendravaram (East Godavari District).[73] In this record the goddess is identified as the form of Uma (Parvati), an indication of her Saivite co-option.

Some of the tenth- and eleventh-century CE inscriptions mention certain names of *gramadevatas* and state that they are residing on the boundaries of the village, and the description resembles the current worship pattern in several Andhra villages. An Eastern Chalukyan ruler, Amma II, in his tenth-century CE inscription, mentions a couple of *gramadevatas*, Potyavva of Chuntur village and Bhatarandu of Pallikollu.[74] Other names of *gramadevatas*, such as Poleramma, Ankamma/Ahankalamma, and Nukanamma, find mention in the records issued by local rulers in Andhra and later Vijayanagara rulers and their subordinates.[75] Some names of goddesses given after the name of the villages, such as Maddiravuladevata from Maddiravula and Mavindipati-devi from Mavindipati, indicate that this was a tradition that prevailed for many centuries.[76] Some *gramadevatas*, such as Talakantamma, Chavundesvaramma, and Durgamma, became popular because their devotees constituted the ruling class who, as the inscriptional records indicate, made generous donations to ensure continuous worship.[77]

The suffix in the case of goddesses like Chavundesvaramma indicates how some of these popular goddesses were given Saivite identification. Not as frequently, there were some *gramadevatas* who were brought under Vaishnavite influence. Suffixes, or epithets such as Paramesvari or Isvaramma or Devi, were added to these goddesses's names inconsistently. In some records, these epithets appear, indicating Saivite or Vaishnavite affiliation, only at certain timings, but as time passed they retained their original names. This was the case with the goddess Talakantamma, who was mentioned as Talakantidevi in the records, but at present is known as Talakantamma. Irugalasani in Tekaprolu (Nellore District) is another *gramadevata* whose name is mentioned in one inscription of the thirteenth century CE as Irugalasani and in another issued in the same shrine as Irukala Paramesvari, while she is presently known as Irukalamma.[78]

These records also bring out an interesting fact about how some of the *gramadevatas*, such as Ellamma, never entered Sanskrit literary traditions in their original forms, in spite of rulers' subscriptions and public acknowledgments. There might be multiple factors responsible for this phenomenon. One explanation could be that copies of these goddesses or their hybrid forms had already entered into these traditions, thus eliminating the need for embracing these specific local goddesses. On the other hand, the Sanskrit versions lost their primary identity with fecundity, thus leaving space for the original *gramadevatas* to continue to be relevant at the village level. Examples of this could be the cults of Sri Lakshmi and Parvati, goddesses who retained only positive aspects in their Sanskrit renderings. At times Sanskrit renderings have to split the identity of these goddesses so that the negative side of the goddess has been assigned to a different incarnation, as in the case of Jyestha, who is described as inauspicious and whose appearance is rendered as ugly, a split-off form of Sri Lakshmi.[79] In the same way, Kali functions as the split-off form of Parvati, standing in opposition to the good-natured and filial Parvati.[80] This does not mean to say that the *gramadevatas* have remained unchanged over the years. In the same way that the fertility goddess evolved over time to become goddesses of Vaishnavism and Saivism, numerous fertility cults of the *gramadevatas* accommodated some changes in their iconography as a result of the reappropriation of *brahmanic* forms.

A thirteenth-century CE Telugu work, the *Simhasana Dvatramsika*, mentions *sudras* (non-*brahmin* agricultural castes) worshiping various goddesses such as Kamakshi, Mahakali, Chandi, Ekavira, etc.[81] Note that the goddess Ekavira finds mention along with other *gramadevatas*. That the *gramadevatas* were approached by barren women seeking offspring and by pregnant women wanting healthy children is known from the *Simhasana Dvatramsika* and another contemporary Telugu work, *Hamsa Vimsati*.[82] Personal names that appear in these works, such as Ellamma and Maramma, are given after the names of other specific local *gramadevatas*.

What I have demonstrated in the above discussion, which referred to contemporary mythology, past inscriptions, literature, and sculpture, is that the goddess started her career in agricultural societies with fecundity as her main function. As the functions of the fertility goddess diversified, so did her iconography. Her cultic representations, from naked image to that of fierce forms in the act of killing demons, reflect her diverse devotees and their needs. Like the names of the present *gramadevatas*, the goddess names varied in the past depending on location and popularity. A certain *gramadevata* could be named after the name of a village, or a *gramadevata* could become so popular that her name is used for other *gramadevatas*. A *gramadevata* assumed even more functions when she became the guardian deity of a particular ruler. This warrior function changed her imagery. Further changes and diversification came to the fertility goddess when she was appropriated by various religious orientations.

The changes that have occurred in the religious space of the goddess can be put into two broad categories. In one instance the earliest form of the fertility goddess was appropriated by various religious orientations to make her a central functional part of their religious constructions. In the second instance, these various religions tried to bring many different fertility goddesses under their wing by tweaking goddess mythology, iconography, and ritual to fit into their more general orientations. In the former, goddesses were implicated in the path of religious quests per se. In the latter, they functioned more in relation to this-worldly needs in a manner that complemented, rather than competed with, the values and powers associated with established deities such as Vishnu and Siva, and *bodhisattvas* and *tirthankaras*. I illustrate further in the following section how the interplay of various religious orientations with that of *gramadevatas* influenced the development of cultic activity.

Goddess Hariti as Erukamma. Erukamma is a goddess worshiped in a small but busy temple in Dondaparthy, a village that forms part of the city of Visakhapatnam in coastal Andhra (Figure 4.9). As is the case with many village goddesses in Andhra, Erukamma is attended to by a non-*brahmin* priest. But unlike a typical village goddess, Erukamma possesses a distinct iconography and a unique myth. The image of Erukamma in her shrine depicts her with a cut-off head lying in front of her and her right arm wrapped around a kidnapped child, who is sitting on her lap. (Hariti images were traditionally depicted with her own child in her lap). The myth of the goddess as narrated by the current priest of the temple goes like this.

FIGURE 4.9 Erukamma, Dondaparthy

A woman named Erukamma was causing horror by stealing the children in the village and devouring them in a secret place on the village outskirts. A man of the Erukala (basket weavers) caste happened upon her while she was devouring a recently kidnapped child and immediately cut off her head. After her death, people feared the potential malevolent effects of her revenge. To placate her, they worshiped her and through their petitions were able to redirect her powers for the purposes of village protection.

This rather crude story contains the basic outline of an extensive myth preserved in classical Chinese Mahayana Buddhist texts about how the goddess Hariti came to be worshiped by the laity as a boon-conferring *bodhisattva* who symbolizes not only the well-being of the *sangha* (monastic community), but who is especially adept at providing young or barren couples with children. In those traditions, Hariti was originally a child-devouring *yaksi* who was converted by the Buddha when he kidnapped one of her own five-hundred sons, causing her to suffer the pain of such a loss so that she could understand the pain she had inflicted on others.[83] The Buddha was able to elicit compassion in Hariti and to make her sympathize with those whom she had made suffer. Having quenched her insatiable appetite for devouring children, the Buddha promised that in the future she would be, instead, fed rice by his monks for as long as his *sangha* prospered. And so she came to symbolize the material well-being of the Buddhist community in general and was also venerated by laity seeking offspring.

As a form of Parvati, Erukamma is now served liturgically by a *brahman* priest during the rituals constituting her annual festival. But on all other days, a non-*brahman* belonging to an agricultural caste acts as the ritual preceptor. Worship of Erukamma is usually done directly by the devotees themselves who offer fruits, coconuts, saris, and blouse pieces to the goddess after applying turmeric and vermilion. But on the special annual occasions, the *brahman* priest conducts rites on behalf of all devotees for a price. Animal sacrifices are rare, and devotees still take pride in saying that this goddess does not like non-vegetarian food, probably a reflection of middle-class sensibilities of her contemporary worshipers more than the Buddhist associations in her mythic past.

That her cult was popular in Andhra, as it seems to have been in many other parts of the Buddhist world as well, is amply attested by scores of sculpted images of Hariti, usually seated with a child sitting on her lap, found outside the remains of refectories of Buddhist monastic complexes at such places as Nagarjunakonda and Sankaram (Visakhapatnam District). At Nagarujunakonda, a temple from the second century CE is dedicated to goddess Hariti.[84] The upper part of the image has been broken; the only section still intact is from the waist and below, and this part is seated on a throne (Figure 4.10). Hariti's image at Sankaram is better preserved. She is flanked by two attendants (Figure 4.11). In spite of the Buddhist story portraying Hariti's origins as an ogress, a Kushana sculpture of the first to second century CE portrays Hariti more like a goddess of the fertility cult. Hariti has antecedents as a *yakshini*. She has been associated with symbols like the *purnakumbha*, reflecting the probability of her origins in a fertility cult. The fact that some of her images are not just depicted with children and husband, but that they also denote wealth and abundance, reflects how her functions have been elaborated as she became the deity for rulers as well.[85] In Andhra, one of the Eastern Chalukya rulers styled himself as Haritiputranam ("son of Hariti") and Matriganaparipalanam ("ruled by a group of mother goddesses").[86] The first epithet, son of Hariti, reflects the fact that the ruler considered Hariti as his favorite deity and as a kind of mother deity. The second epithet indicates the ruler's perception that all his actions were governed by a group of mother goddesses. While I discuss the subject of the group of mother goddesses in the next subsection, suffice it to say here that the Chalukya ruler considered Hariti as part of the group of mother goddesses who themselves form part of a fertility cult.

FIGURE 4.10 Hariti, Nagarjunakonda

FIGURE 4.11 Hariti, Sankaram

Among the intact figures of the fertility goddess from the early historic period, there is a bronze sculpture from the third to second century BCE of a figure sitting on a pedestal (indicating its probable use for worship on an altar), holding a child in her left hand and resting her right hand on her knees (Figure 4.12).[87] Unlike many naked goddess images of this period, this figure seems to be clothed. She clearly resembles the later goddesses such as Hariti.

The name Hariti appears in a Buddhist text along with a group of feminine supernatural beings referred as *rakshasis* (demons) who were said to have given a *mantra* (magical charm) of protection by the Buddha.[88] As noted, fertility goddesses were incorporated first into the Buddhist tradition and then later into Sanskritic Hinduism. D. D. Kosambi, in his *Myth and Reality*, notes how the cults of many village goddesses in Maharashtra were first influenced by Buddhism during the middle of the first millennium CE.[89] Many of these goddesses have been portrayed in rock-cut relief sculptures in various Buddhist cave complexes and continue to be venerated today in nearby villages. The incorporation of Hariti and her continued veneration would seem to be an analogous case in Andhra.

FIGURE 4.12 Bronze Mother

With the total eclipse of the Buddhist tradition by the eighth or ninth century CE in Andhra, and the concomitant sweeping wave of Saivism of the same period, many folk deities became identified with aspects of the Saivite cult.[90] The vicious campaign led by militant Saiva sects against Buddhism left little trace of Buddhist influences on these goddesses. A Telugu Virasaiva text of the eleventh century CE serves as a testimony to the way the Saivites led their aggressive campaign against Buddhists.[91]

This is what must have happened to the previous identity of Erukamma, whom devotees now identify with Siva's spouse, Parvati. The icon of Erukamma seems much older than the Saivite affiliation of this tradition, however. The precise origin of this icon, though evidently quite ancient, is not known to the local people or to temple administrators. The image clearly represents the local myth about this goddess, and no iconographic elements can be linked to Parvati whatsoever.[92]

What these details about Erukamma indicate is a very rich and varied amalgamation of practices and beliefs encompassing aspects of religious cults originating from pre-Buddhist, Buddhist, Saivite, and village origins. Erukamma, in her former incarnation as Hariti, started her origins as a small-pox deity but travelled to Andhra in the incarnation of her Buddhist rendering.

In post-Buddhist Andhra, when her sculpture was worshiped as the mother of the village, with the name Erukamma, she might be viewed as a small-pox goddess who, at the height of the epidemic, was the devourer of children and whose protective power can be invoked by appropriate propitiation. In the absence of smallpox and in a suburban context, now her protective function is extended to the well-being of families and especially as a goddess with the power to produce male offspring. This is probably the reason why she is identified by devotees as a form of Parvati, who as Siva's mate is considered an ideal wife and mother of two sons. There is, however, remarkable evidence of amalgamated sources in the narrative and ritual traditions associated with Erukamma, and it is precisely this amalgamation that contributes to her continuing appeal to a diverse congregation.

When Hariti was worshiped as a smallpox deity in the northern parts of India, Buddhists were likely to have felt a responsibility for diverting people away from violent forms of worship. The result was that Hariti, herself, became a Buddhist goddess. When Hariti's cult was presented in Buddhist guise, the lay people, in fact, were happy that they could continue to worship the mother to ask for their favorite boons, while remaining as Buddhists. Buddhists themselves consciously attributed the same Hariti myth to other guardian deities as well. For example, John Strong mentions the conflation of the cult of Kunti with that of Hariti in the Mathura region.[93] In Erukamma's form, Hariti not only brings her past imprints of village characters as well as Buddhist soteriology, but also embraces a new identity as the form of Parvati. But in all of these vicissitudes, either as Hariti or Erukamma, her basic identity remains.

Realizing the universality of the fertility cults, Buddhists indeed tried their hands at transforming these goddesses into *bodhisattvas*. But they met with only partial success, as *bodhisattvas*, with the exception of Avalokitesvara, usually do not alleviate the needs of villagers that are concerned with the everyday harsh realities of life. The Saivites seemed to have understood this problem and thereby approached the goddess cults from a very different angle. Being the successors, they were more aggressive and ambitious in their approach. Rather than transforming fertility goddesses into soteriologically significant figures, they simply added their Siva as a husband and the stamp of authority. This proved to be a brilliant stroke, in that the cults of the all-pervading goddess helped the Saivites to spread their religion at the grassroots level.

Akka Devatalu. The great variety of *gramadevatas*, with their specialized functions and names, are often referred to in Telugu village mythology as *akka devatalu* ("sister goddesses"). Their counterparts appear in *brahmanic* temples, as the *saptamatrika* ("seven mothers") figures. My discussion in this section is concerned with the current mythology, worship, and iconography of *akka devatalu* as *gramadevatas*. In order to understand the types of influences that have affected the cults of these sister goddesses over the years, I have also traced their ancestry and their *brahmanization* here. The discussion also includes the contribution of *saptamatrika* figures to the iconography of *gramadevatas*.

The imagery of *saptamatrikas* in *brahmanic* temples shares similarities with that of the fertility goddess, exhibiting evidence of how the goddess in her various forms entered the Sanskritic tradition. The tree as associated with the fertility goddess has been imported into the Sanskrit tradition as part of the iconography of sister goddesses, as noted by H. Krishna Sastri in his early twentieth-century ethnological account of gods and goddesses of south India, a study that included parts of Andhra.

> Some of these goddesses are said to have each a tree specially sacred to them, e.g., Kaumari has the fig-tree (udumbara), Vaishnavi, the pipal, Varahi, the karanja, Indrani, the celestial tree kalpadruma, and Chamunda, the banyan. The Saptamatrikas thus described are generally found figured together in a group on the same panel and are quite a common sight in South-Indian villages and Siva temples. When installed within the enclosure of a temple, they are seen often without a shrine built over them, and may receive such attention as the other minor deities of that temple. In villages and in Pidari temples built exclusively for goddesses, they are worshipped regularly. The Selliyamma temple at Alambakkam in the Tanjore district possesses an important shrine for the Saptamatrikas. [94]

In this way, Saivites brought the *gramadevatas* as minor deities into their temple precincts by providing them with a sectarian identity. In general, all *gramadevatas* are understood to be *akka devatalu*, although in some villages they are worshiped specifically as *eduguru akkalu* ("seven sisters"). In many instances, a group of *gramadevatas* of any specific number may be worshiped collectively.[95] For instance, in Anantapur District, these *akka devatalu* are treated either as a single goddess, Akkamma ("sister-mother"), or as a group of goddesses, Akkammagarlu ("sister-mother madams") or Akkagarlu ("sister madams"). In Rallahalli, all seven goddesses are seen as one huge rock, whereas in Mavinamardhanahalli, seven earthen images are worshiped annually for three days.[96] In this context, the goddess is understood simultaneously as a single entity, as well as in multiple forms.

There are many different myths in play about the origin of these goddesses and their numbers. A very brief version of one of these myths was recorded by Elmore.[97] There used to be a group of seven sisters who fought fiercely among themselves, which resulted in their deaths. As a result, the spirits of the unhappy sisters started causing diseases among the living; when worship was initiated to appease them, they became goddesses.

There is another oral tradition prevalent in many villages of Andhra that claims the *gramadevatas* are really one hundred and one sisters.[98] The myth is narrated thus. In ancient times, there were one hundred and one kings who ruled over specific regions. Due to their devotion to Siva, they were all granted the boons of immortality and of invincibility in battle. With this power, they invaded many other kings, who in their conditions of distress also sought refuge in Siva. Siva, in a human incarnation, also joined the fight against the one hundred and one kings only to be defeated. But Vishnu came to his rescue and advised him to take up the form of a pipal (ficus religiosa) tree by the water tank used for bathing by the wives of the one hundred and one kings. As they were devoted wives, they had miraculous powers to make brass pots out of sand to carry water back to their houses to cook food, which nourished their husbands. Vishnu then appeared as a sage to the wives and advised them to embrace the tree if they wished to beget children. They did as he said, but in doing so they were really making love to Siva with the result of losing their fidelity. Consequently, they lost their power to make brass pots out of sand and only could carry water with ordinary pots to cook food for their husbands. Once they had eaten this food, the kings lost their strength and were then easily destroyed by Siva. Soon the wives conceived and gave birth to one hundred and one daughters. These daughters, knowing their real father, went to Siva and asked for their means of living. Siva told them to go into the world as *saktis* and to demand from people their food and to receive propitiation as their birthright.

This myth shares a claim made in a number of other earlier myths, establishing namely that all the goddesses at the village level are the daughters of Siva. This was a convenient way for the Saivites to recognize the multiplicity of *gramadevatas* and, at the same time, to assert their hegemony over them. An additional element in this myth is the role played by Vishnu as a facilitator for Siva to gain the upper hand. This infusion of Vishnu probably indicated a period when Saivites shared religious space with Vaishnavites. Not only does this myth represent the subordination of the *gramadevata* to *brahman*ical deities, but by virtue of the manner in which the wives of the hundred and one kings are portrayed as being unwittingly duped by Siva, it also identifies them as the vulnerable elements in traditional society. Even though the wives were not conscious of any violation, they were held responsible for the downfall of their husbands' plights.

As evident in the discussion of the goddess Hariti, there were several *gram-adevatas* that came under Buddhist influence. The Saivite wave that came later to incorporate all those goddesses probably erased most of these memories. But in some myths, like the ones I am going to mention here, the Buddha's presence seems to be retained. In the first instance, it is the seven sister goddesses popularly known as *Akkagarlu* (sister madams), in a shrine in the hills of Tirumala below the temple for Lord Venkatesvara, who are believed to be the daughters of Munisvara (a sage), who very well could be the Buddha.[99] Since there is no mythology connecting these goddesses to Siva or Vishnu, they can be regarded as very independent deities. *Akkagarlu* are understood by the local people as young virgin girls who roam in the hills, forests, and water holes (lakes and wells) during three specific times of the day at noon (12 p.m.), dusk (6 p.m.), and night (1 a.m.). These goddesses can appear either in the form of seven young girls or as just one young girl representing all of the sisters. This is an acknowledgement that the goddess is one but takes multiple forms as seven sisters. If people witness these sisters while bathing in the water holes at noon, it is believed that they will die repeating the name of the goddess, *akka* (sister). These goddesses are worshiped in an open shrine in the forms of seven bricks. The devotees offer the *akkagarlu* not just auspicious gifts, such as turmeric, vermilion, black bangles, mirrors, combs, flowers, fruits, etc., but also married symbols such as black beads, indicating that the goddesses are in married status. In addition, the devotees acknowledge the goddesses as playful little girls by offering them toys, especially the toys that represent the vehicles, such as elephant, horse, tiger, lion, fox, etc., that they believe these goddesses ride. These details explain how the goddesses are seen as part and parcel of the animal kingdom on the one hand and on the other as seven young girls who are married. Peta Srinivasulu Reddy, who collected the mythology and worship pattern of *gramadevatas* in Tirumala and Tirupati regions, suggests that these goddesses, who are seen as provoking sexual desire among the young by appearing in enticing forms, have absorbed the cults of virgins who experienced sudden deaths and, as a result, have been deified.[100]

Leaving the discussion of the deification process for later, I will turn my attention to the next myth. Here the Buddha is known as Muniraju, the sage king. Seven sisters were born to Parvati, the consort of Siva, after she quenched her thirst, which was derived from practicing austerities, by taking seven handfuls of water from a tank. The sisters were Peddamma, Mahankalamma, Mutyalamma, Gandamma, Maisamma, Pochamma, and Ellamma. Siva also gave her a boy, Poturaju, to rear along with the seven daughters. When all the daughters came into their youth, they wanted to marry Muniraju, their uncle and the brother of Parvati. But Muniraju rejected all of their proposals and went to the forest to perform austerities. Six of the sisters became angry at this rejection and started troubling people by bringing on diseases. But the seventh sister, Ellamma, persisted and succeeded in negotiating all the ascetic ordeals prescribed by Muniraju as a precondition. Thus she finally won over his heart and married him. Whether or not the other sisters succeeded in their aims, people started worshiping all these seven sisters along with Poturaju.[101] Note that it is the seventh sister, Ellamma (symbolizing the correct path of true religion), who by practicing austerities, wins the affection of her elder male relation, while her six sisters, though worshiped, remain as potentially dangerous phenomena who can bring sickness and disorder to the lives of the villagers. The special status given to Ellamma in this myth is interesting, considering the historicity of her name, mythology, and identity with the ancient form of the naked fertility goddess. Because of her ancient origins, Ellamma just might have gone through a Buddhist adaptation before the Saivite version. However, the fact that the Buddha is understood as having taken a wife shows the Saivite influence at play.

There is no doubt that in this myth, in relating how these *gramadevatas* were born as the daughters of Siva and Parvati, there is an attempt to bring them under the Saivite wing in a different format. Metaphorically, we are not incorrect to see in these myths that goddess religion needs to be recast in *brahman*ical norms so that the goddess undergoes a second, or may be even a third birth, to provide an ordering of her power. Even if this new birth is just metaphysical window dressing, it often worked for the Saivites in capturing the grassroots, where the strengths of the goddess lie. In this and in some other myths I related earlier, *gramadevatas* are not the wives, but the daughters of Siva through Parvati. Parvati, as we have discussed, takes her own origins from the fertility goddess. It is well-known that Siva himself probably had tribal origins before he was identified with the Vedic deity Rudra.[102]

In any case, the various versions of the myth of the *gramadevata* reveal not only the attempts of a range of religious orientations to incorporate the fertility goddess cult, but also the hierarchical social tensions within a typical village. Some versions also speak about the tensions between *brahman* and non-*brahman* communities. Because *brahman* families, like the rest of the village, need the blessings of the *gramadevatas*, it is obvious that they tried to bring the *gramadevata* into conformity with their accepted norms of female behavior. A local legend prevalent in the village of Vidavalur (Nellore District) shows that their attempts were not always successful. A *brahman* by the name of Ayyangarappa had seven sisters: Ankamma, Mahalakshmamma, Poleramma, Gruddi Kunkalamma, Charu Mudamma, Aretamma, Gangamma, as well as a brother Poturaju.[103] While all the other sisters and the brother settled down in different villages, Ankamma followed her elder brother Ayyangarappa to his *agraharam*.[104] Along the way, as she was a form of *sakti* who needed sacrifices to be sustained, she stopped at the boundaries of a village to stay with her sister Mahalakshmamma, who previously had settled there. As Ayyangarappa proceeded to his village alone, Ankamma changed into a beautiful girl and went into the village. Knowing that she was a *brahman* girl, the village head put her into the care of a *brahman* priest. One day, she suddenly disappeared but reappeared in the village headman's dream, saying that she was none other than *sakti*, and as such, needed a temple. A temple was built and a wooden image was prepared and installed. Since then she cared for the village and even killed the enemy's army when they came to fight. Meanwhile, Ayyangarappa found a good match to marry Ankamma and came with all his relatives to celebrate the marriage with great pomp. Ankamma acceded to her brother's wish, but during the marriage ritual, the bridegroom was terrorized to find *sakti svarupini* (the natural form of *sakti*) as his bride. He fled away in fear. Daunted by this, Ayyangarappa left for his village. Ankamma, on the other hand, accompanied by her other sisters, went around the village in a procession, in a state of immense joy.

The *brahmanic* way of subjugating the independent nature of the goddess is to marry her off and bring her into the patriarchal fold. This myth makes it clear that this attempt failed and that the will of the goddess prevailed so that the goddess retained her independence and untamed or undomesticated nature. The relationship of *saktis* as the sisters to a *brahman* (the elder brother Ayyangarappa) is an attempt by *brahmans* to gain affinity with these *gramadevatas*. This might also symbolically show how these *gramadevatas* were introduced as *saptamatrikas* into *brahmanic* temples and how this attempt was not completely successful, as they always remained on the periphery. For the myth spells out clearly that the *gramadevatas* are fiercely independent and their primary nature is to care and defend the borders of the village.

On the other hand, those *brahmans* who live in villages need the same kind of protection from the *gramadevatas* as do the rest of the villagers. For example, while seeking progeny, some *brahman* families still follow a form of traditional worship to the seven sister goddesses. In this worship, seven married women fast on an auspicious day, sit in devotion, and sing a song in the name of Kamesvari devi and her sister goddesses.[105] They end the fasting after making vegetarian offerings to these goddesses. In the neighboring state, Tamilnadu, there is another tradition of worshiping the seven sisters by *brahmans* and other villagers whenever there is a sickness in the family. Their worship of seven goddesses brings both the *gramadevatas* and the *saptamatrikas* into one category, which shows their common source. Here I quote Krishna Sastri's remarks:

> The Saptamatrikas of the Tantras are also counted among village deities and are, perhaps, the same as "the Seven Kanniyamar (unmarried girls)" or the "Seven Sisters." They are frequently appeased by special worship when any unforeseen and sudden illness takes hold of a man. The local fortune-teller, often a woman of the Korava caste, being consulted, says that the patient is possessed by the "sisters" while walking alone in untimely hours of the day near tanks, gardens or groves. Once the goddesses are propitiated, a temporary shrine is constructed. Seven small stones are planted in a row, near a tank, almost touching the edge of the waters, and a small shed erected over them with leaves and flowers. Coconuts, plantains, fried rice and pulse are then offered to the stones and not infrequently also a fowl. Even Brahmanas worship the "Seven Sisters" in this way, but when a fowl is to be sacrificed they get a Sudra to do it. The worship is enjoined to be performed in wet cloth after bathing.[106]

While the various versions of myth and different forms of worship explain the diverse interests, influences, and adjustments that have occurred over the centuries, some current examples of iconographic details of the *gramadevatas* throw light on the recent past as well as on current sociological changes. Out of the many forms of fertility goddess that have eventually appeared in *brahmanic* art and literature, it is goddesses like the *saptamatrikas*, and the manner in which their images have been executed in the *brahmanic* temples, that traditionally has influenced the iconography of the *gramadevatas*. Unlike the rest, goddesses like Durga and Kali, while retaining the essential qualities of *gramadevatas*, simultaneously acquired a special place in *brahmanic* literature and in *brahmanic* temple religion. Probably because of this, their *brahmanic* iconography is, in turn, emulated at the village level, creating a kind of circular effect. Once the iconography was introduced at the village level to Durga and Kali, it created a chain reaction, as many other village goddesses came to be fashioned in the same way, as will be shown in the consideration of a tenth-century CE goddess image toward the end of this section.

An early eighteenth-century iconographic description of a typical *gramadevata* in neighboring Tamilnadu is very useful for understanding the norms of that period. Here, I will quote Ziegenbalg's description of Ellamma (called Ellammen in Tamil), who in some versions is considered as one of the seven sisters.

Ellammen is represented in a sitting posture, with a red skin, a fiery face, and four arms and hands. On her head she wears a crown, round which there are serpents; for these heathens say that her pagodas are abodes of serpents; and when they see snakes, they call on Ellammen to drive them away. On her forehead she has three streaks of sacred ashes, and on the whole she is adorned like the other goddesses. In her four hands she holds respectively a kind of drum, called Damaru; a trident, called Sula; a bundle of ropes, called Pasa, and the skull of Brahma's fifth head, which was cut off by Siva. Of this skull it is said that it attracts all the blood shed on earth, and does nevertheless never get full; and inasmuch as the Gramadevatas receive bloody sacrifices, they usually hold it in their hands. An image of the above description, cast of metal, is found in her pagodas; but her principal image, to which offerings are made, is of stone, representing but her head, in the earth, to indicate that only her head was made alive, and put on the body of another woman.[107]

While mentioning the special features of Ellamma and her acquired Saivite connections, Ziegenbalg actually gave an account of a typical representation of *gramadevatas* in iconic form. No doubt, these iconographic features are very different from the early naked images of the goddess. The fearsome features can be attributed to the warrior goddesses who were tutelary deities to various rulers or to the goddesses of smallpox who, like Hariti, were described by Buddhists as ogresses. Although there are several *gramadevata* images still in worship in Andhra meeting these standards, in the absence of warfare and in the wake of the eradication of deadly diseases, there is a trend to soften the appearance of *gramadevatas*. In cases where *gramadevatas* go through an urbanization process, they lose their agricultural leanings and become the forms of Saivite Parvati or Vaishnavite Lakshmi, representing the role of an ideal docile wife. In addition, there are regional trends as well. Especially in coastal Andhra, there is a tendency to identify all of the *gramadevatas* as forms of Durga. But in some recent urban contexts this tendency is changing. I will quote a few examples to illustrate these different cases.

A typical *gramadevata* iconography in its variations is seen in the following representation of three goddesses in Peda Waltair in the city of Visakhapatnam. In 1994, these images were still being worshiped in their stone form.[108] But now all three images are covered by a layer of silver, indicating the acquisition of affluence in the last decade and half (Figure 4.13). The stone image of the main goddess Polamma, said to have been recovered from the ocean by the fishermen folk in the sixteenth century CE, is a standing figure with four

FIGURE 4.13 Polamma

hands. She holds a *parasu* (axe) and *khadga* (sword) in her right hands and *naga pasa* (snake in the form of noose) and *rudhira patra* (bowl to drink blood, which is also seen as the fifth head of Brahma as explained above) in the left hands. But the drinking bowl is described by the priests as *kumkuma bharani* (vermilion box) to indicate her blessings for a long and prosperous married status for women devotees. This *kumkuma bharani* has become an essential item held by all the newly executed images of urbanized *gramadevatas*. Two other goddesses, Nilamma (also called Nilamamba) and Kunchamma (also called Kunchamamba), stand on either side of the image of Polamamba in her shrine. Nilamma is depicted in a sitting posture with four arms. She is holding a *trisula* and *khadga* in her right hands, and in the left, *naga pasa* and *rudhira patra*. Kunchamma is shown seated on a pedestal with two arms holding a *khatvanga* (curved knife) in her right hand and *rudhira patra* in the left. All the three images are worshiped as *gramadevatalu*. These images are benign in appearance despite the weapons they carry. In general, their iconographic features conform to the iconographic texts, where multiple forms of Devi are described.[109] The temple sells photos of the fully decorated image of Polamma, presently known as Polamamba, with three snakes spreading their hoods over her crowned head. The snake is a critical symbol revealing her nature as a *gramadevata*. The temple is presently known as Sri Sri Sri

Karakachettu Polamamba devasthanam. While the epithet of "Sri Sri Sri" indicates that now *brahmans* are the priests using Sanskrit liturgy and performing *brahmanic* rituals, the name "Karakachettu" indicates the original affiliation of the goddess with the tree, *terminalia chebula*. The temple houses seven other goddesses (Nestalamma, Kanakadurgamma, Pidugulamma, Bangaramma, Dandumaramma, Sattemma, and Mutyalamma) who represent the fourteen villages that worship Polamma as their regional goddess. It is in this sense that these *gramadevatas* are considered as sister goddesses.

In contrast to the goddesses discussed above, sometimes a *gramadevata* is borrowed from *brahmanic* tradition to serve as a guardian deity of a village. Actually speaking, this is a re-borrowing. This is what has happened with the goddess Kanaka Durga, who takes the form of Kanakamma in the village of China Waltair. The image of the goddess Kanaka Durga that resides in China Waltair was brought some three hundred years ago from the temple of Vijayawada Kanaka Durga, ostensibly with her blessings (Figure 4.14). (The goddess Kanaka Durga of Vijayawada has her own village origins, as I will discuss in the next subsection.) This *brahmanized* form of Durga has been worshiped as a *gramadevata* by the name of Kanakamma. As the village grew into a cosmopolitan suburb of Visakhapatnam city, the growing middle class who worshiped the goddess on a regular basis called her Mahalaksmi. As the

FIGURE 4.14 Kanakamma

income of the temple increased, the Department of Endowments took over its administration, registering the goddess's name as Kanaka Mahalaksmi. But when it was reinstalled and consecrated, the *pandits* (Vedic scholars) recognized its details and declared that it was Simhavahini ("lion rider") and therefore Kanaka Durga, an incarnation of Parvati, corroborating the local oral tradition. The image stands on a pedestal made of a coiled serpent, depicting a goddess with a proportionate body with four hands holding *pasa* (noose) and *sruk* (spoon) in the right hands, and *naga-damaru* (kettle drum with a coiled snake) and *aksaya patra* (vessel that perennially supplies food) in the left. This iconography conforms to the description of Tulaja Bhavani, a food-offering incarnation of Parvati, as recounted in normative iconographic texts. Tulaja Bhavani is said to hold a jeweled vessel containing food in one hand and a spoon in the other to distribute food to her devotees, with her two additional hands holding a noose and a trident. [110]

While there are not many permanent images in many Andhra villages, the norm has been such, as in the case of Polamma and Kanakamma, to meet the iconographical prescriptions of the forms of Devi. At least this has been the tradition from as early as the sixteenth century, if we go by the story of Polamma's ancestry. I will cite earlier examples later. We know that this was the case in the eighteenth and early twentieth century, as noted by Ziegenbalg and Krishna Sastri respectively. The recent image-making, however, is subject to changes brought about by urbanization and the technology used in creating images.

Although both Polamma and Kanakamma are typical *gramadevatas*, *brahmanic* anthropomorphic images have been installed as consecrated images and are liturgically celebrated by a *brahman* priest. Yet, village folk characteristics remain predominant in their typical annual rituals and occasional animal sacrifices. Both are still considered to be earth mothers who are believed to assume the form of snakes to protect the village from all calamities. In both cases, devotees may sacrifice animals, especially chickens, to the goddess to show their gratitude on special occasions.

An instance of where the devotees want a docile form of goddess is evident in the cult of Durgalamma in Velampet in Visakhapatnam City. According to the lore, Durgalamma's original worship started with a diamond dealer who, on his way through Visakhapatnam City, worshiped a stone as a form of Durgalamma. Although it is not clear when exactly the goddess acquired an anthropomorphic form, the image that was worshiped until 1997 had fearsome features. The devotees felt the need of a softer form and, as a result, the present image was made (Figure 3.33). The goddess in this image has eight hands, holding a *trisula*, axe, club, and sword in the left hand and a snake, bow, lotus, and *kumkuma bharani* (vermilion box) in the right. The vermilion box replaces the traditional *rudhira patra* that is often seen in *gramadevata* images or in the images of Kali and Durga. A *brahman* priest has been appointed to conduct regular worship for the new image. A non-*brahman* woman who attended to the old image now works as an attendant to keep the surroundings clean. A cloister hall was built behind the temple to set up the *utsavamurthy* (a smaller image of the goddess taken out in processions, a feature in all *brahmanic* temples), where special worship is done at the request of devotees. Since 1997, sacrificing animals and birds within the temple has been stopped. Those who would like to offer blood sacrifices bring their sacrificial animal to the entrance, where they show it to the goddess as an offering before taking it to their own place to sacrifice. In spite of these changes, the goddess image, like in the above instances, is still accessible to the devotees who go into the sanctum to make their offerings. The iconography of the goddess reflects the enthusiasm for *brahmanic* associations among her contemporary devotees who want to regard her not as a "mere village goddess," but as a form of Lakshmi, the docile wife of Vishnu. What is intriguing here is that the identification of Durgalamma is with the goddess Lakshmi, but not with the great goddess Durga. The reason might be, as in many instances in Visakhapatnam, that the majority of the present devotees are middle-class housewives who do not see the need for a warrior goddess, but rather prefer a docile wifely goddess like Lakshmi, whose function is to protect their husbands and provide health and wealth to their families. This profile better fits with the now dominant Hindu norms and, as such, reflects how social ideals are so often articulated through the expressions of religious culture. Nevertheless, despite these iconographic changes, the residual *gramadevata* basis of the goddess is reflected in her garland of skulls, the sword she wields, and the kneeling demon at her feet. These iconographic features reflect her earlier incarnation of fighting enemy armies or diseases, such as small pox. In both cases, the goddess is understood as needing bloody sacrifices. It can be explained that the residual features are necessary for those devotees who still understand her need for blood sacrifices and who continue to offer them outside the temple.

In a different case, the *gramadevata* Pydamma of another village was also absorbed into the city of Visakhapatnam, and came to be viewed by the people who moved into the area as the incarnation of the goddess Durga. The homologization of Pydamma with Durga is expressed in different ways, most clearly in the contemporary iconography of the goddess, where Pydamma is made to resemble the goddess Durga (Figure 4.15). She is depicted with four arms, which hold *trisula* (trident), *khadga* (sword), *naga-damaru* (kettle drum with a wound serpent), and *rudhira patra* (cup to drink blood). She is

FIGURE 4.15 Pydamma, Visakhapatnam

beautifully rendered, sitting on a throne with her right leg folded up and her left leg draping down to rest on the demon's (Mahisasura's) head. Given the weapons she holds and the head of the demon being crushed under her foot, she appears aggressive, although her face looks benevolent. In this way she represents a fiercely protective yet benign character. Devotees of Pydamma, on the one hand, are eager to identify their goddess and their form of worship as *brahman*ic and yet they still observe animal sacrifices during the annual hot season ritual and on other special occasions. Enthusiastic educated devotees have introduced *yantra* meditation practices in which the goddess acts as the object of meditation. This aspect of devotion emphasizes that the goddess is also capable of bestowing *moksa*. The *diksa* (vow) that is practiced by the devotees of the famous Kanaka Durga in Vijayawada has also been introduced.[m] After being initiated by a *brahman* priest, participants in the vow maintain a special vegetarian diet and undertake ascetic practices (including celibacy) for somewhere between nine and forty-one days. Devotees also wear only saffron-colored robes, sleep on the floor, observe restraint in speech, and spend leisure time only in praise of the goddess.

Having lost its typical rural characteristics many years ago, the village has ceased to view this goddess as a caretaker of crops and cattle, and she is no longer associated with children's diseases. Village forms of ritual have also been mostly supplanted with *brahman*ic ritual forms, except for the animal sacrifices occurring during the annual festival and other special occasions. The contemporary cult of Pydamma is, therefore, a jumbled mixture of village and *brahman*ic forms of worship, reflecting the sentiments of her wide variety of devotees.

In the case of the *gramadevata* Satyamma *Talli* (mother) from Ambaripeta (Krishna District), the circumstances are yet different again. Since her shrine is located at the junction of a busy highway, the goddess became popular for saving the lives of those who travel on the road. As such, many passersby, particularly truck drivers, make a point to stop in front of the temple and to pray for their own and their vehicle's safety. Satyamma *Talli*, in typical fashion for sister goddesses, is seen in the shrine in both anthropomorphic and snake forms (Figure 4.16). *Utsavamurty* (the image used in public processions) is placed on the left side of her anthropomorphic form. Because of her location, her protection extends to all those who travel on the treacherous roads. Most vulnerable are the truck drivers who drive long overnight hours and often get into serious accidents. Probably because of this, the truck drivers find solace in praying to their favorite *amma*s of local and popular pan-Indian status, the latter including Kanchi Kamakshi, Madhura Minakshi, Kasi Visalakshi, and Kanaka Durgamma Talli. Seeking their protection, many drivers will print the

FIGURE 4.16 Satyamma, Ambaripeta

FIGURE 4.17 Truck with Goddess Names

names of these goddesses on their vehicles (Figure 4.17). This is an excellent testimony to how a fertility goddess can change or extend her functions to suit the evolving needs of her devotees.

While the discussion so far is about how *gramadevatas* who are considered as sister goddesses have evolved over time to fit into the needs of contemporary devotees, here I will turn my attention to look into the history of the seven sisters as forms of the fertility goddess. Like many forms and symbols of goddesses, the concept of seven goddesses is traced to Indus seals, one of which shows seven female figures standing in a row in the context of a religious scene.[112] These seven figures have been identified by some scholars as a proto-*matrka* (mother) group of goddesses.[113] Katherine Harper is of the view that the concept of the *saptamatrkas* emerged from two separate traditions, "folk" and "Vedic," before their characteristics were merged in art and iconography.[114] While the Vedic goddesses traced to the *Rig Vedic* heptads are described as pacific and auspicious, Harper has argued that the "folk" goddesses, with their origins in the Indus, are understood as standing for inauspicious and dangerous qualities. Attributing all negative qualities to the "folk" goddesses and positive qualities to the very vague reference of Vedic heptads is problematic. Parpola, who takes a different stand, found no differences in this regard between Vedic and Indus goddesses. In fact, in order to show how aspects of Indus religion continued to appear in the Vedic and later Vedic texts that continue into current Hindu practices, Parpola stated that six of the seven figures of the Indus seal are "the mothers or wet-nurses of the war god Rudra-Skanda in the Vedic as well as in the Hindu religions."[115]

It is not until just before the Common Era period and in its early centuries that texts like the *Mahabharata* mention a group of mothers possessing various dangerous and inauspicious qualities, such as the propensity to kill infants.[116] As these goddesses started to make their ways into Buddhism, Saivism, and Vaishnavism as *matrika* (mother goddess) figures, their number oscillated in the beginning from seven to eight or more.[117] But the later reified relevant Sanskrit texts, as well as the evolving iconographic orthopraxy, settled for seven mothers, the *saptamatrika* figures. The story of the origin of these mothers, as mentioned in the *Mahabharata* and in later Saivite texts, reflects their subordination to *brahman*ic deities on the one hand, and their nature as bloodthirsty beings on the other.[118] These mothers were often mentioned only to show how Skanda, the son of Siva, controls and contains their evil nature, a strategy obviously deployed to bring them into subordination to the emerging pantheon of male deities. A simultaneous and consistent effort by Saivites to subvert the goddess is also seen through the textual descriptions, such as the *Skanda Purana*, and the placement of images of *saptamatrka* in relation to Siva.[119] With their various agendas, the *Purana*s vary widely in their accounts of *matrika*s. The *Devibhagavatapurana* describes Devasena as the best of the *saptamatrika*s, the mother of *naga*s, who wears cobra gems and lies in a snake bed.[120] This description conforms to the popular perception of Renuka/ Ellamma as the goddess of snakes and the association of *gramadevata*s with snakes in general. The ambiguity of how these goddesses are introduced into these texts shows the attempts made by Saivites and Vaishnavites to bring these goddesses under their fold. While the Saivite texts claim to employ the *saptamatrika*s in assisting Siva's fight with the *rakshasa*s or *asura*s (demons), the Vaishnavite text, *Kurmapurana*, claims that Vishnu Narasimha changed their natures to become benevolent beings.[121] The *Devipurana*, dedicated to advocate the supremacy of the goddess, gives a different version: the *matrika*s are benevolent for children and care for the animate and inanimate world.[122]

Sara Schastok is right in noticing the coincidence of the composition of the *Devimahatmya* that gives primacy to the goddess and the appearance of the *saptamatrka* figures in temples from the sixth century to argue how in some quarters there was a renewed emphasis on bringing the goddess to the forefront.[123] There are three stages that can be distinguished in the iconographic evolution of *saptamatrika*s.[124] The first representation of *saptamatrika*s after the Indus is displayed in the second- to third-century CE Kushana art in Mathura, where they are seen standing or sitting with two hands, the right in *abhayamudra* ("fear not" gesture) and the left holding a *kamandala* (water vessel). In the second stage, they are shown as holding babies. In the third stage, however, different *vahanas* (mounts) were added to each of the figures to distinguish them from one another and also to relate them to *brahmanic* male deities. These mounts, originally associated with various fertility goddesses, were later appropriated as the mounts of various male *brahmanic* deities. Even later, these mounts were given back to the goddesses in their *brahmanic* form of *saptamatrikas* only to show their spousal status in relation to the male *brahmanic* deities. But this spousal status was also made peripheral, as they were relegated to minor deities by the usual placing of their images outside the main shrine. Arguing how the famous shrines of fertility goddess were taken over by Saivites by manipulating all the symbols and icons of goddess imagery, Bolon cites the Ramesavaram shrine in southern Tamilnadu as an early example of how the *saptamatrika* figures became Saivite.[125] In this instance, the goddesses, by being Saivite, lost their centrality of place but remained in multiple forms in diminutive status.

There are some early records to show that members of the ruling class of Andhra were devotees of these mothers. An inscription issued by the Western Chalukya ruler, Pualakesin I, in the early fifth century CE, reflects his devotion to the *saptamatrikas*.[126] But their first iconic appearance in Andhra as Brahmi, Mahesvari, Kaumari, Vaishnavi, Varahi, Indrani, and Chamunda was within Western Chalukya temples dedicated to Siva.[127] These are typically styled as two-armed females and without any vehicles or any distinctive features to separate each other.[128] On stylistic grounds, these figures are assigned to the eighth and ninth century. CE. More often, the *saptamatrika* figures are seen in the company of the naked images of the goddess Lajja Gauri, showing their close links with her.[129] Panels of the ninth century and later contain four armed figures, bejeweled with crowns and halos around their heads and with their distinctive vehicles: the swan, bull, peacock, eagle, buffalo, elephant, fox, and mouse. Sometimes, there is either Ganapati or Virabhadra on one end of these figures to reinforce their identification with the Saivite pantheon.[130] In the same way as the mythology of various *gramadevatas* was recast to establish Saivite predominance, the *saptamatrikas* were shown assisting Siva in his fight with *Andhakasura*, perhaps a personification of the earlier religious culture of Andhra that the Saivites had sought to subdue.

While the process of incorporating several fertility goddesses as *matrikas* was underway for many centuries, their presence in *brahmanic* temples did not substitute entirely for the function of *akka devatalu*, either as individual *gramadevatas* or as a group of unaccounted for deities known from the archeological or inscriptional records. For example, *akka devatalu* of an unspecified number are at times referred to in inscriptions as *gramadevatalu,* such as Ammanambroli *gramadevatalu* ("goddesses of the village Ammanambrolu").[131] Although the archaeological evidence traces the worship of fertility goddess to the pre- and proto-historic period, it is not until the eighth and ninth century that there is some evidence in inscriptions and literature to show the widespread worship of what was specifically called *gramadevata* in image form. One of the rare examples of the image of a *gramadevata* is from the tenth century in a ruined temple at Choppanandi (Karimnagar District).[132] Of the sculptures exposed in this temple, one is of *nandi* and another is a seated goddess figure named Choppanandi devi, named after the village. She is a youthful goddess, seated with four hands and carrying *kathvanga, khadga, kavacha* (shield), and *rudhira patra* (Figure 4.18). She has bejeweled ears and upper and lower arms. With a skull necklace and a crown with snakes on either side, she has the essential iconographic features typical of a *gramadevata*. There is another image clearly reported as a *gramadevata* by name of Baddi Pochamma who now is lying outside of her shrine.[133] In the absence of any inscriptional records, there is no clear date assigned to this image.

Earlier, I mentioned the contemporary practice of worshiping *saptamatrikas* by *brahmin* women. As is mentioned in a fifteenth-century Telugu work, *Kridabhiramamu,* this practice by *brahmin* families is a centuries-old tradition.[134] According to this source, a householder who was seeking children worshiped

FIGURE 4.18 Choppanandi Devi

the goddesses by asking seven sisters from a Jakkula family to fast, sing, and dance in devotion to the goddesses.[135] The *eduguru akka devatalu* in this text are described in the form of *yakshinis*, or the goddesses of Manibhadra, the youngest of which is mentioned as Kameswari. Their *yakshini* identification and their relation to Manibhadra point out their possible past Buddhist affiliations. Except for the variation of contemporary practice, where married *brahmin* women themselves worship and sing, the format of fasting and singing in praise of goddess Kamesvari appears to be the same as in the sixteenth century.

The mythology of *akka devatalu* reflects the attempts of Saivites to bring the goddesses under their purview. This resulted in the sculpted execution of *saptamatrika* panels in *brahmanic* temples. As discussed earlier, this was yet another layer of goddesses that the Saivites introduced in their attempts to replace the *gramadevatas*. This attempt, like other attempts, did not successfully erase the function of the *gramadevatas*. Ironically, the iconographic depictions of *saptamatrikas* and their sculpted execution in *brahmanic* temples gave a boost to the iconographic imagery of *gramadevatas*. The forms of worship of the *gramadevatas*, as reflected in the case of *brahmin* women, also seems to have diversified.

Tribal Goddess. A tribal goddess is a goddess whose origins lie with the people who comprise the hill tribe people of the mountainous regions. In most cases, it is difficult to ferret out the details of these tribal cults, as many of their aspects were imported into the cults of *gramadevatas* from a very early period. As different tribes became part of village life over the centuries, their goddesses added diversity to the *gramadevata* cult. While these were lesser known and fully merged with village deities, there are well-known goddesses of tribal origins, such as Kali and Durga, who accumulated Sanskrit mythologies and liturgies within the context of their veneration in *brahmanic* temples. Even so, in some contexts and in isolated places, these goddesses still retain their tribal nature. But more importantly, their transitions into the cults of *gramadevatas* continue. In this section, I explore the cultic aspects of these goddesses in Andhra as well as the development and growing popularity of the Andhra-specific tribal cult of Sammakka and Sarakka. In tracing the changes and evolution of these goddess cults and putting them into historical perspective, I will discuss and compare their tribal origins and the reasons and circumstances for their assimilations.

Durga and Kali are goddesses of tribal origins who made their journeys from the mountains to the plains to become not only *gramadevatas*, but important deities of *brahmanic* tradition as well. The contradicting and conflicting natures of goddesses Durga and Kali have been amply articulated in the fifth-century text, the *Devi Mahatmya*.[136] Their association with mountains, their desire for blood, and their fierce battles against demons are known through popular mythology that is recited throughout India during the annual ten-day festival called Dasarah. These characteristics place their origins with hunting and gathering societies on the one hand and foreshadow their later transformation within the context of agricultural societies on the other. Durga's current association with agriculture and fertility, for example, is evident through the ritual observations that are held for her on important agriculturally based occasions.[137] In the same way, Kali, regarded as a beloved daughter, is venerated especially during the Deepavali festival in Bengal.[138]

In their popularity as pan-Indian deities, these goddesses were able to subsume other tribal goddesses of a regional nature. For example, Sangam literature, particularly the second-century Tamil epic *Cilappatikaram*, mentions not only these two deities but also their identification with Korravai, a fierce battle goddess of the southern tribe, Eyians.[139] What is interesting is that the description of this tribal goddess Korravai corresponds perfectly with the profile of a *gramadevata*. Here I quote the description of Korravai as mentioned in the epic:

> *The goddess wore the silver petal of the moon*
> *on her head. From her split forehead blazed*
> *An unwinking eye: her lips were coral.*
> *Bright as silver her teeth, and dark*
> *With poison was her throat. Whirling the fiery serpent*
> *As a bowstring, she bent Mount Meru*
> *As a bow. Her breasts smothered*
> *Inside a bodice the venomous fangs of a snake.*
> *In her hand, piled with bangles, she bore*
> *A trident. A robe of elephant skin covered her...*[140]

The mythology and imagery of the *gramadevata* in Andhra that I have so far described is synonymous with the description of Korravi. From this early description, we can gather that the tribal deities largely retained their features when they became *gramadevata*s. But by doing so, they conflated with similar cults such as those of Kali and Durga, who by this time had become popular throughout the subcontinent. For example, Sara Caldwell reports this phenomenon in Kerala, as several tribal goddess cults of the Western Ghats merged with the cult of the goddess Kali.[141] Like its southern neighbors, the inscriptions and literature in Andhra indicate that several *gramadevata*s took the identity of Durga and Kali. Records issued from the fourteenth through the seventeenth century identify some *gramadevata*s with the epithets Kali,

Durga, and Sakti to indicate that all these are various names for one Sakti.[142] This reflects the amalgamation of many *gramadevata*s into the forms of either Kali or Durga.

Durga is first mentioned as Durga Vairochini in the *Taittiriya Aranyaka* (X.1.7). A female figure on the Satavahana coins of the Kolhapur series (second to third century CE) is said to be the goddess Durga.[143] A representation of a standing two-armed goddess facing downward with braided hair, standing on a pedestal while holding a wreath on the left and a four-pronged object on the right, with a snake on her right is described in a legend in Gupta script as Durga, as seen on an oval seal of sunburned clay from Rajghat.[144] The first iconographic form of Durga in Andhra can be traced to a fourth to seventh-century plaque in which the goddess is seen killing the buffalo demon.[145] This evidence, along with the steady appearance of Durga figures from the seventh century onward as part of Saivite and Vaishnavite shrines, reflects how people in Andhra had begun to acknowledge her as a *brahmanic* deity. In the coastal districts of Andhra today, Durga is popularly identified as Kanaka Durga of Vijayawada. As Kanaka Durga, the goddess shared village origins before she became conflated with the pan-Indian goddess, Durga. Kanaka Durga still functions both as a *gramadevata* as well as a *brahmanic* deity. Her influence is extended in such a way that almost all *gramadevata*s in coastal areas of Andhra are seen as the forms of this goddess.

Kanaka Durga. A close look at the background of Kanaka Durga shows an interesting mixture of various cults and historical transitions. While the *purana*s of the seventh century and later identify Kanaka Durga as a form of *Sakti*, a tenth-century inscription by a Chalukya ruler mentions his attendance at her annual *jatara* (festival) for a *gramadevata*. An inscription issued in 1518 CE by Singayyaraju, a subordinate of the Vijayanagara dynasty, on a partially ruined pillar in front of the goddess's temple in Vijayawada, states that the issuer's ancestors ruled from Vijayawada.[146] If Madhavavarma's capital was Vijayawada, it is likely that the goddess Kanaka Durga served as a guardian deity for his fortress, as the ruins of a fort of an early period are still seen behind the present Kanaka Durga temple.[147] A priest and scholar who has done substantial academic research on the Kanaka Durga temple has pointed to the two lakes on the west side of the Kanaka Durga temple and has argued that they were part of a moat protecting this early fort.[148]

The legend in which Sankaracharya converts Kanaka Durga's *ugrarupa* (fierce form) into *saumyamurti* (pleasing form) by introducing the *yantra* (*chakra*) form of worship and then marrying the goddess to Siva confirms her former *gramadevata* profile, or the status of guardian deity.[149] Her fully developed Saivite affiliations are confirmed by a twelfth-century inscription.[150]

FIGURE 4.19 Kanaka Durga Ugrarupa

The iconographic history of Kanaka Durga supports the above evidence of her career trajectory from *gramadevata* to guardian deity to that of Saivite deity. One of Kanaka Durga's images that was formerly worshiped as a main icon supports her *ugrarupa* (Figure 4.19). In this painted image, the goddess is shown with her very prominent lolling tongue spreading out as a dangerous weapon threatening to wipe away all demons. The heads of a group of demons resembling human heads are shown on her tongue as if they are small food particles that the goddess is about to swallow. She is portrayed holding various weapons in her twenty hands, ten on each side. Her legs are shown far apart from each other as though she is running. But, in fact, this pose indicates how her stretched legs fill all the space of the universe. To exaggerate this point further, her head is flanked by the sun and moon while the sky spreads like an umbrella above her. This image is accompanied by three other images carved and painted on the same side of the cave. The first of these images has three heads and eight hands, and is trampling a demon with her two feet (Figure 4.20). The second image, located at the entrance, has five heads and her eight hands are holding weapons (Figure 4.21). This image is shown in the act of kneeling, with her left knee firmly placed on the ground to show her force in piercing the demon. The third image close to the first image has ten heads and ten hands that are fighting the demon

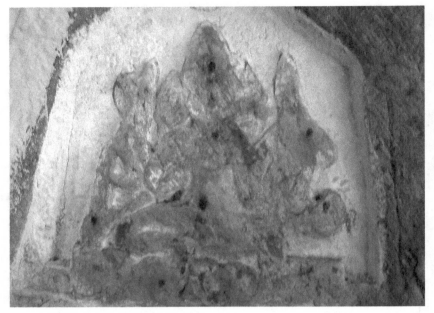

4.20 Three-Headed Kanaka Durga

4.21 Five-Headed Kanaka Durga

that has been forced to the ground (Figure 4.22). It is possible that these images were executed during different timings, as the goddess is imagined in successive centuries as having more heads and more hands. These are rare images, as Durga is not often shown with more than one head. There are other smaller and not so small-sized crudely carved images, most of which are naked (Figure 4.2). These images have been carved out of the rough surface of the cave wall that extends into a huge semicircle shape. Occasionally, a few women devotees who have knowledge of these early images of the goddess drift into this place to offer turmeric and saffron powder to the painted image and to touch the naked images of the goddess so as to be blessed with progeny. In contrast, her present-day image, at least the one now worshiped as the central icon, conforms to the iconography of Mahishasuramardini. It is an impressive four-foot-high stone image of the goddess riding a lion with eight hands holding different weapons, trampling the demon Mahisha (buffalo) with one of her legs and piercing him simultaneously with a trident held in one of her eight hands. Despite this warrior profile of the goddess, a *brahman* especially appointed for the decoration of her image presents her daily in her most pleasing queenly countenance by carefully painting her face, bedecking her with elaborate precious jewelry befitting a heavenly empress, and adorning her with variegated flower garlands and a lavishly brocaded

FIGURE 4.22 Ten-Headed Kanaka Durgav

pure silk saree.[151] Except for the trident shining as an ornament in front of her, neither her other weapons or her trampling of the demon are apparent in this enchanting form.

It is not uncommon in a *gramadevata*'s worship to have more than one image or form to worship in practice. For example, the present temple lore points to the *svayambhu* (self-manifestation) nature of the goddess as the natural rock itself.[152] In fact, some devotees who choose to climb up the stairs start their worship with the image of Kanaka Durga placed at the foot of the hill by the steps and continue their worship at each step of the temple (*metla puja*) until they reach the top of the hill, indicating that the hill itself is the form of the goddess. In this context, her *svayambhu* nature becomes genderless. She is neither female nor male and at the same time she is both female and male.

The goddess in her many functions and forms is understood not just as the form of water and mountain, but as many other forms as well. For instance, after visiting the goddess in the sanctum, some devotees make a point of venerating the snake hole that is located in the temple precincts. Once a year on the fourth day of the new moon, this snake hole attracts crowds of married women devotees who bring offerings of milk and sesame seeds mixed with jaggery to offer to the goddess and to be blessed with healthy children. What they are worshiping here is both the snake hole that is fecund soil and the snake inside. Some devotees also visit the Ashwattha tree located in front of the temple, where some of them tie a cloth laden with turmeric to one of its branches to signify that they just fulfilled their vows to the goddess (Figure 4.23). Here the goddess is in the form of vegetation.

While all of this points to a series of transitions for Kanaka Durga, there is yet another identification of her, known from a couple of stories connecting her origins to human women bearing the name Kanakamma.[153] The first story is about a woman of the *komatie* (business) caste who fell sick and had a dire craving for meat. The sick woman's craving was unabated, unsatisfied and later she died. After her death, when cows started dying of diseases, people feared that it was Kanakamma who was eating their flesh. Immediately, Kanakamma was propitiated with blood offerings. Because she was regarded as Sakti, the name Durgamma was added to initiate her worship as Kanaka Durgamma. The second story is quite different from the first one, though it is about another woman named Kanakamma, who was a sister of seven *brahmin* brothers. When the brothers suspected her of having an affair, she killed herself by jumping into a well. After her body was taken out and cremated, people started worshiping her and soon built a temple at the site. It is said that she was viewed as a *gramadevata* who in her regular rounds wanders into the hills. The name Durgamma was given to her. The common theme in both

FIGURE 4.23 *Mudpulu* (Vow-Fulfilling)

these stories is that deified woman who had to be appeased with blood sacrifices were conflated with the cult of the *gramadevata*. The popular mindset in Vijayawada connects these deified women cults to the goddess Durga, thereby indicating the merging of these two cults with *gramadevata* themes and the cult of Kanka Durga per se.

Although temple lore suggests that the goddess's worship has changed since the installation of a *srichakra*, allegedly by Sankaracharya, until a few years ago an annual allowance was made for the goddess to receive animal sacrifices during her annual ritual.[154] This sacrificial ritual was performed very quickly by non-*brahman* priests, without any public viewing. At present, with the ban on animal sacrifices in the precincts of the temple, this tradition is observed only in a nominal form, and even more briefly, by bringing sacrificial sheep to the deity and by touching one of its ears with a knife. However, the temple administration prefers to keep this ritual out of the public gaze, as they do not think that many of their educated devotees would approve of this practice. Devotees who still prefer to worship the old form of the goddess continue with their animal sacrifices to one of her old images that has been set up by the steps at the foot of the hill (Figure 4.24).

FIGURE 4.24 Kanaka Durga at the Foot of the Hill

The extension of the Kanaka Durga cult is seen in instances such as Kanaka Mahalakshmi in China Waltair, as I have summarized earlier. But the following incident shows how Kanaka Durga is still remembered in one of her earlier forms as a goddess of cattle. In the late 1950s, in the village Nandigudem (Krishna District), there was an outbreak of viral disease among the cattle herd of a person by the name Venkanna. A *yadava* (cattle herder caste) tried to prevent it by sprinkling curd rice because the goddess who was believed to have caused the disease among the cattle was fond of it, and being satisfied by eating curd rice, would leave the cattle alone.[155] Later, Venkanna was possessed by the goddess Kanaka Durgamma and told the villagers that if a temple was constructed for her she would protect the village. Funds were raised and a temple with the image of Kanaka Durga installed, and for whom the annual *jatara* is held.

Thus, it would seem that the basic elements found in the historical transformation of the cult of Kanaka Durga fit into my earlier demonstration of the evolution of the fertility cult. A fertility goddess in the agricultural and household contexts was worshiped in her naked form. When the goddess was seen as the bringer and curer of diseases, or as a battle queen, she manifested ferocious forms and served the common people and the rulers in her respective attributes. From time to time, the goddess also incorporated aspects of the ferocious tribal cults, such as Durga as in the above context, and yet managed to retain relative independence even after becoming *brahmanic*. In the same pattern, in local contexts, deified women's cults merged with the cultic veneration of *gramadevatas*.

Bhadrakali and Mahankali. While Durga is prominent in coastal Andhra, Kali, her counterpart in western Andhra, does not claim the same degree of influence. Kali as a widely venerated deity in Andhra is known from the sixth century.[156] As stated earlier, the *Simhasana Dvatrimsika* also mentions the worship of goddesses such as Kali and Chandi.[157] A stone inscription from Dighasi mentions a *brahman* couple worshiping Kali.[158] But Kali in Andhra has a very different career than Durga. Although Kali has been worshiped widely at least since the twelfth century, as the literary and inscriptional evidence suggests, there is no example of a Kali temple rivaling the same stature of Kanaka Durga's. A temple devoted to Bhadrakali on the top of a hill in the outskirts of Warangal is said to have been built by the Western Chalukyas in the seventh century. But the present temple does not support this evidence. It is said that the later Kakatiya rulers (from the eleventh to fourteenth century), whose primary fort is in close vicinity, worshiped Bhadrakali, whose identity seem to have merged with their guardian deity, Kakatamma.[159] Kakatamma, as mentioned earlier, was considered to be the counterpart of the goddess Renuka or Ellamma. In this sense, it is possible that the present Bhadrakali has incorporated the identities of a guardian deity as well as that of a *gramadevata*. The original stone image of the seated goddess Bhadrakali was very fierce, with lolling tongue and with various weapons in her eight hands. This form of Kali shares features with some *gramadevatas* whose iconic images were made prior to the twentieth century and who are seen wearing skull garlands and holding a skull cup as *rudhira patra*.

Of late, some of her devotees have preferred to see Bhadrakali as a form of Tripura Sundari (a pleasing form of Parvati) (Figure 4.25). One of the devotees recounted to me that a few years ago one of the politicians of the Warangal area facilitated the reinstallation of the image after its protruding tongue was broken. Later, I interviewed the wife of the main priest who has served the goddess since the temple's restoration in 1950s. She confirmed these details. During the installation, a *yantra* was carved in front of the deity to assuage her anger. In addition, her original form is often presented with a sumptuous variety of fruits and vegetables to show her as *prakriti* (earth goddess). During her annual ritual in the lunar month of Sravana (August–September), she is decorated to represent various forms of Devi.

FIGURE 4.25 Bhadrakali, Warangal

In some ways, Bhadrakali's transition from a fierce to a pleasing form shares similarities with the goddess Kanaka Durga. But neither the inscriptional evidence nor the contemporary identifications show the extension of the Bhadrakali cult to other parts of Andhra in the same way as the spread of Kanaka Durga. However, there are some scattered images of Bhadrakali throughout Andhra, like one reported from Karimnagar District, where a small image holds a *khadga*, a shield, *trisula,* and the head of a demon.[160] The Saivite understanding of a head being held by a goddess is not that the head is of a demon but rather it is the fifth head of Brahma that was cut off by Siva, a head that cannot be satiated with any amount of blood. In any case, the head essentially replaces the *rudhira patra,* but signals the same message that the goddess needs blood sacrifices. Later in this region, Kali gained prominence in such a way that local *gramadevata* cults were conflated with her.[161] For instance, all of the *gramadevatas* (including the regional goddess Maisamma) in Hyderabad and Secunderabad are now seen as forms of Kali. The goddess is known as Mahankali in Secundrabad, though her origins are not traced to Bhadrakali, but to Mahankali of Ujjain in Madhya Pradesh instead. In any case, Kali's connection to various local goddesses at times is tenuous, as will be explained later in this section.

The worship of Mahankali in Secundrabad began a couple of centuries ago as a *gramadevata* cult and still exhibits some of her *gramadevata* features.

According to oral traditions, Suriti Appaiah, an army mason during his posting in Ujjain, became a devotee of Ujjain Mahankali when smallpox killed several people. In gratitude for surviving, on his return home, he made a wooden image of Mahankali, built a temporary shrine, and started *puja*. Gradually, as the city grew around the shrine, the number of devotees to the goddess grew, leading to the development of a permanent temple first administered by his son and then later by a temple committee. An image identified as Manikyamba was found during the excavation for the new temple and was installed to the left of a newly carved stone image of Mahankali (Figure 4.26). Their procession images are placed in front of them to receive daily worship. Since these installations, Vedic rituals have been performed by a *brahmin* priest who has been hired to conduct regular *puja*. There is no explanation about why the other image has been identified as Manikyamba. Earlier I have mentioned that Manikyamba is a deified devotee of Siva who takes precedence over Parvati in the Bhimesvara temple at Draksharamam. Occasional Vedic rituals, such as *chandi homam*, are conducted to maintain the *brahman*ic status of Mahankali. The worship of the goddess in the form of a large neem tree on the premises of the temple and the animal sacrifices during her annual ritual belie her earlier original identity as a *gramadevata*. Since the structure of the temple occupies the area in which the neem

FIGURE 4.26 Mahankali & Manikyamba

tree continues to grow, the trunk of the tree is in the main hall, where it is robed with a saree and decorated with the image of the head of the goddess, such that the trunk gives the illusion of the goddess in her anthropomorphic form (Figure 5.2). Another interesting aspect of this temple is the worship of Matangi here understood to be the servant of the goddess (Figure 4.27). This image is placed in a low shrine facing the Mahankali image across the hall. Devotees treat Matangi as a form of Ellamma. In keeping with the tradition of Ellamma's imagery, the temple has only her head and neck carved out of the stone. Some devotees come to make vows and special offerings to Matangi. In this way, the Mahankali temple has established relations with another popular *gramadevata* (Ellamma). In fact, Ellamma and Kali vie with each other in their popularity in and around Hyderabad, with respective temples present in virtually every Telugu neighborhood. Given the ubiquity of each goddess, it is a clever ploy by the temple administration to bring Ellamma into subordination on the one hand and on the other to bring those devotees of Ellamma into the Kali temple. This is analogous to the history of the subordination of goddess to male gods. In this context, just as the human Matangi is seen as a *dasi* (servant) of Ellamma, Ellamma, by taking the name Matangi, in this temple is understood to be the *dasi* of Mahankali.

FIGURE 4.27 Matangi

Unlike Kanaka Durga, the forms of Kali, Bhadra Kali, and Mahankali were imports from outside of Andhra, with their original tribal connections long forgotten. Even so, they made a transition to fit into the local environment, first in the fierce form of the battle queen, as in the case of Bhadra Kali, or as a *gramadevata* in the case of Mahankali. But in the contemporary urban milieu both have changed their appearances into pleasing forms in just the same way as the goddesses I mentioned before in the coastal city of Visakhapatnam.

Sammakka and Sarakka. Even when considered together, the goddesses Bhadrakali and Mahankali cannot compete with the popularity of Kanaka Durga in coastal Andhra. It might be because of this vacuum in western Andhra that the tribal cult of Sammakka and Sarakka is increasingly drawing the attention of millions of Hindu devotees in this region. It is not unknown in history for various tribal cults such as Sammakka and Sarakka to merge with the cults of a *gramadevata*. As I have argued throughout, there were many local tribal cults in history that merged with *gramadevata* cults. One such contemporary example is the goddess Kondalamma (mother of hills) introduced by tribals of the agency area of East Godavari District and adopted as the *gramadevata* by the villagers. She is feted with an annual festival celebrated in her honor.[162]

By studying the names of various cults of *gramadevatas* from tenth to fifteenth-century inscriptions and literature, it is possible to surmise that different tribal people were assimilating with the mainstream village society of the time. The names of the goddesses of these groups appear in inscriptions as Irukalasani, Kuruva-Bhattarika, Tanku-bhattarika, Pallikanti-bhatarandu, Kanamoti, Brosniamma, Kondapoti, among others.[163] The same identification has been given to the goddess Kondapoti who is known as Kondapotidevi in a thirteenth-century inscription on a pillar in a temple at Singavaram (Srikakulam District).[164] The literal meaning of Kondapoti in Telugu is the goddess "Poti who represents the hills." "Poti" might be a female as opposed to the word, "Potu" meaning male.

Tribes in Andhra like the Koyas and Sugalis worship goddesses such as Sammakka, Sonalamma, Peddamma, and Uppalamma, who are regarded as the presiding deities of various viral diseases.[165] Whenever a disease or an epidemic breaks out, they propitiate the deity who is believed to preside over that particular disease. For this, they decorate a stone and worship it by offering a sacrifice of fowls, a goat, or a sheep. In the states of Madhya Pradesh, Orissa, Chattisgad and Jharkhand, tribals such as Baiga, Pardhan, Santal and Gadaba worship many goddesses of this nature. The religious universe of the Baiga, for example, comprised some twenty-one goddesses who cause various diseases.[166] Like the *gramadevtas*, these goddesses are appeased by blood sacrifices. As stated earlier, some of these tribal goddesses who become *gramadevatas* from time to time enter the Hindu *brahmanical* mainstream to become conflated with popular goddesses such as Durga and Kali, who themselves went through the same process. For example, for the last half century or so, Koy goddesses Sammakka and Sarakka have started to attract large Hindu populations in Western Andhra. The Koyas are a hill tribe who traditionally live in the forest of Eturunagaram (Warangal District), which is now a Tiger Reserve. Telugu literature of the twelfth century mentions their practices of human sacrifice. Many Koy practices must have changed because of their long-standing contacts with mainstream Telugu-speaking society, as human sacrifice has been extinct for a long time. This long interaction with the people living in agricultural plains resulted in many cultural borrowings. This is especially reflected in their language, which contains a substantial number of Telugu words used to refer to various practices and activities. They maintained semi-independence under successive Telugu rulers by paying tribute. Failing to pay such tribute during the time of the last Kakatiya ruler Prataparudra (1290–1320) resulted in a battle that, according to mythic traditions, led to the heroic death and worship of Sammakka.

Sammakka's legend begins with tribal leaders finding Sammakka as an infant in the midst of the forest and raising her as the gift of Kondadevara, the god of the hills. Many auspicious signs afterward made the tribe believe that Sammakka was the incarnation of Kondadevara. The childless sought her blessings. She was believed to ride tigers and lions. This belief is analogous to that of Durga riding lions and tigers and Sammakka shares the command of power over the wilderness. In her prime, Sammakka was married to Pagididda Raju, the tribal head of Medaram village. The couple raised a son and two daughters, Jampanna, Saralamma, and Nagulamma, respectively. The older daughter, Saralamma, was married to Govindaraju. At this time, there was a famine in the forest for four successive years, during which time Pagididda Raju piled up debts, thereby angering Prataparudra. In a fierce fight that ensued by a rivulet called Sampenga vagu between the Kakatiya army and the Koy tribe, Pagididda Raju, Saralamma and her husband, Govindaraju, along with many others, lost their lives. Seeing this, Jampanna jumped into the Sampenga vagu that had turned red by this time with all the blood shed and took his life. After this incident, the rivulet came to be called as Jampanna vagu. Although this was shocking news, Sammakka decided to restore the morale of her tribe by putting herself at the helm. While she was fighting valiantly, a soldier came from behind and struck her. In order not to be caught alive, Sammakka fled into the woods toward the east of Medaram. Those who followed her found only a vermilion box at a snake hole under a tree called Nagavriksham (snake tree). The villagers understood that Sammakka had assumed the form of the vermilion box at this place of her liking. The place became her shrine. Initially, tribal women gathered once every two years at this place to worship. As devotees increased in number, the tribal elders moved the venue by cutting the wood from the tree over the snake hole and making it into a *gadde* (throne) for Sammakka under a different tree. They built a second *gadde* for her daughter Saralamma, also known as Sarakka, next to Sammakka's. Some devotees spotted a snake in the snake hole under the tree where the *gaddes* were placed. They believed that the snake was Sammakka's husband, Pagididda Raju. A little water hole called *deyyala madugu* (water hole of spirits) in the vicinity also receives worship as the form of Jampanna.

This legend contains several tribal cultic expressions, such as Sammakka as a form of Kondadevara riding the lion and tiger. In this detail, this goddess resembles her much better known counterparts, Durga and Kali. Although Sammakka died in the battlefield, she fought the battle valiantly in the same way as Durga and Kali have done after their male associates were defeated. Her association with the snake hole and tree and her representation in the form of a *gadde* (throne) using the branches of the tree are typical of tribal veneration. The snake hole and tree, of course, also have been the symbols of the *gramadevata*. It makes sense that the symbols of snakes and trees would come from forests to the villages, but not the other way around. Throughout history, successive rulers made efforts to woo tribes to cultivate virgin lands and to produce food. It is natural that they brought their cults along with them. In addition to the traditional tribal symbols, such as the snake hole and tree, the Sammakka cult seems to borrow the symbol of the vermilion box that is typical of the *sati* cults to mark a perpetual married status. It is common in Andhra that some *satis* become *gramadevatas*. As seen earlier, it is an increasing trend that *gramadevatas* in urban contexts will take soft forms, wherein the *rudhira patra* is replaced by the vermilion box. In Sammakka's case, she is no doubt a deified martyr for the tribals. But she also qualifies to be a *sati* as she jumped into the battle scene knowing that she would lose her life in just the same way as her husband and her other family members. When she received a fatal blow, she disappeared into the woods to save her body from falling into the enemy hands. In this way, her act can be interpreted as following her husband into the other world. This is the reason why the Hindu worshipers interpreted the cobra roaming around the *gadde* of Sammaka as a form of her husband. As I will explain in the next chapter, a common understanding in *sati* cults is that husband-and-wife couples are seen in cobra forms. Moreover, the inclusion of a second relative, in this case, Sarakka, to accompany the deified Sammakka, is a pattern commonly seen in the cults of deified women in Andhra.[167] This practice is what followed in reinstallation of the image of Mahankali along with the image of Manikyamba. Thus the cultic symbolism is a mixture of tribal, village, and brahmanic traditions. In part, that may be one of the reasons that the bi-annual jatara festival has been a draw for huge crowds of devotees from Hindu communities and other tribes from Maharashtra, Madhya Pradesh, Karnataka, Chattisgad, and Jharkhand. In recent years, as part of brahmanic influence, the husbands of Sammakka and Sarakka—Pagididdiraju and Govindaraju—are also given due importance by adding separate gaddelu (thrones) to them. This feature is analogous to the presence of Siva as a husband in the shrines of popular gramadevatas, an obvious assertion of brahmanic patriarchal values.

The jatara in Medaram, 110 kilometers from Warangal city, is held for Sammakka and Sarakka for four days starting on the full moon day of the lunar month Magha. The gaddes are decorated with new clothes two weeks before the festival. It is a custom that one of the Koya boys will receive a vision of the deity and will roam in the forest without food and sleep for a week before he brings the goddesses in the form of vermilion boxes which represent the main deity Sammakka and her daughter Sarakka, both tied to a piece of bamboo. A day before the festival begins, Sarakka's vermilion box, decorated with peacock feathers, pots, and bells, is brought from the neighboring village of Kannepalli. On the main festival day of the jatara, Sammakka's vermilion box, which is covered in vermilion and turmeric, is brought with a guard of honor by the police chief of the state of Andhra Pradesh, who fires three shots into the air to begin the jatara. Music, songs, and dances commence. In 2010, it was the chief minister of the state who brought the offerings to the goddess, carrying them on his head.

The road from Warangal that was built in 1998 certainly helped to increase the crowds. The huge numbers of devotees follow the traditional rites prescribed for Sammakka, such as offering an amount of jaggery equal to their weight, worshiping the bamboo, and performing animal sacrifices. For example, young tribals consuming copious amounts of liquor dance their way to gaddelu to a drumbeat. A large number of them claim to be possessed by the deity. While these traditions were followed by Koya and other tribes who visit the deity without any notion of purity, the mainstream Hindus have been adding other components. Many male devotees shave their heads in reverence to the goddess. Some devotees bathe in the Jampanna vagu to purify themselves before they approach the deity, a brahmanic way of preparing to worship deities. They also believe this dip will cure them from all diseases. Some devotees bring cooked food in pots as an offering to Sammakka, a feature in the ritual for gramadevatas. Some men and women walk for miles while being possessed by the deity. Possession is also typical to the rituals of both *grama-devata* and tribal cults. The Jatara, music, songs, and dances of possession are common in *gramadevata* festivals. As the devotees diversify from villagers to urban low- and middle-class populations, to politicos and celebrities, such as popular film actors and actresses, the petitions to the goddess increasingly vary from personal and familial to that of society-at-large. For example, some politicos and celebrities made a trip in recent years to Medaram to pray for a separate Telengana state, a political movement that is still in full swing into the second decade of the twenty-first century. It was reported in 2010 that the four-day festival attracted eight million people. The private media, music, and film industries have vied with each other to participate in dessiminating the power of the goddess. This shows how Sammakka's cult is cutting across not just tribal lines but also class and political lines as well. The symbols of goddesses, the vermilion box, the pot, the bells, and the peacock feathers are a mix of tribal and *gramadevata* cults. The guard of honor, the gun-fire and other martial forms of expression are derived from colonial traditions introduced by the British.

The cult of Sammakka is not confined to the deep forest receiving new influences from outside forces. In recent years, biennial *jatara*s are being held in many parts of western Andhra at the same time as at Medaram. What causes these extensions can probably be explained through a devotee's words. This devotee, a retired lecturer at a degree college in Warangal, believes in the power of Sammakka to fulfill the wishes of devotees. She went to attend a biennial ritual at Medaram to redeem her vow taken a few years ago that if her daughter would get a good husband, she would pay a visit to Sammakka in Medaram. After her daughter was married to a handsome husband who settled abroad with a good job, the mother went, in gratitude, to pray to Sammakka. Her experience of visiting Sammakka during the biennial *jatara* was an arduous task, as it involved waiting long hours in traffic jams and then wading through a sea of people to reach Sammakka's *gadde*. Even so, she was glad that her health and time enabled her to do this. Not many devotees are as brave and adventurous as this particular one. Thousands of devotees who cannot make their pilgrimage to Medaram constitute the patrons of the new shrines and mini-*jatara*s for Sammakka and Sarakka that are increasingly held in many places in western Andhra.

It is possible that this cult, like some tribal cults, will eventually merge as an extension of a *brahmanic* cult, as in the case of Kondamma (mother of a hill) from Singupuram (Srikakulam District), who is served by a *brahmin* priest with vegetarian offerings.[168] In fact the songs, the videos, and a new Tollywood film have been made for the consumption of Hindu devotees who want to identify Sammakka as Sakti, the preeminent goddess who rules the whole world. She is also, of course, identified as Siva's wife and Vishnu's sister. The images distributed as Sammakka and Sarakka also reflect an uncanny resemblance to the great goddess Durga. In this imagery, Sammakka is riding a tiger and Sarakka, a stag.

The trend reflecting the mainstreaming of the Sammakka and Sarakka cult into the cults of *brahman*ic deities is seen in instances like their growing association with Venkateswara, whose main temple in Tirupati (Chittoor Distict) is considered the second-wealthiest temple in the world, (the first is the Vatican in Rome). There are innumerable temples all over the world to this deity, some of which receive financial help from Tirupati. Venkatesvara, a form of Vishnu, has become something of a Telugu national deity. As early as 1977, Sammakka and Sarakka Devasthanam (temple organization) provided financial help to develop a Venkatesvara temple in Jeella Cheruvu (Khammam District). This association of Sammakka and Sarakka with Vekatesvara might be correlated with the early attempts of bringing Durga and Kali into *brahman*ic temples.

While it remains an open question regarding the future course of the Sammakka and Sarakka cult, it is clear that for various reasons some cults have long-lasting and extensive influences, while some in varying degrees maintain their independence, merge with the more influential cults, or disappear totally. While the gender issues involved in the deification of women will be explored in the next chapter, here it is sufficient to say that the origins of a cult, as in the case of Sammakka and Sarakka, can start with a deified woman who becomes a tribal deity, who will then transcend that status to be worshiped as a *gramadevata,* then as a *brahman*ic spousal deity, and finally as the preeminent *sakti.* Some of the forms and symbols of worship might be as old as that of the Megalithic period in Andhra, and some might be of recent origin. Pan-Indian tribal deities like Durga and Kali may merge with local deified deities or lesser-known *gramadevata*s; or they may metamorphose to the needs of locals as well as the elite, as in the case of Kanaka Durga, Mahankali, and Bhadra Kali. In the recent trend, like some *gramadevata*s, the cults of Durga and Kali went through a similar transition both in their principal functions and appearances.

5

Bala Perantalu

AUSPICIOUS VIRGIN MOTHERS

HUMANS SURVIVE ON hope. To counter suffering and grief, often their hopes lead them to think beyond death. In what form human life exists after death is imagined in various cultures in different ways. In the religious cultures of India, this impetus for the religious imagination has resulted in the belief that the present life is but one of many cycles of rebirths. This belief is so ingrained that people of all classes and castes commonly name their children after a dead parent or grandparent, believing that the dead family member has been reborn. In these cases the family member has usually died naturally. But not all deaths are natural. There are accidental and sudden deaths that are believed to have occurred through human or divine agency. These premature deaths are viewed in various ways in Buddhism, Jainism, and Hinduism. The popular Hindu interpretation of premature death is that it is foreordained by events of the past. It is karma that takes life away suddenly and causes anguish among the living. While karma dominates reflections on death, there are other modes of reaction that seek to deny death's finality, i.e., deification of the dead.

In final discussions in the previous chapter, specifically those concerned with the emerging popular cult of Sammakka and Sarakka, I began a transition to the primary focus of what constitutes this and the following two chapters of this book: the deification of women. Deification of the dead arises primarily from the belief that a sudden violent death creates a disturbance and fear. It upsets the equilibrium of the family. But more importantly, it registers a profound disappointment and apprehension: how can an abrupt premature death so frustrate the hopes and aims of those who have yet to live their full span of years? What happens to the unspent energy of the deceased? Will the dead seek revenge for their unjust end? Who is responsible? As a way of consoling and cajoling departed souls and tapping their energies for the good of the living, deification may take place.

This chapter and the next two considers the stories of women who have met sudden deaths. My aim is to try to understand gender issues, on the one hand, and on the other, the relationship between deified women and *gramadevatas*. Some historians of religions have suggested that contemplation on the meaning of death may have given rise to the first collective rituals marking the origins of religious cultures. Whether or not this is the case, reflections on the meaning of death are, in fact, reflections on the meaning of life. In studying the cults of deified women in Andhra, what I have discovered is that because of the manner in which women are expected to behave, or because of the manner in which they are often treated, the feminine has come to be valorized in the form of various goddess cults.

Stuart Blackburn finds contrasting beliefs that exist between what he has called "Folk Hinduism," on the one hand, and the "Hinduism" based on the Sanskrit texts, on the other.

> If elsewhere in Hinduism death separates humans from gods, in these folk cults it joins them together. However, not just any death has this effect; only a special kind makes the dead hero an object of worship. First, the death must be premature, an end that cuts short a person's normal life span. Second, and more important, the death must be violent, an act of aggression or a sudden blow from nature.. .
>
> However, unlike the problem of theodicy, this deification does not depend on the innocence of the victim. Indeed—and this cannot be overemphasized—it is not moral considerations but violence that transforms humans into deities.[1]

As I show in this and the following chapters, what Blackburn says about the violence of death that causes deification holds true to a large extent. But violence and premature death is not necessarily a precondition for deification. While violence causing death, irrespective of victim's innocence, can result in deification, in some cases it is clear that the particular circumstances that lead to victimization determine the kind of worship and the functions associated with the deified being.

Blackburn states that the participants and patrons of these cults constitute "middle and low levels of the caste and class hierarchies" with almost no cases involving *brahmins*.[2] If the term "middle caste" for Blackburn constitutes also former ruling *kshatrya* castes, then his statement might hold true to some extent in Andhra. Otherwise, this generalization ignores a lot of complexities. For example, a majority of the deified victims discussed in this and the following chapters come from castes such as the *Reddy* and *Kamma*, who are traditionally known for farming, fighting, and ruling. In demonstrating how the folk cults and the *sraddha* ceremonies have been developed as rituals for the dead in different directions, Blackburn argued that those castes who follow the *sraddha* ceremonies in detail are usually not involved in cults to local gods and goddesses.[3] For the most part, this phenomenon is true in Andhra. But as Blackburn himself has pointed out, the degree of Hindus worshiping various local deified gods and goddesses depends mainly on local factors, such as the religious dispositions of local social groups. I argue that these Hindus, at times, include the *brahmin* caste as well. In fact, there are instances, as I explain in this chapter and in the following two, where deified women themselves, or local patrons or participants, include *brahmins*. This chapter considers the death and deification of virgin girls.

Central to the popular Hindu religion of goddess veneration in India is the figure of the virgin mother. At first glance, the words "virgin" and "mother" seem wholly incompatible: virgin, connoting youth and asceticism (abstaining from sexual activity), is antithetical to mother, connoting reproductive sexuality. Hindu tradition is not alone in combining these antithetical conceptions of the feminine within a single image of the divine: the Virgin Mary of Roman Catholicism immediately reminds us that this notion of virgin mother is certainly not confined to the popular religion of rural India, but has surfaced powerfully in a number of other religious contexts as well. What may be unique in the Hindu instance, however, is the process of how and why this image of virgin as mother has been created and sustained.

As stated in previous chapters, ancient goddesses are often associated with fertility and their origins are traced to agricultural societies of the prehistoric period, when raising crops and engaging in animal husbandry was the main stay. Fertility, observed as the essential power to raise crops and successfully breed animals, has been venerated and sacralized, essentially because of its perceived efficacy and necessity to the continued vitality of the community. In this view, then, goddesses are simply anthropomorphic projections of the power of female fertility. Although the biological role of the male in procreation was known, it was not over-emphasized. Portrayal of male figures or symbols along with the goddess figures clearly reveals the awareness of prehistoric people about the roles played by male and female in procreation. Yet, since it was the female that actually gives birth, her association to fertility was treated as fundamental. In annual rituals to the goddess, both in ancient agricultural societies and in the present context of rural India, a male animal is sacrificed to the goddess with the belief that the goddess mates with him as her lover to ensure prosperity and abundance for the coming year.[4] Thus, the goddess in ancient times was seen as the ultimate symbol of fertility, but not as a chaste virgin. Linking the issue of chastity with patriarchal notions of marriage and tracing its historicity, Lynn Gatwood argued that the goddess, as a fertility symbol, was central to the people of Indus civilization whose society was based on egalitarian values:

> With regard to marital independence, the hypothesized goddess may or may not have been married to the Shiva prototype; there is, however, no indication that marriage was a relevant factor in the determination of her ethical nature.[5]

According to Gatwood, it was the arrival of Aryan warrior tribes and their patriarchal values that led to the gradual change of social morals, thereby reducing the status of the fertility goddess in the divine sphere as well. Miriam Dexter, on the other hand, traced the process of the goddess being tamed to around 3000 BCE in the ancient world of the Near East and Old Europe, when god-worshiping nomadic warrior cultures coming from the north of the Black Sea invaded the existing agricultural societies.[6] But both Gatwood and Dexter are in agreement that there had been a long process of accommodation and adjustment before the patriarchal values dominated these beleaguered societies. Their statement about the institution of marriage bringing woman's sexuality under man's control might be true, but one must note that the initial norms of marriage, compared to later times, were much more relaxed. Chastity among virgins, although desirable and much glorified, was not viewed, at least until almost the beginning of Common Era, as compulsory. For example, characters like Satyavati, Kunti, and Madhavi from the famous epic *Mahabharata* bore sons by famous personalities before their marriages and yet were considered as "virgins" until they were married. In these contexts, virginity was not tied to chastity. Whether married or not, their matriarchal ability to produce sons was what determined their epic roles. As patriarchal values begin to tighten, the notions of chastity and virginity among females gained prominence. In any case, the argument of patriarchal values being introduced only by Indo-Aryan groups is questionable. It is simply not possible to trace the origins of these goddesses to matriarchal societies in any conclusive manner.

It is true that in the divine sphere of the religious imagination in Europe, many goddesses of agricultural origins, who did not fit into Christian patriarchal values, either gradually disappeared, or their power was restricted in such a way that they conformed to the newly emerged notions. For example, the profiles of many agricultural goddesses from the old world were sometimes merged with a new incarnation of Virgin Mary.[7] Unlike the European Christian experience, Hindu tradition, a conglomeration of often contrasting and opposing religious systems, although predominantly patriarchal, did not succeed with the same degree of intensity in transforming the values associated with the indigenous goddesses that were encountered. One of the obvious reasons for the continued relevance of fertility goddesses in India is that agriculture continuously has been the economic main stay. Even today, the Indian population remains 75 percent rural and directly connected to agriculture. On the other hand, the cumulative Hindu tradition, through its often inclusive nature, has repeatedly reinvented itself. Bayly has mentioned that in south India, the alliance between the small chieftains and *brahmin* priests transformed many agricultural and tribal goddesses into martial virgin goddesses.[8] This alliance might have lead to the superimposition of *brahman*ic notions of purity and virginity over fertility goddesses and thus created an ambivalence. Here, the existence of *brahman*ic notions based on Sanskrit manuals does not necessarily mean that these principles have their origins solely in the Vedic tradition. As has been argued earlier, while Vedic literature itself incorporated ideas of other groups to a degree, the Sanskrit manuals that were composed in different regions of India before the Common Era and in its early centuries contain divergent religious and cultural traditions that at times are quite contradictory. This complexity is reflected in the historical understanding of the power of virgins. For example, there are specific early tribal associations with virgin goddess worship. Thurston, in the early twentieth century, reported that tribal groups such as the Eravallur from the Cochin area and the Irulans from the Nilgiri hills, Tamil Nadu, worship seven virgin goddesses.[9] The veneration of these tribal goddesses was introduced into mainstream Hindu society very early on. Sangam literature, such as the epic *Cilappatikaram*, mentions tribal goddesses such as Korravi, Kali, and Durga as virgin goddesses possessing a sacred power called *ananku*.[10] In fact, the name of the one of the seven virgin goddesses is mentioned in *Cilappatikaram* as Ananku. The ancient Tamil word *ananku* indicates not just the abstinence of sex, but "chastity filled with sacred power."[11] The fact that the tribal goddess Korravi was adopted as a warrior goddess by the rulers of the Sangam age, and in addition, along with the recognition of Kali and Durga, Korravi was considered among the seven chaste virgin goddesses, attests to how the notion of a virgin's sacred power was deeply entrenched, not just among Tamils but in *brahman*ic ideology as well.

While the notion of virginity is revered in relation to the divine sphere, the same virginity in a Hindu normative view led to suspicion because of the belief that female sexuality without man's control leads to chaos or even destruction. This dichotomy is addressed in the religious imagination by subduing the aggressive virgin goddess and turning her into a shy bride who demurs when she meets her suitor. A good example of this process is seen in the case of the goddess Kanya Kumari ("young virgin") at Cape Comorin (Tamilnadu) in the south. Kanya Kumari's antiquity goes back to the first century CE, if not earlier, since her presence is also known from other parts of India.[12] Actually, in Andhra, elements of her tradition can be traced to the third to second century BCE. Naked goddess images with a parrot, and the inscription with the name Kumari, have been found at Dhulikatta (which I mentioned previously). While some of these goddesses went through the above said transformation to meet the patriarchal standards of the society in the name of Saivite and Vaishnavite traditions, many goddesses in rural areas retained their function of fertility as their central focus. Thus, the independent nature of these goddesses sometimes stands in contrast to the social values pursued by villagers. These factors alone create enough ambiguity between the spheres of divine and human levels. These goddesses are hardly role models to emulate. There remains a tension between the character of goddesses as they have been portrayed and the normative social experiences and expectations of women.

While the fertility goddesses that came under the *brahmanic* sphere of influence were sometimes endowed with the virtue of chastity, there are cases like the ones I examine below where fertility is combined with chastity. In this context, the notions of virginity, fertility, and power, rather than just fertility and power, have been indelibly linked. In what follows, I will try to show the process by which the powers of virginity were transformed into the protective power of mother goddesses and how this is the product not only of the complementarities of agricultural and urban valorizations, but also the result of at least two other factors: patriarchal reactions to the premature death of young virgins and religious perceptions of the transformative power of heat (energy or *sakti*).

In traditional Hindu south India, virginity is regarded as a sacred quality, not only of the divine feminine, but also of unmarried girls. Virginity, in fact, is an expected status of all unmarried girls. Moreover, in many parts of India and Nepal, because of their virgin statuses, young girls are worshiped on special ritual occasions.[13] Their virginity connotes purity. Because of this Paul Hershman, who conducted his field work in the state of Punjab, observed that a virgin girl who can command divine power and high status can lose it all as soon as she is married.[14]

In northern India, an unmarried *brahmin* girl is often addressed as Devi-ji ("respected goddess"). It is significant that these girls are not required to touch a person's feet, not even those of their parents. It is only after marriage, the losing of their virginity and the ceding of their power to their husbands, that they must touch the feet of their husbands as well as their parents.

Though a virgin girl receives respect, she is subjected to close super-vision and discipline. Sudhir Kakar has described how a girl is trained to emulate the roles of Sita and Savitri, the archetypal epic and *Puranic* female characters.[15] The character Sita comes from the epic *Ramayana,* which was composed when patriarchal values were solidified in such a way that a hus-band was described as a woman's personal god. Sita's character meets these patriarchal standards when she is perceived as leading her life in singular devotion to her husband.

To further characterize the orientation of a young girl in India, I begin with reference to a case study that was done by Vanaja Dhruvarajan in a traditional village in Karnataka, a neighboring state of Andhra Pradesh.[16] Dhruvarajan's observations about how girls are treated until their marriages were based on her interviews with villagers of various castes. The strategy that parents play in bringing up a girl is to make the girl understand her position in relation to men. In the words of Dhruvarajan,

The son evokes feelings of pride, anticipation, fulfillment, hope, and elation... the daughter, on the other hand, evokes feelings of pity, con-cern, and affection... Even though a daughter means a pleasant and positive influence on the quality of life, since she makes life tender and sweet, the realization that she is a transient member of the family puts her in a marginal position. The family has the responsibility to train her properly so that she will bring a good name for the family. But the painful feeling is always there that the parents have to go through a lot of trouble to see her settled and watch her suffer if things do not go right for her [after marriage].

[In] the ritual during the first menstruation... women sing songs elaborating themes about the meaning of becoming a woman... how a woman should behave—the qualities of docility, shyness, patience, and tolerance are stressed as being the most important qualities of a woman. After puberty the older women in the household take active interest in instilling proper dispositions and attitudes in her. It is made very clear to her that the impulsive carefree days of childhood are over and it is time that she trains herself to become a woman.... [P]ermission from adults is mandatory even when she goes chaperoned. She is dis-couraged from talking to strangers, particularly men, and is no longer allowed to sit in male company. She is told to pay more attention to how she dresses and combs her hair. She is given lessons in cooking and housekeeping. At this stage she is no longer observing but is learning her future role actively by doing.[17] [Brackets are mine.]

What Dhruvarajan found to be true in the above village correlates well with my own understanding of how young girls are raised in rural parts of Andhra Pradesh. Young girls in Andhra and other parts of south India are not venerated like their counterparts in northern parts of India. But usually the daughters, from a young age on, are referred to affectionately as *amma* by their parents. This affectionate term might indicate the reality that the daughter, in essence, is a future mother, but for the time being, she is a beloved "little mother" to the family. In women's rituals of vow-taking for long-married status blessed with many children, married women called *"perantalu"* (auspicious women) are invited to participate. Unmarried girls are welcome at these functions, in which they are referred to as *bala perantalu* (auspicious girls) and are offered all of the married symbols, such as turmeric, vermilion, and a blouse piece. This gesture indicates the girls' imminent future status as married women. From birth, a girl is regarded as a future wife and mother of another household and is trained to fit into that role. While a son may be expected to provide food and protection for the parents, a daughter is expected to bring a good name to her parents by her appropriate behavior. Given these scenarios, the question could be asked: why is it that only daughters, and not sons, after meeting sudden or tragic deaths, are deified?

Bruce Tapper, who considered the role of *Gavara* caste women in farming communities in Andhra Pradesh, reported that both men and women felt that a female's desire/hope continues more prominently than a man's beyond her lifetime, and this was the reason why usually it is female ghosts who come back to disturb the living.[18] Why is a female's desire stronger than a male's? One way of answering this question is that in a traditionally patriarchal world, the females are expected to exercise patience even under trying circumstances. Here the comments made by Veena Das about the Punjabi understanding of the female body are relevant:

> On the one hand, then, the female body is seen as constantly transformed by use, as being progressively polluted. On the other hand, it is the very capacity of the woman to absorb the negative forces of the cosmic and social world that allows men to be regenerated.[19]

Thus this ambiguity surrounding the female body reflects society's perspectives of women as inferiors on the one hand, yet, on the other hand, they seem to possess boundless enduring power. In spite of this ambiguity, a female is expected to give her unflinching attention to her husband even when she has been mistreated by him.

What I am specifically interested in exploring here, however, is what can happen if a virgin girl dies suddenly or accidentally without fulfilling this defined role set for her.

By citing several local stories that I have collected during my fieldwork in Andhra Pradesh, I will try to illustrate a process of deification in which young girls come to be regarded as virgin mother goddesses endowed with protective powers.

The first instance of deification I want to cite comes from Vizianagaram, where a locally famous goddess by the name Paidimamba has two temples and is regularly venerated in liturgical worship, led by a *sudra* (agricultural caste) priest.[20] People believe that every year she resides for six months in one temple near the main bathing tank of the town and for another six months in another temple in the midst of the town. This tradition resembles the custom in the worship of some *gramadevatas* where a permanent temple is called the "in-law's place" and a temporary hut or a canopy made for her annual ritual is called her "native place." Another reason might be that Paidimamba, according to a legend, was initially deified by the common folk after they had retrieved a goddess image from the bathing tank and enshrined it. Later, her royal family relations constructed another shrine to worship her as their family protectress. Although the descendants of her family remain the traditional political rulers of this area and act as treasurers for these temples, they respect popular sentiments toward this goddess by allowing non-*brahman*ical priests to officiate the ritual activities performed for the cult of their goddess relation. Usually, in conventional Hindu temples, a *brahmin* from the priestly caste who has been trained in ritual performance according to the traditional texts acts as a priest. But here, either a man or a woman from any non-*brahmin* caste, without any formal training, can function as priest.

The legend of the goddess Paidimamba begins with an account of the tensions that once existed between the official representative of French East India Company and two regional rulers in the mid-eighteenth century, the rulers of Vizianagaram and of Bobbili. The representative of the French was a man named Bussi, who had been given commercial control over the coastal regions of Andhra by the Nizam (the Muslim potentate at Hyderabad). At this time, most of the petty Hindu rulers in this region did not want to acknowledge the suzerainty of the Muslim Nizam. Meanwhile there developed some jealousy between Vijayaramaraju, the ruler of Vizianagaram, and his neighbors, the Bobbili rulers, in spite of continuing formal social meetings between these families. Vijayaramaraju wanted to crush the power of the rival Bobbili rulers by taking the help of the Frenchman Bussi. So, he not only acknowledged the authority of French, but also extended his help to bring Bobbili rulers under French control. However, his designs for ruining the Bobbili rulers were not shared by his wife and his loving younger sister, Paidimamba, who had made it clear to her brother that neighborly rivalry would lead to mutual destruction. Paidimamba and her sister-in-law were unsuccessful in persuading Vijayaramaraju not to go to war. In this context of tension and imminent warfare, Paidimamba became ill with smallpox (the significance of which we shall soon understand). While she was bedridden, she heard that the Bobbili rulers had been killed and that Bussi, in turn, was planning to kill her brother too, thus bringing into fruition her intuitions of mutual destruction. As Vijayaramaraju was in the warfront, it was impossible to send a message to warn him, so Paidimamba herself started with an assistant to go to Vijayaramaraju to warn him of Bussi's design. As she was on the way, she heard that her brother already had been killed. Hearing this news, she fell unconscious. When her assistant sprayed water on her face, she woke up and said that she was leaving the world, but she could be worshiped in the form of a stone image to be found in the bathing tank of Vizianagaram. And so a stone image was indeed found in the tank and people started worshiping the image as Paidimamba, the virgin goddess.

While interviewing worshipers at her temple, I was told repeatedly that people especially remembered Paidimamba's genuine concern to stop the war of destruction and to save her brother's life. These people often wondered if Paidimamba had been a boy, how effective she could have been in those circumstances. This particular comparison is very common among the people who believe in patriarchal values and at the same time recognize the strong will and ability of a particular girl or a woman that could not reach its full potential, given the restrictions placed on female gender. They believe that Paidimamba, after her death, acquired the power of protection that she desired but could not exercise while alive.

Paidimamba, in a sense, was a traditional and typical virgin girl whose concern was to protect her family as much as she could. A traditional adolescent Hindu girl generally acts second to her mother in caring for the family. Paidimamba, being a member of a ruling family, showed her concern not only for her brother, the head of the family, but also for the whole region, by trying to avert the war. In the popular mind, she seems to represent something of the prevailing sentiment of resistance against "outside" political and economic control (Muslim and French). My sense is that one of the reasons why her cult had such an appeal to the people of Vizianagaram is that they saw in her a potential protective power that was never realized, a theme that I will return to again later in this chapter. In addition to the resistance and protective aspects, another element of this story that I wish to stress is that, in the popular mind, smallpox itself, as I have mentioned before, is regarded as a goddess of heat (energy/*sakti*) that embraces whomever she likes. Once a person gets small-pox, that person is also viewed as having been touched by the goddess. In this myth, we see something of this popular belief at work. Paidimamba's goddess stature is signaled by the presence of this disease. Thus, in her virgin fig-ure, we find combined virtues of family and political protection as well as the religio-magical association of miraculous manifestation. It is in the tragedy of her early death that we find the catalyst for belief in her continuing power.

Another instance of deification of a young virgin I will cite concerns Rangamma *perantalu*, a goddess worshiped in a place called Telaprolu in the Krishna district. Rangamma was born into a *sudra* family in the mid-nineteenth century. At the age of only eight years old, she died from smallpox. Soon after her death, many calamities occurred, especially the sudden appearance of fire that would burn down houses or ignite clothes. Frightened people left the vil-lage and built their houses elsewhere. The same happenings occurred at the new place too. At this time, a bangle seller came to the village inquiring about the house of the parents of Rangamma. He reached their house and asked for the money for the bangles he said that he had just sold to Rangamma on his way into the village. After this event, villagers determined through a medium that it was Rangamma's troubled spirit that was upsetting the village. Then the medium proclaimed that Rangamma wanted to be worshiped by the villagers as a *perantalu*, the auspicious goddess. At this stage, an image was prepared and installed in one of the two rooms of a temple (Figure 5.1) along with the image of *gramadevata* Ankamma in the second room. It is often the case that deified women are enshrined along with other goddesses in the belief that giving company to the deity will ward off any outcome of evil. In this scenario, the temple is named after the deified woman. In this case, it is Rangamma *perantalu gudi* (temple of Rangamma Perantalu). The epithet *perantalu* not only identifies the auspicious status of the deified woman but also separates her from the *gramadevata*. A neem tree is present in the precincts, for the devotees to offer chicken and cooked food. An annual festival conducted by a priest who is the descendant of Rangamma's family has been held ever since, in the same fashion as for a *gramadevata* with animal sacrifices.

At first, it would seem that the story of Rangamma is similar to many other stories of the departed that attribute disturbing and unusual events to a trou-bled spirit who has not been properly put to rest. For example, a similar inci-dent of a bangle seller selling bangles to a dead daughter is told in Attili (West Godavari District) in relation to the virgin goddess, Kollapati Venkamma. Later, the dead daughter appeared in the dreams of her parents to confirm the claim of the bangle seller. This led to the initiation of her worship in an annual

FIGURE 5.1 Rangamma *Perantalu*

jatara. An image is made during this occasion and is taken in procession during which she is offered turmeric and vermilion, symbols for *perantalu*.

We do not know the details of the death of Kollapati Venkamma. But the story leading to the deification of Rangamma is also consistent with that of Paidimamba insofar as what is actually celebrated is the potential power of the feminine that was never realized in life. In both instances, potential unrealized power is associated with a virgin's status. Here again, the smallpox that claimed Rangamma's life indicates the presence of the goddess. A manifestation of the goddess's "heat" was understood by the villagers in the form of the fires plaguing them, fires symbolic of the goddess's frustrated energy. Like Rangamma, when Venkamma made her appearance to a bangle seller declaring that she wanted to wear bangles, it alarmed her family and the villagers that her restive spirit was wandering around to fulfill her unrequited desires. Bangles, vermilion, and turmeric are the important signs symbolizing the auspiciousness of Telugu women. For young girls, these symbols indicate their potential to be wives and mothers. By venerating or placating these virgins, what villagers are actually attempting to do is to transform the channels of their manifest divine power from destructive tracts to constructive conduits. The presence of heat, yet again in this story, also signals a transformative process at work.

In another story I have collected, which is also situated in the nineteenth century, young female twins were deified as one goddess after their accidental deaths. This took place in Elamanchili in the Visakhapatnam district. The twins by the names of Ramamma and Chandramma had been born into a *brahmin* family and had lost their mother soon after their birth. When they were nine years old, their father wanted to arrange marriages for them, as in the custom of those days, and went to talk to prospective bridegrooms' families. But neither of these girls was willing to marry, and each made their stubborn attitudes known to their anguished father. As their father did not return in time, they began to worry about him and walked into the outskirts of the village with the intention of meeting him on the way. As the sun went down, they lost their way and fell into an unmarked well and drowned. Later they appeared in a dream to their father and also to a village elder, declaring that they were now living in the form of an anthill and should be worshiped by the name of Ramachandramma. The village elders then constructed a temple beside an anthill and initiated celebrations biannually, with the help of a priestess from the *kapu* (agricultural caste) family. All devotees on the first day of celebrations gather near the anthill in front of the temple at the foot of a small hill to witness the manifestation of the goddess in the form of lightning. This lightning is said to appear three times: first on the top of a nearby hill, second behind the hill, and third in the sanctum sanctorum of the goddess's shrine immediately after a verse in praise of the goddess is read by a man who has fasted for a whole day. Celebrations continue for a month, just like the celebrations for a typical *gramadevata*.

Sharing similarities with the above myth is that of the goddess Guttalamma ("mother of hills or anthills"), alias Puttalamma ("mother of anthills"). In fact, the meaning of both of these names is the same, as both indicate anthill, the abode of snakes. In this case, the name of the deified young woman is forgotten or was never known. But the story reports that a *brahmin* of the Kamalanabhuni family was bringing his young daughter, who was at the age of attaining puberty, to a river so that he could build a hut for her overnight stay on an island between the rivers, as per the dictated tradition of their family. When they arrived in Nallapadu (Guntur District), he asked her to wait outside the village while he would fetch some food. When he returned, he found a big anthill had grown over her. A shepherd of the Chigurupati family told him that the girl had called out to him and informed him that she would be living in the anthill and that the villagers should initiate worship for her. In the annual *jatara* that was held into 1950s, a member of the Kamalanabhuni family visited.[21] The first *bonam* (food offering brought in a pot) was offered by a member of the Chigurupati family, after which the ritual was held in the same fashion as it is for a *gramadevata*, with blood sacrifices.

There are some curious aspects to the cult of the two goddesses just discussed. In the first instance, though the goddesses are purportedly of *brahmin* origins, they are fed with animal and bird sacrifices. Thus, virgin *brahmin* girls, vegetarians, have been rendered into bloodthirsty *gramadevatas*. Identifying their abode as anthills is an authentication of their status as *gramadevatas*. Almost all agricultural goddesses, as discussed in the previous chapters, are believed to live in an anthill in the form of a snake to make the earth fertile. Furthermore, the twins drowning in the water, the potent symbol for sustaining life, make them unite with the goddess Ganga. Secondly, as in the case of *gramadevatas*, the ritual specialists of this temple are non-*brahmin*, and in one case, a woman. Moreover, these two developments would seem to indicate the non-*brahmanic* impetus for the process of deifying virgin goddesses. That is, the cult of virgin goddesses represents a quest for the realization of power as it has been conceived beyond the conceptions of the *brahmanical* priestly community. Finally, in the case of Ramachandramma, the presence of the goddess's heat or energy/power/*sakti* is perceived in the form of lightning, analogous to the fire we noted in the immediately preceding case, and in the previously cited instances of smallpox as well. Here, however, the villagers are assured of bringing the power under control through proper ritual veneration and non-vegetarian offerings.

The next story I need to discuss is about Vasavidevi, a beautiful young girl born to a *vaisya* (merchant) couple, Kusuma Sreshti and Kusumamba, in Penugonda, purportedly hundreds of years ago.[22] When Vasavidevi was still young, the ruler of that region, Vishnuvardhana, visited Penugonda. As the head of the trading community, Kusuma Sreshti paid a visit to the king, and he brought his daughter along.[23] The king fell in love with Vasavi at first sight, and after returning to his capital, he sent word to Sreshti that he wished to marry Vasavi. Though Sreshti agreed to this proposal, his daughter did not. Sreshti had no choice but to refuse the king's offer. When the king learned of the refusal, he was so infuriated that he came to invade Sreshti's community and to abduct Vasavi. Hearing of the king's plan, young Vasavi committed suicide by jumping into a fire. Before her suicide, she cursed the king and blessed the *vaisya* community so that they would prosper and establish trade empires across the oceans. She proclaimed that henceforth the girls of her community would be born without beauty, so husbands should compensate for this by providing beautiful clothes and jewelry. She also admonished *vaisya* males not to cheat people for more profits and not to visit prostitutes. After her death Vasavi was identified as an incarnation of Parvati, and she became famous as Kanyaka Paramesvari (a virgin form of Parvati, wife of Siva). Eventually, she became the goddess of the entire *vaisya* community in Andhra. Wherever a considerable number of the *vaisya* community live, there is a temple to this virgin goddess. *Vaisyas* are vegetarian and they appoint *brahmin* priests to their temples.

In addition to the reasons I have already given regarding why the deaths of virgins can lead to perceptions of great potential power, this myth is particularly revealing in multiple ways. First, it is a myth often cited in traditional circles for the justification of child marriage. If a beautiful young girl is already betrothed, then the possibility of her being taken away by wealthy noblemen or royalty for their harems is prevented. Second, the myth clearly reflects caste tensions between the merchant *vaisya* community and the warrior ruling class. Third, by her admonitions to *vaisya* men, this virgin goddess has come to symbolize the moral standards of the community. And fourth, she shares the virtue of strong-willed independence that preserves the pride of the *vaisya* caste in showing defiance to the ruling *ksatrya* caste. Moreover, the motif of fire is present again to indicate unbridled energy or fierce sakti. Vasavi's transformation into a goddess occurs when she enters into the fire.

Another instance of virgin deification I will cite is somewhat similar to the theme broached above, reflecting the strong-willed independence on the part of a young girl. This story as has been mentioned previously in chapter 3, is known with some variation throughout several villages in the East Godavari District.[24] Nearly two centuries ago, a young woman, assuming her bridegroom was handsome, agreed to a marriage arranged by her father. In traditional marriage arrangements, it was common in those days that bride and bridegroom would not see each other until the formal ceremony of marriage. On the day of her marriage, the bride found the groom to be disgustingly ugly and became very upset. As she could not prevent the marriage, she jumped into the fire that was prepared for cooking the food for the marriage party. Later, her father saw her in his dream wearing ankle bells (indicating that she was in happy mood) and carrying a *garaga* (a decorated earthen pot) on her head. The *garaga*, as discussed earlier, has been a symbol of fertility and auspiciousness since ancient times and as such understood as a symbol of the *gramadevata*. After the father's dream, the dead young woman became famous as Garagalamma ("mother of pots") and temples for her were constructed, to be worshiped by the entire village.

In this story, the element of male guilt seems to have been introduced. It is curious that in many of the oral myths I have collected that involve the untimely death of young virgins, the dead appear to male relations in dreams directing them to begin worshiping them as goddesses. Could it be that in some instances that the occasion of the death of a young virgin still under the care of her male relatives spawns propitiation in response to feelings of remorse? Or generates propitiation for what has been lost, what has not been realized? Is it a recompense for a failure of sorts? What is more curious is that her father's dream contains a happy image of her with a water pot on her head indicating a transformed status, a symbol of fertility. Married women in the annual rites for *gramadevatas* often participate in processions in such a fashion. This might be the belief of the father that his daughter continues to live in some other plane to care for her children who now would consist of the whole village. Thus, in this case, as in the case of the cult of Ramachandramma, we seem to have found again the coalescence of virgin and mother goddess types.

I will cite here a couple of examples to show how a virgin girl becomes a *gramadevata* of either a specific village or a smallpox goddess for a number of villages. The details of this particular virgin girl, Tallamma, who becomes a typical *gramadevata* are not known, except that she was the daughter of the Yerrammareddy family in Gudur (Nellore District) and offered fire to the elders to light their tobacco cheroots. Although the circumstances leading to her death are not clear, we do know that now she is treated as the *gramadevata* for the town of Gudur. Her temple is located in the outskirts of the town, typical for a traditional *gramadevata*. Her image in the temple reflects the traditional fearsome features of a *gramadevata* with round wide eyes and two protruding side teeth as fangs, and she is shown holding *khadga*, *naga*, *trisula*, and *patra* (vessel) in her four hands. Devotees add bangles to the *khadga* and treat the *patra* as a vermilion holder, both of which are probably recent phenomena. Devotees worship her every Sunday with blood sacrifices to fulfill their vows. The annual festival to this goddess is typical for that of a *gramadevata* except for a couple of unique features. These include bringing an annual *prasadam* (food offering) from a neighboring village goddess, Mudigedamma. The *gramadevata* Mudigedamma is worshiped with sand in the river and this is brought and kept in the house of Yerrammareddy on the previous day of the annual ritual to the goddess. On the day of ritual procession, a pot of turmeric and vermilion, along with a sand offering, is brought to the temple and mixed with the cooked food to offer to Tallamma. After sacrificing a goat, the blood is added to the food offering and sprinkled over the fields and village boundaries with the belief that it kills off insects and other pests. On this festival day, the villagers invite their daughters and offer them clothes, in addition to vermilion and turmeric.

In this way, Tallamma fulfills the role of *gramadevata* both in her image and in her ritual function. The detail of the girl serving fire to the elders of the village invokes the motif of fire that was discussed earlier in the deification of a number of virgin girls. In spite of all the trappings of a *gramadevata*, it could be said that the offerings such as bangles, vermilion, and turmeric, although not uncommon to the *gramadevata*, could also be identifiable signs for the virgin goddess.

Yet a further example of virgin goddess and her conflation with a *gramadevata*, in this case Mutyalamma, has it origins in the Garrala family of the Bobbili rulers. As was mentioned in the story of Paidimamba, the Bobbili rulers were both friends and foes to the Vijayanagar rulers. Unlike in the case of Paidimamba, we know very few details of Mutyalamma except for her dying of smallpox and that she came to be worshiped as a family deity. But when the family dispersed to several parts of Andhra after the fall of the Bobbili fort, her cult spread to many villages, where the villagers appropriated her as a smallpox goddess. The reason she is worshiped as a smallpox goddess is probably related to her dying of smallpox. While family members worship her with non-vegetarian offerings, in many villages of Andhra Mutyalamma is worshiped as a typical *gramadevata*. In chapter 4, I explained one of the rituals held in honor of Mutyalamma with the expectation of rains. Mutyalamma's origins are essentially the same as Paidimamba's: royal families treated them as family deities with non-vegetarian offerings, while the larger public appropriated them as *gramadevatas*.

While these two previous instances indicate how certain virgin goddesses become *gramadevatas*, it is clear in other cases, such as Rangamma, that some cults, although they acquire the features of *gramadevatas*, remain separate, especially with the identifiable epithet, *perantalu*. The following event of deification helps to understand the meaning of this epithet further. A girl in China Erukapadu (Krishna District) grew up worshiping a deified *sati*, Vuyyuru Veeramma, who was popular in the region. It is said that the girl, before her death, told her parents that she was Veeramma in her previous birth and asked them to build a temple for her. The poor couple sold their piece of land and built a temple in her name, *perantalu gudi*. In this instance, the word *perantalu* clearly extends from the woman who performed *sati* to that of the young virgin girl. The understanding here is that if the girl had a chance to grow up and become a wife, she would have realized the potential of a steadfastly devoted wife who would die for her husband if needed. By worshiping her, the unspent power of single-minded devotion of the dead young woman is realized by the village community.

The theme that is consistent throughout the above stories is that if a young virgin dies, her unrealized protective powers may remain in this world manifest in the form of a mother goddess and often articulated through symbols of fertility. In the first story, after the death of Paidimamba, people believed that she acquired the power of protection that she could not exercise while alive. Paidimamba, with her selfless concern for her brother and the people under her family's protection, makes for an ideal goddess: her unspent life's powers can be tapped in the present. Her death by smallpox symbolizes the transformative and purificatory function of heat. It can be understood as a kind of rite of passage, a purified death that renders her and other goddesses like her a powerful force. Although the reasons for the death of the *vaisya* girl, Vasavi, were different, in her curses and admonitions, she stood as a protector of her whole community. Vasavi's death is legitimized because, like Paidimamba's, it is understood as occurring for the sake of her community. Perhaps their stories also arouse a certain degree of guilt in the ranks of male devotees. In this instance, both Paidimamba and Vasavi share certain common features with Garagalamma, features that resemble the *sati* cult. While I leave the discussion of *sati* for later, here I would like to further underline that the guilty feelings on the part of the male relations are consistent throughout the above stories. Despite the presence of guilt in the surviving male relations, in the deaths of Rangamma, Venkamma, and Ramachandramma, there does not seem to be any anger or frustration toward the family or other patriarchal enforcers.

Rangamma was powerfully transformed through the process of fire/heat brought on by her fatal encounter with smallpox. The virgin girl who is a potential mother and nurturer is taken away by the goddess of heat, the presiding deity of smallpox. Meeting her death, she is united with the goddess of smallpox. By being one with the smallpox goddess, her potential energy is shown in the form of fire, the same notion of transformative energy of heat but reflected in this instance in a different form. In the story of Garagalamma, on the other hand, the young virgin embraces fire out of anger and frustration at her own family. The palpable feelings of guilt and remorse of the families can easily extend to the rest of the villagers, who knew well that they put the societal norms of patriarchal values above the individual desires of these young women. The twins representing Ramachandramma and the nameless Puttalamma share similarity in the sense that they, in their temporary state of abandonment by their parents, met sudden deaths to become one with the *gramadevata*. The reasons for abandoning these young girls had to do with the process of subjecting them to patriarchal societal norms. In the first instance, it was to marry the twins off before puberty, and in the second instance, to confine the young girl overnight on an island so that she would be eligible for marriage. This collective feeling, combined with the desire of converting the impending energy of the girl into a positive force, may be what makes her the object of a cult for the whole village.

In each of our stories, although cultic contexts were not exactly the same, a basic pattern emerges: virgin mother goddesses are the product of untimely and youthful deaths of young women whose futures as wives and mothers were short-circuited. That is, their powers of fertility and their contributions to the ongoing nurturance of their families and communities were aborted. Symbolically, what leads to their transformation from virgin girl to mother goddess is a purification process by heat, fire, or water. Heat or fire is traditionally associated with the power generated by *tapas*, or ascetic practice, while water is considered as the supreme purifying element. In each of our stories, there is certainly an element of sacrifice present in the manner in which these virgin girls are understood. Their trials by fire, heat, or water are considered ascetic and transformative. Psychologically, we may see in these dynamics an attempt to cope with loss, or perhaps to deal with feelings of guilt, for the premature death of potentially reproductive females. The powers of these goddesses, understood as fertile and protective, are thus the displaced hopes for a life of which never realized its auspicious potential.

A young woman in a traditional family is expected to be a devoted future wife, a daughter-in-law, and carries on her head the burden of the honor of two families, natal and agnate. Because of this, people think that a female child has immense potential powers of patience and understanding, and moreover, the motherly qualities of taking care of family members. As soon as a girl marries, she is expected to produce children. This means virginity is understood as a temporary state, a state in which a young girl's energies lay dormant. Once she attains puberty, a girl must be married off for her own good and for the good of the entire society to channel her energies as a caretaker. It is even better if the girl is married before she attains puberty, as this will not raise any suspicions of her lack of chastity and will make her an ideal bride, wife, and future mother. Since a girl is raised to be inside the home, her whole world is nothing else but her family. Thus, if a female meets any kind of unusual death, people still see her hopes and future dreams of caring for the family as her latent power that has not yet been realized. In deifying her, they are trying to tap the unspent powers of her "motherhood." This is probably why she is viewed as the caretaker of the community, as illustrated in the story of Vasavi and others. When transmuted so that she takes on village well-being as a whole, therein lies the stimulus to make her a *gramadevata*.

6

Perantalu

AUSPICIOUS WIVES

IN THE FIRST chapter, we observed that many scholars have argued that there has been a tendency in India for regional customs to become associated with pan-Indian traditions articulated in Sanskrit literary culture. In this way, customs of a particular region gain popularity and validation. At the same time, local traditions draw inspiration from seemingly similar pan-Indian traditions, while retaining their local rootedness. I argue in this chapter that the tradition of *sati* developed as pan-Indian with *brahmanic* interpretations, but only after drawing inspiration from local traditions. Having been established, the pan-Indian tradition, in turn, influences the behavior of each locality. This is a reflexive process.

In the pan-Indian tradition the term *sahagamana* is used to refer to those women who have died by entering the funeral pyre of their husbands. *Anumarana* is the term used for those women who make a special fire for themselves after the cremation of their husbands. In either case, in Indian tradition, self-immolation of women after the death of their husbands has been generally termed by historians as *sati*. *Sati* takes place mainly because of society's expectation for a chaste wife to join her husband after his death to continue to help cancel out the karmic effects of his shortcomings in this life, and to continue to assist him through making her ascetic powers available to him in the other world. *Sati* has never been compulsory in India and various examples can easily be found illustrating the efforts of relatives to dissuade widows from committing to the act. Incidents of *sati* have always drawn the attention of foreigners, whose reports have helped to create a powerful, widespread condemnation.[1] Obviously within Hindu tradition, there is considerable ambivalence about the practice.

In a traditional and extreme view, self-immolation is the ultimate expression of a woman's *dharma* (duty) in relation to her husband. In modern India, the intense controversy surrounding a 1987 *sati* in Rajasthan quickly became a lightening-rod political issue between progressive women's movements on the one hand who, for obvious reasons, expressed their outrage that such an event could occur in modern India more than a century and a half after it had been legally banned by the British, and Hindu fundamentalist groups, on the other hand, who saw in *sati* a symbolic assertion of traditional Hindu cultural values, values which they see as under siege by the secular and Western forces of modernity. In general, Indian society is both patriarchal and hierarchical, like the majority of societies in the world. There is no doubt that practices of *sati* have reduced women's position further. But the history and context of *sati* occurrences, and the circumstances in which *sati* came to be validated, present a more complex picture than the general assumption of *sati* as a cultural imposition on hapless women.

In the following pages, I will discuss what is generally understood as the history of *sati* and what other factors should be taken into account in order to gain a more holistic picture of how and in what context *sati* came to be practiced in Andhra. Contrary to conventional understanding, I show that the origins of the tradition of *sati* lie not in northwest India, but in the far south of the subcontinent, and that the original ethos of *sati* is related closely to the cult of *gramadevatas*. This argument serves as a background to the stories of Andhra *satis*, who are called *perantalu*, that I present in this chapter. To illustrate the meaning and worship of *perantalu*, I will discuss the individual and collective significance of these stories and then compare the symbolism within these stories with the *sati* traditions of neighboring Tamilnadu and Karnataka, as well as with Rajasthan. By doing so, my intention is to show how the Andhra *perantalu*, in its cultic worship, shares more similarities with its neighbors in Tamilnadu and Karnataka than with the clan-based *sati* understandings of Rajasthan. With examples of non-*sati* events, I will also show how the word *perantalu* incorporates a wider meaning than *sati* and how it adds a local affectation to these cults.

Much Treaded Path. A. L. Basham once stated that the tradition of *sati* should be understood as part of a very widespread complex of custom and belief, arising independently in many parts of world, and not as something uniquely Indian.[2] Even within India, the practice seems to have had different origins. Although Greek observers in 316 BCE mention witnessing the wife of a military general belonging to a tribe referred to as Kathaioi burning herself along with her dead husband, this incident has been treated by historians as an isolated event.[3] What most scholars conventionally have agreed upon is that the practice of *sati* began in the fifth century CE in the northwestern parts of India and that its cult was institutionalized by the eighth century CE.[4] The *Padmapurana*, written around eighth century CE, can be quoted to corroborate this view.⁵ It mentions how the authors of *smriti* literature competed with each other in promising generous rewards for *satis*.⁶ In spite of these references in *smriti* literature and in the *Padmapurana*, there is still a need to reassess the origins and the logic of encouraging the act of *sati*. It is true that the tradition of *sati* took on its own life in colonial times, when the events of ritual burning multiplied. Although many indigenous rulers had discouraged this custom in the past, British opposition and its legal prohibition of the custom in 1829 met with defiance by many widows who were adamant in carrying out their wishes for *sati*. But the reasons for the apparent rise in the number of ritual burnings varied across regions. For instance, there seems to have been an economic motive at work in Bengal, where wives inherited the property of their dead husbands. According to Kane, with an eye to capturing this inheritance, relatives sometimes encouraged the wives of rich Bengali *brahmins* to join their dead husbands.⁷

Bringing the South into the Mix. Since the more abstract and religious understanding of *sati* tradition is largely based on Sanskrit sources, I will direct my attention further south. The earliest epic story that refers to *sati* in south India comes from the Tamil epic *Cilappatikaram* of the second century CE.⁸ In this story, the heroine, Kannaki, leaving her palatial home in the Chola kingdom, faithfully follows her unlucky and fickle husband, Kovalan, on an arduous journey, even after all his failings to be truthful to her. In the events that ensue in the Pandyan city, Kovalan falls victim to a royal goldsmith's machinations to frame him for theft, leading to the ruler's unfortunate misjudgment against him. Seeing her husband's dead body, Kannaki turns into a rebel who curses the king, sets fire to the city by hurling her left breast as a fiery ball and climbs a cliff to join her husband in heaven. Thereafter, Kannaki assumes the name Pattini (the "chaste wife"), after her cult was instituted by a Chera ruler. The statement in the *Cilappatikaram* sums up why Pattini is an important goddess:

> It is true that even the gods adore her—[the one]Who adores no god but her husband.⁹ [brackets mine]

In this story, which is also preserved in other folk forms, Kannaki exceeds the standards of what later understood as *sati*, the loyal wife, not just in following her husband into death, but in taking on the responsibility of proving her husband's innocence. Pattini is still venerated in parts of south India and Sri Lanka by those who seek long fruitful marriages and family welfare.

The *Manimekhalai*, another Tamil epic belonging to the same period, not only explains how and why chaste wives prefer to die after losing their husbands, but also mentions the practice of *sati* by all four castes.[10] The explanation of why widows resort to self-immolation, or torture themselves to death, comes from another contemporaneous Tamil text, the *Purananuru*, which says that while a chaste wife is a source of power to the king, a widow possesses dangerous negative power. Such widows should take extreme measures to shun all worldly pleasures.[11] Urn burials of the first century BCE corroborate references in this text in which a woman requests a potter to make a burial urn for her dead husband spacious enough so that it will hold her bones as well.[12] The idea of women possessing sacred power articulates not only ancient Tamil society's ambivalence toward females, but also shows how this notion got into mainstream Indian tradition. George Hart demonstrates, with examples about how the Vedic tradition was liberal in regard to women's expression of sexuality and then how the more restrained Tamil notions of womanhood, along with the necessity to control her sexuality, started to influence Sanskrit tradition as early as the third century BCE. [13] In this context of Tamil influence, Hart has pointed out that Greek visitors noticed the aforementioned incident of *sati*. Considering the widely prevalent custom of wives immolating themselves on the death of their warrior husbands throughout the world and in west Asia, it is difficult to say with certainty that it was Tamil influence that prompted the Kathaioi tribe to follow suit. But what is important to note is the significant change in the attitude of *smriti* literature toward women and its insistence on controlling their sexuality. The following quotation is an example of how the Tamil concept of an ideal wife was appropriated by *Manu Dharmasastra:*

> She who, controlling her thoughts, speech, and acts, violates not her duty towards her lord, dwells with him (after death) in heaven, and in this world is called by the virtuous a faithful wife (*sadhvi*). [14]

Sacrifice, however, was not the express prerogative of women per se in Tamil society. In fact, evidence shows that it was the male warrior cult that coerced women to follow suit. There are certain features that indicate specifically how values of the Tamil warrior cult permeated other social and religious arenas. While good men give their lives in guarding the land and its ruler, the good women sacrifice themselves in protecting their husbands and families. In turn, this culture of self-sacrifice soon spread beyond the Tamil country. *Sangam* literature from the early centuries of the Common Era reflects the intense nature of the belief that by sacrificing oneself in war, one's place in heaven could be assured. This belief became so powerful that even those who died naturally were ritually sliced with swords before they were buried.[15] Also, the merit of sacrificing oneself in war, or in devotion to one's king, who was also seen a divine incarnation, was extended to the self-immolations performed in devotion to one's chosen deity.[16] Both the *Cilappatikaram* and *Manimekhalai* mention that self-immolation in fanatic devotion to a chosen deity was not uncommon at this time.[17] Males are mentioned as the participants in these forms of sacrifices.

A female's role as protector of the family was thought to be empowered by her *ananku* ("chastity").[18] *Sangam* literature states that an attractive girl from the time of her puberty possesses sacred power, which she has to protect by maintaining her chastity before and after marriage, refraining from all forms of immodesty (speaking but few words, cultivating patience, and expressing no sign of harshness even when her husband sees other women). Her sacred power, maintained by her singular devotion to her husband, protects him while he is alive but causes destruction on his death, which can be attenuated only by her entering the fire. Kannaki's story fits into this context, although it is atypical from other examples mentioned in the literature.

The similarities between a typical *sati* and other forms of self-immolation in Tamil society can be uncanny. Dennis Hudson, in describing the act of self-immolation by a Saivite Chola king depicted in *Sangam* literature, compared the saint-king's act as equivalent to that of *sati* performed by a warrior's wife when her husband has died away from home.[19] This drives the point home that while Tamil men, inspired by the ideology of earning honor and heaven, were ready to give their lives either in the war or in devotion to their ruler or chosen deity, so Tamil widows, worrying about their own negative power, chose self-immolation to claim the same honor and heaven.

Influences Traced. Although there are copious references to *sati* in early Tamil literature, there are very few stone memorials that have come to scholarly attention. On the other hand, in the neighboring state of Karnataka, there are several inscribed stone memorials from around the fifth through the seventeenth century that were raised for those who were either killed in war, took their lives in devotion to Siva, died from the asceticism of the Jaina tradition, or mounted the funeral pyre of dead warrior husbands.[20] If we rely on this evidence, we can surmise that Karnataka was a fertile ground for the hero cult that received influences from Jaina sources in the north and Saivite and *sati* sources from the south. Most of the *sati* stones speak of *sati* performed by wives of dead rulers and soldiers.[21]

The sheer number of *sati* memorials in Karnataka testifies to the prevalence of the *sati* tradition in this region. In spite of this prevalence, there is very little evidence to show that these historical *satis* were worshiped, except for a couple of rare exceptions.[22] In the first case of deification, the wife performed *sahagamana.* The second instance was a case of *anugamana*: a betrothed woman of a dead man. There are single-room shrines to these two *satis* in their respective villages; the shrines have no doors, as closing the shrine is believed to offend these deified women. Each of these *satis* is known locally as *"mastyamma"* (the Sanskrit word *maha sati* means "great wife," used colloquially as *masti* to which the Dravidian suffix "amma" is added).

The first *mastyamma* is worshiped annually with animal sacrifices in the same fashion as *gramadevatas*. A special feature of her festival is the wedding of the goddess to her husband, after which the village farmers undertake their first plowing of the fields to start their agricultural activities with blessings from the goddess. The marriage ritual of the goddess is analogous to that of other popular goddesses in Tamil Nadu: Durga, Minakshi of Madurai, and Kamakshi of Kanchi, all of whom get married to Siva. While these goddesses were thoroughly influenced by Saivism, ordinarily, in *gramadevata* festivals, the sacrificial animal is considered the husband of the goddess, who through the sacrifice is able to unite with the goddess.

The second *masti* shrine is ritually attended to by a widow who acts as its priestess. Only prepubescent girls and unmarried men are allowed to visit this goddess, for there is a fear that the presence of married men and women would offend the goddess's purity. The married men and women of this village do not have any confidence that they can get any blessings from this *masti*. Even the fact that girls, after their puberty, are not allowed to go to this temple indicates the inauspicious nature of this goddess. Although called *masti*, this goddess is basically treated as an inauspicious widow, a belief that is similar to the ancient Tamil understanding of a widow's chaste power as negative. The local assumption might be that the virgin widow in question had experienced a self-imposed widowhood for a brief period before she immolated herself and thereby accumulated negative power. In the case of first *masti*, Karnataka villagers make sure that the inauspiciousness of the *masti* is driven away by marrying her annually with her husband and thereby revivifying her auspicious quality each year. Otherwise, it appears that the *masti* cult in Karnataka is not associated exclusively with the function of assisting families with their welfare, which is a primary focus of a Rajput *sati*.

This prompts us to ask what exactly is the tradition of Rajput *satis*. Rajasthan, although regarded as the forerunner of the *sati* tradition from the fifth century CE, actually possesses evidence only from the seventh century.[23] In relation to the erection of memorials, Chattopadhyaya, quoting Hermann Goetz, argues that it was the central Indian tribal memorial pillars for the dead that influenced the Rajputs in Rajasthan to use stones for their dead warriors and their wives, the practice of which also gave sanction to *sati*.[24]

Lindsay Harlan has explained how this cult was systematically articulated in Rajput traditions:[25] a woman becomes *sati* through the acquisition of virtue or goodness—that is, through the realization of *sat*, a term that not only means "goodness," but also "being." *Sat* is realized through three stages—*pativrata*, *sativrata*, and *satimata*. During the first stage a woman vows to protect her husband by serving him and performing ritual vows on his behalf. If he predeceases her, she is regarded as culpable. Here she escapes the suspicion of sin by taking a vow to die for him. At this point she enters the second stage. A true *sativrata*'s death occurs, it is believed, when the moral or ascetic "heat" or *sat* that she built up while holding her vow as a *pativrata* explodes into flames when she mounts her husband's pyre. It is her purifying "heat" that immolates her. In the process of dying, the *sativrata* becomes a *satimata* or *sati* mother. As a *satimata,* she is capable of protecting not only her husband, but her earthly household as well. As a transcendent being, the *satimata* personifies auspiciousness or good fortune (*saubhagya*), for she remains married to her husband eternally. No matter how many *satis* might have occurred within a given Rajput family, they all referred to as a singular *satimata*, a deified feminine condition of powerful, purified, fertility and protection. *Satimata* is an institutionalization of this deification functioning as a dominant, transcendent being while reflecting *pativrata* selfless morality. She not only protects the family, but also patriarchal values by issuing warnings to women about their negligence in their service to their husbands. She is worshiped for all domestic functions and rituals, especially the ritual of the first tonsure of children. Although it is said that some *satimatas* in Rajasthan function "in some respects like a village goddess (*gramadevata*)," it is clear that this is an exception to the rule and even when a *satimata* acts like a *gramadevata*, those functions are added to her essential responsibility of caring for families.[26]

Rajput notions of *sati* seem to have improvised upon the earlier concept found in Tamil literature. When an ancient Tamil woman died, it was feared that her negative power would inhibit her ability to join her husband in heaven. But a Rajput widow, on the other hand, redeems herself and her husband with her accumulated chastity to live in heaven for eons. Except in Kannaki's case, whose sacrifice and resolve to clear her husband's name in this world gives her special powers to curse the king, there are no references at this early period to show how women possess any power to curse their relatives if they have been dissuaded from committing *sati*. But then the story of Kannaki is out of the ordinary. The story recounts instant deaths of pious wives upon the death of their husbands. But Kannaki, another pious wife of this category, postpones her death until she seeks justice for her dead husband and until she meets him in his heavenly body. The story's popularity in oral and written traditions must have helped to hone the concept of what is presently known in the Rajput *sati* tradition. The concept of a chaste devoted wife accumulating *sat*, a sort of virtuous electricity in her body that she discharges at will, has an uncanny similarity to Kannaki using her breast as a fireball to gut the whole city of Mathurai.

The Andhra region, because it is contiguous to Tamil land, through peasant migrations and the expansion of the Chola kingdom, not only shared and participated in many aspects of Tamil culture, but also acted as a conduit to pass on influences coming from the north. At the same time, the region also seemed to have developed its own culture that separated it both from the north and the south, of which the memorials and hero stones point us to a northerly direction.[27] A lone piece of sculptural evidence from a second to third century CE *sati* at Nagarjunakonda (Guntur District) shows Andhra's awareness of the *sati* concept on the one hand, and on the other its reluctance to adopt it into its culture.[28] What is remarkable, however, is that this incident predates the first occurrence of *sati* reported in Rajasthan. By the twelfth century, we notice the regular mention of the practice of *sati* in the context of widely spread self-immolation ideology coming from within and outside of Andhra. First, in the ninth century, we know that tribals of southern Andhra who served local rulers were reported performing *kilgunte* ("self-immolation") to show their utmost loyalty to their rulers. According to this tradition, loyalty to one's ruler was considered as the highest form of virtue and, as such, the loyal servant would die before the dead body of the master was laid on the earth. Rulers such as Vaidumbas, Nolambas, Chalukyas, Kakatiyas, Reddys, and the Royas of Vijayanagar not only encouraged this tradition, but also gave it much publicity. A soldier by the name of Achkunjundu offered his head to the *grama-devata*, Padlasani, seeking victory for his king, Birudugamaya.[29] As a way of promoting this tradition, memorials were set up for those who died practicing *kilgunte*. This is known from inscriptions of the ninth century and later, issued during the time of the Vidumba rulers in Chittoor and Anantapur Districts.[30] These two districts constitute part of the tribal area of Andhra. With the aim of attracting people to clear woods and to promote the cultivation of land, rulers in Andhra also honored those who were killed as they fought wild animals, in the act of protecting cattle and humans.[31]

Starting from eleventh century, Telugu literature and inscriptions mention militant Saivite sects promoting the culture of self-sacrifice and self-torture as an extreme devotion to deities such as Bhairava, Virabhadra, and Kali.[32] The devotees of militant Saivism, of course, included women as well.[33] But there is no evidence that the devotees who sacrificed their lives have been deified.

It is during the height of the hero cult that we note incidents of *sati* being performed by royal and noble women.[34] For example, it is stated in a twelfth-century work that after her husband sacrificed his life for the sake of the king, his wife performed *sati*.[35] A record dated 1210 from Nidubrolu (Guntur District) reports that a wife of a treasury officer to the ruler Gonka II joined her husband in *Sivaloka* (what Saivites considered heaven).[36] The reason for the death of the officer was unknown, but nonetheless, his wife gave up his life on his death. However, this does not mean that acts of *sati* in Andhra were totally homegrown. The chronology and the geographical spread of the incidents of *sati* in the regions of Karnataka, Maharashtra, Madhya Pradesh, Gujarat, and Rajasthan indicate the floating and mixing of ideas that culminated in the formal cult of *sati*, which by this time was validated by tracts of Sanskrit literature, such as the *Padma Purana*.[37]

In Andhra, at least from the thirteenth century, commemorated stones called *mastikallu* (Tamil word *kallu* for stones is added to the colloquial Sanskrit word *masti*) constructed as part of *virakallu* (hero stones) point to influences coming from Tamil and Sanskrit sources.[38] The word *mastikallu* was common in this period to both the regions of Karnataka and Andhra, showing not only a shared inspiration, but also the cultural influences that they received from both the north and south. The Sanskrit tradition, as I have argued earlier, itself imbibed regional and tribal traditions containing strong components of Tamil notions of chastity and loyalty. By the thirteenth century, royal wives joining their dead husbands who had fallen in the war seems to be commonplace, as mentioned in the literary work *Palnativiracharitra*, which recounts a destructive war that ensued two centuries ago between two cousins claiming the same kingdom.[39]

In any case, the incidents of *masti* occurred only in certain situations when husbands had died in chivalry.[40] Telugu literature, imitating the *puranas*, promotes *masti* in fifteenth-century works such as *Kasikhandam* and *Rukmangada Charitramu*.[41] These works prescribe *masti* to chaste wives so that not only *satis* and husbands, but also seven generations of natal and agnatic families will go to heaven. These assurances must have generated a percolator effect, as there is evidence that lower strata imitated this act not only to secure heaven in the other world, but also to claim honor for their families in this world. The custom became more popular by the Vijayanagara period (fourteenth to seventeenth century), as noted by Mahalingam.[42] Inscriptional evidence in Andhra indicates that since the fifteenth century, *satis* were referred to with the Telugu word *perantalu*, which means a married woman (who is auspicious). The change of the usage of *sati* to *masti* and then to *perantalu* in Andhra shows its gradual transition from a pan-Indian to a local character. Unlike in north Indian *sati* stones, the size of many *sati* figures in Andhra, such as the ones coming from the Kurnool District, are as large as their husband's stones, probably to honor the acts of *sati*s as equivalent to that of their husbands' chivalry.[43] The feudal polity seemed to have vested interests in promoting *sati*, as noted by Reddy:

> The sati memorials also have the feudal basis. Subordination, loyalty and...[a] subservient mentality promoted [the] sati custom in the medieval times. The relationship became almost homologous to over lord-vassal relationship or deity-devotee relationship. The wife or the life partner has to follow her dead husband by throwing herself into the funeral pyre.[44] [brackets mine]

As part of the process to encourage people to cultivate the wilderness, rulers honored those who were killed putting up resistance to wild creatures.[45] Many stories of *sati* incidents that I collected from the Vijayanagar period (fourteenth to seventeenth century) mention husbands being killed by tigers.[46] While the cult of hero worship faded away by the twentieth century, the worship of *perantalu* remained strong.

Perantalu in Their Own Milieu. In its local usage, the word *perantalu* has a somewhat wider meaning than *sati*. If a married woman immolates herself for some noble cause (not only after the death of her husband but for another reason during his lifetime), or if she is killed at any time during her married life, she is worshiped as *perantalu*, an auspicious one. Note that unlike the word *sati* (chaste wife/good woman), the word *perantalu* is generic to any woman who is married as well as unmarried. As discussed in the previous chapter, deified virgins are also often labeled as *perantalu*. In this sense, the connotation of *perantalu* implies the more independent nature of Andhra women with regard to *sati* than is seen in the Rajput version of *sati*. Also, unlike Rajput tradition, the Andhra *sati* is now a phenomenon of the past, as no occurrences have been recorded in the past century or so. On the other hand, like in most parts of India under colonial rule, despite protests from villagers and the illegality of the practice since 1829, there were incidents reported from almost every district of Andhra Pradesh after the ban. In this chapter, I will provide representative examples of *sati* as well as other self-immolations of married women, in order to compare any common traits between these two categories and to capture local cultural expectations and understandings. I will also examine each *sati* incident to assess its independent as well as shared traits with the northwestern understandings of *sati* traditions.

Motifs of Cow and Bull The three instances I cite below show the affiliation of *perantalu* with cattle and bullock, recalling these important motifs of *gramadevatas*. In honor of Achchamma *perantalu* in Pungur (Nellore District), an annual festival is held in which cows are invited from the surrounding villages to receive water, flowers, and cooked pulses. One of the cows is picked to fast for this occasion and is given the first offering. Achchamma *perantalu* is believed to possess the cows that come running to their offerings. In this sense, the ancient notion of cow as fertility goddess continues to apply to emerging goddesses like Achchamma.

Represented by three smooth stones set up in a shrine under a tree like some *gramadevatas*, Amasamma *perantalu* in Chinnarajupalle (Anantapur District) also has an established association with the bullock. When Amasamma's husband died while passing through the village, Amasamma requested the villagers of Chinnarjupalle and its neighboring village, Yerramballi, to arrange the funeral. A pair of bullock were used to cart the firewood needed for the funeral pyre. Before joining the funeral pyre herself, in recognition of the services given by the bullock, Amasamma instructed the villagers not to put the bullock to work during her annual festival. Since then, the villagers have followed her instructions to avoid any unforeseen calamity to them or to their bullock. To secure her blessings in the annual festival, the villagers bring decorated bullock carts to circumambulate her temple. While Amasamma shares her association with the *gramadevata* in her form and ritual, she also displayed the aspects typical of *satis* by giving instructions to villagers before entering the fire.

Narayanamma *perantalu* of Gudur (Nellore District) is also associated with cattle, but in a different way from Amasamma and Achchamma, as the elaborate details that led to her *sati* indicate. These details also tie her to *gramadevatas* in a very direct way. During the Vijayanagara period, when Gudur was under the Palegars (military chieftains), young Narayanamma's husband, Papireddy, traded in cattle. One year during the annual ritual to the *gramadevata*, a woman devotee possessed by the *devata* asked for a young healthy bull to be stamped in her name. Papireddy, who was assigned to this task, set off with his brother and a group of friends and found a good animal that was fit to be the bull of the goddess. On the way back, Papireddy fell ill and survived only until he got to Gudur to see the celebration of the stamping and the inviting of the new bull on behalf of the *gramadevata*. Narayanamma, who was still young and living in her parents' home, heard the news. She not only convinced her parents, but also, it is told, due to her supernatural power, sought the needed permission to become *sati* from the Palegars (chieftains) of the Vijayanagar period, whose messengers met the village servants half way.

FIGURE 6.1 Narayanamma *Perantalu*

It is often the case in *sati* incidents that the rulers needed convincing reasons before they allowed widows to immolate themselves. After performing *sati*, Narayanamma's image was installed in a shrine (Figure 6.1) and is approached by those who have lost cattle, as well as by young women seeking long married life. Her image with just two hands, one holding a *trisula* and the other in *abhaya mudra* ("fear not" gesture) is pleasing in appearance. As part of worship, a *kalasa* topped by a blouse piece is placed in front of her image, indicating her fertility. It is believed that those married women who clean her courtyard, sprinkle water, and decorate it with *muggu* (patterns drawn with rice flour on prepared ground) every morning will be blessed with marital longevity, family prosperity with children, grandchildren, good crops and good milk. As discussed in one of the previous chapters, the patterns of *muggu* are to honor the goddess and connote the same in the case of *gramadevatas*.

The age-old relationship between the fertility goddess and the bull is resurrected once again in the above two stories, identifying the *sati* as the fertility goddess. The logic appears to be simple in that the bull has played a prime role in agricultural societies for centuries until the recent introduction of mechanization. Narayanamma's husband's death in finding a village bull for the *gramadevata* and Narayanamma's subsequent *sati* performance makes her eligible to take on multiple functions other than just finding cattle, such as ensuring good crops and milk. Narayanamma also fits into the *sati* tradition, in which she acquires miraculous power by taking a vow of joining her husband in death. With this power, she gets permission from the rulers to perform *sahagamana*, an act that enables her to bless women with long married lives.

Tree and Serpent. In addition to cows, bulls, stones, and rocks, the *satis* of Andhra, like *gramadevatas*, are often seen in the forms of tree and serpent. Timmamma, a daughter of one of the chieftains under Vijayanagar rule who was born in 1394 CE, performed *sati* in her native place, Gutibylu, in Anantapur District, after the death of her leprosy-stricken husband, Gangaraju Bala Veeraiah.[47] In spite of dissuasions from all quarters, she is said to have arranged her own funeral pyre with four dry branches of the banyan tree and burnt herself into ashes. One of the branches was unburned and eventually grew into a big tree covering an area of five and a half acres of land. A small temple was constructed for Timmamma *perantalu* and an annual festival is still celebrated there. In spite of the presence of the shrine, the banyan tree is still viewed as the incarnation of Timmamma. The tree is referred to as Timmamma Marrimanu ("Timmamma's banyan tree").

The serpent or *naga* is another prominent symbol that *satis* share with the *gramadevata*. In *sati* temples, the image of the *naga* is often present. The story I now relate serves two purposes. It shows that, although rare, incidents of *sati* did occur among the lower castes. It also reflects how deceased persons are viewed, especially when they are victims of some kind of injustice either by fate or by some human act. In either case, they are now perceived to be living in the form of serpents. The legend is as follows.[48] A *madiga* caste man, along with his wife and son, were in the service of a local chieftain in Koruprollu Mallavaram (East Godavari District). One day when he was cutting down a tamarind tree, the *madiga* fell down and died. His wife performed *sahagamana* on his funeral pyre. Later people of the village believed she was transformed into a serpent and lived in an anthill beside a village well. One day, the lone son of this deceased couple, while passing by the well, was bitten by a snake and died instantly. People believed that the snake was, in fact, the form of the dead boy's mother who had come to take her son to her world by turning him also into a snake. This incident was seen as a validation of the goddess living in a serpent form in the anthill. People still worship this anthill as *perantalamma gudi* (temple), where they seek fertility and the enforcement of justice. This nameless *perantalu* resembles some *gramadevatas* who go by the generic name *uramma* (village mother). Here the understanding of this *perantalamma* who lives in serpent form legitimates her status precisely because of the serpents' affiliation to *gramadevatas*.

Another instance of the *naga* form and *sati* that I relate here involves a further mix of cultic features. When Nagireddy was killed by a tiger in Yerragunta (Anantapur District) while guarding his small field, his wife Chinna Nagamma collected his bones, prepared a pyre, and burned herself. Her deification was not realized until she appeared to a passerby named Rangaswamy, to whom she promised a boon, one that would allow him to acquire the power of cleansing away the sins of those people he touched. He was seen as possessed by the goddess. This incident led to the worship of an anthill at the cremation site on Tuesdays and Fridays and also the celebration of an annual ritual. As Chinna Nagamma *perantalu* is believed to remove barrenness, offerings to her included small silver cradles and snake hoods. The snake's hood, as with Ellamma, is considered a fertility symbol. When children are born, their tonsure ceremonies are held as a fulfillment of their vows. This ritual of holding tonsure ceremonies at the goddess's shrine resembles one of the functions of Rajasthani *sati* cults.[49] In the context of Andhra, the name Nagamma ("snake mother)" must have helped to forge the identity of Nagamma with the goddess Ellamma.

Enforcer of Social Norms. The following story illustrates the *sati*'s role in establishing caste hierarchy.[50] This story resembles certain myths relating to *gramadevatas* in establishing the norms of caste hierarchy. On hearing of the death of her husband, Buchamma, from the *kamma* (agricultural) caste, hurried to find out what the arrangements were for his funeral, only to find that the arrangements were already made. She intercepted the plans and mounted the funeral pyre with him after making proper arrangements, and she prevailed on reluctant bystanders to set the fire. Four days later, when a piece of her unburned cloth was pushed with a stick into the fire pit by a passing *madiga* caste person, Buchamma took offense and appeared to her father in a dream asking him to purify her; thereupon, her father retrieved her jewels and gold *mangalya* (wedding symbol) from the ashes and set them up in a pot for worship. Thereafter, a stone image of Buchamma was made, and a shrine was built to worship her as *perantalu*.

To put into context Buchamma's feelings about purity, one needs to more fully understand the nuances of caste in Andhra, which work somewhat differently from that of northern parts of India. As Burton Stein explained, historically, certain warrior groups, in the absence of the *kshatriya* class, who were categorized as *sudras* by *brahmins*, occupied very powerful positions.[51] These groups, belonging to many agricultural castes, such as the *Kamma* mentioned above, considered themselves as high-caste in relation to the other castes who served them. Here, the act of Buchamma signifies the confirmation of her caste status in society, on the one hand, and on the other, glorification of her natal and agnate families. My own intimate connections with my aunts and other female relations and extensive interviews with elders of my families reveal that until the middle of the twentieth century, the women of land-owning families in most *Kamma* villages observed the practice of *ghosha* (not being seen in the public).[52] Possibly, this practice might have been adopted due to the impact of the Persian Nawabs ruling in western Andhra until 1948. Wealthy agricultural caste families in Andhra saw themselves as equal to the ruling class (second only to *brahmins* on the caste ladder) and, as such, emulated the ruling Muslim class in keeping women indoors. On rare occasions when these women ventured out, they covered their heads and shoulders or traveled in covered coaches, accompanied by their men. They learned folk songs through their elders and their entertainment consisted of listening to various storytellers and singers who wandered from house to house, praising the chivalry of various heroes including *perantalu*. The stories of devotion of *perantalu* to their husbands served as an inspiration for this class of women. The rituals they performed, such as worshiping Bodemma and Batukamma for long happy marriages, influenced their mindsets so that their ideal goal was to lead a chaste wifely life, assuming the role of caring for husband and his parents.

When *sati* had become more prevalent, women like Buchamma, who understood themselves as devoted wives, were eager to fulfill their roles. They were intent upon proving their chastity by following the rules of purity and pollution and the rules of caste hierarchy. Losing a husband, for these women, on the one hand connoted delinquency in their duties, and on the other meant the potential of living a disgraceful life as an inauspicious widow whose face was not to be seen favorably by others. So, Buchamma, who took her life to avoid this inauspiciousness, naturally would have believed that the touch of a low-caste person leads to contamination. In the village's annual festival, Buchamma is offered a sheep with the belief that she, like a typical *gramadevata*, will be appeased by the blood flow. The assumptions might be either that her intolerance toward the low caste is interpreted as that of a goddess needing appeasement with a blood sacrifice, or that her antecedent association with the agricultural caste made her want an animal sacrifice. Her prejudice reminds us of the enraged pox goddess Gangamma at her discovery of her husband's identity as an untouchable. Goddesses like Buchamma and Gangamma act as enforcers of the traditional hierarchical value system.

Another trajectory in this story is Buchamma appearing in her father's dream. The dead person appearing in the dreams of family members or the villagers is a recurrent theme that we have seen before and will continue to see in the following chapter as well. A dream is a liminal state of consciousness and thus a congenial time and space for linkages between the living and dead. The dead appearing to the living in dreams indicates that the power of the deceased is still potent in the minds of the living. The cult of the goddess is born in a dream as an exercise of religious imagination.

Cultic Spread and Influence. I have discussed earlier that the *sati* cult in Andhra was introduced within the context of the practice of other forms of sacrifice. But the stories I relate show that the practice of *sati* continued even after other forms of self-immolation disappeared. What factors nourished this tradition? How did *sati* continue into the nineteenth century, even after the disappearance of the warrior cult? I quote Bruce Tapper to show how Telugu women of farming communities have kept the ideology of the chaste wife alive even in the late twentieth century.

> Women themselves internalize this ideology of the ideal wife as one who, through her devotion and faithfulness to her husband, keeps him alive and herself in an auspicious status. Consequently, stories about faithful wives, *pativratalu*, such as the story of Balanagamma [a story of a chaste wife whose abduction is similar to that of Sita in the *Ramayana*] are among the most popular themes of stories followed by village women. Interestingly, all of this amounts to an ideology of marital stability and female subordination in a society in which, as we have seen, there are considerable tendencies to marital instability, and both real and imagined challenges to male dominance.[53] [brackets mine]

In addition to listening to stories like that of Balanagamma, women intently heard the stories of *sati*s sung by professionals in the annual rituals to these goddesses. Following are some examples to show how the process of the perpetuation of *sati* goddess traditions gained wider popularity.

Tirupathamma *perantalu* in Penuganchiprolu (Krishna District) has received devotees for the last two centuries from the districts of Khammam, Krishna, and Guntur. The story of Tirupathamma not only mentions her devotedness to her husband, but also the difficulties she faced at the hands of her mother-in-law.[54] Hailing from the village of Anigallapadu and descending from the *kamma* caste, she was married to Goparaju of Penuganchiprolu. When Goparaju was killed by a tiger while grazing a cow given to his wife as a gift from her parents, Tirupathamma, who was also in the fields at that time, brought his body home. After obtaining permission from the district collector, she performed *sati*. Her image was made soon after and installed in a temple for daily worship. Unlike the cases of other *perantalu*, the ritual to this goddess is held twice a year. Fowls are sacrificed to the goddess.

Tirupathamma *perantalu* became so popular that branches of her temples began to appear in other villages as early as a century ago. In one instance, her devotee was a tribal by the name of Banathu Chandraiah who, on receiving instructions from the goddess, brought her image to his village, Kanur (Krishna District), and installed it in a big temple constructed especially for her.[55] The annual celebration at this temple is attended by neighboring villagers as well.

One of the reasons for the popularity of Tirupathamma *perantalu* seems to be the difficulties she encountered with her mother-in-law. It was a tradition that married women at a young age came to live with the husband and his parents. In winning her husband's affections, a young woman found herself in competition with her mother-in-law, who controlled household affairs. Often it is the case that a jealous mother-in-law subjects the daughter-in-law to various hardships. Tirupathamma's difficulties at her mother-in-law's hands are elaborately narrated by the professional storytellers at her annual festivals, in the process capturing the empathy of women in the audience who can identify with the role of a victimized daughter-in-law. Another element that captures the attention of women is Tirupathamma's ability to carry her husband's dead body home, despite her most distressed state.

While the above instance gives a sense of the spread of one particular *perantalu* cult, the following example illustrates other factors that contribute to the geographical spread and perpetuation of a particular *sati* cult. A few centuries ago, Veeramma, a beautiful girl, was born into a Yadava (cowherd) family in Vuyyuru (Krishna District). She was married in her youth to a cowherd boy, Veeraiah, of the same village.[56] Karanam, the head of the village, was attracted by her beauty and made advances. Veeramma resented this and complained to her family members. Fearing the power of Karanam, the parents advised her to comply with his demands. But Veeraiah encouraged his wife not to comply with Karanam's advances. Taking a grudge against Veeraiah, Karanam had him murdered. Veeramma cursed her parents and swore that she would swing in her next birth above the ruins of Karanam's house; in other words, she would dance on his grave. Later, in spite of the objections from her parents and villagers, with her supernatural power, she sought permission from the Nawab who was passing by and entered the funeral pyre of her murdered husband. Both her natal and agnate homes were then converted into temples where the two images of the victim couple were worshiped. Over the years, the rulers of the region patronized this celebration. The growing popularity led to the recent construction of a bigger temple with a *dhwajastambha* (flag post) installed in the front with *brahmans* chanting Vedic liturgy. Probably because of this *brahmanical* element, sacrificial birds and animals are just displayed to the goddess and later are sacrificed in private homes. In other ways, the worship and annual fortnight festival is similar to that of *gramadevatas*, in which the neighboring villages participate (Figure 6.2).

Quite clearly, this is a story of a woman's resistance to the social pressures of family and local political power. Her story portrays her as being enraged before her death, somewhat similar to how a *gramadevata* defends her interests, and like many *gramadevatas*, she is propitiated with the sacrifice of rams, swine, and cocks. Normally, we think of *sahagamana* as a symbolic statement of traditional Hindu values. But in this instance, the act constitutes a rebellion against the village head, whose belief seemed to be that he could gain a hold on women like Veeramma. By joining her husband in his death, not only did she make herself unavailable to Karanam but also showed her preference to be with her husband if not in this world then in the next. Indeed, I would argue that she is a goddess born of anger and rebellion on the part of women,

FIGURE 6.2 Festival to Veeramma *Perantalu*

women who were unjustly victimized and share the same traits as the goddess Pattini, which I have discussed above. But the aspect of cursing those who obstruct the widow committing *sati* shares the belief in pan-Indian tradition that people are afraid of upsetting a *sati*'s decision of self-immolation in any manner. In the annual ritual, her story is recited by *yadavas*, the professional singers for many *gramadevata* rituals as well. Branches of Vuyyuru Veeramma shrines are being built in other parts of coastal Andhra, including a major shrine in Narakodur (Guntur District). The popularity of her cult shows how her victimization captured the hearts of many. Over the years this goddess inspired other *sati* events, such as the ones described below.

It is said that about two centuries ago, a married Yadava woman by the name of Buchamma from Mudunur (Krishna District) worshiped Vuyyuru Veeramma, Siva, and Parvati with devotion.[57] When her husband died of fever while grazing the sheep, Buchamma obtained the permission of her parents and mother-in-law and performed *sahagamana* in a plot in their fields. In a typical fashion for a *sati*, Buchamma proceeded to the site accompanied by music and jumped into the fire pit. From the pit, she uttered the name of her husband thrice, replied to the grief-stricken audience thrice, and died. On the place of the fire pit a temple was constructed.

Belonging to the same caste as Veeramma, Buchamma of Mudunur followed in Veeramma's footsteps. The details of her *sahagamana* show how the ritual has acquired a normativity. Later, another woman in the village by the name of Pilla Kotamma performed *sahagamana* in the same manner as Buchamma. A tank next to Buchamma's temple was constructed in memory of the *satis* performed by both Pilla Kotamma and Buchamma. Pilla Kotamma also has a temple of her own. But the annual ritual for these two deities, along with the *gramadevata* Gangamma, is performed at the same time with animal sacrifices. This annual festival is analogous to the annual festivals held in some villages, grouping all *gramadevatas* as sister goddesses. During this festival, fasting barren women with wet clothes prostrate themselves before Buchamma's image until, in ecstatic fits, they see her. Sometimes, their prostrations can last as long as three days. As a result, those who beget children name them after Buchamma. In this instance Buchamma functions like a Rajasthani *sati*, in which she is seen as imbued with specific powers to bless women with fertility. On the other hand, unlike Rajasthani *satis*, these *perantalu* like Buchamma do establish their own cultic followings.

Ambivalent Satis. In spite of the great respect and devotion given to *satis*, there is an element of ambivalence that comes through in their deification. An example of this is seen in the deification of Papamma from Singavaram (Kurnool District). When villagers killed her husband, thinking that he was stealing hay,

Papamma, who was known to be a pious woman, made arrangements to perform *sahagamana*. When worried villagers begged her not to self-immolate, she tried to reassure them. She asked them to place two stones on the spot of her sacrifice to represent her husband and herself. As a result of worshiping them, they would gain prosperity. Later, villagers erected a temple on the very spot of her *sati*, which is a distance of one-eighth mile from the village. The villagers believe in her power to keep the village safe from pestilences. They attribute village prosperity to her kindness. In the annual festival, a lacquer image of Papamma is made to take around the village in procession before it is thrown into the fire. Like many *perantalu*, Papamma receives animal sacrifices.

In this story, the element of ambivalence starts with the fears expressed by villagers that her death might bring calamities upon the village. The reason for this might be a feeling of collective guilt, as well as the fear that Papamma might be planning revenge. Whether or not it is intentional, Papamma's assurances only establish their belief that her restless spirit needs appeasement in the form of worship. Her worship started right on the spot outside the village, an ideal location for a *gramadevata*. The ritual procession of her image and getting rid of it at the end of the festival serve the same purpose as in several *gramadevata* festivals. The ritual message is clear: the villagers give her a fitting festival and afterward they hope that she will go back to wherever she resides in the other world and leave them in peace for the remainder of the year. The villagers are satisfied that they are worshiping Papamma as instructed and the goddess is keeping her promise of taking care of the village's welfare. In the final analysis, however, ambivalence remains, typical of a *gramadevata* who needs periodical sacrificial appeasement to rejuvenate her protective energies.

Besides the other example of Papamma from Singavaram (Kurnool District), the second example comes from Raghavapuram (Krishna District). There, it is said that Peddamma lived as a chaste wife and possessed some magical powers: through holding hot coals, she would not be burned; or while walking in the rain, she would not get wet. As a chaste and devoted wife, when her husband Nagireddy died, she performed *sahagamana*. After this, images of this couple, along with the image of a *gramadevata*, Ankamma, were installed in a temple. As I mentioned above, it is not unusual to have a husband's image installed next to a *sati* for worship. Nor is it unusual in deified women's shrines to add an image of a *gramadevata*. In these cases, the focus of worship is always the *satis*. What is unusual in Peddamma's case, however, is that her annual ritual contains not just animal sacrifices, but various forms of pain-inflicting asceticism, or even the torture of animals, a rare form of cultic behavior done to appease some angry *gramadevatas*. In the case of Peddamma, sometimes a goat or a man is fixed to a wooden stake by means of iron hooks pierced through the back. Then the goat or the man is taken on a circumambulation around the temple. Afterward, the goat would be sacrificed to the goddess. This violent form of practice was seen as necessary by the villagers, probably because of Peddamma's death by burning herself alive. On the other hand, her *sati* status is also acknowledged in a very different ritual followed by women devotees who clean their houses, observe fasting, and offer fruits, flowers, vermilion, and turmeric to married and unmarried women as part of their efforts to seek longevity for their marriages.

In the case of Akkamma *perantalu* from Mukkamala (West Godavari District), the ambivalence is articulated differently. All couples in the village, before their weddings, will go to ask for the blessing of the goddess out of fear that their marriages will not be successful otherwise. In this case, Akkamma has some element of the young *masti* from Karnataka whose presence is feared by the married.

A *Sati*'s Vengeance. The following story of Yerukamma *perantalu* from Srungavarapukota (Vizianagaram District) is another instance of belief and fear in the power and miracles of a chaste woman after she joins her husband on the funeral pyre. Around the middle of the eighteenth century, when young Yerukamma's husband from the *dasari* (a middle rank) caste was killed by a tiger in the fields, neighboring farmers recovered his head and sent word to Yerukamma. Wailing, Yerukamma went to the Raja of Vizianagaram to request a small piece of land to cremate her husband. The king rejected her request, inciting her curse that he should go blind. Knowing her power, the king granted her three acres of land, the act of which restored his eyesight. Yerukamma then prepared a funeral pyre and jumped into the *gundam* (fire pit) with her husband's head in her hands. A temple in front of the *gundam* was built to worship her. All the villagers, except for *vaisyas*, participated in Yerukamma's worship. This disrespect on the part of *vaisyas* enraged the goddess and so she cursed them as well: at any *vaisya* weddings in the village, the bridegroom would die before the marriage celebration was over. The curse came true when soon thereafter a young *vaisya* bridegroom died during his wedding festivities. Since then, *vaisyas* have joined in the worship of Yerukamma, although they never again have celebrated any of their marriages in the village. Devotees believe that the goddess gives them strength to cope with any difficulties in their lives. The annual ritual for Yerukamma *perantalu* is held for twelve days and neighboring villages also participate. However, no animal sacrifices are made to this goddess.

Like the previous three stories, this story reflects a degree of ambivalence. But in this case, the ambivalence started before the *sahagamana*, when the angry Yerukamma punished the king. Her vengeance continued afterward and is thought to be in play to this day in that the *vaisyas* are forced to worship her and yet they do not seem to trust her completely. In exacting her vengeance, Yerukamma shares a characteristic of Rajasthani *satis*, who are feared from the time they determine to do *sahagamana*. In Andhra, Yerukamma is an anomaly.

Doubly Heroic Deeds. Performing *sahagamana* requires great courage. Even securing approval requires heroism, as several stories of *perantalu* indicate. The story I relate now purports to have taken place under British rule, when *sati* was illegal. This story reveals tensions between local and pan-Indian traditions, on one hand, and western insensitivity, on the other. This story and similar stories are preserved in the form of folksongs among some villagers.[58] Here, the heroine's name is Kamamma and the story starts directly with the death of her husband, Marayya, sometime during colonial rule. When Kamamma expressed her wish to be a *sati*, her brother-in-law, Reddanna, discouraged her because of the near impossibility of getting permission from various officials and that she should think about a long and possibly fruitful future awaiting her. But Kamamma wanted to exercise her will anyway. As a beginning, she approached the wife of the town headman who advised her to remarry her brother-in-law in order to avoid widowhood. Kamamma was angry at this suggestion and cursed the headman's wife. Subsequently, the headman's wife was stricken with a severe stomachache and was on the verge of dying. In distress, the headman pleaded with Kamamma to retract her curse. In return, he would construct a temple for her and would conduct a festival every year (after she became *sati*). He gave her permission to go on to other higher officials. Kamamma then went to the collector of the district in Kakinada (district headquarters), who was very difficult to deal with. The song says that in similar early cases he subjected women to severe tests before he granted permission for *sati*. In Kamamma's case, he made her stand in hot sand under the blazing fire of the sun. For seven days Kamamma was not given food or water. Meanwhile, arrangements were made for her husband's cremation. When the body was being cremated, Kamamma stopped breathing. Thinking that she was dead, her brother-in-law and her uncle were asked to take her to Samarlakota. On the way back she got up and vowed that she would get permission from the higher authority in Chennapatnam (the capital of the province) to undertake *sati*. However, first she went to her husband's cremation ground and took hot burning coals along with the bones of her husband in a pot and planted a branch of the pipal tree. She asked her uncle to take care of the plant and went into her house, closing the doors behind her. She then appeared in the dreams of the head of the state and got permission from him for her cremation with her dead husband's ashes. Kamamma got her wish fulfilled and is considered by the common folk as a heroine who did not waver in her determination at any odds.

The story reveals a number of interesting aspects. The superimposition of the *sati* ideal on native traditions is very clearly seen, when Reddanna, her brother-in-law, tries to convince Kamamma that she is yet to see and enjoy worldly pleasures and that she would be assured of his brother's property. Further, when Kamamma complained that she didn't want to lead the life of widow, the headman's wife asks her to marry her own brother-in-law. In agricultural castes in Andhra, remarriage for widows is not unusual. But *sati*, which became such a pan-Indian ideal, was powerful enough to alter or modify local traditions. Moreover, in the wake of foreign rule, *sati* functioned as a political or cultural tool to articulate native defiance. Also, common people very much wanted to see their victory over their lords or the administrative heads in some form. *Sati*s who defied the laws laid down by foreign rulers were viewed as heroines, while they were also worshiped as goddesses for their heroic conviction to join their husbands in the burning fire. Lastly, *sati*s, who as women could hardly exercise their will in a patriarchal world, also might have seen this as an opportunity to defy the societal norm and establish their will once and for all. If indeed this was the case, their act becomes doubly heroic.

Anomalies. The following story of Ammaneni Siddhamma from Ramasagaram (Nellore District) is an example of the choice made by some affluent families.[59] The reason I want to indicate the specific nature of this *sati* worship is to show the possibility of some cults taking on a *brahman*ic form. Siddhamma, as in many instances of *sati*s, was still young and living with her parents of the Duttaluru family of the *kamma* caste in Arambaka near Kalahasti in Tamilnadu. When her husband was killed on his way to see her from his village, Veera Bayallu (Nellore District), she performed *sahagamana*. Later, she appeared in the dreams of her natal and agnate families, asking them to set up a shrine in a village where families of the Duttaluru and the Ammaneni live. They found Ramasagaram as this place and set up a temple with a grove behind and a pond in the front. The two affluent families offer daily worship to the deity through *brahmin*s, believing that she chose them to fulfill their family's desires. The villagers, on the other hand, remained aloof from this goddess. In this sense the goddess with her *brahman*ic form remained distant to the villagers.

Sati, as I have explained earlier, can be performed either *sahagamana* with the husband or *anugamana* separately, after the cremation of her husband. In either case it is understood that a *sati* is consumed by fire. Although rare, there are cases of *satis* not consumed by fire but just buried alive, as in the case of Adi Lakshmamma in Kuricherlapadu (Nellore District).[60] It is said that Adi Lakshmamma was traveling with her husband and when he died, she opted to be buried alive in a tomb. This live burial is called *jeevasamadhi*. She is worshiped annually with animal sacrifices.

Non-*Sati* Perantalu. As discussed earlier, *perantalu* incorporates not just *satis*, but deified virgins and those who experience deaths while in married status. In order to compare and contrast with *satis*, I will consider the following examples, in which the protagonists are women whose husbands were alive at the time of their own immolations.

The same theme of rage that appears in *sati* stories continues in the following story, although the circumstances are very different. The significance of this story, unlike others, is that in this story, as reported by Elmore, Lingamma, a *sudra* caste woman, worked along with her husband in a rich man's house; when some valuables went missing in the house, and Lingamma's hand was suspected, the employer was ready to take legal proceedings against her; Lingamma, humiliated, ended her life by jumping into a well. [61] Despite the troubles he experienced in his household and despite Lingamma's appearance in his dreams threatening worse disasters, the employer did not institute a proper worship for her. But when Lingamma appeared as a devil to villagers and brought a scourge of cholera, finally the employer, along with the rest of the village, prepared Lingamma's image and enshrined it in a well-built temple. Here, Elmore reports that although Lingamma appeared as a devil to villagers, because she died as a married woman, they worshiped her as *perantalu*. There is yet another case reported by Elmore where a married woman named Usuramma ("of good deeds") died naturally before her husband and was deified as *perantalu* because of a threat she had made known to bring trouble to the village unless she was worshiped.[62] While the stories of these two married women, Lingamma and Usuramma, establish the point that performing *sati* is not a precondition to becoming a *perantalu*, it also features one interesting aspect that these *perantalu* have: an ambivalent status of causing trouble to the village unless they are propitiated. While a typical *gramadevata* shares this ambivalence, there is also a specific reason for the notion of attributing malevolence to the dead soul of a married woman. Lingamma's temporary status as a devil who will eventually be accepted as *perantalu* stems from the belief that any young woman who dies as a married woman is believed to be capable of returning as a ghost to haunt relatives. Describing special funerary rites held for a married woman, Bruce Tapper, in his study of rural parts of Visakhapatnam district, reports how a dead woman is propitiated for her "auspicious wifehood [from being a] *perantalu* on the one hand and on the other the suspicion of her returning as a ghost because of her strong ties to her family and especially if she left children behind and her jealousy if her husband brings a new wife." [63] In the funerary rights for the *perantalu,* a woman who acts as a surrogate to the dead woman makes a mud image to which all the auspicious offerings are made. Making sure through the surrogate that the dead woman is appeased and will not return, the image is thrown into a tank at the conclusion of the veneration.[64] This ceremony shares similarities with the annual ritual of a *gramadevata,* in which, after the conclusion of the ritual, the goddess image is taken to the outskirts of the village and thrown away. This is a symbolic gesture of asking the *perantalu*/goddess to go away with their offerings and leave the village in peace. This feature is analogous to the ritual burning of *sati* Papamma's image.

Instances like this prompt us to ask what particular fears the villagers have about these dead women. In Lingamma's case it was clearly her anger toward her employee that caused her to take her life. The villagers might have perceived that this suppressed anger made her spirit wander as a devil needing appeasement to harness her positive energy. Interestingly, for very different reasons, villagers presumed that their lack of gratitude to Usuramma's good deeds created anger in Usuramma. In this sense, Usuramma shares similarity with the *sati* Peddamma, whose annual ritual contains a gruesome feature.

Following now is a story that shows how the family members of a dead woman control the deification process. The story shares some similarities with Sidhamma, except that in this case it is the death of young married woman and not a widow. At age twelve in 1953, Sarojini, a married girl of the *kamma* caste, was burned while cooking in her parents' home in Thotacherla (Krishna District). When villagers saw her in their dreams asking for propitiation, her affluent grandfather built a temple for her with a *brahmin* priest to attend on her ritually. On the priest's advice, the grandfather set up an eight-faced *dhwajastambha* and a lion vehicle facing the image of Sarojini in the shrine. This indicated that Sarojini was the incarnation of the goddess Durga. Although the temple soon received many devotees from the village and outside, the family started experiencing troubles. According to Sarojini's younger surviving brother, the installation of a deified woman as the form of Durga with Vedic rituals caused calamities in his family. He tried to have a second installation of the image, adding images of Ganapathi, Kumaraswami, and Hanuman as well so that the energy of the goddess would be diffused. But the calamities never stopped. On seeking advice from some *brahmin pundits,* he submerged the image in a river. Now the temple is an abandoned site without any image inside except for a *trisula,* a remnant, probably held by the image. The neighbors believe that the goddess would have protected them if worship continued. Like in the case of Ammaneni Siddhamma and virgin goddesses, such as Pydamma and Mutyalamma, this affluent family decided to have *brahmanic* worship to the deified *perantalu*. But a family descendant decided to stop the worship, believing that it was causing harm to their family. Unlike the case of Pydamma and Mutyalamma, Sarojini's cult was not taken over by the public, leaving her fate entirely in the hands of her family. The reason for this seems to be that the villagers were hesitant to take over the worship that was initiated by a *brahmin* priest. So, Sarojini's cult remained aloof. In this instance, Sarojini's cult shares similarities with Siddhamma's. In both cases, the villagers felt that these cults grew out of their hands, and that they no longer need their attention.

The following story of Pydithallamma from Anakapalle (Visakhapatnam) is antithetical to *sati* in some ways. But nonetheless, Pydithallamma is worshiped as a *perantalu*, as she died a married woman. Pydithallamma, the only child in a rich *kapu* family, was given in marriage to her uncle in the same village. Pydithallamma, not finding any happiness in her marriage, spent her time in worshiping Lord Rama. Stricken with sorrow, she renounced food and sleep and died. Later she appeared in her father's dream asking him to construct a temple for her and to celebrate an annual festival. According to her wish, the father constructed a temple and appointed a *yadava* woman to offer daily worship.[65] An annual festival is celebrated in Pydithallamma's honor, in which the poor are fed and clothes are given to a *sadhu* (ascetic). The devotees in the neighborhood trust her help in their times of distress. In this case, although Pydithallamma was never devoted to her husband, people seemed to understand that she was not allowed to fulfill her role as a wife. Because she died unable to fulfill her role as a wife and mother, people tap her latent power in the same way as if it were from a virgin goddess. Since the circumstances of her death were grievous, women devotees believe that the goddess understands their grief and will help them to find strength.

Atypical *Perantalu*. As in a story related earlier involving worship in a tomb, a Muslim named Tanishabibi is worshiped by Hindus under the name of Masanamma, thus reflecting how Hindu devotees have made her their *amma*. The story begins by reporting that during the time of the Mughal emperor Aurangazeb, a pious woman by the name of Tanishabibi in Ullipalle (a former village close to present Sanjamala in Kurnool District) had the ability to predict the future. During Aurangazeb's invasion of the south, Jayaram Reddy, an estate ruler of Sanjamala, went to her to ask about the fate of Golkonda Nawab and learned that Nawab had been taken as prisoner by Aurangazeb. Soon, Reddy was summoned by Aurangazeb, after Tanishabibi had told him that he would be imprisoned without trial. On Reddy's departure, in spite of her pregnant state, Tanishabibi undertook fasting for Reddy's release. On the eighth day of her fasting, Tanishabibi announced to the community that she and the twins she was carrying would die for the welfare of their king and then the situation would return to normal. As per her prediction, she and the twins died. Later she appeared in a dream to Aurangazeb, entreating him to release Reddy. Aurangazeb released Reddy and gave him a black marble stone on an elephant for the construction of Tanishabibi's *samadhi*. It is said that on his return, Reddy embraced the religion of Islam, transformed his temple into a mosque and constructed a *samadhi* for Tanishabibi with the black marble stone (Figure 6.3). Next to her *samadhi* stands a neem tree, as if to affirm her deified status as a mother. Both Hindus and Muslims of Sanjamala take part in her annual festival in which the public is fed. In this story, Tanishabibi's sacrifice was not as a *sati*, but her devotion to the ruler and to the people of the estate was equivalent to the devotion of one's own husband. It is for this reason that for Hindus she is an "*amma*" while for Muslims she is "bibi," but for the whole village community she is a savior and her *samadhi* has become a shrine.

Stitching Together. To recap what I have presented above and to reiterate the significance of the Andhra *perantalu*, I argue the following. In the

FIGURE 6.3 Tanishabibi *Samadhi*

south, the concept of a wife sacrificing her life after her husband's death arose from two different but related aspects: 1) the culture of sacrificing one's self in extreme loyalty to rulers and later on in ecstatic devotion to gods; 2) the Tamil notions of a woman possessing sacred power and how it turns dangerous when she loses her husband unless she controls it by either dying along with her husband or living an impossibly austere life. In considering the dating of relevant sources, the practice of dying with one's husband in the south would seem to predate the practice of *sati* in the north. In sum, it appears that although *sati* in the north took its origins in the custom of *jauhar*, the ritual was later emulated by the wives of warriors and others as well because of the atmosphere of self-sacrifice created by the warrior cult on the one hand and on the other, the burden of chastity that women were supposed to display through self-sacrifice. Rajput culture served as an appropriate breeding ground to develop the concept of *sati* further. The practice of *sati* that emerged was validated by *brahmanic* literature as a pan-Indian tradition. In the context of other forms of sacrifices, the *sati* tradition spread to various regions such as Karnataka and Andhra. Because of their location, these regions received influences both from the north and the south.

In Andhra, the *sati* tradition spread mostly among middle and lower castes as a way of bringing honor to caste and family. Telugu literature supported Sanskrit literature in announcing generous rewards for those women who became *satis*. When it came to deification, these *sati* cults shared similarities with the cults of deified virgins and married women. That the common term *perantalu* was used to identify these deified women, including *satis*, proves that in the view of common people they function more or less the same way. The question that still remains is why a *perantalu* is worshiped.

As in the case of Pattini, as well as in the worship of Rajput *satis*, married women in Andhra believe that worship of *perantalu*, including *satis*, prolongs the lives of their own husbands in such a way that if they die as married women, they will bring auspiciousness into their deaths. I have observed and participated in the rituals of widows as well as those who have died as married women. A married woman's death is celebrated by distributing symbols of marriage to other married women as a blessing from the dead woman.[66] If a woman outlives her husband, she can keep her marriage symbols signifying auspiciousness until the day of *pedda karma* when her husband's spirit departs from this world. This usually falls within a fortnight or so of the day of death. The evening before *pedda karma*, she is supposed to take a purifying bath, wear all auspicious signs of a married woman as though to appear as a *perantalu* to the married women in the village who visit her to celebrate her last signs of auspiciousness and to dispel any inauspiciousness that arises later from seeing her as a widow devoid of marriage symbols.[67] The following morning, she takes an early-morning bath and wears all of her auspicious signs, after which she is taken to the site of her husband's cremation, or near a tank where she is stripped of all of her decorations, a way to declare her widowhood. She will take yet another bath to transform herself into a widow, an inauspicious one. From then onward, she is an official widow who is not a welcome sign to any auspicious events, such as the puberty ceremony held for girls, weddings, etc. Every married woman dreads thinking about this last ceremony and considers it as very unfortunate. Technically, all those women mentioned in these stories were still considered as auspicious women when they joined their husbands in their deaths. So, unlike as it is in Karnataka, wives who still were not technically widows before their deaths are considered auspicious and thus are called *perantalu*, the auspicious women who are perpetually married. This might be the reason why even those who die as married women, as in the case of Lingamma and others, are treated in the same way as a *perantalu*. But at the same time it is clear that the ancient Tamil notion of widows possessing negative power is as strong in Andhra as it is in Tamilnadu. To avoid this patriarchal notion of negative power, *satis* lived their lives like a penance. Consequently, they accumulated power that could be used either for protection or for destruction. This is why devotees in Andhra appease *satis* with sacrificial offerings. In this sense, Lingamma, an angry goddess for a different set of reasons, also needed the same kind of appeasement.

Bayly has noted the spread of Andhra *sati* cultic veneration to Tamilnadu, while referring to the migration of *vaduga* warrior culture.

Women who die by sati (self-immolation on their husbands' funeral pyres) also came to be worshipped as power divinities in many parts of south India. . . . Like the proliferation of goddess cults in south India, the spread of this tradition was associated with the enhanced power of local predator groups and with the immigration of "Vaduga" warrior cultivators from Andhra and the Deccan. A typical example is the shrine known as the Vadugachaikovil near the hill fort site of Tirumayyam, which once divided the home territories of the Ramnad Marava chiefdom and the Pudukkottai Kallars: as the name suggests, the temple or kovil on this spot is devoted to a Vaduga woman who was deified after committing sati. In the seventeenth and eighteenth centuries sati became widespread among the Kallar and Marava ruling lines; until recently royal sati sites were still important places of pilgrimage in the former warrior chiefdoms.[68]

Bayly's finding supports my argument about how some cults of *perantalu* transform into *gramadevatas*, those goddesses that she has referred to as "power divinities." The spread of the Andhra *sati* cult to Tamilnadu, as Bayly confirms, shows how the tradition of borrowing between Tamilnad and Andhra historically turned into a two-way street.

The cults of *perantalu*, therefore, closely resemble in symbol and ritual other village goddesses rather than the clan-based *satis* in Rajput tradition that are more esoteric in nature. It is undeniable, though, that *perantalu* symbolizes the auspiciousness that arises from a perpetual married status. But the wider meaning of *perantalu* itself explains that for a woman to be a *perantalu*, *sahagamana* is not mandatory. The blessing of married women, though a function of *perantalu*, is not primary. As such, their acts of sacrifice have been interpreted not for the benefit that they bring to their husbands, nor just as the benefits they bring to their families, but rather as sacrifices benefiting the entire village. The primary quality of a giving nature that these women displayed to their families while living was where their energy was focused. The worship of these women is an attempt to tap this great resource so that these women adopt the whole village as their family. So, the females, whether they are virgins, married women, or widowed, all inherited this potential for sacrifice, an obligation they were born and bred into and are expected to carry out beyond their current lives. In this critical sense, these women are hypostasized symbols of feminine power, power often denied to women in social reality. The phenomenon of *perantalu*, historical women raised to the status of goddesses, represents one more instance in a tradition that is unrivaled in the manner in which the feminine is worshiped in the form of the goddess, though the power of women remains socially repressed in most everyday settings.

Deifying Victimized Women

SACRIFICES AND MURDERS

IN THE LAST two chapters, I have focused my discussion upon the deification of women, very young and not so young, those who have died either of natural causes or from their own volition. In this chapter, I shift to a discussion of stories about those women whose lives ended at the hands of others. The reasons for these premeditated deaths are varied but chiefly revolve around two aspects: attempts to please a supernatural power or punishment of the victims for their perceived violations of moral or social codes. The former reason constitutes a ritualistic act that has been universally identified as human sacrifice. In the latter instance, the deaths are actually killings, either rationalized capital punishments or, in some cases, intentional calculated murders. Deification of these victims is dependent upon the circumstances in which they died.

Sacrifices. Sacrificing humans, animals, and birds has been a religious rite observed in many ancient cultures. The rationale for sacrifice has always been the same: to please the gods. There is pictographic evidence to show that both animal and human sacrifices were known in the Indus River Valley civilization. For example, one of the terracotta tablets from the Indus period shows the sacrifice of a buffalo. Here, a human being is shown placing one of his feet between the horns of the buffalo's head while piercing the animal with a *trisula*. Another person who sits in the lotus posture wearing a mask watches.[1] In another seal, a human sacrifice is shown with a deity standing by in what appears to be a sacred fig tree, looking down on the kneeling worshiper, who seems to be offering a human head placed on a stool next to him.[2] We also know that the *Rig Vedic* people believed in the notion that sacrifice gives birth to life. Indeed, the following hymn from the *Rig Veda* (X. 90) became one of the most favored accounts of creation.

When gods prepared the sacrifice with Purusha as their offering,
Its oil was spring, the holy gift was autumn; summer was the wood.

They balmed [sic] as victim on the grass Purusha born in earliest time. [10]
With him the deities and all Sadhyas [11] and Rishis [12] sacrificed.
From that great general sacrifice the dripping fat was gathered up.
He fanned the creatures of the air and animals both wild and tame.
From that great general sacrifice, Richas and Samahymns [13] were born:
Therefrom the metres were produced, the Yajus [14] had its birth from it.
From it were horses born, from it all creatures with two rows of teeth:
From it were generated kine [cows], from it the goats and sheep were born.
When they divided Purusha how many portions did they make?
What do they call his mouth, his arms? What do they call his thighs and feet?
The Brahmin [15] was his mouth, of both his arms was the Rajanya [16] made.
His thighs became the Vaisya [17], from his feet the Sudra [18] was produced.
The Moon was generated from his mind, and from his eye the Sun had birth;
Indra and Agni [19] from his mouth were born, and Vayu [20] from his breath.
For from his navel came mid-air; the sky was fashioned from his head;
Earth from his feet, and from his ear the regions. Thus they formed the worlds.
Seven fencing-logs had he, thrice seven layers of fuel were prepared,
When the gods, offering sacrifice, bound, as their victim, Purusha.
Gods, sacrificing, sacrificed the victim.[3]

In this hymn, the word "Purusha" literally means "person" or "man," which in this mythical context is the primordial "man." So, the differentiated and variegated natural, social, and cosmic existence is understood as coming alive through a sacrifice. In other words, for *Rig Vedic* people, sacrifice is what generates life. The annual rituals for *gramadevata* still practiced in contemporary times share in this basic concept. But this does not mean to say that the primary source for the sacrifices at the village level derived from the *Rig Veda*. As mentioned before, sacrifice in all its forms has been practiced at least from the Indus times. As I will show in the following pages, human and animal sacrifices were practiced by various isolated and wandering tribes. In previous chapters, I have repeatedly noted that in the annual ritual held for the *gramadevatas*, animal sacrifices are made and blood is mixed with cooked food and then sprinkled over the fields for renewal and regrowth. While this particular concept of sacrifice leading to new life is basic in many *gramadevata* rituals, sacrifice at the village level also signifies many other concepts, a number of which have converged over the years. I shall now ferret them out.

Among many famous goddesses known for their tribal origins is the goddess Kamakhya of Assam. The *Kalika Purana* of the ninth to tenth century, dedicated to the glorification of goddess Kamakhya, mentions buffalo and human sacrifices as a form of ritual to Kamakhya and to other *saktis*.[4]

In Andhra, as I have recounted in previous chapters, many tribal cults and practices eventually became mainstreamed as a part of the amalgamated Hindu tradition. As noted in the fourth chapter, several tribal goddesses either became *gramadevata*s or were assimilated with popular goddesses such as Durga and Kali. The *Simhasana Dvatrimsika*, the twelfth-century Telugu work mentions tribal peoples like the Gond or Koya practicing human sacrifices in their temples devoted to deities like Bhairava, Virabhadra, and Kali, all deities who became identified eventually with militant Saivism.[5] These temples, most of them located in isolated and desolated places, are called *champudu gullu* ("killing temples"). Indeed, there is one particular inscription that mentions a devotee offering the goddess Bhattarika his flesh from nine different parts of his body before he offers his own head.[6] Bhattarika later came to be identified as the goddess Durga. The *Yasasthilaka*, a Jaina literary work written by Somadeva in the tenth century, mentions the worship of Durga in remote places where blood sacrifices were regularly made by female priests.[7] These references point to how "blood-thirsty" goddesses of tribal cults were either eventually embraced by militant Saivism or became identified with the cults of Durga, Kali, or one of the *gramadevatas*.

Early 20th c. ethnological studies refer to human sacrifices practiced by wandering and isolated tribes, such as the Lambadas and Thodas.[8] The sacrifices made in these instances also resemble the similar ritual sacrificial appropriation of power reflected in contemporary *gramadevata* myths and rituals.

There are some scholars like Susan Bayly who have located this appropriation of power in relation to a long tradition of south Indian rulers engaging in the practice of consuming the blood of their enemies. Relating a historical incident in which the ruler of Chandragiri (Chittoor District) receives his enemy's head from one of his chieftains and in return grants him a wife from among his enemy's women, along with new titles and new lands, Bayly states that the "consumption of the dead chief's blood and body is now complete, and the new dominion is confirmed through these newly constituted blood and kinship ties."[9] Bayly draws a correlation between how Telugu and Tamil rulers treated their subjugated enemies and the sacrifice of animals for *gramadevatas*. She notes how in both instances the head of the victim is offered in sacrifice. In the instance of the *gramadevata* cult, she notes how "the worshippers offer up a severed buffalo's head in token of her [the goddess's] victory."[10] Agreeing with Heesterman, Bayly finds a connection of this tradition with Vedic sacrifices:

This notion of dominion being created out of blood sacrifice and dismemberment is very pervasive in the Tamil and Telugu country. It is closely related to the ancient Vedic theme of divine sacrifice: in the Vedas the gods create the world and its human social order through an awesome and ambivalent act of sacrifice.[11]

Madeleine Biardeau takes a similar route in her elaborate study, in which she not only connects Vedic sacrifices with that of the *gramadevata*s, but also, in quoting the *Mahabharata*, likens that epic war to a sacrificial ground where "the warriors refer to their opponents as victims of the sacrificial war."[12] These motifs pointed out by Bayly and Biardeau are, no doubt, seen similarly in many *gramadevata* rituals, especially in the cases of goddesses who have acted as guardian deities to rulers. The myth of the *Devimahatmya* and its local and somewhat crude versions told in many Andhra villages, such as the version about Renuka fighting on behalf of her father, help to identify the roots of this myth in the incessant wars waged by political rulers. However, this does not mean that the sacrifices offered to various *gramadevata*s in annual rituals or in other contexts convey the same meaning as described above. Variation in myths, rituals, and worship from village to village and region to region, as I demonstrated with examples in chapters 2 and 3, show that the rural religion is much more complexly layered than just a continuation of one particular tradition, whether that is Vedic or pre-Vedic or a combination of both. How the tribal tradition of Kilgunte was embraced by mainstream society, as mentioned in the previous chapter, shows how these occurrences from time to time add complexity to ritual practices. Moreover, ritual cults in Andhra villages are not simply reflective of the celebratory and malicious behavior of victorious politicos who exacted tribute.

Some scholars argue that the present form of *puja* can be traced to human sacrifices. There is some truth to this if one considers the way some devotees treat coconuts as a substitute for the old practice of sacrificing human heads. Whether or not this is true, in one of the deified *sati* temples located in Gudur (Nellore District), I came across three coconut offerings painted as human faces. These are now understood as demons that the *gramadevata* has subjugated. This idea reminds me of the ferocious form of Kanaka Durga drawn on the natural rock of Indrakiladri in Vijayawada, in which she is sucking on demon heads that are shown floating on her tongue.

Unlike the display and promotion of chivalry and heroism by respective rulers in pre-modern times, very little in the form of evidence about the practice of human sacrifices is found in Andhra. However, I will refer to a couple of incidents that are known as "volunteered sacrifices." In the first of these two, a woman by the name Musalamma from the village of Bukkarayasamudram voluntarily sacrificed herself when the bund of the irrigation tank in Anantasagaram

(Anantapur District) was breached. This event is recorded on a memorial stone.[13] The bund, in this instance, came to be known as Musalamma *katta*. Musalamma has since been worshiped annually on the day when the waters are released for irrigation. Animal sacrifices are then made to this goddess. The second instance involves an irrigation tank in Rayalacheruvu (Anantapur District), which was constructed at the instigation of the Vijayanagar ruler, Sri Krishnadevaraya (1509–1529 CE). The legend says that when the construction was finished, the tank leaked. The worried ruler had a dream that the leak would stop only if a human was buried alive in the embankment. Hearing of his dream, it is said that one of his daughters offered herself up as a victim. This story is so popular that it is claimed as the story of other large irrigation tanks, such as the one at Punganur (Chittoor District), which was built in the territories ruled by Rayas.[14] Although it can't be true that several daughters of this one particular ruler offered themselves to be sacrificial victims for the well-being of these tanks, it does tell us that in this part of Andhra during this time, there was a prevalent notion that a human sacrifice would help prevent a disaster such as the breaching of these huge tanks.

What causes this particular belief is a question worth probing. One direction to look within is the history of this region, where the tradition of *kilgunte* was prevalent from the ninth through the fifteenth centuries. It is possible that this tradition of giving life in devotion to some person or to some cause promoted the concept of humans sacrificing themselves voluntarily and heroically. But there are incidents in which victims seemed to have not known about the fact that their lives were about to be sacrificed. So, another explanation could be the perception that the goddess Ganga was perceived as hungry and would take the entire population of the village if not appeased. Sacrificing a human was thought to mollify her. Probably for this reason, Gangamma is worshiped in many villages of Chittoor and Nellore districts in her fierce form with rituals that include the impaling of animals on stakes attached to a cart that is taken in procession. The ferocity of the goddess is experienced by villagers when there are heavy rains and the tank water overflows or breaches its bunds to submerge villages with little notice. In this case, Gangamma is like a smallpox goddess who, without appeasement, is understood as capable of wiping out villages in her great wrath. Uncontrolled, Gangamma is perceived to revel in taking human lives through inundations. The sacrifice of one human is believed to be the cure to save many. A conclusion that can be derived from this and other similar sacrifices is that there was an assumption that the goddess Ganga would be pleased, especially if the victim was a young woman.

Usually this cure comes in the form of a divine order and dreams are often the medium through which the orders are delivered. As discussed in the last chapter, dreams are a liminal state of consciousness, and as such, serve as a linkage to the world that is beyond the realm of the living, whether it is the world of the dead or the divine. The realms of the dead and the divine are not always neatly defined. In cases when dead ancestors become divinities, the line between the realm of the dead and the divine is blurred. When the human efforts of keeping Gangamma in her confines are futile, it is expected that she will reveal herself to explain what satisfies her appetite. Possession and dream are two of the most important mediums through which a goddess conveys her messages to devotees. Two of the following incidents of human sacrifices occurred as a result of dreams.

In Dornipadu (named after a person known as Dori of the *yadava* caste who lived in Kurnool District) there was an instance of human sacrifice performed in order to secure the functioning of a well.[15] Frustrated after digging a stepped well a hundred feet deep and not finding water, Dori dreamed of the goddess Ganga, who asked him to sacrifice his seventh daughter-in-law, Akkamma, in her bridal attire. The next day, after Akkamma was asked to dress up, Dori decorated her with jewelry and sent her to bring the pot that he said that he had forgotten in the stepped well. The instant when Akkamma picked up the pot at the bottom of the stepped well, water gushed, drowning her in it. The stepped well since then has been known as Akkamma *gadhi bhavi*. The lore is that until a few decades ago, those who wanted to borrow jewelry for wedding functions went to the well and prayed to Akkamma imploring her to help and jewelry has appeared on the steps of the well. The "borrowed jewelry" is always promptly returned. In addition, Akkamma is offered food and prayer by those locals who are beginning to learn how to swim.

Akkamma shares some features of the goddess Gangamma. Ganga, as the goddess of waters, is also the deity of the *yadava* caste who protects their cattle. So, it is not so surprising to learn that Dori, as a *yadava* person, dreamed that the goddess Ganga was craving a human sacrifice in exchange for providing the life-generating water. Note that young Akkamma shares the quality of bearing the generative capacity of giving birth to new life. The concept of giving one's life to sustain many lives is recurrent here. Akkamma, who was decorated before her drowning, is analogous to a sacrificial animal that is decorated and worshiped before being sacrificed. But in Akkamma's case, the preliminary act of "worship" did not occur, as the sacrifice itself was kept as a secret from her. While Dori was guilty of deceiving Akkamma, the villagers share this guilt as well. This commonly shared guilt is what translates into paying respects to her as an innocent victim following her sacrifice.

The story of the sacrifice of Chinnamma in Thenepalle (Chittoor District) more or less resembles that of Akkamma's. The difference here is the victim was not a daughter-in-law but a daughter.[16] In this case, it was a *reddy* caste man who engaged in constructing an irrigation tank but encountered the problem of a leak in the bund. He dreamed of a stranger telling him that he could prevent the leak only after he had sacrificed his daughter. It is not clear whether he offered his daughter Chinnamma with or without her approval. It probably was the latter, because her approval would have been made public in such a way that the detail would have gotten into the legend in the same way as it was in the story of the great ruler, Raya. Nevertheless, Chinnamma, like Akkamma, possessed the generative power that was dormant. So, Chinnamma, after her sacrifice, in the same way as in the case of Akkamma, has become a deity for villagers who offer her worship once a month on a Friday. This goddess, also like Akkamma, is understood as a passive victim who was not aware of her fate.

In a third case from Eradikera (Anantapur District), the details are different. To begin, the innocent victim was a pregnant woman (named Bandamma) from the *madiga* caste.[17] Her sacrifice seems to have been a result of a collective decision made by villagers, who bought the victim from a poor family. It might have been assumed that a pregnant woman who was carrying new life in her womb would make for a more potent sacrificial offering to the river goddess. When the tank in Eradikera was breached, a deal with Bandamma's family to give a land grant on behalf of the village was struck and the pregnant Bandamma was sacrificed. The land grant is still enjoyed by Bandamma's family descendants. Nevertheless, villagers believe that in the early morning hours, the crying of Bandamma's child, and Bandamma singing a lullaby, can be heard. Soon after the sacrifice, Bandamma was worshiped in a temple set up on the tank bund.

The circumstances leading to the sacrifice of Bandamma are a clear case of collective guilt. In addition, there seems to be a realization or fear of the possibility of not one but two wandering spirits potentially causing harm to the villagers. It is an interesting point that Bandamma is still considered alive in villager's minds, not in her pregnant form with an unborn child, but as a mother consoling her child. This seems to acknowledge their belief that this dead woman continues to live with a newly born child in the world of the dead.

The common theme in these three instances of sacrifice is that the victim was a young female possessing reproductive capacity. The last case, a pregnant woman who becomes a victim, highlights this especially. It could be argued that by sacrificing these young women, the villagers were trying to assuage the goddess so that she would help the village sustain and flourish with new crops.

These instances, in their number and location, reflect the remote nature of this practice. Yet, the evidence shows that this belief and practice, although limited to certain areas and sections of society, has continued to survive into the present day in different forms. These different forms of sacrifices might reflect the traditions of different tribal groups who are becoming part of the mainstream society.[18] More research needs to be done in these areas. Daily newspapers report the rare but persisting phenomenon that human sacrifices are attempted with the intention to ward off any potential hazardous short-comings when inaugurating industries, mills, and schools. One report about an attempt to sacrifice boys for a new school building in Pasunur (Karimnagar District) was published by the International Humanist and Ethical Union on the Internet in 2007.[19] Another unfortunate incident came to light only after the sacrifice of a young boy in 2008 in Jagityal (Karimnagar District).[20] In 2010, a similar ill-fated incident of a sacrificed young boy in a Siva temple in Srisailam (Kurnool District) was reported.[21] Another recent report, how-ever, cites a thwarted attempt of sacrificing a three-year-old girl in Pangri (Rangareddy District).[22] The areas of Andhra where these incidents have occurred are also where poverty and illiteracy are quite high. It is heartening to know that there are organizations, like Spoorthi, working to educate villagers and to develop awareness among people about the harm and ultimate futility of such sacrifices.

Murders. Unlike ritual sacrifices of human beings, assassinations or mur-ders are not bound to any one region in Andhra. Some murder victims have been deified, depending on the contexts in which these assassinations have occurred. If the victim is a virgin or a married woman, unlike in the cases of sacrifices, she may be deified as a *perantalu*. In this sense, the victim shares similarities with the *perantalu* of other categories that have been discussed in the two previous chapters. I will explore what these similarities are and whether they vary according to the victim's station in her life. The stories of the victims, therefore, are examined in three categories: 1) virgin girls; 2) mar-ried women; and 3) a widow.

The Murder of Virgin Girls. In 2009, an Indian magazine entitled *Frontline* ran a cover story about honor killings that are still taking place in northern parts of India.[23] Within the article, an interview with a south Indian folklorist by the name of A. Sivasubramanian was published. In this interview, Sivasubramanian regaled two different versions (official and alternative) of stories about two "virgin deities" in the state of Tamilnadu. The official ver-sions of these two cases are similar to the story of Vasavi Devi in which the deified girls were known to have killed themselves as a result of advances made by local landlords. But alternative and hushed-up versions collected by Sivasubramanian are quite different. According to Sivasubramanian, the girls, after their encounters with lascivious landlords, were suspected of losing their virginity and were killed by family members to preserve the honor of their families. The Tamil notions of chastity and virginity and their connection to honor, a theme that I discussed in the previous chapter, is basically the same in traditional Andhra society, especially among middle and upper castes. This is why dying while protecting a woman from molestation in ancient times was believed to bring the reward of heaven. A testimony to this is found in the memorial stones set up in honor of those heroes who were killed in protecting women from marauders.[24] The flip side of this, however, was that if a girl lost her virginity before her marriage, it reflects a failure on the part of the family to protect her. Since this failure brings shame on family members, the "solution" in these instances was homicide, which was then often portrayed as a suicide. In these stories, either the girls were victims of "honor killings," or intense coercion of some kind worked on them to take their own lives, as in the case of Vasavi, mentioned in chapter 4. So, both the official and hushed up versions of the stories of these deaths point to these highly gender-biased values in which the bottom line is that the girls were expected to treat their virginity as more valuable than their own lives. But yet, when these girls fulfill the societal expectations by taking their lives, they become not only role models for other girls, but also symbols of fertility, who in their death gain the ability to bestow children. Thus, in their death they fulfill the role of mothers that was stunted or taken away from them in real life. In the case of the Andhra "honor killings," as I cite below, the loss, or the suspicion of loss of chastity, are the instigating reasons.

The deification of a Virasaiva maiden in Agali (Anantapur District) is the first case in point. A story published in the District Gazetteer in 1962 mentions that two centuries ago, Bandamma, a young woman of Virasaiva orientation, took her life to save the honor of the family, and that people worship her for this reason.[25] The alternative story that I have collected from villagers, however, says that Bandamma's wanderings as a Virasaiva female ascetic follower caused embarrassment to family members and, as a result, they killed her. In traditional Andhra society, it is atypical for a virgin to choose the life of asceticism and to leave her parental home. This very well could have caused the stir within and outside the family that finally led to her death. The young woman might have been thrown into a well, because for many years, she has been worshiped in the form of a well, called "the Bandamma well," in which all of her paraphernalia were purportedly thrown. Recently, a new generation of her devotees sent money from abroad leading to the construction of a temple in which she is worshiped in the form of a bamboo basket (3.19). Since she was a Virasaiva, no animal sacrifices are offered to her. During her annual festival, all the married daughters of the village are invited and all of these daughters, irrespective of their ages, are worshiped with offerings of turmeric, vermilion, and clothes. The gifts are considered by family members to be expressions of gratitude to the Virasaiva female ascetic.

In closely knitted societies, as in Andhra's rural areas, it is difficult to keep any family secrets. At the same time, living by the same value system, the village, as in the case of Agali, accepts a manufactured story as the official version, while dealing with guilt in the form of worship. Worship, in this particular case, translated into the eventual worship of one's own living daughters. This yearly worship of daughters can be understood as an attempt at appeasement so that the daughters, in return, would not trespass patriarchal norms. A point should be made here, however, about how the influence of the idiosyncratic nature of Bandamma's background is seen in the milder form of her worship. For example, unlike in other cases of virgin deification, there is no attempt to harness the power of the maiden so that she would become a goddess of fertility. Instead, her power is seen as now in the possession of the village's living daughters who, through propitiation, can be coerced into observing normative behavior. This is a way of preventing their daughters from trespassing normative social behavior, even if it inhibits their desire to embark upon some higher spiritual quest.[26] In this way, Bandamma is worshiped not to hold her life up as an ideal to be emulated, but to learn a harsh lesson about what might be the consequences of crossing boundaries that bring dishonor to the family or village. The point here is that a young woman's energies, along with her sexuality, should be carefully channeled for family welfare so that she could make an ideal wife and mother.

The following incident is not so much involved with the issue of chastity, but it is certainly concerned with the honor of the family. Maddi Ravamma was a girl from the Karnata *reddy* family. The family was in the midst of a feud with other *reddy* families in the village and so boycotted any of their rival's social functions. When a wedding was held among the opposing faction, Maddi Ravamma, as a child, attended the wedding and ate at the function. Later it was revealed that Ravamma had attended the wedding, a public act that caused a tremendous humiliation to the Karnata family. The outraged family beat Ravamma to death. The dying Ravamma flew into the sky and spoke to all the villagers that unless all of them forget their differences and worship her together, the village would not flourish in the future.

Because of the interrelation between a girl's chastity and her natal family's honor, it is expected that a girl should guard herself at all times from outside elements and follow the rules laid down by the family. Even if it is not directly involved with chastity, patriarchal values imposed on a girl are expected to be observed with a force as significant as observing the veritable legal laws of a particular locality or household, the violation of which can have disastrous effects, such as in the case of Ravamma. The family might not have intended to really kill Ravamma, but their anger knew no bounds and resulted in her death. If the punishment was intended to teach Ravamma a hard lesson in patriarchal values by crushing her independent spirit, they succeeded only by stopping her physically. If the girl's spiritual death would not make the family feel remorseful, the physical death certainly must have brought them to their knees, as they seemed to have worried about what her free spirit might do to them in the future. Again, it was not just Ravamma's family who was implicated in her death, but the entire village, as they all seemed to have known that they were complicit in Ravamma's family's effort to protect their honor. The cumulative effect of the collective remorse was the realization that the only way to avoid incidents of this nature in the future was to stop bickering with each other and to worship her together. This is what they imagined that Ravamma's free spirit had advocated.

Murders of Married Women. Here I will relate a couple of examples to show how deified married women relate to other *perantalu*, while also simultaneously sharing affiliation either with *gramadevatas*, or with one of the pan-Indian deities, as the context may be.

The first is the story of Lakshmi Perantalamma of the *kamma* caste.[27] Lakshmi is said to have been born a couple of centuries ago at Durgi (Guntur District). She went to live with her husband in Lingalapadu (Krishna District) and had a daughter by him. It is a tradition in Andhra to marry daughters with the sons of the siblings of the opposite sex or to maternal uncles. Lakshmi's sister-in-law wanted Lakshmi's daughter to marry her son, while Lakshmi was set to give her daughter in marriage to her younger brother. Angry at Lakshmi's refusal of the proposal, her mother-in-law and sister-in-law concocted tales of extramarital affairs about Lakshmi and passed them on to her husband. Believing the words of his mother and sister, the enraged husband knifed Lakshmi to death. Later, signs of Lakshmi's presence appeared in the form of the family's cattle straying away and clothes catching fire suddenly. After these signs, Lakshmi appeared in the dreams of her two brothers-in-law in image form and directed them to construct a temple for her and to initiate worship. They followed her directions and built a temple, installing her image made of wood and lacquer. Some people say that the temple was actually built by Lakshmi's parents.

Since the initiation of worship, Lakshmi Perantalamma *jatara* is celebrated annually for six days with animal sacrifices. *Yadavas* act as priests in her temple. Her story became so popular that, in the 1950s, two feature films were made with Lakshmi as a protagonist victim who acquires powers in her death. Following the release of these films, the goddess earned even wider popularity with devotees coming from far away distances to participate in her *jatara*. Lakshmi Perantalamma's image in her temple is flanked by the images of her granddaughter and great-granddaughter. Each of these images is seen holding *khadga* (sword) in their left hands and a vermilion box in the right. On the far left is the image of the husband of her granddaughter, who is shown raising his hands holding up his three fingers. Her daughter's image, however, is conspicuously absent. When asked about her absence, the priest's response was that because the daughter had lied to the authorities that her father was not responsible for her mother's death, she thereby was not qualified for worship. The granddaughter, her husband, and their daughter, on the other hand, were considered to be pious and took considerable interest in developing Lakshmi Perantalamma's temple. Therefore, they were qualified to accompany her in the shrine. The temple has two rooms, with a *gramadevata* Ankamma's image installed in the next room. She holds *khadga* and a vermilion box and is accompanied by a brass-hooded snake image. Next to the *perantalamma gudi* is a low structure housing a stone as the form of Mutyalamma located under the shade of a tree. Ankamma's presence here in Lakshmi Perantalamma's shrine resembles that of Rangamma, the *bala perantalu*, and some *sati perantalu*. In these cases, their affiliation with the *gramadevata* is confirmed. But Lakshmi Perantalamma holding the *khadga* resembles the imagery of a *sati perantalu*. As in the worship of many *sati perantalu*, the upright *khadga* is used as a bangle holder by devotees when they offer bangles, clothes, turmeric, and vermilion in exchange for protection for family and children. In her story, there is a clear message that Lakshmi Perantalamma was a victim at the hands of her in-laws and husband. Even the daughter who did not strive to bring her father to justice is seen as a traitor. In this instance, the *perantalamma*'s image holding a *khadga* can be interpreted as a symbol of the aspiration to bring those who were culpable to justice. Nonetheless, the symbolism of holding a *khadga* seems to function in the same way in the *sati* images as well.

The second story about a married woman in some ways resembles the story of the virgin maid Bandamma in terms of how the details of the death were camouflaged. But the reason I relate this story is not only to make note of the above point, but also to illustrate how a murdered *perantalamma* can be equated with a *bala perantalu* or a *sati perantalu* on the one hand, and a pan-Indian goddess on the other. This incident also indicates that, as in some cases of *bala perantalu*, a ruling family may initiate the deification process. Around a century ago, Venkamma was a young married woman from Ramavarappadu (Krishna District), which is now part of the city of Vijayawada.

[28] Venkamma became pregnant before the official nuptials were observed and her brothers suspected an extramarital affair. The family belonged to the *raju* (ruling) caste. On the mission of taking her to her husband's home in Narasannapalem (West Godavari District), they arranged for Venkamma to be murdered. Later, the repenting family initiated her worship. Promotional literature for this goddess, however, omits these details leading to Venkamma's death, but only mentions that she appeared in a dream to a professional image-maker in Kondapalli and directed him to make an image and initiate her worship in Ramavarappadu. The literature then locates Venkamma *perantalu* in the category of other *perantalu* goddesses in the neighboring region, such as Rangamma *perantalu* (the same one as mentioned above), Vinukonda Venkamma *perantalu*, and Penuganchiprolu Tirupatamma *perantalu* (both died as *satis*) among others. In addition, Venkamma *perantalu* is described as a form of Lakshmi.

To support her identity with other *perantalu* and also the goddess Lakshmi, Venkamma *perantalu*'s image is flanked by the images of Vinukonda Venkamma and Mahalakshmi in a temple located on a very busy street in the city. As in the case of Lakshmi *perantalu*, Venkamma's natal and agnate families are involved in the annual *jatara* with a *yadava* acting as a priest. The annual festival is held during Sankranti (the harvest festival that falls in mid-January) and commences with descendants of Venkamma *perantalu* inviting her to their home for turmeric, vermilion, and clothes. The *yadava* priest sacrifices a sheep, after which the goddess receives new clothes by a donor family and then is taken in procession through the streets for a couple of days. In fulfillment of vows, some devotees carry oil lamps on their heads during the procession.

After the procession, the goddess's image is placed on a sumptuously decorated float in the canal behind her temple and then is taken to a swing under a pipal tree also located close to the temple. The swinging ceremony is held for many deified goddesses, as well as for some *gramadevatas*, during their annual rituals. The day when the goddess returns to the temple, a large-scale public free feast takes place. It is common during the popular *jataras* of *gramadevatas* and deified goddesses, such as Venkamma *perantalu*, for groups of professional musicians and storytellers to arrive from some distance away to volunteer their services. In these cases, the temples give them donations in cash or kind as a way of recognizing their services.

The devotees of Venkamma *perantalu* are a mix of city dwellers and suburbanites who seek help with their daily problems, as well as with important life decisions. It is not uncommon to find young women seeking marriages, sick people seeking success in their medical treatments, business people seeking prosperity in their transactions, etc. As though she is a *gramadevata*, some devotees who keep buffaloes bring the first milk products to this goddess as an offering. Since the temple draws a huge income from these activities, the management has been brought under the purview of the state government.

While Venkamma *perantalu* is accompanied by Lakshmi in her shrine, the adjacent shrine is occupied by Siva and Subrahmanyesvara, the serpent god of Siva. Venkamma *perantalu*'s association with Lakshmi, rather than with the *gramadevata*, and the presence of Siva and Subrahmanyesvara replacing the snake, tree, and other forms of the *gramadevata*, is clearly an attempt to cater to the needs of middle-class city dwellers.

At any rate, the above two deaths occurred because of perceived violations of the marriage code. The stories of these deified women emphasize victimizations. Both were innocent of the suspected acts: Lakshmi and Venkamma did not have any extramarital affairs. Highlighting their innocence captures the sympathies of devotees so that they understand why the goddess is angry at any slight infraction; the flip side of this is that it reinforces patriarchal norms. It sends the message that if women were to commit the actions that were suspected of these deified women, they would deserve to be killed or severely punished.

Widow. There is yet another category of the goddesses that neither falls within the orbit of the *perantalu*, nor is an instance of being a sacrificial victim. This is the deification of a widow. Whitehead described an instance of a widow by the name of Ramamma, who lived in a village located between the capital city of Hyderabad and the town Vijayawada.[29] She farmed her husband's land by hiring some servants. She was accused of having a sexual affair with one of her servants, one Buddha Sahib. Her brother was so angry that he killed them both. Later, there occurred a cattle plague in which several cattle died. Villagers thought it was the wrath of Ramamma and started to worship her. Whenever there is a cattle plague in this area, people prepare wooden images of Ramamma and Buddha Sahib and worship them along with other deities.

The reasons for the death of Ramamma are similar to why Venkamma was killed, that is, for violation of patriarchal norms. The issue that surfaces here again is non-conformance to patriarchal sexual mores. In this case, it was not just Ramamma who suffered punishment for violations, but it was also her alleged lover, who was a poor, low-caste person without much social standing. This is what made the worship extend to him as well. Actually, Ramamma was twice oppressed by the patriarchal moral code by having forbidden sex, on the one hand, and disrespecting social hierarchy by courting a person outside of her caste, on the other.[30] The collective fear and guilt because of this incident led to the realization that shutting off all the avenues for a young woman, in the name of gender and caste, might generate the spirit of Ramamma's anger at society for the values that resulted her death. It remains an interesting case that reflects the manner in which some degree of ambivalence has been managed.

Ramamma's widowhood disqualified her from becoming a *perantalu*. But this does not prevent the deified Ramamma from becoming a *gramadevata* or merging with one of the pan-Indian goddesses such as Durga, in the same way as Vijayawada Kanaka Durga. This brings the essential nature of the *gramadevata* to the surface: fertility takes preeminence over the patriarchal notions of auspiciousness. Ramamma, though a widow, still possesses this potential fertility. Curtailing this potential by taking her life away makes her an ideal candidate for becoming a *gramadevata*.

To sum up in relation to what has been discussed in the previous two chapters, virgins as *bala perantalu* are understood as symbols of mothers in the aftermath of their deaths; married women as *perantalu* are suspended in time, as it were, to retain their status; and those who become *satis* revert to when they were living in their auspicious married status. The common theme in all these cases is that these goddesses are perceived to be in control of time in such a way that they are perceived as divine mothers and auspicious wives who fulfill the wishes of their devotees who, in turn, approach them not just for offspring and longevity for their husbands, but for all those concerns of well-being in their lives that fall within the domain of their village/town. In this sense, these deified women become the guardians of the whole village or urban neighborhood. The nature of their food offerings is dependent upon how appeasement of each of the deities corresponds to the blessings that their devotees seek.

Sacrificial victims, on the other hand, are a different kind unto themselves. Although their deaths are the result of violence, there is a rationalized justification that violence was necessary to prevent a larger scale disaster. These women, seen as a sacrificial offering to a deity, by default actually assimilate to the power of the deity. It is probably for this reason that no elaborate annual festivals are held in honor of these deities. However, mention should be made of how sacrificing male animals to *gramadevata*s is a norm in Andhra. One popular explanation for this is that the *gramadevata*, as a fertility goddess, does not encourage the sacrifice of female animals that have the power of reproduction. A related aspect that comes through, one that I have repeated often in this study, is that for rejuvenation and for reproduction to occur, the female goddess needs to unite with her male lover. The sacrificial animal is seen as just that.

It is important to note that sacrificing female animals and birds puts the villagers at an economic disadvantage, as one of the reasons for sacrifice is to multiply domestic animals and birds. This nature of the goddess, however, does not square up with the explanation of why the goddess accepts a young female human victim. Wanting a young human female victim is probably coming from a very different source than what is assumed to be the normative expectation of a *gramadevata* in village Andhra. As discussed in the beginning of the chapter, one of the sources could be newly merging tribes bringing new traditions with them. As I have discussed in previous chapters, divergent streams joined the *gramadevata* tradition when new rituals and myths led to the invention of new cults, such as the deification of women.

Referring to the cults of *gramadevatas* and *satis*, Susan Bayly has mentioned how these spread to the south, as cultivators migrated from coastal Andhra. I have discussed how *sati* tradition was a result of the conglomeration of various influences from the south as well as from the north. In the case of the *gramadevata* cult, however, the tradition goes deeper. As the stories indicate, *sati* and other deified cults primarily imitate *gramadevata* features in their iconography and ritual while at the same time exhibiting traits specific to the circumstances of their deaths and to the locales in which the deaths occurred. These diverse forms of worship reflect the fact that it is not always the appropriation of the power of the dead that motivates deification, but a complex web of reasons that can either conform to or oppose the values of the normative Hindu tradition.

Conclusion

GODDESS TRADITIONS ROOTED in the valorization of fertility can be traced within many agricultural societies in the world. The Indus Valley civilization, one of the oldest of these, is the earliest society in the Indian subcontinent in which the fertility cult functioned as the dominant pattern of religious culture. This pattern of religious culture has been sustained historically, despite the rise of patriarchal and highly philosophical religions with universal pretensions that attempted to absorb and subordinate its various dimensions of meaning. Over millennia, adaptation and transformation by these other religious orientations did not significantly diminish the religious culture of the goddess, but instead refracted an astonishing array of new goddess articulations who were then worshiped within assorted types of ritual practices in the form of distinctive iconographic representations that were, in turn, provided with powerful mythic warrants.

Entering into this bewildering and complex religious scene three centuries ago were western Christian missionaries and European colonialists seeking Christian converts and colonial wealth, respectively. With the exception of a few who recognized the need to understand the natives in order to achieve their ends, a majority bore the burden of establishing what they perceived as their own superior credentials by finding fault with the natives. An exceptionally few missionaries, like Ziegenbalg in the early eighteenth century and Whitehead in the early twentieth century, along with colonials like Thurston in the late nineteenth and early twentieth centuries, can be compared to indigenous religious reformers of the Indian past, insofar as they understood that in order to eradicate or to subordinate goddess religious culture, they needed to make an effort first to understand it. In spite of their interests, or because of their ulterior motives to disestablish it, western understandings of goddess religious culture remained remarkably skewed, such that generations of educated Indians today consider the worship of *gramadevatas* as irrational, superstitious, and detrimental to the evolution of a modern society. Neither the colonial west, nor the majority of the educated Indians, grasped the constructive significance of *gramadevatas* in the religious lives of village people because they simply could not imagine how these goddess cults have emerged out of, and then informed, the on-the-ground lived experiences, and the concomitant value-producing perspectives, of people who exist in an agriculturally based village environment.

By the middle of the twentieth century, when a politically independent India finally surfaced from colonial rule, the dominant paradigm for understanding the complexity of emergent Hindu society and culture was dependent upon the historical perception that superior Aryan and *brahmanic* principles of moral hierarchy had provided a salvaging order to the welter of confusing and morally impaired Dravidian customs. That is, whatever was considered civilized was attributed to the former and whatever was in need of being civilized was attributed to the latter. But many scholars in the latter half of the twentieth century, western as well as Indian, who approached the study of Indian society and culture in its village forms, developed alternative frameworks to interpret its significance. Various conceptual schemes and relevant vocabularies were proposed in order to interpret the complex social and cultural patterns they encountered. Yet the derisive western colonial attitude toward India's village cultures in which *gramadevatas* played a central role had left such a huge cloud of misunderstanding that it has taken a half-century for scholars not only to take up the *gramadevata* as their focus of study, but also not to frame her as intrinsically subordinate to her Sanskrit counterparts.

My argument in this study has been this: not only is the *gramadevata* not culturally inferior to the goddesses of Sanskrit tradition, but, in fact, she is the contemporary form of what was originally an ancient fertility goddess. Some of the symbols used to represent the fertility goddess as early as 3000 BCE are still relevant in contemporary *gramadevata* rituals. The various symbols used to represent the fertility goddess, still articulated by aspects of her current mythology, reveal that the nature of the *gramadevata* has been complex from the time of its known origins, possibly as early as in Indus civilization. Moreover, the fact that the goddess seems consistently to have been conceived in paradoxical ways has produced a multipurpose and adaptive cult. For example, because the *gramadevata* has been understood essentially as a shapeless and even genderless procreative force, her imagined forms reflect a propensity to assume a presence in virtually any inanimate or animate beings that conform to a logic of association with her power. As such, the *gramadevata* has often been imagined as a human female figure giving birth to nature, as a mother who bears the universe in her womb. In this sense, she is creation as well as creator. She is also seen as capable of destroying what she creates. What has been striking in this study is that the symbols, images, and mythology of the ancient fertility goddess correlate with contemporary understandings of the *gramadevata* as a creator, nurturer, and destroyer. She may be worshiped as the body of the village, with her naval stone planted in the center of the village, or kept at a safe distance at the edge of the village. In the former instance, she brings fertility and prosperity to the villagers by bringing timely rains if worshiped properly. In the latter, she is a goddess of poxes or other forms of illnesses afflicting humans, domestic animals, birds, and crops, who needs to be appeased so that she will stay away. Whether she is a loving mother or a wrathful ghoul punishing villagers for their missteps, the *gramadevata* remains an integral feature of village identity.

Centuries ago, emerging nascent ascetic religious teachers intent on the establishment of Buddhism, Jainism, and Vedic Brahmanism, understood this basic fact very well. To popularize their abstruse philosophic teachings, they courted the vocabulary familiar to the agricultural folk. First, they adopted the very symbols of the fertility goddess to depict their religious exemplars, such as the Buddha, Jaina *tirthankaras*, or the *sramana* traditions or the powerful deities Siva and Vishnu of *brahmanic* traditions, or they deployed symbols of the goddess in strategic places in their shrines, to infuse an auspicious quality as a way of making their religious articulations attractive to agricultural folk. Their promotion of textual and visual representations was so effective that symbols of the goddess became identifiable markers of important paradigmatic religious personalities. Thus, we find the *mahapurushalakshanas* on the Buddha and Jaina statues, the *srivatsa* on Vishnu's chest, snakes on the body of Siva, and the lotus as a pedestal for virtually all Hindu, Buddhist, and Jain supernatural personalities. This first step resulted in symbols assuming multivalent meanings, thereby losing their exclusive meanings in association with the fertility goddess. This appropriation was likely not enough to turn whole populations into enthusiastic listeners of their messages, but a second type of appropriation seems to have been exceedingly effective. In this strategy, symbols associated with the fertility goddess evolved to take on human female shapes of the goddess, who were subordinated to serve the respective orientations of power and soteriology in these emergent religious traditions. In addition to the deployment of these new iconographies, various *gramadevata* mythologies were reworked to demonstrate how these goddesses were really "at home," or domesticated within the newly enlightened, disciplined, or transcendentally realized cosmologies. *Gramadevatas* were portrayed as reverent to the buddhas, bodhisattvas, and *tirthankaras*, or devoted support-ers or spouses of Siva and Vishnu in their wondrous exploits, as the case may be. Thus, symbols intrinsic to the fertility and *gramadevata* cult evolved into the anthropomorphic shape of subordinated goddesses. The *purnakumbha*, *srivatsa*, and lotus became chaste and devoted anthropomorphized spouses to Siva, Vishnu, and Brahma, that is, as Parvati, Lakshmi, and Sarasvati, respec-tively. The role of these goddesses in these instances served to promote the ideology that focused on the ultimate power attributed to these gods, as well as the patriarchal value system legitimated by that power.

However, the evolution of fertility symbols orchestrated by these emergent religious traditions does not mean that goddesses had not been conceived in antecedent anthropomorphic forms. Anthropomorphic female forms of the goddess are as old as her other symbols. The ancient anthropomorphic female form that emphasized the fertility aspect had been depicted by scenes of the goddess giving birth, by prominently exhibiting her vulva, by simply being portrayed in a naked youthful form, or by being fully or partially clothed and holding a child. As the political structures developed beyond villages, the asso-ciation of villages, to chiefdoms, kingdoms, and empires, the functions of the goddess diversified from village protectress to battle queen, from providing rain and respite from disease, to becoming a dispenser of wealth (Lakshmi), education (Sarasvati), and a model of wifely *dharma* (Parvati and Sita). The imagery of goddesses developed to represent her in these many forms.

The diversification of her forms and imagery was also due to other social and political processes, such as the merging of various tribal and other groups with the *dharma*-minded Hindu mainstream society. Some villages in contact with various tribes and castes cultivated the worship of *gramadevatas* either as clan or caste deities. The fluidity of village religion was also often a reflection of the fluidity of its economy. As various groups of families practiced their livelihoods (either by providing assistance to farmers or by pursuing comple-mentary professions such as fishing and hunting), the diverse *gramadevata* goddesses that they venerated were either mythologically understood as sis-ters of the same divine family or, in other cases, combined together and wor-shiped as the one versatile mother of the village.

While the appropriation of these goddesses into Saiva and Vaishnava tra-ditions created a subordinated position for the goddess, patronage extended by rulers to some *gramadevatas*, such as Durga and Kali, eventuated in their exalted appearances in Sanskrit compositions and their liturgical worship in *brahmanic* temples as powerful warrior goddesses. In view of the fact that the power of the goddess was ascertained as immanent in nature, *brahmanic* the-ology sometimes recognized a feminine principle of nature as the primordial energy of creation: *prakrti, maya,* and *sakti.* One of the results of this recognition was the emergent Mahadevi ("Great Goddess") in *brahmanic* thought, who was equated with prakriti, *sakti,* and *maya,* thus reinforcing her ontological nature further.

In Andhra, this process occurred mostly in the waning period of Buddhism's demise and was the byproduct of Vaishnavites and Saivites, who were making attempts to bring warrior goddesses into their fold. But because these goddesses had already made their debuts in written traditions and had received patronage from powerful rulers, the subordinations of these goddesses to Siva and Vishnu remained something of a mere theological veneer within the context of the newly emerging urban temple religion. At the same time, the cults of *gramadevatas* remained strong in the outlying hills and agriculturally based villages. Experiencing competition from each other and also from the continued strength of *gramadevata* worship and the more recently established cult of Mahadevi, the Buddhist, Jaina, Saiva, and Vishnava clerics introduced fierce forms of independent goddesses as *tantric* deities. Whether or not this strategy worked for the benefit of the survival in Andhra of Buddhism and Jainism is debatable. But their attempts contributed to an enormous diversification of goddesses.

Eventually and more recently, the emerging *brahman*ized profiles of popular goddesses such as Durga and Kali, who were likely tribal goddesses in their origins, became paradigmatic for understanding the nature of those *gramadevata*s whose locales had become part of urbanized settings. One of the reasons for this development can be traced to reactions of reform to the colonial western idea perception of the *gramadevata* tradition as irrational and superstitious. Indigenous Hindu reformers of the eighteenth and nineteenth century sought refuge in the sophisticated Sanskrit *brahman*ical textual philosophical traditions deemed as authentic in order to recast their understandings of the goddess's significance. This movement continues to hold its sway today among educated and middle-caste people who have distanced themselves from *gramadevata* worship. This tendency plays a major role in explaining why rural goddesses in their transition to an urban environment are identified with popular deities of Sanskrit mythology so that the goddess will appear more respectable to the more cosmopolitan-oriented population.

Buddhists, Saivites, and Vaishnavites incorporated some specific *gramadevata*s directly. Buddhists tried to identify some *gramadevata*s as bodhisattvas. While some of these, such as Hariti, subsequently traveled widely as Buddhism spread throughout and beyond the Indian subcontinent, in Andhra they left only a few faint memories. The growing popularity of Saivism not only wiped out Buddhism with few traces left behind, but it also managed to bring *gramadevatas* into its fold by treating the *grama-devata* as either a spouse or daughter of Siva. In a few regions of Andhra where Vaishnavism managed to dominate, some *gramadevatas* were identified as the spouse of Vishnu. Although Saivite and Vaishnavite connections with specific *gramadevatas* remained tenuous, they did influence the societal value system and, as a result, affected ritual practices held within the context of annual festivals in honor of *gramadevatas*. For example, although almost all of the emergent religious movements (Buddhism and *bhakti*, for instance) became popular in the quest to connect to common people, Saivism and Vaishnavism in their final stages yielded to hierarchical *brahmanic* values reflected in caste and gender segregation. A typical *gramadevata* ritual is now often used to reify traditional caste and gender hierarchy despite the fact that the independent goddess and the fertility nature of the *gramadevata* cults stand in direct opposition to *brahmanical* understandings of gender.

The profile of a fiercely independent *gramadevata* who produces at will without benefit of a husband is hardly a role model to a traditional Hindu woman, whose fertility power is controlled by the patriarchal value system. This discrepancy between the divine and human realms created a strange situation, leading to the deification of women who became victims of the uneven value system. Dead women, especially those whose lives ended abruptly and whose unhappy spirits are perceived to be still hovering around, often return in the dreams of male relations asking for deification, a recompense for their victimization. Yet the cults of some of these deified women, merging with the cult of *gramadevatas*, also, ironically, result in the reassertion of patriarchal norms.

In spite of the prevalent nature of the worship of *gramadevata* in rural, semi-rural, and even urban areas, there is a tendency in Hindu society as a whole to imbibe the norms of *brahmanic* codes of behavior. For example, the idea of deification of women might be borrowed from autochthonous religious beliefs, but the contexts that lead to this deification are often *brahmanical* in nature. The injustice often met by women frequently derives from patriarchal beliefs and customs influenced by Sanskrit manuals. This does not mean to say that the source for these manuals comes only from Vedic tradition itself. It is likely, for example, that the Tamil notion of *ananku*, a potentially harmful power when unharnessed that resides in the female's body, contributed to the rise of the conceptualization of *sakti*, an understanding in Sanskrit tradition that begs the necessity of controlling female energies.

Vows made by traditional Hindu females to be good daughters, daughters-in-law, wives, and mothers, deriving from their staunch dedication to their families, reflect their enormous hidden strength regarded as *sakti*. When a young virgin girl dies unexpectedly, her potentially unbridled energy, or her *sakti*, is a force to be feared. Controlling this *sakti* by deifying her is a strategy often deployed. However, there is a remaining ambiguity in chaste virgins becoming divine mothers. In the case of auspicious married women who were dedicated to their husbands in life and in death, villagers feel assured that these deified women (*perantalu*) would bless them in their afterlives by vowing to become caretakers of the entire village. This understanding of *perantalu* itself is a patriarchal construct in which the goddess's primary function is seen not so much as fertility, but rather as giving the blessing of long lives to the husbands of married women.

In spite of the institutionalization of patriarchal notions regarding the control of *sakti*, some *gramadevatas* still maintain an independent and non-conforming stature. This is seen in instances of the deification of young widows who still have the power of reproductive capacity but whose lives have been short-circuited by actions inspired by patriarchal norms. Nonetheless, in all these cases within rural village contexts, deified women share with *gramadevata*s the function of protecting the village. In most cases, these goddesses are understood to be appeased in the same way as *gramadevata*s because of the fear that they might punish transgressive villagers with their wrath. In some villages, it is actually a deified female who acts as a *gramadevata*. One of the important aspects that I have referred to in this study has to do with how the cult of deified women springs from a sense of moral guilt and outrage. In this context, the goddess seems to symbolize an abiding faith in the intrinsic morality of the cosmos. She would seem to be a figure that demands restitution for contraventions of justice. In other words, it would seem as if she represents not only the material well-being of the community (e.g., the fertility and prosperity celebrated in her annual festivals), but also the moral conscious or moral identity of the community as well.

Having said this, I also need to reiterate a notion associated with the fertility goddess that continues to be present in *gramadevata* rituals, as well as in Sanskrit textual descriptions of the goddess. The *gramadevata* is not simply a human being elevated to divine status, but rather the form and power of various natural forces that create and take away life. Yet power to create or destroy is also attributed to the human female. Believing in this notion is what prompts a wife to accept her failure to protect her dead husband and to consequently join him in death. On the other hand, it is the goddess's wrath that is projected onto those women who have died of social injustice and then purportedly seek deification. In some cases, blood sacrifices are made to these goddesses in the same way as they are made to *gramadevata*s. Here the sacrifice conveys the same meaning of reenergizing and renewing the power of goddess so that she would be efficacious in providing fertility and protection.

In this connection, we can see more clearly why the feminine figure of the goddess is such an apt symbol for village life. It is the village agricultural economy that lies at the heart of the general society's economic wealth. Whatever ruler could command taxes and influence the network of agricultural production in Andhra's vast network of villages gained power over the wealth of the region. That is, whoever could subordinate the village gained economic control of the means of production. Here the parallel between subordinating the feminine in order to secure the cosmological order—and subordinating the village in order to ensure a prosperous economic order—is just too obvious to ignore. The goddess, then, in this vein, represents the very power of the village, whether or not this power is championed as a symbol of resistance or as a symbol of what must be subordinated. That is, whether or not she is seen to be the symbol of village economic prosperity and moral order by villagers themselves, or as a symbol of what must be subdued and controlled by those who would act imperially, she is a personification of the village power per se. Having said this, I now want to further emphasize this point specifically in relation to women.

When I have tried to probe into what I take to be the relatively original folkloric indigenous religious culture that is separate from *brahmanic* traditions, I notice that aspects of this religious culture can be seen as still very prevalent among the lower castes of society who live in rural villages and follow their age-old professions. I do not mean to assert that they are totally free from *brahmanic* traditions. In fact, they, themselves, often view aspects of the *brahmanical* tradition as civilized and, as I have noted, utilize many opportunities to follow pan-Indian *brahmanic* traditions of symbol and ritual. But because the lower castes in village society have been kept away from actively mingling into higher levels of society for many centuries, they still retain many unaffected traditions. "Scheduled," "outcast," or "untouchable" women are exempt from the closely knitted chains of *brahmanically* defined womanhood and, in fact, enjoy much more social freedom than the "classical" middle- or upper-caste Hindu woman. This social freedom sometimes has been ridiculed by followers of the "*dharma*-minded" Hindu hierarchy as "uncivilized" behavior, labeled as immoral in the same way that the *gramadevata* has been labeled as *ksudra devata*. From both *brahmanic* and village points of view, what the *gramadevata* seems to symbolize is the relatively unbridled power, or freedom, or social creativity of the village woman. It is the people of the middle castes, most of whom own land and possess relatively more economic power, who are the most ardent followers of the *brahmanic* value system. For example, *sati* traditions, although they have their origins in non-Sanskritic cultures such as the Tamil culture of the south, have received validation under the *brahman*ical system, after which they became the ideal for the women of middle classes and middle castes, by which they could prove their status, dignity, and devotion. That is the reason why incidents of *sati* were seen mostly among these sections of society. That women of these families would regard suicide as an ultimate act of fulfilling their ideals of *dharma*, while such a thought would rarely enter into the head of a lower-caste village woman, is perhaps an apt commentary on the relative comparative status and aspirations of the feminine in their respective religio-cultural contexts. Other married women deified as *perantalu* either committed suicide or were murdered for their perceived failure to measure up to the *brahman*ically inspired value system. These women also came mostly from these middle castes. Incidents leading to fatality as a result of women receiving punishments have been motivated by the *brahman*ical values asserting that women's sexuality should be controlled at any cost by male members of the family. Within families of small farming communities, the divide between gender roles is much less defined than in affluent urban societies more highly informed by textually based Sanskrit-oriented religious culture. Wealthy middle castes who define themselves in such a way as to argue for their sophistication in terms of the *brahman*ical patriarchal value system were the chief executives of the *sati* tradition.

While saying this, I am quite conscious about exceptions (those villagers who still want to emulate higher-caste norms) and present-day changes that have affected society that attenuate the above conclusion. With government efforts since independence, Indian society has witnessed, at least in urban areas, less caste distinctions (though they appear in a different form depending on the present-day policies) and more of a mixture of people from different castes living in one locale and pursuing similar careers. Yet, this atmosphere has also created a tendency among people of lower-caste origins or background to emulate, as much as possible, the high-caste customs and traditions so as to be appear to be "more civilized." As a result and most often, women in these urban contexts lose their freedom and are confined to a life of domesticity in their houses, a newly reincarnated form of *ghosha*. While this is one feature of this mixture, yet another side is seen when middle- or high-caste women who pursue new careers in the changed world are appropriating the features of modernity in which women are trying to find their freedom when they come out of their households. This process is affecting a small amount of people who live in urban areas, while ironically in the *brahman*ized village context it remains a very slow process and is sometimes not felt at all.

The history of the *gramadevata* and its religious ramifications, as a reflection of the history of Indian society, is very complex indeed. Given the vicissitudes it has traversed, from hills, to agricultural plains, to urbanized regional towns, and to cities, over a period of five millennia, the cult of the *gramadevata* still remains, in the twenty-first century, intimately connected to those who seek to reap the fruitful benefits of nature or of immediate existential relief.

Notes

INTRODUCTION

1. B. Ziegenbalg, *Genealogy of the South-Indian Gods* (Delhi: Unity Book Service, 1984; originally published in 1869).
2. Edgar Thurston, *Castes and Tribes of Southern India.* 7 vols. Madras: Government Press, 1909; W. T. Elmore, *Dravidian Gods in Modern Hinduism; A Study of the Local and Village Deities of Southern India,* The University Studies of the University of Nebraska vol. XV (Lincoln: The University of Nebraska, 1915); Henry Whitehead, *The Village Gods of South India* (New York and London: Garland Publishing, Inc., 1980 Reprint of the second ed., 1921).
3. K. Viswanadha Reddy. "Ganga Jathara—A folk festival in a small city—Tirupati and the neighboring villages in Andhra Pradesh," *Folklore* 17 (1976): 237–242; Bruce Elliot Tapper, *Rivalry and Tribute. Society and Ritual in a Telugu Village in South India.*(Delhi: Hindustan, 1987); Velcheru Narayana Rao. "Tricking the Goddess: Cowherd Katamaraju and the Goddess Ganga in the Telugu Folk Epic," in Alf Hiltebeitel, *Criminal Gods and Demon Devotees* (Albany, New York: State University of New York Press, 1989), pp. 105–121.
4. Biardeau, Madeleine. *Stories about Posts.* Trans. by Alf Hiltebeitel (Chicago: University of Chicago Press, 2004).

CHAPTER 1

1. Romila Thapar, *Early India* (Berkeley: University of California Press: 2002–2004), pp. 157–159.
2. Two versions of his manuscript have been published: 1. B. Ziegenbalg, *Genealogy of the South-Indian Gods* (Delhi: Unity Book Service, 1984, First Edition: 1869); 2. Daniel Jeyaraj, *Genealogy of the South Indian Deities* (London: Routledge Curzon, 2003).

3. Ziegenbalg, 131.

4. Jeyaraj, 210.

5. Jeyaraj, 45–46 & 114–143.

6. Jeyaraj, 6.

7. Theodor Griesinger. *The Jesuits: A Complete History* vol I (New York: G.P. Putnam's Sons, 1883), p. 92.

8. Voltaire, *Lettres sur l'origine des sciences et sur celle des peuples de l'Asie* (Paris: de Bure, 1777), letter of December 15, 1775 in http://en.wikipedia.org/wiki/Goa_Inquisition.

9. Griesinger, 90–92; Ram Chandra Prasad, *Early English Travellers In India,* (Delhi: Motilal Banarsidass, 1965), pp. 6–7 & 13.

10. Griesinger, 88–89; John Patrick Donnelly, ed. & tr. *Jesuit Writings of the Early Modern Period, 1540–1640* (Cambridge: Hackett Publishing Company, Inc., 2006), p.67; a quote from Xavier's letter: "After they had helped me with great toil for many days, we translated the prayers from Latin into Malabar, beginning with the sign of the Cross, confessing that there are three persons in one sole God, then the Creed, the Commandments, the Our Father, Hail Mary, Salve Regina and the Confiteor." See also fn. 5; http://www.global12project.com/2004/profiles/a_code/hindu3.html.

11. Joan- Pau Rubies, *Travel and Ethnology in the Renaissance: South India Through European Eyes, 1250–1625* (Cambridge: Cambridge University Press: 2002), p.7, fn.13.

12. Ram Chandra Prasad, 17.

13. Rubies, 321.

14. *Sixteenth Century Journal*, Vol. 32, No. 3, p. 844.

15. John Patrick Donnelly, ed. & tr. *Jesuit Writings of the Early Modern Period, 1540–1640* (Cambridge: Hackett Publishing Company, Inc., 2006), pp. 101–111.

16. Henriette Bugge, *Mission and Tamil Society: Social and Religious Change in South India (1840–1900)* (Richmond: Curzon Press Ltd. 1994), p. 45.

17. Stephen Neill. *A History of Christianity in India 1707–1858.* (Cambridge: Cambridge University Press,1985), pp. 28–29 & 35–36.

18. Arno Lehmann, *It Began at Tranquebar* (Madras: The Christian Literature Society, 1956), p.7.

19. Hudson, 17.

20. Neill, 33. Also see Matthew Atmore Sherring. *The History of Protestant Missions in India: From their commencement in 1706 to 1871* (London: Trubner & Co., 1875), p. 2.

21. Jeyaraj, 351.

22. Bugge, 57.

23. Jeyaraj, 36–37

24. Neill, 31–32.

25. Jeyaraj, 40.

26. Ziegenbalg, xv.

27. Jeyaraj, 9. For example, "[h]e asked his teachers to explain ancient Greek and Roman architecture in such a way that they leave out the 'fables [i.e., religious mythologies] that might mislead or confuse the minds' (Francke, 1702, 56 f.) of the students because they were nothing but mere concocted stories [brackets mine]."

28. Jeyaraj, 235–236.

29. Jeyaraj, 235.

30. *Asiatic Researches*, Vol I, 1788, pp.415–431.

31. Cynthia Ann Humes, "Wrestling with Kali, South Asian and British Constructions of the Dark Goddess," in Rachel Fell McDermott and Jeffrey Kripal eds., *Encountering Kali* (Berkeley: University of California Press, 2003), pp.145–168.

32. Garland Cannon ed., *The Letters of Sir William Jones*, vol. II (Oxford: The Clarendon Press: 1970), p. 856. fn. 3. "The Santa Casa, Mary's Nazareth house, is said to have been miraculously transported by angels to a spot near Loretto in 1294, after the Virgin's appearance."

33. Ward, p. xxxviii.

34. Dubois, 609–610.

35. Dubois, 595–596

36. Dubois, 606.

37. George Bruce, *The Stranglers* (London: Longmans, 1968), p. 183. "For Kali, like Satan tempting Christ with riches on the high mountain, offered all the treasure in India to those of her followers ready to kill for her. In contrast to Christianity, Islam and Hinduism, she imposed no moral code, set down no limits to man's animal nature, made no call to his flickering spiritual being to burn with a flame so bright and hard that he would live in illumination. On the contrary, her creed amounted to defiance of all that true religion held sacred."

38. Humes, 155–161. In this chapter, Humes enumerated the Indian literary sources criticizing the goddess Kali to show where Sleeman drew his source for his account. Humes also argued how Sleeman's claims were manufactured in such a way to show that the culture of worshiping a female Goddess as against a male God is amoral. Humes also discusses how the goddess Kali was imagined by the British as "murderous," "inhuman," "sexualized she-devil and consort attacker," symbolizing the darker Hindu woman who was marginalized by the British male as a sex partner.

39. Thapar, 3 & 11; Ram Sharan Sharma, *Sudras in Ancient India* (Delhi: Motilal Banarsidass Publishers Pvt. Ltd., 1958), p. 3. Revealing the real intentions behind Jones's Sanskrit translations, Sharma quoted Jones supporting the English Company's mission of adopting original institutes in India so as to please the millions of India and help the British to amass wealth.

40. The East India Company's charter in 1813 was amended to allow for missionary activity.

41. Rev. Alexander Duff, *India and India Missions: Including Sketches of the Gigantic System of Hinduism, Both in Theory and Practice*, 2nd ed., Edinburgh: John Johnstone, Hunter Square, 1840, pp. 50–52: "The decree hath gone forth—and who can stay its execution?—that India shall be the Lord's,—that Asia shall be the Lord's; yea, that all the kingdoms of this world shall become the kingdoms of our God and of His Christ!...[T]hey [the missionaries] must become acquainted with the learned language of the country, and through it with the real and original sources of all prevailing opinions and observances, sacred and civil;—and have not our Joneses [William Jones and other contemporary Indologists], and our Colebrookes [H. T. Colebrooke and other philologists] the whole, to prove subservient to the cause of the Christian philanthropist?" [brackets mine].

42. Robert Caldwell, *A Comparative Grammar of the Dravidian or South Indian Family of Languages* (Madras: University of Madras, 1856), p. 108: "The introduction of the Dravidians within the pale of Hinduism and the consequent change of their appellation from Mlechchas to that of Sudras appears to have originated, not in conquest, but in the peaceable process of colonization and progressive civilization....All existing traditions, and the names by which the Brahmanical race is distinguished in Tamil, viz., 'Eiyar,' *instructors, fathers*, and 'Parppar,' *overseers*, (probably the *episkopoi* of Arrian), tend to show that the Brahmans acquired their ascendancy by their intelligence and their administrative skill." This quote clearly shows Caldwell's intention of elevating *brahmins* as a race of intelligent people and the descendants of Aryans who helped to civilize the Dravidians in just the same way as the British and the Christian missionaries in the contemporary period.

43. John Murdoch, *Religious Reform: Popular Hinduism*, 3rd ed. (London: The Christian Literature Society for India, 1896), p. 10.

44. Jeyaraj. 242–245.

45. Ziegenbalg, x; also see, *Genealogy of the South-Indian Gods Published in the Original German*, Text with Notes and Addition by the Rev. W. Germann, Late of the Leipsic Missionary Society (Madras: Higginbotham and Co., 1869); page xvi, Rev. Germann said: "The name of the venerable author secured an interest for the work in various directions. The Right Reverend Dr. Gell, Lord Bishop of Madras, by his kind encouragement in word and deed, strengthened my resolution to have the work printed; and the Rev. Mr. Kenneth, Secretary to the Christian Knowledge Society (the same Society which once aided Ziegenbalg so well), managed to remove all hindrances to the printing."

46. Ziegenbalg, xiv. Metzger says this clearly in his translator's note, "...and one Mediator between God and men, the holy God-man Christ Jesus, in whom God reconciled the fallen and rebellious world unto Himself, and without whom no man can come to the Father. And that also this little work may, by its faithful exposure of the religious errors of the Hindus, be subservient

to the spreading of the saving knowledge of the Truth, is the earnest prayer of the translator." P. xvi: Germann supports the belief indirectly in a simple statement as a conclusion to his preface, "May the blessing of God rest on the great work of propagating the Gospel in India and on all faithful labourers in churches and schools, near and dear to me..."

47. Some of the works include: H. H. Wilson. Trans. *Vishnu Purana* (London: John Murray, 1840); Max Muller edited *Sacred Books of the East*, translated by various Oriental scholars (Oxford: Clarendon Press, 1879–1910); Gustav Oppert, *On the Original Inhabitants of Bharatavarsa or India* (Westminister: A Constable & Co., 1893; 2nd ed., New York: Arno Press, 1978); Sir H. M. Elliot, *The Races of the North-West Provinces of India*, 2 vols. (London: Trübner, 1879).

48. Jeyaraj, 114–115.

49. Jeyaraj, 131, footnote.

50. *Life and Letters of the Rt. Hon. Friederich Max Muller*, Vol. I (London: Longmans, Green, and Co., 1902), p. 328.

51. Hugh B. Urban, "India's Darkest Heart," in Rachel Fell Dermott and Jeffrey J. Kripal. eds., *Encountering Kali* (Berkeley: University of California Press, 2003), p. 174 and fn. 23.

52. David Kopf, "British Orientalism and the Bengal Renaissance: the Orientalist in Search of a Golden Age," in Thomas R. Metcalf, ed. *Modern India* (New Delhi: Sterling Publishers Private Limited, 1992 [first edition, 1990]), pp. 35–37.

53. Kopf (1992: 80).

54. Kopf (1992: 79–82).

55. Sir Monier Monier-Williams, *Indian Wisdom* 3rd edition (London: Wm. H. Allen & Co., 13, Waterloo Place, S.W., Oxford, 1876), pp. ix-x.

56. Williams (1891: 223).

57. Williams (1891: 225): "I need not repeat here that the god's energy is supposed to be located more especially in the female half of his nature, and that the divine mothers are variously classified according to various degrees of participation in that energy, the highest being identified with different forms of his supposed consort, the lowest including human mothers downwards, who are all worshipped as incarnations of the one divine productive capacity of nature....In all likelihood every one of these, though declared by the Brahmans to be separate forms of Siva's consort Kali, is really the representative of some local deity (Grama-devata), worshipped by the inhabitants from time immemorial."

58. Murdoch (1896: iv). Also mentioned by Caldwell (1856): 75 & 79.

59. Murdoch (1896: 8).

60. Murdoch (1896: 3–38).

61. Isaac Taylor, *The Origin of the Aryans: An Account of the Prehistoric Ethnology and Civilization of Europe* (New York: Scribner & Welford, 1890), p. 212.

62. Gustav Oppert, *On The Original Inhabitants of Bharatavarsa or India* (1893; New York: Arno Press, 1978).

63. Oppert (1893: v-vii & 9–13 & 451–452).

64. Oppert (1893: 12, 451 & 503–04): "The outward appearance of the Dasas or Dasyus—these were the names with which the new-comers honoured their opponents—was not such as to create a favourable impression, and they were in consequence taunted with their black colour and flat noses, which latter made their faces appear as if they had no noses... Neither it can be denied that the worship of the aborigines has secured access into Brahmanism, with the result that not only did the Kshetradevatas enter into the Brahmanic liturgy, but also that superstitious Brahmans still sacrifice at the shrines of the popular deities of the lower orders.... [T]he presence and assistance of Brahmans at the feasts of the Gramadevatas, a participation which may be scorned by many pious and intelligent Brahmans, but which is nevertheless a well-known fact, proving the influence which superstition exercises on the human mind, however free it may boast to be."

65. Oppert (1893: viii-ix).

66. Ramakrishna, T., *Life in an Indian Village* (London: T. Fisher Unwin [Unwin Brothers], The Gresham Press. 1891, p. 67.

67. Ramakrishna (1891:73).

68. Edgar Thurston, *Castes and Tribes of Southern India*. 7 vols. (Madras: Government Press, 1909).

69. Edgar Thurston, *Ethnographic Notes in Southern India*. (Madras: Government of Madras, 1906), pp. 487–501: "In some cases it would appear that the observance has led to loss of life. This would, of course, justify the interference of the magistracy, and in future, any occurrence of this nature should lead to the prohibition of the ceremony of the village where it happened. The best method of discouraging this objectionable practice must be left to the discretion of the different magistrates, but the Governor in Council feels confident that, if it be properly explained that the object of Government is not to interfere with any religious observances of its subjects, but to abolish a cruel and revolting practice, the efforts of the magistracy will be willingly seconded by the influence of the great mass of the community, and more particularly of the wealthy and intelligent classes who do not seem to countenance or support the swinging ceremony."

70. A. Berriedale Keith, "Indian Mythology" in Louis Herbert Gray, ed., *The Mythology of All Races*. 13 vols.), Vol. VI (Boston: Marshall Jones Company, 1916) pp. 230–232.

71. Keith (1916: 245).

72. Henry Whitehead, *The Village Gods of South India* (New York and London: Garland Publishing, Inc., 1980; reprint of the 2nd ed., 1921).

73. Whitehead (1980: 13).

74. Whitehead (1980: 11–13).
75. Elmore, 1915.
76. Elmore (1915): 10–11.
77. Elmore (1915): 6.
78. W. Crooke, "The Cults of the Mother Goddess in India," *Folklore* 39 (1918), p. 302. The last sentence was footnoted to, W. Ward, *The Hindoos*, 2nd ed., ii., 115 et seq.; *Gazetteer of Oudh*, 1877, i., 367 et seq.; H. H. Oldfield, *Sketches from Nepal*, ii., 293 et seq.
79. H. Krishna Sastri, *South-Indian Images of Gods and Goddesses* (Delhi: Bharatiya Publishing House, 1916; reprinted in 1974 by Asian Educational Services, Madras), p. 7.
80. Sastri (1974: 226).
81. Sastri (1974: 227), footnote 1: "Some of these inhuman practices seem to be but remnants of the older human sacrifices which were once quite a common feature of Sakti worship. Epigraphical evidence has been adduced to show that voluntary human sacrifices were offered even to the male deity Virabhadra."
82. John Marshall, "First Light on a Long Forgotten Civilization," *Illustrated London News* 20 (September, 1924), pp. 528–532 & 548. Within a week of Marshall's publication, Henry Sayce, a professor of Assyriology, wrote a letter to the editor in which he established Indus relations with Susa of 3000 BCE, thereby putting Indus in that time slot. In another week, two Sumerian archaeologists reconfirmed Sayce's opinion by quoting the location of Proto-Elamite tablets in the sites of Susa and Babylonia. See C. J. Gadd and S. Smith, "The New Links between Indian and Babylonian Civilizations." *The Illustrated London News* 4 (October, 1924): 614–616.
83. Sir John Marshall, ed., *Mohenjo-daro and the Indus Civilization* 3 vols. (London: A. Probsthain, 1931; reprinted by Asian Educational Services, 1996).
84. Marshall (1996: vol I: 111).
85. Mortimer Wheeler, *The Indus Civilization* (Cambridge: University Press, 1953), pp. 83.
86. Louis Dumont. *Religion/Politics and History in India* (Paris: Mouton Publishers, 1970), p. 21.
87. M. N. Srinivas, *Religion and Society Among the Coorgs of South India* (Bombay: Asia Publishing House, 1952; reprint, 1965), pp. 213–214.
88. Srinivas (1965: 214–215).
89. Srinivas (1965: 225).
90. M. N. Srinivas, *The Remembered Village* (Berkeley: University of California, 1976), pp. 167–176.
91. McKim Marriott, ed. *Village India. Studies in the Little Community* (Chicago: The University of Chicago Press, 1955, reprint, 1986), pp. 217–18; Surajit Sinha, "Tribal Cultures of Peninsular India as a Dimension of Little Tradition in the

Study of Indian Civilization: A Preliminary Statement," in Milton Singer, ed., *Traditional India* (Austin: University of Texas Press, 1959), pp. 298–312.

92. Paul C. Wiebe, "Religious Change in South India: Perspectives From a Small Town," in *Religion and Society* 22 (1975): 27–46.

93. McKim Marriott, ed., *Village India: Studies in the Little Community* (Chicago: University of Chicago Press, 1955; reprint, 1986), pp. 211–212.

94. S. C. Dube, *Indian Village* (London: Routledge & Kegan Paul LTD, 1959; originally published in 1955), pp. 38–39: "It is probable that their social exclusiveness reflects an attitude which was developed in ancient times when a great fusion of Aryan and non-Aryan groups was taking place in Indian society and Hinduism was consolidating itself."

95. Dube, 94.

96. Alan Beals, "Conflict and Interlocal Festivals in a South Indian Region," The Journal of Asian Studies 13 (1964): 99–113.

97. Thomas Coburn. *Devi-Mahatmya: The Crystallization of the Goddess Tradition* (Columbia, Missouri: South Asia Books: 1985), p. 8.

98. Coburn (1985: 7). As a representative sample, Coburn quotes the following works: A.L. Basham. *The Wonder That Was India* (New York: Grove Press, 1959), p. 311; R. G. Bhandarker, *Vaisnavism, Saivism, and Minor Religious Systems* (Varanasi: Indological Book House, 1965) p. 142–143); A. K. Bhattacharya, in "A non-Aryan Aspect of the Devi" in D. C. Sircar, ed., *The Sakti Cult and Tara* (Calcutta: University of Calcutta, 1971), pp 56–60; Brown (1961), p. 5); Sudhakar Chattopadhyaya, *Evolution of Hindu Sects* (New Delhi: Munshiram Manoharlal, 1970), pp. 151–52.

99. Some more examples of these are: Eva Rudy Jansen, *The Book of Hindu Mythology* (Diever: Holland: Benkey Kok Publications, 1993), p. 127; John R. Hinnells & Eric J. Sharpe, ed., *Hinduism* (New Castle upon Tyne, England: Oriel Press, 1972), p. 52; Jitendra Nath Benerjea, "The Hindu Concept of the Natural World," in Kenneth M. Morgan, ed., *The Religion of Hindus* (New York: The Ronald Press Company, 1953), p. 66.

100. Norman Brown, "Mythology of India," in Samuel Noah Kramer, ed., *Mythologies of the Ancient World* (Garden City, NY: Double Day and Co., 1961) p. 311.

101. Milton Singer, *When A Great Tradition Modernizes* (New York: Praeger Publishers, 1972), pp. 43–44.

102. Singer, 45.

103. David Mandelbaum, "Introduction: Process and Structure in South Asian Religion," in The *Journal of Asian Studies* 13 (1964): 5–20.

104. David Mandelbaum, "Transcendental and Pragmatic Aspects of Religion," *American Anthropologist* 68 (1966): 1174–1198.

105. Pauline Mahar Kolenda, "Aspects of Religion in South Asia," *The Journal of Asian Studies* 13 (1964): 71–81.

106. Kolenda: 71–81.

107. Edward Harper, "A Hindu Pantheon," *Southwestern Journal of Anthropology* 15 (1959): 227–234.

108. Harper (1959), 228.

109. Lawrence Babb, "Marriage and Malevolence: The Uses of Sexual Opposition in a Hindu Pantheon," in *Ethnology* 9 (1970): 138.

110. Lawrence Babb, *The Divine Hierarchy* (New York: Columbia University Press, 1975), p. 212.

111. Babb (1975): 229.

112. Harper (1959): 227–234).

113. Susan Snow Wadley, *Shakti: Power in the Conceptual Structure of Karimpur Religion* (Chicago: The University of Chicago, 1975), p. 54.

114. Wadley, 107–145.

115. Wadley, 121.

116. Susan A. Bean, "Referential and Indexical Meanings of Amma in Kannada: Mother, Woman, Goddess, Pox, and Help!," in Journal of Anthropological Research 31 (1975): 313–330.

117. Edward Harper, "Ritual Pollution as an Integrator of Caste and Religion," *Journal of Asian Studies*, 13 (1964): 151–197.

118. Harper (1964):185.

119. Harper, 1964.

120. Harper, (1964): 184.

121. Dumont (1970): 28.

122. Dumont (1970): 28.

123. Gabriella Eichinger Ferro-Luzzi, "Ritual as Language: The Case of South Indian Food Offerings," in *Current Anthropology* 18 (1977): 509.

124. Ferro-Luzzi, 509.

125. Michael Moffatt, *An Untouchable Community in South India* (Princeton: Princeton University Press, 1979), pp. 219–220.

126. Moffatt, 220–221.

127. Bryan Pfaffenberger, "Social Communication in Dravidian Ritual," *Journal of Anthropological Research* 36 (1980): 196–219.

128. Diane Mines, *Fierce Gods* (Bloomington, IN: Indiana University Press, 2005), p. 17.

129. Tapper (1979): 1–31.

130. Tapper (1979): 1–31.

131. Brenda E. F. Beck, *Perspectives On a Regional Culture* (New Delhi: Vikas Publishing House Pvt Ltd, 1979), p. 5.

132. Brenda E. F. Beck, *Peasant Society in Konku* (Vancouver: University of British Columbia Press,1972), p. 79.

133. Beck (1972):111–116.

134. Beck (1972: 99). F. J. Richards has provided a suggestive parallel here in his article "Village Deities of Nellore Taluk, North Arcot District," *The Quarterly Journal of the Mythic Society* 10 (1920): 116.

135. Stein (1980): 173–215.

136. Stein (1980): 78–86 & 323–331.

137. Susan Bayly, *Saints, Goddesses and Kings Muslims and Christians in South Indian Society 1700–1900* (Cambridge: Cambridge University Press, 1989), pp. 27–30.

138. Bayly, 30.

139. Bayly, 45–46. Although an effort had been made to preserve some independence of Sanskrit and various Dravidian traditions during the medieval period, Stein opines that the existence of two independent traditions—Sanskrit and Dravidian—was a false conception and so was the notion that *brahmins* were outsiders. Stein admits that there were tensions between *brahmin* and non-*brahmin* savants and religious teachers in the thirteenth century, but the issues were not related to indigenous culture versus outside culture, as there were *brahmins* who were advocates and transmitters of non-Sanskritic cultural variations, while there were a number of non-*brahmin* Sanskrit scholars as well. So, the competition, as he states, was primarily among the upholders of cultural variants to gain the approval from the powerful. See Stein, 51–52.

140. David Kinsley, *Hindu Goddesses* (Berkeley: University of California Press, 1988) p. 217.

141. Kinsley (1988): 197–211.

142. Kinsley (1988): 155.

143. Gavin Flood. *An Introduction to Hinduism* (Cambridge: Cambridge University Press, 1996), pp. 23–50.

144. Flood, 50.

145. Madeleine Biardeau, *Stories about Posts* Trans. by Alf Hiltebeitel (Chicago: The University of Chicago Press, 2004): *passim.*

146. Biardeau (2004): 307–308.

147. Madeleine Biardeau, "Brahman and Meat-Eating Gods," in Alf Hiltebeitel, ed., *Criminal Gods and Demon Devotees* (Albany, New York: State University of New York Press, 1989) pp. 20–21.

148. David Knipe, "Goats Are Food Divine: A Comparison of Contemporary Vedic God and Hindu Goddess Sacrifices in Coastal Andhra," 29th Annual Conference on South Asia, University of Wisconsin—Madison, October 13, 2000.

149. Alf Hiltebeitel, "Draupadī's Two Guardians: The Buffalo King and the Muslim Devotee," in Alf Hiltebeitel ed. *Criminal Gods and Demon Devotees*, pp. 362–363.

150. Narendra Nath Bhattacharyya, *The Indian Mother Goddess* (New Delhi: South Asia Books, 2nd edition, 1997 [first 1970]); Jitendra Nath Banerjea, *The Development of Hindu Iconography* (New Delhi: Munshiram Manoharlal, 1974); Shantilal Nagar, *Indian Gods and Goddesses* vol. I (Delhi: B. R. Publishing House, 1998).

151. Parpola (1994):168.
152. Parpola (1994):172.
153. Sjoberg (1971): 240–272 and Maloney (1975): 1–40.
154. Sjoberg (1971): 240–272.
155. Jane McIntosh, *A Peaceful Realm* (Boulder, CO: Westview Press, 2002), pp. 116–117.
156. David Kinsley, *Hindu Goddesses* (Berkeley: University of California Press, 1988), pp. 212–220.
157. Lynn E. Gatwood, *Devi and the Spouse Goddess* (Riverdale: Riverdale Co., 1985).
158. Sara Caldwell, "Margins at the Center, Tracing Kali Through Time, Space, and Culture," in Rachel Fell McDermott and Jeffrey Kripal, eds., *Encountering Kali.* (Berkeley: University of California Press, 2003), pp. 251–253.
159. Caldwell (2003): 251–253. See also Friedhelm Hardy, *Viraha-bhakti: The Early History of Krsna Devotion in South India* (Oxford: Oxford University Press, 1983), p. 123.
160. Lynn Foulston, *At the Feet of the Goddess. The Divine Feminine in Local Hindu Religion* (New Delhi: Sussex Academic Press, 2003).
161. Eveline Meyer, *Ankalaparamecuvari, A Goddess of Tamilnadu, Her Myths and Cult* (Stuttgart: Steiner Verlag Wiesbaden GMBH, 1986), pp. 39–40.

CHAPTER 2

1. I use the word "symbol" in this book to indicate that a particular sign is not just what it appears to be, but also stands for something else. For example, the lotus is just a lotus but it will also function as a symbol when it is not just representing the lotus flower, but standing for the universe and understood as the womb of the goddess.
2. N. N. Bhattacharya, *The Indian Mother Goddess.* (New Delhi: South Asia Books, 1997; originally published in 1970), p. 155.
3. Sumathi Ramaswami, *The Goddess and the Nation: Mapping Mother India* (Durham, NC: Duke University Press, 2010).
4. Nayani Krishnakumari, *Telugu Janapada Geya Gathalu (Telugu)*, (Hyderabad: Telugu Academy, 1990), p. 225.
5. Nayani (1990): 211–212. It is possible, as suggested by one of the anonymous reviewers of this book manuscript, that the name Mahuramma derives from the name of the town, Mahur, in the state of Maharashtra to which the western Andhra region is in close proximity. This Mahuramma might be conflated with the cult of Ellamma.
6. The translation of the Sanskrit phrase *adi maha sakti* is as follows: Adi=beginning; Maha=great; Sakti=energy, power or goddess (who is synonymous to the power and energy): "the primordial great goddess."

7. The main components of the ritual descriptions come from my observation of the annual festival held in honor of Kanaka Mahalakshmi in China Waltair, Visakhapatnam in 1993.

8. It is not uncommon to hold rituals for *gramadevatas* in different seasons, especially when multiple goddesses are worshiped at different timings. These rituals could be observed once in several years.

9. Vermilion, also called *kumkuma* in Telugu, is a red powder used in worshiping the goddess. One theory of the significance of this powder is that it represents the menstrual blood of the goddess, symbolizing the fertility aspect. Hence wearing this powder on one's forehead indicates auspiciousness.

10. In religious ceremonies, gifts are always accompanied by betel leaves and areca nuts.

11. *Poturaju*, who is considered as a brother or a servant of the *gramadevata*, is impersonated by a male in some parts of Andhra. *Poturaju* carries a whip and goes in the procession beating himself or others who come forward to receive these blows as blessings from the goddess. The relationship of the goddess to *poturaju* and the sacrificial animal is explained eloquently by Madeleine Biardeau. See Madeleine Biardeau, "The Sami Tree and the Sacrificial Buffalo," in *Contributions to Indian Sociology* (New Series) 18 (1984): 1–24.

12. For details of animal sacrifices in the early twentieth century see Whitehead (1921): 49–70.

13. The sacrificial animal is considered as the form of the goddess herself. Some myths, such as the myth of Renuka that will be explained in the next chapter, tell of her violent death leading to her deification. This is analogous to the violent deaths of human females who are turned into *gramadevatas*, whose stories are enumerated in successive chapters. In all these cases, before they became *gramadevatas*, these females were victims like the sacrificial animal. While their stories and myths indicate the connection of their sacrifice with rebirth and rejuvenation, the reenactment of sacrifice in the annual worship of the goddess through an animal victim ensures this revitalization. One theory is that the *gramadevata*, a victim at the hands of a male (sometimes those of her husband), asks for a sacrifice of a male animal representing her husband. In the act of sacrifice, the goddess is seen as mating with her husband. Whether the animal represents the goddess or her husband or a male relative, the goddess becomes the sacrifice causing renewal and rebirth.

14. Coburn (1985).

15. Menstruating blood and the blood during the delivery of a human baby are seen as signs of fertility that extends to the fertility of crops, herds, etc. For this reason, it is considered important to reinvigorate the fertility goddess by offering blood. The rice that is mixed with blood is believed to be potent in killing pests and nourishing fields.

16. Thurston (1909: 299). The word "Matangi" is derived from Sanskrit, the translation of which is "person possessed by the mother." In this sense, Matangi is a person who acts as a vessel to the goddess. See chapter 4 for more detailed discussion on Matangi.

17. Whitehead (1921): 67–68.

18. David Kinsley, *Hindu Goddesses* (Delhi: Motilala Banarsidass, 1987), p. 33.

19. Elaine Craddock, "Reconstructing the Split Goddess as Sakti" in Tracy Pintchman, *ed.*, *In Search of Mahadevi* (New York: State University of New York Press, 2001), pp. 148–167.

20. Velury Venkata Krishna Sastry, *The Proto and Early Historic Cultures of Andhra Pradesh* (Hyderabad: The Government of Andhra Pradesh, 1983), p. 197, fig. 22; a *svastika* pattern is noticed in the ground plan of burial monuments in the districts of Mahaboobnagar, Karimnagar, and Warangal; see pp. 57, 64, 66, and 79; the Ujjain symbol representing four quarters could be a representation for the goddess as the head of the world, p. 110. The symbols such as the trident, endless knot, and snakes are depicted on Megalithic rock paintings, brushings and coins: p. 111. Also, the *svastika* and other symbols have been in use as graffiti marks starting from the pre-historic period of Andhra to the present day. See Velury (1983): pp. 107, 109–111; plate 17(b), fig. 8).

21. Lal (1960): 21; H. D. Sankalia, "The Nude Goddess in Indian Art." *Marg* 31 (1978): 4–10; http://www.harappa.com/indus/90.html, (Harappa 1996-2008), 90; a molded tablet from the Indus period shows the symbol of the *chakra* as a sign of the goddess. The symbol of unending knot in proto-historic Andhra is identical with the symbol at Harappa. See Asko Parpola, *Deciphering the Indus Script*. (Cambridge: Cambridge University Press, 1994), pp. 55–56, fig. 4.6 a.

22. See C. Sivaramamurti, *Sri Lakshmi in Indian Art and Thought*, fig. 62.

23. Velury (1983): 47, 50 and 116, plate 13 (e) and 112. The early phase of the Megalithic period in Andhra was assigned to seventh to eighth century BCE, which overlapped with the Neolithic phase that lasted for nearly 1500 years.

24. The nude mother goddess tradition is traced to Indus times, where the goddess is seen naked in several representations: http://www.harappa.com/indus/90.html, http://www.harappa.com/indus/34.html.

25. Parpola (1994): 256, fig. 14.32: Parpola interpreted the naked goddess image as a priestess.

26. Bhattacharyya (1997): 152–153.

27. Velury (1983): 46–47, 68, 109–111, plate 12.

28. Susan Huntington, *The Art of Ancient India, Buddhist, Hindu, Jain* (New York: Weather Hill, 1985), fig. 2.11.

29. Huntington (1985): 19–20.

30. Parpola (1994): 14.16.

31. Parpola (1994): fig. 6.3a & 10.11)

32. Parpola (1994: fig. 14.16.

33. The Buddha is often portrayed as the bull mounted on the pillars and pilasters of the Buddhist stupas in Andhra and elsewhere. The Adinatha, or Rishabhanadha, is portrayed with a bull on his pedestal, as it is at Kolanupaka in Nalgonda district. See Sripada Gopala Krishna Murthy, *Jain Vestiges in Andhra* (Hyderabad: Government of Andhra Pradesh, 1963), p. 62 (the author identifies the sculpture as belonging to Jaina Adinatha from the emblem on his pedestal).

34. John Marshall, *Mohenjo-daro and the Indus Civilization*. 3 vols. (London: Arthur Probshtain, 1931), vol. I, plate 12, no. 18.

35. *The Hymns of the Rgveda*. Tr. Ralph T. H. Griffith. 4th ed. 2 vols. (Banaras: Chowkhamba Sanskrit Series Office, 1963), Vol. I. Book 1. 22, 159, 160, 185; Book 4. 56, Book 6. 70; Bhattacharyya (1997):153.

36. Kinsley (1988): 9–10.

37. Wendy Doniger, *The Rigveda: An Anthology* (London: Penguin Books, 1981), p. 38. Interpreting *Rig Veda* 10:72, Doniger says that the creation myth identifies the goddess Aditi as giving birth to the universe. She crouches with legs spread in just the same way as the naked goddess is often depicted in early sculptures. Carol Radcliffe Bolon, *Forms of the Goddess Lajja Gauri in Indian Art* (Pennsylvania: The Pennsylvania University Press, 1992), p.16, fn. 22 mentions R. C. Dhere, *Lajja Gauri* (in Marathi) 1978, p. 172; Raymond Allchin, "The Interpretation of a Seal from Chanhu-daro and Its Significance for the Religion of the Indus Civilization," in Janine Schotsman and Maurizio Taddei, eds., *South Asian Archaeology: Papers from the Seventh International Conference of the Association of South Asian Archaeologists in Western Europe*, Brussels 1983 (Naples: 1985), 371–383.

38. David Kinsley, *Hindu Goddesses* (Delhi: Motilal Banarsidass, 1987), pp. 9–10.

39. Velury (1983): 223–224.

40. Kinsley (1998): 68–70.

41. Bolon (1992):16 and 39, figs. 73, 77, 81, 99 and 102. The author discusses the frequent presence of the bull in association with the goddess in early art predating Saivite art to explain how the bull's virility is needed to fertilize the earth goddess.

42. H. K. Narasimhaswamy, "Mother Goddess from Nagarjunakonda," *Epigraphia Indica* (EI) XXIX, p.137.

43. *Nellore District Inscriptions* (*NDI*), Vol. I, p. 238, Atmakur, 28 and 50, Vol. II, p. 767; Nellore 3, Vol. III, pp. 1069 and 1221; Rapur 10, Ongole 12. 90, 92; *South Indian Inscriptions* (*SII*), Vol. X, No. 577 and Vol. XVI, Nos. 21, 55, 64 and 285; P.V. Parabrahma Sastry, ed., *Inscriptions of Andhra Pradesh, Cuddapah District*, 1981. Vol. II, p. 240.

CHAPTER 3

1. Although there is a reservation system in educational institutes and government employment to improve the lot of formerly untouchable castes categorized as "scheduled castes" in India's constitution, a majority of members of these castes still experience social and economic inequality.

2. This case has parallels with the one described in Bernard S. Cohn's "The Changing Status of a Depressed Class;" see in Marriott (1955): 53–57.

3. A priest serving at Nalla Pochamma temple in Secundrabad related this story.

4. *Census of India 1961 Vol II. Andhra Pradesh. Part II, VII- B (12). Fairs and Festivals: Mahaboobnagar District*, p. 117.

5. Elaine Craddock, "Reconstructing the Split Goddess as Sakti" in Tracy Pintchman, ed., *Seeking Mahadevi*, pp. 151–159.

6. *Census of India 1961, Chittoor District*, p. 41.

7. *Census of India 1961, Srikakulam District*, p.6.

8. *Census of India 1961, Srikakulam District*, p. 35. This practice resembles the ritual of mixing the blood of the sacrificed animal with the cooked rice and spreading it over the village and the fields in order to drive away diseases. Whitehead records the practice of cooked rice soaked in blood sprinkled over houses to protect them from evil spirits in several places in Andhra. See Whitehead (1921): 52–57.

9. Parpola (1994): 240–283, figs. 14.25, 14.26, 14.32, plate XCIII. 307; E. J. Mackay, *Further Excavations at Mohenjodaro* (Delhi: Manager Publications, 1938), plate XCIV–430; the evolution of the tree into the anthropomorphic form of goddess appears in the early Buddhist art of Andhra. See C. Sivaramamurti, *Sri Lakshmi in Indian Art and Thought* (New Delhi: Kanak Publications, 1982), plate 62.

10. Parpola, figs. 7.13b (reverse of a faience tablet), 13.18 and 14.5 (terracotta tablets).

11. James Fergusson, *Tree and Serpent Worship* (Delhi: Indological Book House, 1971), p. 209, plate LXXXVII, fig. 3; to learn about what physical traits constitute *Mahapurusha Lakshanas* for the Buddha, refer to K. Rama, *Buddhist Art of Nagarjunakonda* (Delhi: Sundeep Prakashan, 1995), pp. 183–184; P. Chenna Reddy, ed., *Phanigiri: A Buddhist Site in Andhra Pradesh* (Hyderabad: Department of Archaeology and Museums, Government of Andhra Pradesh), p. 25: e and f.

12. Sivaramamurti (1982): fig. 65.

13. Sivaramamurti (1982): 69, fig. 119.

14. Sripada (1963): 7 and 42, fig. 25b; I. K. Sarma, *Jaina Art and Architecture in Andhra* published online: http://jainology.blogspot.com/2008/11/jaina-art-and-architecture-in-andhra.html.

15. Sivaramamurti (1982): 33, fig. 69.

16. K. Ramammohan Rao, *Perspectives of Archaeology, Art and Culture in Early Andhra Desa* (New Delhi, Aditya Prakashan, 1992), pp. 90–92, plate 13.

17. Velury (1983): 107, 109–111 and 197, plate 17b, fig. 8). The *srivatsa* in the form of endless knot is depicted on pottery and coins. Also, the *srivatsa*, along with other symbols, have been in use as graffiti marks starting from the prehistoric period in Andhra.

18. P. Chenna Reddy, ed., *Mahatalavara Coins: A Hoard from Phanigiri, Nalgonda District* (Hyderabad: Government of Andhra Pradesh, 2008), pp. 3–26.

19. Velury (1983): plate 64.

20. Bolon (1992): 55, fig. 121. Bolon also mentions the evolution of the *srivatsa* as the form of the goddess at Sanchi and Bharhut. See p. 56, figs. 10, 111, and 122.

21. Bolon (1992): 56, fig. 112.

22. Bolon (1992): fig. 111.

23. C. Sivaramamurti (1982): figs. 87 and 89.

24. Bolon (1992): fig. 110.

25. Bolon (1992): 47, figs. 126 and 127.

26. Bolon (1992): figs. 122–125 and 128.

27. Huntington (1985): 21, figs. 2.13 and 2.18.

28. I. K. Sarma, "Lead Coins of King Satavahan from Sannati," in A. V. Narasimha Murthy, ed., *Studies in South Indian Coins*, Volume 3 (Madras: South Indian Numismatic Society, 1993), pp. 65–80; Veluri (1983): 201, pls. 101a and b).

29. Huntington (1985): 78–79, fig. 5.29.

30. Rama (1995): 69–74, 80; plates 17, 18, 20 and 24).

31. Huntington (1985): 140, fig. 8. 17.

32. P. Arundhati, *Brahmanism, Jainism and Buddhism in Andhra Desa* (Delhi: Sundeep Prakashan, 1990), p. 232; these depictions represent the scenes in the Jataka stories. See E. B. Cowell, ed., *The Jataka*. 6 Vols. "Ayacitabhatta Jataka," No. 19 (pp. 53–54); "Baka Jataka," No. 38 (pp. 95–97); "Dummedha Jataka," No. 50 (pp. 126–128), "Vessantara Jataka," No. 547 (pp. 246–305) as mentioned in Srivastava (1979: 65).

33. C. Sivaramamurti (1982): fig. 83.

34. Fergusson (1971): 223.

35. Sivaramamurti (1942): 57.

36. Fergusson (1971): plate XXVII.

37. Stone (1994): figs. 171–200.

38. Stone (1994): figs. 176 and 186; Arundhati (1990): plate 23.

39. Sivaramamurti (1982): 32, fig. 67: Sivaramamurti identified the Yakshi figure as the proto-form of Sri. But there is no evidence that the Buddhists called this goddess Sri. There is, however, sufficient evidence to show that she could be the proto-form of Sirima devata, who in Saivism and Vaishnavism takes the name of Sri Lakshmi. According to the *Khuddaka Nikaya*, Sirima was a courtesan who repented her deeds to become the disciple of the Buddha. Read *Khodavagga*, verse 223: http://www.budsas.org/ebud/dhp/i.htm.

40. Kinsley: 20–21.

41. Sripada (1963): 29 and 72: fig. 13a [Durgakonda] and 13b [Gurubhakta hill], plate IV).

42. A long version of this containing many twists and turns and reflecting varied stages of conflict between the goddess religion and that of *brahmanic* is found in Whitehead (1921): 126–138.

43. This is my translation of the original song given in Nayani (1990: 193–196).
44. *Census of India 1961: Srikakulam District*, pp. 61–62.
45. Anantha Krishna Iyer, *The Mysore Tribes and Castes* (Mysore: Mysore University, 1935), vol.1, pp. 297–298.
46. Personal recollection from local people and also found with some variation in the *Census of India 1961, East Godavari District*, p. 100.
47. *Census of India 1961, East Godavari District*, p. 68.
48. *Census of India 1961, Anantapur District*, p. 159, and field visit in January 2010.
49. Velury (1983): 94.
50. Velury (1983): 94.
51. Velury (1983): 195.
52. Sivaramamurti (1982): fig. 35 shows the photograph of the goddess from Kosam; Bolon (1992): 16, fig. 73.
53. Sivaramamurti (1982): 30, fig. 60.
54. Bolon (1992): 14, figs. 115–117.
55. Some of the variations of the brimming pot are: 1) pots with lotuses and coins issuing out of them (*padmanidhi*); 2) pots encircled by serpents; 3) conches replacing pots where lotuses and coins appear (*sankhanidhi*); 4) conches with creepers issuing out of them (*sankhalata*); 5) lotuses with creepers (*padmalata*).
56. Stone (1994): 29, 38, and 45, figs. 88, 91; A. Aiyappan and P. R. Srinivasan, *Guide to the Buddhist Antiquities* (Madras: Director of Museums, 1992), p. 33, plate VIII; Ramamohan Rao (1992): 37, 39, and 43.
57. Huntington (1985): 633, note 36.
58. Sripada (1963): 51–52, 55, 60–61, 72, 80–82 and 84, figs. 58e, f, g, i, 60a and 69; B. Masthanaiah, *The Temples of Mukhalingam* (New Delhi: Cosmo Publications, 1978), pp. 48, 49, 51, 112 and 116, plate 10; J. Ramanaiah, *Temples of South India* (New Delhi: Concept Publishing Company, 1989), pp. 54–55: Bhimesvara Temple at Vemulavada, Karimnagar District: "The Chandrasila at the foot of the *sopana* and the figures of Sankanidhi and Padmanidhi on the balustrade deserve notice."
59. Velury (1983): 107, 109–111.
60. Huntington (1985):158–159, fig. 8.38.
61. Bolon (1992): 14, fig. 5.
62. Bolon (1992): 52.
63. Elizabeth Rosen Stone (1994): Illustrations # 87, 115 and 149–154.
64. Nigam (1980): plate XI; Rama (1995:91, plate 26).
65. Kinsley: 21.
66. Rama (1995): 154.
67. Rama (1995): 154.
68. Ramammohan Rao (1992): 37, 39 and 43; Sripada (1963): 80–81, figs. 58e, f, g i, 59, 60a and 69, plate XXIX; I. K. Sarma, "Early Historical Vestiges at

Vijayawada and some Trimurti Cult Plaques," *Itihas* 7 (1979,): 23–30, plate III-B; Ramanaiah (1967): 57 and 87.

69. Ramanaiah (1967): 187.

70. http://www.harappa.com/indus/52.html, 52. figurine, pot-bellied goddess.

71. Bolon (1992): 13–14, figs. 5, 8, 11, 12, 32 and 106; Janssen, "On The Origin and Development of the So-Called Lajja Gauri," Paper presented at the 11th International Conference of the Association of South Asian Archaeologist in Western Europe, Berlin, July 2, 1991; Stella Kramrisch, "An Image of Aditi-Uttanapad," *Artibus Asiae* 19 (1956): 259–270.

72. Bolon (1992): 45–46, figs. 104–107.

73. Janssen (1991): 46.

74. Bolon (1992): 28, 30–31, figs. 46, 55–57, 60, 63–64; Ramanaiah (1967): 55, 57, 98, 192; Arundhati (1990): 129–130.

75. Janssen (1991).

76. Bolon (1992): 15.

77. Bolon (1992): 53.

78. *Epigraphia Andhrica* (EI) III, pp. 16ff.

79. Heinrich Zimmer, "The Goddess," in *Myths And Symbols in Indian Art and Civilization*, Joseph Campbell, Compiler/editor (New York: Pantheon Books, 1946), pp. 59–68. Balaji Mundkur, *The Cult of the Serpent: An Interdisciplinary Survey of its Manifestation and Origins* (Albany: State University of New York Press, 1983).

80. A. Berriedale Keith, "Indian Mythology," in Louis Herbert Gray, ed., *The Mythology of All Races*, 13 Vols. (Boston: Marshall Jones Company, 1967) 6: 241.

81. Richard Brubaker, The Ambivalent Mistress: A Study of South Indian Village Goddesses and Their Religious Meaning, Ph.D. Thesis, (University of Chicago, 1978), p. 33.

82. Keith (1967): 53; for examples in Tamilnadu, see Ziegenbalg, 136–137.

83. Elmore (1915): 94–95.

84. Sree Padma, "From Village to City: Transforming Goddess from Urban Andhra Pradesh," in *Seeking Mahadevi*, Tracy Pintchman, ed. (New York: State University of New York Press, 2001), pp. 115–144.

85. David Shulman, *Tamil Temple Myths: Sacrifice and Divine Marriage in the South Indian Saiva Tradition* (Princeton: Princeton University Press, 1980), p. 119.

86. Tapper (1979): 166.

87. Nayani (1990): 197.

88. Parpola (1994): fig. 10.11.

89. Velury (1983): 111.

90. Huntington (1985) 22, fig. 2.14; referring to a seal with a figure of a yogi flanked by two kneeling devotees backed by cobras with raised hoods, Huntington observed: "the obvious resemblance of this group to later Buddhist votive scenes in which serpent deities (*nagas*) pay homage to the Buddha."

91. Velury (1983): 224.
92. Velury (1983): 111.
93. Ramammohan Rao (1992): 117, fig. 17.
94. A. Aiyappan & P. R. Srinivasan, *Guide to the Buddhist Antiquities.* (Madras: Director of Museums,1992), p. 31, plate 182.
95. Sivaramamurti (1982): 3.
96. Fergusson (1971): 223.
97. Rama (1995): 69–74 and 101–106, plates 17,18, 30, 31, and 35); Nigam (plate XI: shows the seated Buddha on the coil of *Muchalinda Naga, whose* hood is spread above the Buddha's head); *Indian Archaeology 1989-90 A Review* (New Delhi: Archaeological Survey of India, 1994), p.8; the Thotlakonda Buddhist ruins contain *Muchalinda Naga* sculptures, where the Buddha was worshiped in relic and symbolic forms; Velury (1983): plate 61: *Muchalinda Naga* protecting the feet of the Buddha; M. L. Nigam, *Sculptural Art of Andhra* (Delhi: Sundeep Prakashan, 1980), plate V: entwined serpents around the stupa at Chandavaram, Ongole district; Stone, 29 (1994), figs. 43, 111 show the seated Buddha on the coil of *Muchalinda Naga,* whose hood is spread above the Buddha's head), 148; Fergusson (1971): plates LVIII, LX, LXII, LXVI, LXVII, and LXX.
98. In Bhutan (personal visit in May–June 2011), people collect stones that look like coiled snakes, believing that they are a self-arisen (*svayambhu*) form of *naga* spirits. These stones are given as votive offerings to the Buddhist temples and monasteries, such as at Kichu Lhakhang and Punakha Dzong, where the goddess with snake hoods around her face is worshiped. People believe that the Buddha brought the snake spirits under his influence so that they could use their powers to protect the people of the land. A clear connection with the earth and the *naga* is established in Bhutan, as the earth itself is considered as the form of serpent deity. Because of this, when the earth is dug to lay foundations for a building, an appeasing ritual called *salang* is performed.
99. Nigam (1980): plates XX –XXII); Mukkamala Radhakrishna Sarma, *Temples of Telingana* (Hyderabad: Book Links Corporation, 1972), plates 71, 83, and 94.
100. J. Ramanaiah, *Temples of South India.* (New Delhi: Concept Publishing Company,1967), pp. 62, 82–83, 88, 103 and 125; illustrations # 14, 35, 36, 43, 88, and 144.
101. Sripada (1963): pp. 22, 28, 42, 47: fig. 25c. plate X, p. 43: fig. 26g, plate XI, p. 47: fig. 27, plate XII and fig. 28, plate XIII, p. 48: fig. 13a, p. 52: fig. 32, plate XIV; pp 54, 63, plate XIII, p. 66, fig. 44c plate XXI; p. 69: fig. 50, plate XXII; fig 59, Pl XXIX); I. K. Sarma, (2008) http://jainology.blogspot.com/2008/11/jaina-art-and-architecture-in-andhra.html.
102. Ramammohan Rao (1992): 44; Ramanaiah (1967): 187.
103. *South Indian Inscriptions (S.I.I.)* X, No. 164.
104. *South Indian Inscriptions (S.I.I.)* V, No. 238.

105. Kinsley: 20–21, 105, 111–113.

106. *Census of India 1961, vol. II, Fairs and Festivals, West Godavari District*, p. 29.

107. N. N. Bhattacharya, *History of the Sakta Religion* (New Delhi: Munshiram Manoharlal, 1996), pp. 19 and 21; http://www.spiritualjourneys.net/Venues/ Tantri%20Temples.htm; Bolon (1992): 25.

108. H. Krishna Sastri, *South Indian Images of Gods and Goddesses* (Madras: Government of Madras, 1916), p. 224.

109. Elmore (1915): 19–20 and 80.

110. *Census of India 1961, Vol. II, Andhra Pradesh, Part II VII-B (12) Fairs and Festivals, Mahaboobnagar District*, p. 171.

111. *Census of India 1961, Mahaboobnagar District*, p. 55.

112. Kinsley (1988): 33.

113. Upendra Nath Dhal, *Goddess Laksmi: Origin and Development* (New Delhi: Oriental Publishers, 1978), p. 178.

114. *Census Records, Cuddapah District*, p.70.

115. For why the cow is seen as a symbol of prosperity, read Madeleine Biardeau (1993), "Kamadhenu: The Mythical Cow, Symbol of Prosperity," in Yves Bonnefoy, ed., *Asian Mythologies* (University of Chicago Press), p. 99.

116. *Census of India 1961 Vol II A.P. Part II VII-B (12) Fairs and Festivals*, p. 52.

117. Nayani (1990): 197–198.

118. To understand the symbolism of the Poturaju cult, see George L. Hart, "Ancient Tamil Literature: its Scholarly Past and Future," in Burton Stein, ed., *Essays on South India* (Honolulu: University of Hawaii Press, 1975), pp. 41–63.

119. Bayly (1989): 53.

120. Bayly (1989): 79.

121. Huntington (1985): 52, plate XII; Parpola, (1994): 240–283, figs. 14.25, 14.26, 14.32.

122. Parpola (1994): fig. 10.10 and http://www.harappa.com/indus/89.html, 89. Model tablet of Indus: Gharial (*makara*) in a religious scene.

123. *The Hymns of the Rgveda.* Tr. Ralph T. H. Griffith. 4th ed. 2 vols. The earth is mentioned as the goddess Prthivi, with its limitless resources: *Rg Veda* 1. 6, 22, 159, 185; 4.56; 6.70; 10.18.10–12; 12.1; 12.1.4, 10, 11, 18, 19, 25 and 29. The river Saraswati is termed as a goddess springing from heaven and bringing bounty to the earth: *Rg Veda* 1.2, 3.10–12; 1. 164.49; 5.43.11; 6.61.3, 11–12; 7.37.11; 7.95–96.

124. www.nandanmenon.com/Atharva_Veda.pdf

125. R. Parthasarathy, ed., and trans., *The Tale of an Anklet: An Epic of South India (The Cilappatikaram of Ilanko Atikal)* (New York: Columbia University Press, 1993), pp. 51–52, 131, 156, and 194.

126. The representation of the *makara* in association with the goddess, or as a separate symbol, is interpreted as a form of the fertility cult. Banerjea, commenting on a ring stone of the third century BCE found in Kosam, Uttar Pradesh

that contained the figures of nude goddesses interspersed by three-pronged trees in one band and in the second a row of alligators, and comparing them to two similar ring stones of goddess figures associated with various birds, animals, and vegetation found in Taxila, argued their unmistakable identity with fertility goddesses of the Indus civilization by tracing their evolution from animals, birds, and vegetation to the anthropomorphic forms of goddesses such as Parvati and Durga. See Jitendra Nath Banerjea, *The Development of Hindu Iconography* (New Delhi: Munshiram Manoharlal Publishers Pvt. Ltd., 1974; 3rd edition), pp. 171–172.

127. Velury (1983): 182.

128. *Mahaparinibbana-Sutta*, iii, 13–19, referred to in M. C. P. Srivastava, p. 65, who mentions the legend in a Pali work called *Pathmasambodhi* and its popularity in southeast Asia.

129. C. Sivarmamurthi, *Amaravati Sculptures in the Madras Government Museum.* (Madras: Government Press,1956), plates IV. 24; LXIII. 4.

130. Srivastava (1979): 65. My personal observation of Nang Thorani statues during my travels to Thailand and Laos in 2004 and 2006 confirm this.

131. Stone (1994): figs. 173 and 186; Arundhati (1990): plate 23 and P. Chenna Reddy, *Phangiri: a Buddhist Site in Andhra Pradesh* (Hyderabad: Department of Archaeology and Museums, Government of Andhra Pradesh, 2008), p. 24.

132. Rama (1995): 160–164, plates 53, 54, and 55; Arundhati (1990): 232–233; (Elizabeth Rosen Stone (1994), figs. 176 and 186).

133. E. B. Cowell, no. 41, pp. 19–37 and 165–168 and 539 in Srivastava (1979: 65).

134. Ramammohan Rao (1992): 37–38, 40, 43, and 45.

135. Banerjea (1974): 369 and 374; referring to the Yakshini figures on Bharhut railing, Banerjea describes Candra as standing on a horse-faced *makara* and Sudharshan as standing on a rhinoceros-faced winged *makara*; a female figure sitting on a lotus flower with lotus designs all around her with a mythical *makara* looking at her on a section of a fragmentary coping stone at Amaravati of early second century CE is identified as Sri Lakshmi. See plate VIII, fig. 6.

136. Srivastava (1979): 65; C. Sivaramamurti, *Amaravati Sculptures in the Madras Government Museum.* (Madras: Government Press,1942), fig. 25.

137. Ramanaiah (1967): 67, 185, and 186.

138. Ramanaiah (1967): 186, illustration # 319.

139. Bolon (1992): 57–58, fig. 68.

140. Bolon (1992): No. 505.

141. *Palnativiracharitra* (Telugu), poem 118.

142. Parpola (1994): fig. 14.26.

143. Parpola (1994): fig. 14.25.

144. Banerjea (1974):184.

145. I. K. Sarma (1979): 23–30; Bolon, pp. 47 and 57, fig. 126.

146. Edgar Thurston (1909): 298).

147. Parpola (1994): fig. 14.23 a, b, and c).

148. Kinsley (1988): 95–115.

149. *The Mahabharata of Krishna Dwaipayana.* Tr. By K. M. Ganguly, 12 vols. (Calcutta: Oriental Publishing Co., n.d.), 7.69; *Madeleine* Biardeau, (1993), p. 99.

150. Sivaramamurti (1982: 36), fig. 59.

CHAPTER 4

1.   Bolon (1992): 3–4.

2.   *Census of India 1961, Mahabubnagar District*, p. 54.

3.   Field visit in January, 2010.

4.   Bolon (1992): 26–27, fig. 46.

5.   Bolon (1992): 30–31, fig. 64.

6.   Bolon (1992): 25.

7.   Zeigenbalg (1984): 136–137.

8.   Bolon (1992): 40. "In his study, *Lajja Gauri*, Dhere notes that the name of this famous site, Ellora or Elura, may be derived from the goddess by name Elapaura Ellamma and that Ellamma is also known as Lajja Gauri. . . . Dhere explains that a *verul* or pot, in South India was worshiped from ancient times as a symbol of the *yoni*, or womb, which later came to be the form of the goddess, that the *verul* is a symbol of Renuka (a name applied to Lajja Gauri images), who is the *yoni* of Prthivi (Earth). The river that flows past Ellora is the Verul River (also called Yelganga)."

9.   Matamma is a mix of Sanskrit and Telugu words (Mata +amma), both with the meaning of mother.

10. For those women who appoint themselves as Matammas see Joyce Burkhalter Flueckiger, "Wandering from "Hills to Valleys" with the Goddess: Protection Freedom in the Matamma Tradition in Andhra," in Tracy Pintchman, ed., *Women's Lives, Women's Rituals in the Hindu Tradition* (Oxford: Oxford University Press, 2007), pp. 35–54.

11. Elmore (1984): 22–26; Richard Brubaker, "The Ambivalent Mistress: A study of South Indian Village Goddesses and Their Religious Meaning." Ph.D. dissertation, University of Chicago, 1978, p. 267.

12. For more details see Oppert (1893): 465–466.

13. Whitehead (1921): 68, mentions a devotee worshiping a *gramadevata* at home in Eluru (West Godavari District) by drawing symbols of the sun and moon on the walls as forms of the goddess.

14. The goddess's preference for blood and brains comes alive in the traditional buffalo sacrifice when, after cutting the throat of buffalo, the blood pours on the earth, is mixed with some water, and is then buried. Then, along with cooked rice, a lamp is placed on the buffalo's head and offered to the goddess. See Whitehead (1980): pp. 50–52.

15. Oppert (1893): 301–305; translation is mine.
16. Kinsley (1988): 152. Kinsley says that the text, *Mahabharata*, portrayed mother goddesses such as Surabhi in a negative light as possessing inauspicious qualities. There is a narrow pass between two hillocks in Cumbum (Kurnool District) in Andhra known by the name of Surabesa Kona, where shrines for the Sapthamathas (seven mothers) are reported, as well as for Renuka, Jamadagni, and Mathangi. See A. Madhaviah, *Madras College Magazine* 23 (New Series 5), 1906, quoted by Edgar Thurston & K. Rangachari, *Castes and Tribes of South India*, Vol. 4 (Madras: Government Press, 1909), pp. 300–301.
17. J. N. Tiwari, *Goddess Cults in Ancient India* (Delhi: Sundeep Prakashan, 1985), pp. 10–11.
18. Krishna Sastri (1916): 223.
19. Saskia C. Keresenboom-Story, *Nityasumangali* (Delhi: Motilal Banarsidass, 1987), p. 57.
20. Keresenboom-Story (1987): 55–58.
21. I have noticed some other shrines going through this same type of transition, one of which is amidst the urban sprawl of Visakhapatnam and which I noted in this chapter. My personal conversation with Joyce Fluckieger reveals that the goddess Gangamma in Tirupathi (Chittoor District) went through a similar change.
22. F. Hardy, *Viraha-bhakti: The Early History of Krsna Devotion in south India* (Oxford: Oxford University Press. 1983) p. 620.
23. Keresenboom-Story (1987): 29ff.
24. *South Indian Inscriptions (S. I. I.)*, Vol. X, No. 12, 59, 70, & 80.
25. Y. V. Ramana, *Draksharama Inscriptions*, (Hyderabad: Andhra Pradesh State Archives, 1982), p. IV.
26. Velury (1983):112.
27. Parpola (1994): fig.14.35, a naked goddess sitting in between the tree branches; Marshall, Vol. I (1931): plate 12, no. 18
28. Velury (1983): 224, plate 104.
29. Pushpendra Kumar, *Sakti Cult in Ancient India*, (Benaras: Bharatiya Publishing House, 1974), pp. 158–159.
30. Velury (1983): 223.
31. Bolon (1992): 57, fig. 124.
32. John Marshall, *Mohenjodaro the Indus Civilization*, (New Delhi: Asian Educational Services, 2004; originally published, London, 1930) I, plates XCV, 20, 24, 29, 30, and Huntington (1985: 17).
33. Bolon (1992): 24, 45, and 64.
34. Velury (1983): 112 and 182.
35. Kumar (1974): p. 157.
36. Velury (1983): 183.

37. G. Hart, "Woman and the Sacred in Ancient Tamilnad," *Journal of Asian Studies*, 32 (1973): 233–250.

38. Velury (1983): 184, Plate 95.

39. Huntington (1985): 157–158, fig. 8.38; C. Sivaramamurti (1982): 4, fig. 5).

40. Bolon (1992): 13–14, figs. 5, 8, 11, 12, 32 and 106; Janssen (1991); Kramrisch (1956): 259–270.

41. Bolon (1992): 11–24.

42. Gail Hinch Southerland, *The Disguises of the Demon* (Albany: State University of New York Press, 1991), p. 143; D. D. Kosambi, *Myth Reality: Studies in the Formation of Indian Culture* (Bombay: Popular Prakashan, 1962; reprint, 1983), pp. 82–109.

43. Janssen (1991).

44. Sripada (1963): 75.

45. Sripada (1963): 51–52, 55, 60–61, 72, and 84.

46. Sripada (1963): 48, fig. 29, plate XIII.

47. Ramammohan Rao, *Perspectives of Archaeology, Art Culture in Early Andhra Desa* (New Delhi: Aditya Prakashan, 1992), p. 89, plate 3.

48. Kinsley (1988): 41.

49. Ramammohan Rao (1992): 90–92, plate 13.

50. Bolon (1992): 47, fig. 126.

51. C. Sivaramamurti (1982): 32, fig. 67.

52. Ramamohan Rao (1992): 92–93, plate 1.

53. Ramamohan Rao (1992): 45, fig. 103.

54. Ramamohan Rao (1992): 46.

55. Janssen (1991).

56. Bolon (1992): 57, fig. 126: left to right: Ganesa, Brahma, Narasimha, the linga form of Siva, Visnu Devi (Durga).

57. Kinsley (1988): 151–160.

58. H. Sarkar and B.N. Misra, *Nagarjunakonda* (New Delhi: Archaeological Survey of India, 1987), pp. 26, 60.

59. Ramanaiah (1967): 55, 57, 98, 192; Bolon (1992): 28, 30–31, figs. 46, 52, 55–57, 60, 63–64; Arundhati (1990): 129–130.

60. *Indian Antiquary* 2 (1878): 241–251 in Bolon (1992): 31, fn. 96.

61. Bolon (1992): 31.

62. B. V. Singarachaya and B. Nalinikantharao, eds., *Kridabhiramamu by Vinukonda Vallabharayudu* [Telugu] (Vijayawada: Victory Publishers, 1997), pp. 29–32, poems, 126–132.

63. *Indian Archaeology* 1967-68, pp. 1–7. See Arundhati (1990): 120.

64. Ramanaiah (1967): 84.

65. B. V. Singaracharya, *Vinukonda Vallabharayani Kridabhiramamu* [Telugu]. (Vijayawada: Emesco Books, 1997).

66. Singaracharya (1997): 29, poem 126 [my translation into English].

67. See chapter 4.

68. "Mapaka, Penubaka, Mahuramu, Nagavaramu were your dwelling places— Orugallu has become the home of blue lotus eyed one..." Singaracharya (1997), poem 128 [my English translation]

69. Nayani (1990):199–206.

70. Ch. Papayyasastri, ed., *Bhimesvarapuranam*, Rajahmundry, 1958, Canto I, V., pp. 99–102.

71. *South Indian Inscriptions*, Vol. X, No. 577; M. Somasekharasarma, *History of Reddy Kingdoms* (Waltair: Andhra University, 1948), pp. 194 and 561.

72. C. Somasundara Rao, "The Aminabad Inscription of Anavema Pedakomati Vema," *Journal of the Epigraphical Society of India* 12 (1985): 69–72.

73. D. Chinnikrsna Sarma, ed., *Srinathakavi Kasikhandam* (Madras: Vailla Edition, 1969), verse 58.

74. *Epigraphia Indica* (*EI*) XXIV, pp. 273ff; *EI* XXXI, pp 37ff.

75. *South Indian Inscriptions* (*SII*), Vols. X, No. 240 and XVI, Nos. 99, 129, 185 236.

76. Butterworth Venugopal Chetty, eds., *Inscriptions on Copper Plates Stones in Nellore District* in 3 vols., Vol. III, Madras, 1905, pp. 1225ff.

77. *SII*, XVI, Nos. 21, 153, 237, 243, 285, 505.

78. *SII*. X, No. 312; the suffix "sani" for the name Irukalasani, is a colloquial Telugu word meaning, "goddess." It translates as goddess Irukala.

79. T. A. Gopinatha Rao, *Elements of the Hindu Iconography*, 2 vols. (Delhi: Motilal Banarsidass, 1985),1, part 2,: 393.

80. Kinsley (1988): 118–119.

81. *Simhasana Dvatrimsika* (Telugu), (Hyderabad: Andhra Pradesh Sahitya Academy, 1960), Canto III, Verse 33.

82. *Hamsa Vimsati* [Telugu] (Hyderabad: Andhra Pradesh Sahitya Academy, 1977), Canto II, Verse 92.

83. For a summary of the story citations of the relevant Taisho texts, see Etienne Lamotte, *History of Indian Buddhism* (Louvain: Peeters Press, 1988), pp. 688–689.

84. *Epigraphia Indica* XXXIV, *Indian Archaeology* (*IA*) 1954–1955, pp. 22–23 1956-1957, pp. 37, site No. VII. Arundhati (1990): 119.

85. Huntington (1985): 147–148, figs. 8.25–8.27.

86. *Epigraphia Indica* V.119 and125; *EI*. XXXI. 40, Arundhati (1990: 119).

87. Velury (1983): 223, plate 82.

88. J. N. Tiwari, *Goddess Cults in Ancient India* (Delhi: Sundeep Prakashan, 1985), p. 11.

89. D.D. Kosambi (1983): 82–109.

90. B. S. L. Hanumantharao, *Religion in Andhra* (Hyderabad: Government of Andhra Pradesh, 1993), p. 228.

91. *Panditaradhya Charitra* (Telugu), Vol. II (Madras: Palkuriki Somanatha, 1936), pp. 1–54.

92. Another possible explanation regarding the origins of this goddess might be connected to the *matrika* (mother goddess) figures who are often portrayed with children in their laps. These *matrikas*, usually seven in number, are considered to fuse aboriginal Vedic symbolism with literature and iconography associated with Skanda, who eventually became a Saivite god when identified as the son of Siva. The seventh mother came to be seen as Parvati, wife of Siva Skanda's mother. This identification seems to have been so popularized that devotees of Erukamma could easily identify the goddess as the incarnation of Parvati, the 7th *matrika*. See Katherine Anne Harper, *The Iconography of the Saptamatrikas* (Lewiston, NY: Edwin Mellen Press, 1989), 47–71, for a discussion of the cult of the *saptamatrikas*.

93. John Strong, *The Legend cult of Upagupta* (Princeton: Princeton University Press, 1982), p. 37.

94. H. Krishna Sastri (1916): 194–196.

95. Biardeau (1984): 1–24.

96. *Census Records, Anathapur District*, pp. 5 and 163.

97. Elmore (1915): 76–77.

98. I have recorded this story in at least four different *gramadevata* temples in coastal Andhra.

99. Peta Srinivasulu Reddy, *Tirumala Tirupati Grama Devatalu* (Tirupati: Rushiteja Publications, 2000) [Telugu], pp. 20–23.

100. Peta Srinivasulu Reddy, *Tirumala Tirupati Grama Devatalu* [Telugu], p. 28.

101. Poturaju, who is believed to be the brother of the goddess, was introduced earlier as a human male acting the role of Poturaju in the annual ritual to the goddess.

102. Gavin Flood, *An Introduction to Hinduism.* (Cambridge: Cambridge University Press,1996), p. 17, 28–29; Stella Kramrisch, *The Presence of Siva.* (Varanasi: Motilal Banarsidass Publication, 1988) pp. 71–74.

103. During the course of my visits to various shrines of folk goddesses, I collected many myths, stories, and narrations of the magical power of goddesses. This is one that I collected in Secunderabad.

104. *Agraharam* is a village given as a tax free grant by the ruling class to *brahmins* in appreciation of their literary talents.

105. Nayani (1990): 218–219.

106. Krishna Sastri (1916): 228.

107. Ziegenbalg (1984): 137–145.

108. Sree Padma, "From Village to City: Transforming Goddesses in Urban Andhra Pradesh," in Tracy Pintchman, ed., *Seeking Mahadevi* (New York: State University of New York Press, 2001) pp. 115–144.

109. T. A. Gopinatha Rao, *Elements of Hindu Iconography* (Delhi: Motilal Banarsidass, 1985), Vol. 1, Part II, pp. 356–368.

110. D. R. Rajeswari, *Sakti Iconography* (New Delhi: Intellectual Publishing House, 1989), p. 32.

111. Kanaka Durga in Vijayawada was originally a village goddess independent of the *brahmanic* tradition. A remnant feature of propitiating her as a village goddess is evident in the offering of animal sacrifices, which takes place very quickly and without much publicity once a year, during the time of her annual festival. There is a tendency among most of the villagers of Andhra Pradesh to identify their village goddess with Kanaka Durga of Vijayawada.

112. http://www.harappa.com/indus/34.html, 34. Seal, Mohenjo-daro; Katherine Harper, *The Iconography of the Saptamatrikas: Seven Hindu Goddesses of Spiritual Transformation* (Lewiston, New York: Edwin Mellen Press, 1989), pp. 5–11.

113. Harper (1989): 5–11; Sara L. Schastok, *The Samalaji Sculptures 6th Century art in Western India* (Leiden, The Netherlands: E.J. Brill, 1985), pp. 60–62.

114. Harper (1989): 45–155.

115. Parpola (1994): 261, fig. 14.35.

116. *Mahabharata*, Vanaparva in Kinsley (1988): 151–52). Instead of killing the children, Kartikeya, the Saivite deity, accepts two requests made by the group of mothers: 1) wanting to be recognized and to be worshiped as great goddesses and, 2) wanting to afflict the children in the form of diseases until they reach age sixteen. This account of converting these goddesses is somewhat analogous to that of Hariti.

117. The names of thirty-two goddesses, divided into four groups of eight each and portrayed as guardian deities of the four cardinal points, are given in the Buddhist text *Lalita-vistara*. The Jaina text *Angavijja* of the fourth century names a number of popular goddesses; see J. N. Tiwari, *Goddess Cults in Ancient India* (Delhi: Sundeep Prakashan, 1985), pp. 10–12.

118. Misra (1989): 2–3.

119. Sara L. Schastok (1985): p. 62. In one particularly strong statement in the *Skanda Purana*, Devi says to Skanda, "women deserve to be reviled. It is the grace of men which brings release from the ocean of existence." [31: O'Flaherty, 1975, p. 26]; "In this sectarian context, Devi is merely a creature of the gods' creation.... As both Elephanta and Ellora cave 21 the placement of the *matrikas* within each ground plan clearly states their containment by Siva... As we shall demonstrate below, the relationship to Siva is further amplified within each group and its immediate setting. Perhaps the most explicit imagery of this type at Ellora is at the Kailasanatha, where there is not only a *matrika* shrine carved into the cliff, but also a large dancing Siva relief on the bridge connecting the temple and the hall before it (fig. 123). At his feet sits a group of *Saptamatrkas* resembling the sculptures in the Kailasanatha's own *matrika* shrine."

120. Nayani (1990): 219.

121. Nayani (1990): 219.
122. Arundhati (1990): 127.
123. Schastok (1985). Cave 14 at Ellora, where a Durga image appears to dominate the program, may well be an example of *Saptamatrka*s as emanations of Devi in the spirit of the *Devi Mahatmya*, but this is more of the exception than the rule.
124. Misra (1989): 7.
125. Bolon (1992): 42–43.
126. Copper plate grant of Pulakesin I, dated Saka 411 (ca. 489–490 CE) in Mistra (1989: 8).
127. Ramanaiah (1967):192–193.
128. Ramanaiah (1967): 81.
129. Bolon (1992): 40.
130. Bolon (1992): 60, 81, 151 and 192–193.
131. *Nellore District Inscriptions*, Vol. III, Ongole 12.
132. Ramanaiah (1967): 73–74 and illustration # 25.
133. Ramanaiah (1967): 56.
134. Singaracharya (1997): xxi.
135. Singaracharya (1997): 32–33, poems 137–139.
136. Kinsley (1988): 99–100 and 116-131.
137. Kinsley (1988): 111–113.
138. Kinsley (1988): 116.
139. Hardy (1983): 223; R. Parthasarathy (1993): 58–59, 117–119, 121–124, and 187–188.
140. Parthasarathy (1993): 121–122.
141. Sarah Caldwell, *Oh Terrifying Mother: Sexuality, Violence Worship of the Goddess Kali* (New York: Oxford University, 1999), pp. 24–25, 96, and 148.
142. *SII*. Vol. XVI, Nos. 285 and 293; *NDI*. Vol. I, p. 238; Atmakur, 50
143. Banerjea (1974): 184.
144. Banerjea (1974): 198.
145. Bolon (1992): 47, fig. 127.
146. B. N. Sastry, *Bezwada Durga Malleswaralaya Sasanamulu [Telugu]* (Hyderabad: Musi Publications, 1991), pp. 139–149; Gordon Mackenzie, *A Manual of the Kistna District* (Madras: The Lawrence Asylum Press, 1883), pp. 218–219.
147. Dr. Velury Venkata Krishna Sastry, who served as the director of State Archaeology and who made several visits to the temple and its environs as a field archaeologist, opines that Madhavavarma III, the last ruler of the Vishnukundin dynasty before he was defeated by the Western Chalukya ruler Kubja Vishnuvardhana (Pulakesin II?) in about 610 CE, made Vijayawada his capital; the ruins of his fort are scattered behind the temple. For the discussion of the end of Vishnukundin power, see K. R. Subramanian, *Buddhist Remains*

in Andhra and the History of Andhra (Madras: Asian Educational Services, 1989; first published 1932) p.128.

148. Kundurti Satyanarayanamurty, *Prachinandhra Mahakavula Devi Pratipatti* [Telugu] (Vijayawada: Bhuvanavijayam Publications, 1989), p. 25.

149. Sastry (1991): 10; Bhavaraju Venkata Krishnarao, *Early Dynasties of Andhradesa*, pp. 116–117 in *Census of India 1961, Krishna District*, pp. 55–60.

150. *South Indian Inscriptions* Vol. X, no. 22.; *Archaeology Survey of India Annual Report* (ASI) No. 536 of 1909; *Madras Epigraphist's Report* (MER), 1901, p. 81 and *MER*, 1910, p. 81; this ruler is identified as Madhavavarman III of the Vishnukundin dynasty by Subramanian (1989): 112–118.

151. http://www.shaktipeethas.org/vijayawada-kanaka-durga-t95.html.

152. Bhavaraju Venkata Krishna Rao, *Early Dynasties of Andhradesa*, pp. 116–117 in *Census of India, Krishna District*, 1961, p. 60.

153. Elmore (1915): 63–64.

154. My interview with Kundurti Satynarayanamurty confirms this. His book traces the goddess Durga as the *gramadevata* with annual *jatara* rituals. See Kundurti (1989): 25.

155. *Census of India, 1961, West Godavari District*, p.41.

156. For details see, David Kinsley (1988): 116–131.

157. Koravi Goparaju *Simhasana Dvatramsika*, puta (page) 103 in Suravaram Pratapareddy, *Andhrula Sanghika Charitra* [Telugu] (Hyderabad: Orient Lajman Pvt Ltd, 2007 [1992]), p. 68.

158. *EI*. Vol. IV, pp. 316–317.

159. Kaluvacheru inscription mentions that Kakati as Parasakti blessed the Kakatiya rulers with sons and grandsons. See Suravaram Pratapareddy, *Andhrula Sanghika Charitra* [Telugu] (Hyderabad: Orient Lajman Pvt Ltd, 2007 [1992]), p. 2; *Kridabhiramamu*, Poem 127. "Perpetual auspiciousness, goddess of *Kali kula* with long braided hair—Adi Sakti, essence of Vedas and Vedic philosophy—Ekavira, possessing the face of full moon—The mother of all worlds, my reverence to you every day." The Kaluvacheru inscription mentions that Kakati as Parasakti blessed the Kakatiya rulers with sons and grandsons. See Suravaram (2007): 2.

160. Ramanaiah (1967): 82.

161. This process is analogous to Korravi or Kottavai, the goddess of Sangam age, transforming into goddess Kali over time. See Hardy (1983): 223.

162. *Census of India, East Godavari District*: p.55.

163. *South Indian Inscriptions (S.I.I.)* vol X, Nos. 107, 289, 713; XI, pp. 147 ff., XII. p. 106; *EI*. XI XXXI, pp. 37 ff; XXXIII, pp. 27ff.

164. *South Indian Inscriptions (S.I.I.)*, vol X, No. 713; *Archaeology Review (AR)*, 1926, No. 634.

165. *Census of India, Warangal District*, p.47.

166. Verrier Elwin, *The Baiga* (London: J. Murray, 1939), pp. 362–365.

167. The deified goddess in some villages is seen with a dead daughter or grand-daughter in the same way as Sammakka is shown in the company of Sarakka. In most cases, the goddess is accompanied by a *gramadevata* or a god or goddess of *brahmanic* status such as Parvati, Lakshmi, Siva, or Hanuman.

168. *Census of India Srikakaulam District*, p. 5.

CHAPTER 5

1. Stuart Blackburn, "Death and Deification: Folk Cults in Hinduism," in *History of Religions* 24 (1985): 255–274.

2. Blackburn (1985): 255–274.

3. Blackburn (1985): 255–274.

4. Elinor W. Gadon, *The Once and Future Goddess* (San Francisco: Harper & Row, Publishers, 1989), p. 99; Parpola (1994): 256–257, fig. 14.32.

5. Gatwood (1985): 27.

6. Miriam Robbins Dexter, *Whence The Goddess* (New York: Pergamon Press, 1990), pp. 51–140. In this book, the author, like many of her predecessors, holds the view that Indo-Europeans, a linguistic group, were responsible for spreading patriarchal ideas throughout the ancient world.

7. E. Ann Matter, "The Virgin Mary: A Goddess?" in Carl Olson, ed., *The Book of the Goddesse Past and Present* (New York: Cross Road, 1983), pp. 80–96; Gadon (1994): 191.

8. Bayly (1989): 19–70.

9. Thurston (1909): 2: 215, 387–90.

10. R. Parthasarathy, (1993): 58–59, 117–119, 120–121, 128, 187–188, and 223.

11. R. Parthasarathy (1993): 329.

12. Michael R. Allen, *The Cult of Kumari* (Kathmandu, Nepal: Madhab Lal Maharjan, 1975), p. 2.

13. Allen (1975): 2; Veena Das, "The Body as a Metaphor—Socialization of Women in Punjabi Urban Families," *Manushi* 28 (1985): 2–6.

14. Paul Hershman, "Virgin and Mother," in I. M. Lewis, ed., *Symbols and Sentiments* (London: Academic Press, 1977), pp. 270–292.

15. Sudhir Kakar, "Feminine Identity in India" in Rehana Ghadially, ed., *Women in Indian Society* (New Delhi: Sage Publications, 1986), pp. 23–68.

16. Vanaja Dhruvarajan, *Hindu Women & the Power of Ideology* (Boston: Bergin & Garvey Publishers, Inc., 1989).

17. Dhruvarajan (1989): 61 and 66.

18. Tapper (1979): 1–31.

19. Das (1985): 2–6.

20. This story has been cobbled together on the basis of interviews at the local temple and the background myth provided in a temple booklet. One of the

interesting aspects of this research involves recognition of how history is either mythicized or how myth is "historicized."

21. *Census of India 1961, Guntur District*, p. 29.

22. This is a famous story, known among all devotees of the goddess Kanyaka Paramesvari, a cult popular among the *vaisya* communities in almost all towns and cities of Andhra Pradesh.

23. A similar story with variations is mentioned by Henry Whitehead (1921): 123.

24. *Census of India 1961, East Godavari District*, p. 100.

CHAPTER 6

1. A. S. Altekar, *The Position of Women in Hindu Civilization* (Delhi: Motilal Banarasidass, 2nd ed., 1983), pp. 135–136; John S. Hawley, *Sati: The Blessing and the Curse* (New York: Oxford University Press, 1994), pp. 3–26.

2. Basham (1954): 186–188. In early times, widow burning was known among the Russians on the Volga, the Teutonic tribes, Heruli, Getae, the Scandinavians, Thracians in Greece, Scythians, tribes in the Tonga and Fiji islands, the Egyptians and the Chinese. See V. N. Datta, *Sati* (Riverdale, Maryland: The Riverdale Company, 1988), p. 2.

3. Altekar (1983): 122.

4. Vidya Dehejia, "A Broader Landscape" in John Hawley, ed., *Sati: The Blessing and the Curse*, pp. 49–53; P. V. Kane, *History of Dharmasastras*, 4 vols. (Poona: Bhandarkar Orient Research Institute, 1973), 2, Part I, pp. 578–579.

5. *Padmapurana*, Sroshtikands, 49. 72–73; see A. S. Altekar (1983): 128–130.

6. Kane (1972), II. I: 631. One work states that she will dwell in heaven as many as 312 crores (each "crore" is a unit equal to ten million) of years and that she will purify three families, viz. her mother's, her father's and her husband's.

7. Kane (197): 635.

8. R. Parthasarathy, trans. *The Cilappatikaram* (New York: Columbia University Press, 1993).

9. R. Parthasarathy (1993): 206.

10. Alain Danielou and T.V. Gopala Iyer, eds. and trans., *Manimekhalai (The Dancer with the Magic Bowl) by Merchant-Prince Shattan* (Delhi: Penguin Books India, 1989), pp. 6 and 25.

11. George L. Hart and Hank Heifetz tr & ed. *The Purannanuru, The Four Hundred Songs of War and Wisdom*. (New York: Columbia University Press, 1999), pp. xx &102: "The nature of a woman's power is clarified by the conduct expected of her when as a widow she was in close association with death. Widows did not wear ornaments (*Purannanuru*. 224, 253, 261), they caked their shaven heads with mud (*Purannanuru*, 280), and they slept on beds of stone (*Purannanuru*, 246)."

12. George L. Hart, *The Poems of the Ancient Tamils: Their Milieu and Their Sanskrit Counterparts* (Berkeley: University of California Press, 1975), p. 107.

13. Hart (1975b): 112–118. In this argument, Hart gives examples of how chastity was not an issue in the Vedic period; *brahmanas* and *sudras* were lenient towards sexual transgressions of a wife, and allowed a childless wife to have children by her husband's brother or to marry him when she became a widow.

14. George Buhler, trans., *The Laws of Manu* (New York: Dover Publications, Inc. 1969), p. 332.

15. Hart (1975b): 41.

16. Dennis Hudson, "Violent and Fanatical Devotion," in Alf Hiltebeitel, ed., *Criminal Gods and Demon Devotees* (New York: State University of New York Press, 1989), pp. 373–404.

17. R. Parthasarathy, *The Cilappatikaram* (New York: Columbia University Press, 1993), Canto 12, p. 120; Alain Danielou, *Manimekhalai* (New York: New Directions Publishing Corporation, 1989), Canto six, p.24: "Within there stands a vast temple dedicated to the black goddess who dwells in the desert...The temple is surrounded by trees, whose long branches bow under the burden of the severed heads hanging from them. These are the heads of fanatical votaries, who sacrifice themselves to the goddess."

18. Hart (1975b): 93–118.

19. Hudson (1989): 396–397.

20. S. Settar, "Memorial Stones in South India," in S. Settar and Gunther D. Sontheimer, eds., *Memorial Stones* (Dharwad: Institute of Indian Art History, 1982) pp. 193–196. We meet one of the earliest instances in the early Kadamba kingdom dated by some in the fourth and by others in the sixth century (f.n. 30: EC VIII, Sb. 523).

21. Settar (1982).

22. M. Chidanandamurti, "Two Masti Temples in Karnataka," in S. Settar & Gunther D. Sontheimer, eds., *Memorial Stones*, pp. 117–131.

23. B. D. Chattopadhyaya, "Early Memorial Stones of Rajasthan," in S. Settar & Gunther D. Sontheimer, ed., *Memorial Stones*, pp. 139–149.

24. Chattopadhyaya (1982): "The stones also gave sanction to the practice of sati, which was becoming increasingly common and the incidence of which was quite substantial among the ruling elite of this period." Hermann Goetz, *The Art and Architecture of Bikaner State* (Oxford: Government of Bikaner State and the Royal India and Pakistan Society, 1950), p. 88.

25. Lindsey Harlan, "Perfection and Devotion: Sati Tradition in Rajasthan," in John Hawley, ed., *Sati* (1994): 79–90.

26. Paul B. Courtright, "The Iconographies of Sati," in Hawley, ed., *Sati* (1994): 27–49.

27. The *Chaya Kambhas* (memorial pillars) of the Andhra Ikshvaku period during the second to third century CE were issued in memory of royal and higher

dignitaries, including that of a queen; these shared characteristics with those of Saka rulers in Ujjain, Central India; and again, the ninth-century hero stones (one of which is suspected to have a *sati* sharing the hero stone) in central India show similarities with those of Andhra, Maharashtra, Orissa, and Bihar. See H. Sarkar, "The Caya-Stambhas from Nagarjunakonda," in S. Settar & Gunther D. Sontheimer, eds., *Memorial Stones* (1982): 199–207; Gunther D. Sontheimer, "On the Memorials to the Dead in the Tribal Area of Central India," in S. Settar & Gunther D. Sontheimer, ed., *Memorial Stones* (1982): 87–99.

28. Arundhati (1990): 143–145, Plate 18.

29. *Annual Reports on Indian Epigraphy (ARIE)*,1939, No. 383, part II, para 62 in R. Chandrasekhara Reddy, *Heroes, Cults and Memorials: Andhra Pradesh, 300 AD–1600 AD* (Madras: New Era Publications, 1994), p. 14.

30. *Andhra Pradesh Archaeological Report (APAR)*, 13/1965; P. V. Parabrahma Sastry, *Cuddapah District Inscriptions*, Part I, No. 64; S.I.I., Vol. IX-X, Nos. 9 & 35; *ARIE*, 742/1917 and 73/1941-42.

31. Reddy (1994): 143–152.

32. Koravi Goparaju, *Simhasana Dvatramsika* I, IV, V: 17; A.R. Ep., 1917/p.125, Para 36; M. L. K. Murthy, "Memorial Stones in Andhra Pradesh" in S. Settar & Gunther D. Sontheimer eds., *Memorial Stones* (1982), pp. 213–218, fn. 12. Telugu literary works like *Vikramarkacharitra*, *Simhasanadvatrimsaka*, Srinatha's *Panditaradhyacaritra*, and Annayya's *Sodasakumaracaritra* praised self-sacrifice for any noble cause as the most desirable form of action; S. Settar (1982:189). The thirteenth-century memorials set up in the pillared halls testify to acts of self-immolation. See Dennis Hudson (1989): 373–404.

33. Sripada Gopalakrishna Murthy, *The Sculpture of the Kakatiyas.* Andhra Pradesh Archaeological Series 12 (Hyderabad, Government of Andhra Pradesh, 1964), p. 34; *Kridabhiramamu* verses 142 & 144.

34. *Annual Reports on Indian Epigraphy (ARIE)*1918, p. 176, para 88; *ARIE.*, 809/1917; *ARIE* 192/1932; *ARIE* 39/1941-42; *ARIE* 155/1946-47; *ARIE* 19/1955.

35. Koravi Goparaju, *Simhasana Dvatrimsika* II, p. 110.

36. *S.I.I.* Vol. VI No. 144.

37. Kane (1972): II. I. 631; Altekar (1983): 130.

38. Altekar (1983): 216–217; The word *mahasati* is Sanskrit and its colloquial form is *masti*. The meaning of Tamil word *Kallu* is "stones."

39. Umakanta Vidyashekharulu, ed. *Palnativiracharitra.* (Guttikonda, Guntur District: Vangmaya Samiti, 1938, first edition, 1911), pp. 19 & 22.

40. Nilakanta Sastri (1965): 195.

41. Mallanna Kavi, *Rukmangada Charitramu* [Telugu] (Madras: Vavilla Ramasastrulu and sons, 1938), p. 56 (4th Canto); V. Ramaswami Sastrulu,

ed., Chinnikrsna Sarma, D., ed. *Srinathakavi Kasikhandam* [Telugu]. (Madras: Vavilla edition 1969), 2nd Canto, verse 90 ff. or verse 90 to 92.

42. T. V. Mahalingam, *Administration and Social Life Under Vijayanagar* (Madras: 1940), pp. 258–262.

43. Reddy (1994): 140–141.

44. Reddy (1994): 151.

45. Reddy (1994): 151.

46. The Raya dynasty ruled Vijayanagara from its capital from 1343 to 1565. After the last ruler, Aliyaraya, was defeated, one of the Raya line ruled a small portion in Andhra, with Penukonda as their capital, until 1632. The majority of *sati* stories claim action that occurred in the seventeenth century under Vijayanagar rulers.

47. *Census of India 1961, Anantapur District*, pp. 113–114.

48. *Census of India 1961, East Godavari District*, vol. II, Part VII-B (3), p. 256.

49. Paul B. Courtright (1994): 27–49.

50. Elmore (1984): 58–59.

51. Stein (1980): 47 ff.

52. For further details, read the autobiography of a woman who comes from these families: K. Lakshmi Raghuramaiah, *Hurricane: Autobiography of a Woman*, (Delhi: Chanakya Publications, 1994), pp. 7–8.

53. Bruce Tapper (1979): 1–31.

54. The temple committee has made her story into film and sells it to her devotees in DVD form.

55. *Census of India 1961, Krishna District*, p. 69.

56. *Census of India 1961 Krishna District*, p. 41.

57. *Census of India 1961, Krishna District*.

58. Nayani (1990): 279–282.

59. *Census of India 1961, Nellore District*, p. 67.

60. *Census of India 1961, Nellore District*, p. 21.

61. Elmore (1984): 60–61.

62. Elmore (1984): 61–62.

63. Tapper (1987): 155–156. Brackets are mine.

64. Tapper (1987): 155–156.

65. It is common that the priests for *gramadevata* rituals are often from non-brahmanic castes such as the *yadava*. It is interesting to note that the professional storytellers in *gramadevata* rituals mostly come from either *yadava* or *mala* and *madiga* castes. This has something to do with the fact that the goddesses of their caste, such as Gangamma for *yadava*s and Ellamma for *mala* and *madiga*, are also popular *gramadevata*s. In any case, in keeping with this tradition, the father of the victim felt it appropriate to have a woman priest from the *yadava* caste to serve in his daughter's temple.

66. See for details, Tapper (1987): 155–156.

67. Tapper (1987): 145–146. Tapper's version in these pages is a variant because the customs in each caste and region are slightly different.
68. Bayly, (1989): 33–34.

CHAPTER 7

1. http://www.harappa.com/indus/89.html, 89. Molded tablet.
2. http://www.harappa.com/indus/34.html, 34. Seal, Mohenjo-daro.
3. http://www.sacred-texts.com/hin/rigveda/rv10090.htm, *Rg Veda* 10: 90, "The Hymn to *Purusha*"
4. Biswanarayan Shastri, *The Kalika Purana: Sanskrit Text, Introduction & Translation in English.* 3 Vols. (Nag Publishers, 1991).
5. Koravi Goparaju, *Simhasana Dvatramsika* I, IV & V: 17.
6. *South Indian Inscriptions (SII).* XII, p. 106.
7. Krishna Kantha Handique, *Yasastilaka and Indian Culture* (Sholapur: Jaina Samskriti Samrakshana Sangha, 1949), p. 422.
8. Whitehead (1921): 60–62.
9. Bayly (1989): 53.
10. Bayly (1989): 53.
11. Bayly (1989): 53–54); also see J. C. Heesterman, *The Inner Conflict of Tradition: Essays in Indian Ritual, Kingship and Society.* (Chicago: University of Chicago Press, 1985), pp. 81–94.
12. Biardeau (1984): 1–24.
13. Sivasanakra Narayana, *Anantapur District Gazetteer* (Hyderabad: Government of Andhra Pradesh, 1977), p. 822.
14. Arthur F. Cox., *A Manual of the North Arcot District* (Madras: Madras Presidency, 1881), p. 822.
15. *Census Of India, Kurnool District,* p. 62.
16. *Census Of India, Chittoor District,* p. 1.
17. *Census Of India 1961, Anantapur District,* p. 5.
18. Tribes like Oran and Khond are known to have practiced human sacrifices: http://www.indianmirror.com/tribes/orantribes.html; http://en.wikipedia.org/wiki/Khonds.
19. http://www.iheu.org/node/2755, August 1, 2007.
20. http://indianchristians.in/news/content/view/2374/45/.
21. http://andhrafriends.com/index.php?topic=58928.0.
22. http://expressbuzz.com/states/andhrapradesh/andhra-human-sacrifice-bid-thwarted/236084.html, January 2, 2011.
23. S. Dorairaj, "Demons and Gods," *Frontline,* August 28, 2009, volume 26, No. 17, pp. 22–24.
24. S. Settar (1982): 186.
25. *Census of India 1961, Anantapur District,* pp. 159–160.

26. See A. K. Ramanujan, *Speaking of Siva* (Baltimore: Penguin Books Pvt. Ltd, 1973). His discussion of Mahadevi Akka touches on the theme of Virasaiva female asceticism and the consequent concerns of her family.

27. Site visit and interviews with locals were checked against the story in *Census of India 1961, Krishna District*: 86–87.

28. I collected this story in 2011 through my interviews with regular devotees to Venkamma temple.

29. Whitehead (1921): 21.

30. This very same set of principles is explored by Arundhati Roy in her provocative novel, *The God of Small Things* (New York: Random House, 1997).

Bibliography

BOOKS

Aiyappan, A. 1965. *Social Revolution in a Kerala Village*. Bombay: Asia Publishing House.

Aiyappan, A., and P.R. Srinivasan. 1992. *Guide to the Buddhist Antiquities*. Madras: Director of Museums.

Allchin, Raymond. 1983–85. "The Interpretation of a Seal from Chanhu-daro and Its Significance for the Religion of the Indus Civilization," in *South Asian Archaeology: Papers from the Seventh International Conference of the Association of South Asian Archaeologists in Western Europe*, eds., Janine Schotsman and Maurizio Taddei, 371–383. Brussels 1983 (Naples: 1985).

Allen, Michael R. 1975. *The Cult of Kumari*. Kathmandu, Nepal: Madhab Lal Maharjan.

Altekar, A. S. 1983. *The Position of Women in Hindu Civilization*. Delhi: Motilal Banarsidass. (originally published 1959).

Arthur, Joseph. 1853–1955. Come de Gobineau, *Essai sur l'ineglalite des races humanities*, 4 vols. Paris: Firmin Didot Freres.

Arundhati, P. 1990. *Brahmanism, Jainism and Buddhism in Andhra Desa*. Delhi: Sundeep Prakashan.

Babb, Lawrence. 1975. *The Divine Hierarchy*. New York: Columbia University Press.

———. 1970. "Marriage and Malevolence: The Uses of Sexual Opposition in a Hindu Pantheon," *Ethnology* IX:137–147.

Balakrishna Mudaliyar, N. K. 1959–1960. *The Golden Anthology of Ancient Tamil Literature*, 3 vols. Madras: South Indian Saiva Siddhanta Works Publication Society.

Banerjea, Jitendra Nath. 1974. *The Development of Hindu Iconography*. 3rd edition. New Delhi: Munshiram Manoharlal Publishers Pvt. Ltd.

———. 1953. "The Hindu Concept of the Natural World," in *The Religion of Hindus,* ed. Kenneth M. Morgan, 48–82. New York: The Ronald Press Company.

Barnabas, A. P. 1961. "Sanskritization," *Economic Weekly,* v. 13, no. 15: 613–18.

Basham, A. L. 1954. *The Wonder That Was India.* New York: Grove Press.

Bayly, Susan. 1989. *Saints, Goddesses and Kings Muslims and Christians in South Indian society 1700–1900.* Cambridge: Cambridge University Press.

Beals, Alan.1964. "Conflict and Interlocal Festivals in a South Indian Region," *The Journal of Asian Studies,* xxiii: 99–113. (June 1964).

Bean, Susan A. 1975. "Referential and Indexical Meanings of amma in Kannada: Mother, Woman, Goddess, Pox, and Help!," *Journal of Anthropological Research,* 31: 313–330.

Beck, Brenda E. F. 1972. *Peasant Society in Konku.* Vancouver: University of British Columbia Press.

———. 1979. *Perspectives on a Regional Culture.* New Delhi: Vikas Publishing House pvt ltd.

Bhandarker, G. 1965. *Vaisnavism, Saivism, and Minor Religious Systems.* Varanasi: Indological Book House.

Bhattacharya, A. K. 1967 "A non-Aryan aspect of the Devi," in *The Sakti Cult and Tara,* ed. D. C. Sircar, 56–60. Calcutta: University of Calcutta.

Bhattacharyya, Narendra Nath. 1997. *The Indian Mother Goddess.* New Delhi: South Asia Books. (First published 1970.)

Biardeau, Madeleine. 1989. "Brahmans and Meat-Eating gods," in *Criminal Gods and Demon Devotees,* ed. Alf Hiltebeitel, 19–34. Albany: State University of New York Press.

———. 1984. "The Sami Tree and the Sacrificial Buffalo," *Contributions to Indian Sociology,* New Series, Vol. 18, No 1: 1–24. (January-June 1984).

———. 2004. *Stories about Posts.* Trans. Alf Hiltebeitel et al. Chicago: The University of Chicago Press.

Blackburn, Stuart. 1985. "Death and Deification: Folk Cults in Hinduism," in *History of Religions,* volume 24, No. 3: 255–274.

Bolon, Carol Radcliffe. 1992. *Forms of the Goddess Lajja Gauri in Indian Art.* Pennsylvania: The Pennsylvania University Press.

Bopp, Franz. 1862. *A Comparative Grammar of the Sanskrit, Zend, Greek, Latin, Lithuanian, Gothic, German, and Sclavonic Languages,* 3 vols. London & Edinburgh: Williams and Norgate.

Brown, Norman. 1961. "Mythology of India," in *Mythologies of the Ancient World,* ed. Samuel Noah Kramer, 309–312. Garden City, NY: Doubleday and Co., Inc.

Brubaker, Richard. 1978. "The Ambivalent Mistress: A study of south Indian Village Goddesses and their Religious Meaning." Ph.D. dissertation. Chicago: University of Chicago.

Bruce, George. 1968. *The Stranglers.* London: Longmans.

Bugge, Henriette. 1994. *Mission and Tamil Society. Social and Religious Change in South India (1840–1900)*. Richmond: Curzon Press Ltd.

Buhler, George. 1969. *The Laws of Manu*. New York: Dover Publications, Inc. (originally published 1794).

Caldwell, Robert. 1856. *A Comparative Grammar of the Dravidian or South Indian Family of Languages*. Madras: University of Madras.

Caldwell, Sara. 2003. "Margins at the Center, Tracing Kali Through Time, Space, and Culture," in *Encountering Kali*, ed. Rachel Fell McDermott and Jeffrey Kripal: 249–272. Berkeley: University of California Press.

Cannon, Garland, ed. 1970. *The Letters of Sir William Jones*, vol. II. Oxford: The Clarendon Press.

Chattopadhyaya, B. D. 1982. "Early Memorial Stones of Rajasthan," in *Memorial Stones,* ed. S. Settar & Gunther D. Sontheimer, 139–149. Dharwad: Institute of Indian Art History.

Chattopadhyaya, Sudhakar. 1970. *Evolution of Hindu Sects*. New Delhi: Munshiram Manoharlal.

Chelliah, J. V. 1962. *Pattupattu, Ten Tamil Idylls*. Madras: Kazhagam.

Chenna Reddy, P., ed. 2008. *Phanigiri: A Buddhist Site in Andhra Pradesh*. Hyderabad: Department of Archaeology and Museums, Government of Andhra Pradesh.

Chidanandamurti, M. 1982. "Two Masti Temples in Karnataka," in *Memorial Stones,* ed. S. Settar & Gunther D. Sontheimer, 117–131. Dharwad: Institute of Indian Art History.

Childe, V. Gordon. 1926. *The Aryans*. London: Kegan Paul, Trench, Trubner & Co.

———. 1934. *New Light on the Most Ancient East*. New York: D. Appleton-Century Company Incorporated.

Coburn, Thomas. 1985. *Devi-Mahatmya: The Crystallization of the Goddess Tradition*. Colombia, Missouri: South Asia Books.

Colebrooke, 1837. Henry Thomas. *Miscellaneous Essays*. 2 vols. London: Wm. H. Allen and Co.

Craddock, Elaine. 2001. "Reconstructing the Split Goddess as Sakti," in *Mahadevi, ed.* Tracy Pintchman, 145–169. New York: State University of New York Press.

Crooke, W. 1918. "The Cults of the Mother Goddess in India," *Folklore* (London) XXIX: 282–308.

Courtright, Paul B. 1994. "The Iconographies of Sati," in *Sati: The Blessing and the Curse*, ed. John Hawley, 27–49. New York: Oxford University Press.

Cox, Arthur F. 1881. *A Manual of the North Arcot District*. Madras: Madras Presidency.

Danielou, Alain. 1989. Trans. *Manimekhalai (The Dancer with the Magic Bowl) by Merchant—Prince Shattan*, with the collaboration of T.V. Gopala Iyer. Delhi: Penguin Books India.

———. 1965. Trans. *Shilappadikaram* (The Ankle Bracelet) by Ilango Adigal. New York: New Directions.

Das, Veena. 1985. "The Body as a Metaphor-Socialization of Women in Punjabi Urban Families," *Manushi* 28: 2–6.

Datta, V. N. 1988. *Sati*. Riverdale, Maryland: The Riverdale Company.

Dehejia, Vidya. 1983. "A Broader Landscape" In *Sati: The Blessing and the Curse*, ed. John Hawley, 49–53. New York: Oxford University Press.

Dexter, Miriam Robbins. 1990. *Whence The Goddess*. New York: Pergamon Press.

Dhal, Upendra Nath. 1978. *Goddess Laksmi: Origin and Development*. New Delhi: Oriental Publishers.

Dhruvarajan, Vanaja. 1989. *Hindu Women & the Power of Ideology*. Boston: Bergin & Garvey Publishers, Inc.

Donnelly, John Patrick, ed. and trans. 2006. *Jesuit Writings of the Early Modern Period, 1540–1640*. Cambridge: Hackett Publishing Company, Inc.

Dorairaj, S. 2009. "Demons and Gods," *Frontline*, August 28, 2009, vol. 26, No. 17: 22–24.

Dube, S. C. 1959. *Indian Village*. London: Routledge & Kegan Paul Ltd. (Originally published in 1955).

Dubois, Abbe J. A. 1906. *Hindu Manners, Customs and Ceremonies*. 3rd ed. Translated by Henry K. Beauchamp. Oxford: Clarendon Press.

Duff, Rev. Alexander. 1840. *India and India Missions: Including Sketches of the Gigantic System of Hinduism, Both in Theory and Practice*. 2nd ed. Edinburgh: John Johnstone, Hunter Square.

Dumont, Louis. 1970. *Religion/Politics and History in India*. Paris: Mouton Publishers.

Elliot, H. M. 1879. *The Races of the North-West Provinces of India*, 2 vols. London: Trübner.

Elmore, W. T. 1915. *Dravidian Gods in Modern Hinduism; A Study of the Local and Village Deities of Southern India*. The University Studies of the University of Nebraska vol. XV Lincoln: The University of Nebraska.

Elwin, Verrier. 1939. *The Baiga*. London: J. Murray.

Erndle, Kathleen. 1993. *Victory to the Mother: The Hindu Goddesses of Northwest India in Myth, Ritual, and Symbol*. New York: Oxford University Press.

Fergusson, James. 1971. *Tree and Serpent Worship*. Delhi: Indological Book House.

Ferro-Luzzi, Gabriella Eichinger. 1977. "Ritual as Language: The Case of South Indian Food Offerings," *Current Anthropology* 18: 507–513.

Flood, Gavin. 1996. *An Introduction to Hinduism*. Cambridge: Cambridge University Press.

Flueckiger, Joyce Burkhalter. 2007. "Wandering from Hills to Valleys with the Goddess: Protection and Freedom in the Matamma Tradition in Andhra," in *Women's Lives, Women's Rituals in the Hindu Tradition*, ed. Tracy Pintchman, 35–54. Oxford: Oxford University Press.

Foulston, Lynn. 2003. *At the Feet of the Goddess. The Divine Feminine in Local Hindu Religion*. New Delhi: Sussex Academic Press.

Gadd, C. J. and S. Smith, 1924. "The New Links between Indian and Babylonian Civilizations." *The Illustrated London News*, October 4: 614–16.

Gadon, Elinor W. 1989. *The Once and Future Goddess*. San Francisco: Harper & Row, Publishers.

Gatwood, Lynn. 1985. *Devi and the Spouse Goddess*. Riverdale: Riverdale Co.

Griesinger, Theodor. 1883. *The Jesuits A Complete History*, vol I. New York: G.P. Putnam's Sons.

Griffith, Ralph T. H. 1963. Trans. *The Hymns of the Rgveda*. 4th ed. 2 vols. Banaras: Chowkhamba Sasnkrit Series Office.

Grimm, Jacob. 1870. *Deutsche Grammatik* 2nd ed. Berlin: Wilhelm Scherer.

Gundry, D.W. 1972. "Professor E. O. James: 1888-1972" in *Numen*, vol. XIX, No. 2/3 Aug.—Dec. 1972: 81–83.

Handique, Krishna Kantha. 1949. *Yasastilaka and Indian Culture*. Sholapur: Jaina Samskriti Samrakshana Sangha.

Hanumantharao, B. S. L. 1993. *Religion in Andhra*. Hyderabad: Government of Andhra Pradesh.

Hardy, F. 1983. *Viraha-bhakti: The Early History of Krsna Devotion in south India*. Oxford: Oxford University Press.

Harlan, Lindsey. 1994. "Perfection and Devotion: Sati Tradition in Rajasthan," in *Sati: The Blessing and the Curse*, ed. John Hawley, 79–90. New York: Oxford University Press.

———. 1992. *Religion and Rajput Women*. Berkeley: University of California Press.

Harper, Edward. 1959. "A Hindu Pantheon," *Southwestern Journal of Anthropology*, vol. 15, No. 3: 227–234. (autumn, 1959).

———. 1964. "Ritual Pollution as an Integrator of Caste and Religion," *The Journal of Asian Studies*, 23: 151–197. (June 1964).

Harper, Katherine. 1989. *The Iconography of the Saptamatrikas: Seven Hindu Goddesses of Spiritual Transformation*. Lewiston, New York: Edwin Mellen Press.

Hart, George L. 1975. "Ancient Tamil Literature: Its Scholarly Past and Future," in *Essays on South India*, ed. Burton Stein, 41–63. Hawaï'i: University of Hawaï'i Press.

———. 1975b. *The Poems of the Ancient Tamils. Their Milieu and Their Sanskrit Counterparts*. Berkeley: University of California Press.

———. 1973. "Women and the Sacred in Ancient Tamilnad," *Journal of Asian Studies*, 32 (2): 233–50.

Hart, George L., and Hank Heifetz, ed. and trans. 1999. *The Purannanuru, The Four Hundred Songs of War and Wisdom*. New York: Columbia University Press.

Hawley, John S. 1994. *Sati: The Blessing and the Curse*. New York: Oxford University Press.

Heesterman, J. C. 1985. *The Inner Conflict of Tradition, Essays in Indian Ritual, Kingship and Society*. Chicago: University of Chicago Press.

Hershman, Paul. 1977. "Virgin and Mother," in *Symbols and Sentiments*, ed. I. M. Lewis: 270–292. London: Academic Press.

Hiltebeitel, Alf. 1989. "Draupadi's Two Guardians: The Buffalo King and the Muslim Devotee," in *Criminal Gods and Demon Devotees*, ed. Alf Hiltebeitel, 339–372. Albany: State University of New York Press.

Hinnells, John R. & Eric J. Sharpe, eds. 1972. *Hinduism*. New Castle upon Tyne, England: Oriel Press.

Hudson, Dennis, D. 2000. *Protestant Origins in India: Tamil Evangelical Christians, 1706-1835*. Richmond, UK: William B. Eerdmans Publishing Company.

———. 1989. "Violent and Fanatical Devotion Among the Nayanars: A Study in the Periya Puranam of Cekkilar," in *Criminal Gods and Demon Devotees*, ed. Alf Hiltebeitel, 373–404.

Humes, Cynthia Ann. 2003. "Wrestling with Kali, South Asian and British Constructions of the Dark Goddess," in *Encountering Kali*, eds. Rachel Fell McDermott and Jeffrey Kripal, 145–168. Berkeley: University of California Press.

Huntington, Susan. 1985. *The Art of Ancient India, Buddhist, Hindu, Jain*. New York: Weather Hill.

Iyer, Anantha Krishna. 1935. *The Mysore Tribes and Castes*. Mysore: Mysore University.

James, E. O. 1959. *The Cult of the Mother Goddess*. New York: Barnes & Noble, Inc.

Jansen, Eva Rudy. 1993. *The Book of Hindu Mythology*. Diever, Holland: Benkey Kok Publications.

Janssen, Frans H. P. M. 1991. "On The Origin and Development of the So-Called Lajja Gauri," 11th International Conference of the Association of South Asian Archaeologist in Western Europe, Berlin, July 2, 1991.

Jeyaraj, Daniel. 2003. *Genealogy of the South Indian Deities*. London: Routledge Curzon.

Jones, Sir William. 1788. *Asiatic Researches*, I: 415–431.

———. 1970. *The Letters of Sir William Jones*, ed. Garland Cannon, vol. II. Oxford: The Clarendon Press.

Jones, Sir William, trans. 1789. *Sacontala; Or, The Fatal Ring: An Indian Drama by Calidas*. Calcutta: The Royal Asiatic Society of Bengal.

Kakar, Sudhir. 1986. "Feminine Identity in India," in *Women in Indian Society*, ed. Rehana Ghadially, 23–68. New Delhi: Sage Publications.

Kane, P. V. 1972. *History of Dharmasastras*, 4 vols. Vol. II. Poona: Bhandarkar Orient Research Institute.

Keith, A. Berriedale. 1916. "Indian Mythology," in *The Mythology of All Races*, 13 Volumes, ed. Louis Herbert Gray, 230–248. Vol. VI. Boston: Marshall Jones Company.

Keresenboom-Story, Saskia C. 1987. *Nityasumangali*. Delhi: Motilal Banarsidass.

Kinsley, David. 1988. *Hindu Goddesses.* Berkeley: University of California Press (originally published in 1986).

Knipe, David. 2000. "Goats Are Food Divine: A Comparison of Contemporary Vedic God and Hindu Goddess Sacrifices in Coastal Andhra." 29th Annual Conference on South Asia, University of Wisconsin—Madison. (October 13, 2000).

Kolenda, Pauline Mahar. 1964. "Aspects of Religion in South Asia," *The Journal of Asian Studies,* Vol. 23: 71–81. (June, 1964).

Kopf, David. 1992. "British Orientalism and the Bengal Renaissance: Chapter II, 'The Orientalist in Search of a Golden Age,'" in *Modern India,* ed. Thomas R. Metcalf, 24–37. New Delhi: Sterling Publishers Private Limited.

Kosambi, D. D. 1962. *Myth and Reality: Studies in the Formation of Indian Culture.* Bombay: Popular Prakashan (originally published 1983).

Kramrisch, Stella. 1956. "An Image of Aditi-Uttanapad," *Artibus Asiae* XIX: 259–270.

Kramrisch, Stella. 1988. *The Presence of Siva.* Varanasi: Motilal Banarsidass Publication.

Kumar, Pushpendra. 1974. *Sakti Cult in Ancient India,* Benaras: Bharatiya Publishing House.

Lal, B. B., 1960. "From the Megalithic to the Harappan: Tracing Back the Graffiti on the Pottery," *Ancient India* 6: 1–24.

Lamotte, Etienne. 1988. *History of Indian Buddhism.* Louvain: Peeters Press.

Lannoy, Richard. 1971. *The Speaking Tree, A Study of Indian Culture and Society.* New York: Oxford University Press.

Lehmann, Arno. 1956. *It Began at Tranquebar.* Madras: The Christian Literature Society.

Ludden, David. 1985. *Peasant History in South India.* Princeton: Princeton University Press.

Mackay, E. J. 1938. *Further Excavations at Mohenjodaro.* Delhi: Manager Publications.

Mackenzie, Gordon. 1883. *A Manual of the Kistna District.* Madras: The Lawrence Asylum Press.

Maloney, Clarence. 1975. "Archaeology in South India: Accomplishments and Prospects," in *Essays on South India,* ed. Burton Stein, 1–40. Hawai'i: University of Hawai'i Press.

Mandelbaum, David. 1964. "Introduction: Process and Structure in South Asian Religion," *The Journal of Asian Studies,* xxiii: 5–20. (June 1964).

———. 1966. "Transcendental and Pragmatic Aspects of Religion," *American Anthropologist,* Vol. 68, No. 5: 1174–1198. (October 1966.)

Marriott, McKim, ed. 1986. *Village India: Studies in the Little Community.* Chicago: The University of Chicago Press. (Originally published in 1955.)

Marshall, John. 1924. "First Light on a Long Forgotten Civilization," *Illustrated London News,* September 20, 1924: 528–32 & 548.

Marshall, John, ed. 1996. *Mohenjo-daro and the Indus Civilization.* 3 vols. New Delhi: Asian Educational Services (Originally published in 1930-1931, London: A. Probsthain)

Masthanaiah, B. 1978. *The Temples of Mukhalingam*. New Delhi: Cosmo Publications.

Matter, E. Ann. 1983. "The Virgin Mary: A Goddess?" In *The Book of the Goddesse Past and Present*. Ed. Carl Olson: 80–96. New York: Cross Road.

Max Muller, Fredrich. 1854. *Learning Languages of the Seat of War in the East*. London: Longman, Brown, Green & Longmans, Paternoster Row.

Max Muller, Fredrich, ed. 1879–1910. *Sacred Books of the East* Trans. by various Oriental scholars. Oxford: Clarendon Press.

Max Muller, Fredrich and Georgina Muller. 1902. *Life and Letters of the Rt. Hon. Friederich Max Muller*, Vol. I. London: Longmans, Green, and Co.

McIntosh, Jane. 2002. *A Peaceful Realm*. Boulder, CO: Westview Press.

Mc Dermott, Rachel and Jeffrey Kripal. 2003. *Encountering Kali*. Berkeley: University of California Press.

Meyer, Eveline. 1986. *Ankalaparamecuvari, A Goddess of Tamilnadu, Her Myths and Cult*. Stuttgart: Steiner Verlag Wiesbaden GMBH.

Mines, Diane. 2005. *Fierce Gods*. Bloomington, IN: Indiana University Press.

Misra, O. P. 1989. *Iconography of the Saptamatrikas*. Delhi: Agam Kala Prakashan, 1989.

Moffatt, Michael. 1979. *An Untouchable Community in South India*. Princeton: Princeton University Press.

Monier-Williams, Sir Monier. 1891. *Brahmanism and Hinduism*. 4th ed. London: John Murray.

———. 1876. *Indian Wisdom*. 3rd ed. London: Wm. H. Allen & Co., 13, Waterloo Place, S.W., Oxford.

Mukkamala, Radhakrishna Sarma. 1972. *Temples of Telingana*. Hyderabad: Book Links Corporation.

Mundkur, Balaji. 1983. *The Cult of the Serpent: An Interdisciplinary Survey of its Manifestation and Origins*. Albany: State University of New York Press.

Murdoch, John. 1896. *Religious Reform: Popular Hinduism*. 3rd ed. London: The Christian Literature Society for India.

Murdoch, John, compiled. 1865. *Classified Catalogue of Tamil Printed Books with Introductory Notices*. Madras: The Christian Vernacular Education Society.

Murthy, M. L. K. 1982. "Memorial Stones in Andhra Pradesh," in *Memorial Stones*, ed. S. Settar & Gunther D. Sontheimer, 209–218. Dharwad: Institute of Indian Art History.

Nagar, Shantilal. 1998. *Indian Gods and Goddesses*. vol. I. Delhi: B.R. Publishing House.

Nagolu, Krishna Reddy. 1991. *Social History of Andhra Pradesh: Seventh to Thirteenth Century: Based on Inscription and Literature*. Delhi: Agam Kala Prakashan.

Narasimhaswami, H. K. "Mother Goddess from Nagarjunakonda," *Epigraphia Indica (EI)* XXIX: 137.

Neill, Stephen. *A History of Christianity in India 1707–1858* Cambridge: Cambridge University Press, 1985.

Nigam, M. L. 1980. *Sculptural Art of Andhra*. Delhi: Sundeep Prakashan.

O'Malley, L.S.S. 1935. *Popular Hinduism.* Cambridge: Cambridge University Press.

Onishi, Yoshinori. 1997. *Feminine Mulitplicity: A Study of Groups of Mutiple Goddesses in India.* Delhi: Sri Satguru Publications.

Oppert, Gustav. 1893. *On the Original Inhabitants of Bharatavarsa or India.* Westminister: A Constable & Co.

Parabrahma Sastry, P.V. 1981. *Inscriptions of Andhra Pradesh: Cuddapah District.* Hyderabad: Government of Andhra Pradesh.

Parpola, Asko. 1994. *Deciphering the Indus Script.* Cambridge: Cambridge University Press.

Parthasarathy, R. 1993. Trans. *The Cilappatikaram.* New York: Columbia University Press.

Pfaffenberger, Bryan. 1980. "Social Communication in Dravidian Ritual," *Journal of Anthropological Research.* 36: 196–219.

Potts, E. Daniel. 1967. *British Baptist Missionaries in India, 1793–1837: The History of Serampore and its Missions.* Cambridge: Cambridge University Press.

Prasad, Ram Chandra. 1965. *Early English Travellers In India.* Delhi: Motilal Banarsi Dass.

Raghuramaiah, Lakshmi. K. 1994. *Hurricane: Autobiography of a Woman,* Delhi: Chanakya Publications.

Rajan, Gita. 2003. *Labyrinths of the Colonial Archive: Unpacking German Missionary Narratives From Tranquebar, Southeast India (1706–1720).* Ann Arbor, MI: University of Michigan Dissertation Services.

Rajeswari, D. R. 1989. *Sakti Iconography.* New Delhi: Intellectual Publishing House.

Rama, K. 1995. *Buddhist Art of Nagarjunakonda.* Delhi: Sundeep Prakashan.

Ramammohan Rao, K. 1992. *Perspectives of Archaeology, Art and Culture in Early Andhra Desa.* New Delhi, Aditya Prakashan.

Ramakrishna, T. 1891. *Life in an Indian Village.* London: T. Fisher Unwin [Unwin Brothers], The Gresham Press.

Ramanaiah, J. 1989. *Temples of South India: A Study of Hindu, Jain and Buddhist Monuments of the Deccan.* New Delhi: Concept Publishing Company.

Ramanujan, A. K. 1967. *The Interior Landscape: Love Poems from a Classical Tamil Anthology.* Bloomington: Indiana University Press.

Ramanujan, A. K. 1973. *Speaking of Siva.* Baltimore: Penguin Books Pvt. Ltd.

Rao, T. A. Gopinatha. 1985. *Elements of Hindu Iconography,* Vol. 1, Part II. Delhi: Motilal Banarsidass.

Reddy, Chandrasekhara R. 1994. *Heroes, Cults and Memorials: Andhra Pradesh, 300 AD–1600 AD.* Madras: New Era Publications.

Reddy, K. Viswanadha. 1976. "Ganga Jathara—A Folk Festival in a Small City—Tirupati and the Neighboring Villages in Andhra Pradesh," *Folklore* 17: 237– 42.

Roy, Arundhati. 1997. *The God of Small Things.* New York: Random House.

Rubies, Joan- Pau. 2002. *Travel and Ethnology in the Renaissance: South India Through European Eyes, 1250–1625.* Cambridge: Cambridge University Press.

Sankalia, H. D. 1978. "The Nude Goddess in Indian Art." *Marg* 31: 4–10 [http://www.harappa.com/indus/90.html, (Harappa 1996-2008)].

Sarkar, H. 1982."The Caya-Stambhas from Nagarjunakonda," in *Memorial Stones* ed. S. Settar & Gunther D. Sontheimer, 199–207. Dharwad: Institute of Indian Art History.

Sarkar, H. and B. N. Misra. 1987. *Nagarjunakonda.* New Delhi: Archaeological Survey of India.

Sarma, I. K. 1979. "Early Historical Vestiges at Vijayawada and some Trimurti Cult Plaques," *Itihas* VII. 2: 23–30.

———. 2008. *Jaina Art and Architecture in Andhra,* http://jainology.blogspot.com/2008/11/jaina-art-and-architecture-in-andhra.html

———. 1993. "Lead Coins of King Satavahana From Sannati," in *Studies in South Indian Coins,* ed. A. V. Narasimha Murthy. Vol. 3: 65–80. Madras: South Indian Numismatic Society.

Sastri, H. Krishna. 1974. *South-Indian Images of Gods and Goddesses.* Delhi: Bharatiya Publishing House (originally published in 1916 by Asian Educational Services, Madras).

Sastri, K. A. Nilakanta. 1965. *The Culture and History of the Tamils.* Calcutta: F.K.L. Mukhopadhyay.

Schastok, Sara L. 1985. *The Samalazi Sculptures and 6th Century Art in Western India.* Leiden, Netherlands: E. J. Brill.

Settar, S. 1982. "Memorial Stones in South India," In *Memorial Stones* Ed. S. Settar & Gunther D. Sontheimer, 183–197. Dharwad: Institute of Indian Art History.

Sharma, Ram Sharan. 1958. *Sudras in Ancient India.* Delhi: Motilal Banarsidass Publishers Pvt. Ltd.

Shastri, Biswanarayan. 1991. *The Kalika Purana: Sanskrit Text, Introduction & Translation in English* (3 Volumes), Calcutta: Nag Publishers.

Sherring, Matthew Atmore. 1875. *The History of Protestant Missions in Inda: from their commencement in 1706 to 1871.* London: Trubner & Co.

Shulman, David. 1980. *Tamil Temple Myths: Sacrifice and Divine Marriage in the South Indian Saiva Tradition.* Princeton: Princeton University Press.

Singer, Milton. 1972. *When A Great Tradition Modernizes.* New York: Praeger Publishers.

Sivaramamurty, C. 1942. *Amaravati Sculptures in the Madras Government Museum.* Madras: Government Press.

———1982. *Sri Lakshmi in Indian Art and Thought.* New Delhi: Kanak Publications.

Sjoberg, Andree. 1971. "Who are the Dravidians?" In *Symposium on Dravidian Civilization,* ed. Andree Sjoberg: 240–272. New York: Jenkins.

Somasekharasarma, M. 1945. *History of Reddy Kingdoms.* Waltair: Andhra University.

Somasundara Rao, C. 1985. "The Aminabad Inscription of Anavema and Pedakomati Vema," *Journal of the Epigraphical Soceity of India, Dharwar,* Vol. XII: 69–72.

Sontheimer, Gunther D. 1982. "On the Memorials to the Dead in the Tribal Area of Central India," in S. Settar & Gunther D. Sontheimer ed., *Memorial Stones*: 87–99. Dharwad: Institute of Indian Art History.

Southerland, Gail Hinch. 1991. *The Disguises of the Demon*. Albany: State University of New York Press.

Sree Padma. 2001. "From Village to City: Transforming Goddess from Urban Andhra Pradesh," in *Seeking Mahadevi*, ed. Tracy Pintchman, 115–144. New York: State University of New York Press.

Srinivas, M.N. 1956. "A Note on Sanskritization and Westernization," *Journal of Asian Studies*, v. 15: 481–96.

———. 1965 (reprint) *Religion and Society Among the Coorgs of South India*. (1st edition 1952.) Bombay: Asia Publishing House.

———. 1976. *The Remembered Village*. Berkeley: University of California Press.

Sripada Gopala Krishna Murthy, 1963. *Jain Vestiges in Andhra*, ed. Md. Abdul Waheed Khan. Hyderabad: Government of Andhra Pradesh.

———. 1964. *The Sculpture of Kakatiyas*, Andhra Pradesh Archaeological Series. Hyderabad: Government of Andhra Pradesh.

Srivastava, M. C. P. 1979. *Mother Goddess in Art, Archaeology and Literature*. Delhi: Agam Kala Prakashan.

Stein, Burton. 1980. *Peasant State and Society in Medieval South India*. Delhi: Oxford University Press.

Stone, Elizabeth Rosen. 1994. *The Buddhist Art of Nagarjuna Konda*. Delhi: Motilal Benarsidass Publishers.

Strong, John. 1982. *The Legend and Cult of Upagupta*. New Jersey: Princeton University Press.

Subramanian, K. R. 1989. *Buddhist Remains in Andhra and the History of Andhra*. Madras: Asian Educational Services (originally published 1932).

Tapper, Bruce Elliot. 1987. *Rivalry and Tribute. Society and Ritual in a Telugu Village in South India*. Delhi: Hindustan.

———. 1979. "Widows and Goddesses: Female Roles in Deity Symbolism in a South Indian village," *Contribution to India Sociology* (NS) Vol. 13: 1–31.

Taylor, Isaac. 1890. *The Origin of the Aryans: An Account of the Prehistoric Ethnology and Civilization of Europe*. New York: Scribner & Welford.

Thapar, Romila. 2002–2004. *Early India*. Berkeley: University of California Press.

———. 2005. "Some Appropriations of the Theory of Aryan Race," In *The Aryan Debate*, ed. Thomas Trautman, 112–115.

Thurston, Edgar, 1909. *Castes and Tribes of Southern India*. 7 vols. Madras: Government Press.

Thurston, Edgar & K. Rangachari, 1909. *Castes and Tribes of South India*, Vol. 4. Madras: Government Press.

———. 1906. *Ethnographic Notes in Southern India*. Madras: Government of Madras.

Tiwari, J. N. 1985. *Goddess Cults in Ancient India*. Delhi: Sundeep Prakashan.

Trautman, Thomas. 1997. *Aryans and British India*. Berkeley: University of California Press.

Trautman, Thomas, ed. 2005. *The Aryan Debate*. New Delhi: Oxford Press.

Turaicami Pillai, Auvai C. Commentator. 1964. *Purananuru*. 2 vols. Madras: Kazhagam.

Urban, Hugh, B. 2003. "India's Darkest Heart," in *Encountering Kali*, eds. Rachel Fell McDermott and Jeffrey Kripal, 169–195. Berkeley: University of California Press.

Velcheru, Narayana Rao. 1989. "Tricking the Goddess: Cowherd Katamaraju and the Goddess Ganga in the Telugu Folk Epic," in *Criminal Gods and Demon Devotees*, ed. Alf Hiltebeitel, 105–21. Albany: State University of New York Press.

Velury, Venkata Krishna Sastry. 1983. *The Proto and Early Historic Cultures of Andhra Pradesh* Hyderabad: The Government of Andhra Pradesh.

Venkataramanayya, N. & V. Parabrahmasastry eds. *Epigraphia Andhrica*, III. Hyderabad: Department of Archaeology & Museums.

Vohra, Ranbir. 1997. *The Making of India*. New York: M.E. Sharpe.

Voltaire, 1777. *Lettres sur l'origine des sciences et sur celle des peuples de l'Asie*. Paris: de Bure. 2011. http://en.wikipedia.org/wiki/Goa_Inquisition.

Wadley, Susan Snow. 1975. *SHAKTI Power in the Conceptual Structure of Karimpur Religion*. Chicago: The University of Chicago.

Ward, William. 1822. *A View of the History, Literature, and Mythology of the Hindoos*, vol. III. London: Kingsbury, Parbury, and Allen.

Wheeler, Mortimer. 1953. *The Indus Civilization*. Cambridge: University Press.

Whitehead, Henry. 1980. *The Village Gods of South India*. New York and London: Garland Publishing, Inc., Reprint of the second ed., 1921.

Wiebe, C. Paul. 1975. "Religious Change in South India," in Religion and Society 22: 27–46.

Wilson, H. H. Trans. 1840. *Vishnu Purana*. London: John Murray.

Wolpert, Stanley. 1997. *A New History of India*. 5th ed. Oxford: Oxford University Press.

Ziegenbalg, B. 1984. *Genealogy of the South-Indian Gods*. (First edition 1869.) Delhi: Unity Book Service.

Zimmer, Heinrich. 1946. "The Goddess," in *Myths And Symbols in Indian Art and Civilization*, Compiler/editor, Joseph Campbell: 59–68. New York: Pantheon Books.

———. 1967 *Philosophies of India*, ed. Joseph Campbell (First edition 1956). Princeton: Princeton University Press.

ARCHAEOLOGICAL RECORDS, GAZETTEERS AND INSCRIPTIONS

Andhra Pradesh Archaeological Report (*APAR*), 13/1965.

Annual Reports on Indian Epigraphy (*ARIE*) 1917, 1918, 1932, 1939, 1941–1942, 146–147, 1955.

Archaeology Survey of India Annual Report (ASI) No. 536 of 1909.

Census of India 1961 Vol II A.P. Part II VII- B Fairs and Festivals: District Records

Mahabubnagar District, Nalgonda District, Khammam District, Warangal District, Cuddappah District, Karimnagar District, Krishna District, West Godavari District, East Godavari District, Cuddapah District, Karimnagar District, Visakhapatnam District, Srikakulam District, Vizianagaram District, Adilabad District, Kurnool District, Nizamabad District.

Cuddapah District Inscriptions, Part I, No. 64.

Epigraphia Indica (EI) V, XI, XXIV, XXXI, XXXIV.

Epigraphia Andhrica (EA).

Indian Antiquary 2, 1878, pp. 241–251.

Indian Archaeology (IA) Publications: 1954–1955, 1956–1957, 1967–1968.

Indian Archaeology 1989–90 A Review 1994. New Delhi: Archaeological Survey of India.

Inscriptions of Andhra Pradesh, Cuddapah District.

Inscriptions on Copper Plates and Stones in Nellore District in 3 vols.

Madras Epigraphist's Report (MER), 1901 & 1910.

Narasimhaswami, H. K., ed. 1988. *Telugu Inscriptions of the Vijayanagara Dynasty, South Indian Inscriptions.* Vol. XVI. New Delhi: Archaeological Survey of India.

Narayana, Sivasanakra. 1977. *Anantapur District Gazetteer.* Hyderabad: Government of Andhra Pradesh.

Nellore District Inscriptions (NDI) Vols. I & III.

Ramayya Pantulu, J. & N. Lakshminarayan Rao, eds. 1986. *Telugu Inscriptions from the Madras Presidency: South Indian Inscriptions Vol. X,* Mysore: The Director General Archaeological Survey of India.

South Indian Inscriptions (S.I.I.), Vols. V, X & XVI.

TELUGU SOURCES:

Chilukuri, Narayanarao., ed. 1939. *Panditaradhya Charitra* Vol. II, Palkuriki Somanatha, Madras: Andhra Granthamala.

Chinnikrsna Sarma, D., ed. 1969. *Srinathakavi Kasikhandam.* Madras: Vavilla Edition.

Hamsa Vimsati. 1977. Hyderabad: Andhra Pradesh Sahitya Academy.

Kundurti Satyanarayanamurty. 1989. *Prachinandhra Mahakavula Devi Pratipatti.* Vijayawada: Bhuvanavijayam Publications.

Mallanna Kavi, *Rukmangada Charitramu.* 1938. Madras: Vavilla Ramasastrulu and Sons.

Nayani, Krishnakumari. 1990. *Telugu Janapada Geya Gathalu.* Hyderabad: Telugu Academy.

Papayyasastri, Ch., ed. 1958. *Bhimesvarapuranam.* Rajahmundry: Andhra Pradesh.

Peta, Srinivasulu Reddy. 2000. *Tirumala Tirupati Grama Devatalu.* Tirupati: Rushiteja Publications.

Pratapareddy, Suravaram. 2007. *Andhrula Sanghika Charitra.* Hyderabad: Orient Lajman Pvt Ltd. (Originally published 1992.)

Sastry, B. N. 1991. *Bezwada Durga Malleswaralaya Sasanamulu*. Hyderabad: Musi
   Publications (Originally published 1985).
Simhasana Dvatrimsika. 1960. Hyderabad: Andhra Pradesh Sahitya Academy.
Singarachaya, B. V., ed. 1997. *Vinukonda Vallabharayani Kridabhiramamu*.
   Vijayawada: Emesco Books.
Vidyashekharulu, Umakanta. 1938. (first edition, 1911). *Palnativiracharitra*. Guttikonda,
   Guntur District: Vangmaya Samiti.

                            WEB RESOURCES

http://andhrafriends.com/index.php?topic=58928.0
http://expressbuzz.com/states/andhrapradesh/andhra-human-sacrifice-
   bid-thwarted/236084.html, January 2, 2011.
http://www.harappa.com/indus/89.html
http://www.harappa.com/indus/34.html
http://www.iheu.org/node/2755, August 1, 2007.
http://indianchristians.in/news/content/view/2374/45/

Index

Page numbers in italics refer to illustrations.